NEW BATTLEFIELDS/OLD LAWS

COLUMBIA STUDIES IN TERRORISM AND IRREGULAR WARFARE

Columbia Studies in Terrorism and Irregular Warfare

BRUCE HOFFMAN, SERIES EDITOR

This series seeks to fill a conspicuous gap in the burgeoning literature on terrorism, guerrilla warfare, and insurgency. The series adheres to the highest standards of scholarship and discourse and publishes books that elucidate the strategy, operations, means, motivations, and effects posed by terrorist, guerrilla, and insurgent organizations and movements. It thereby provides a solid and increasingly expanding foundation of knowledge on these subjects for students, established scholars, and informed reading audiences alike.

Ami Pedahzur, *The Israeli Secret Services and the Struggle Against Terrorism*
Ami Pedahzur and Arie Perliger, *Jewish Terrorism in Israel*
Lorenzo Vidino, *The New Muslim Brotherhood in the West*
Erica Chenoweth and Maria J. Stephan, *Why Civil Resistance Works: The Strategic Logic of Nonviolent Resistance*

EDITED BY WILLIAM C. BANKS

NEW BATTLEFIELDS
OLD LAWS

CRITICAL DEBATES ON ASYMMETRIC WARFARE

COLUMBIA UNIVERSITY PRESS   NEW YORK

COLUMBIA UNIVERSITY PRESS
Publishers Since 1893
New York   Chichester, West Sussex

Copyright © 2011 Columbia University Press
All rights reserved

Library of Congress Cataloging-in-Publication Data

New battlefields, old laws : critical debates on asymmetric warfare / edited by William C. Banks.
  p. cm.
  Includes bibliographical references and index.
  ISBN 978-0-231-15234-1 (cloth : alk. paper) — ISBN 978-0-231-15235-8
(pbk. : alk. paper) — ISBN 978-0-231-52656-2 (ebook)
  1. Humanitarian law. 2. Terrorism—Prevention—Law and legislation. 3. Asymmetric warfare.
I. Banks, William C.
KZ6471.N49 2011
341.6′7—DC23

2011018867

Columbia University Press books are printed on permanent and durable acid-free paper.
This book is printed on paper with recycled content.
Printed in the United States of America

c 10 9 8 7 6 5 4 3 2 1
p 10 9 8 7 6 5 4 3 2 1

References to Internet Web sites (URLs) were accurate at the time of writing.
Neither the author nor Columbia University Press is responsible for URLs
that may have expired or changed since the manuscript was prepared.

Contents

FIGURES AND TABLES   vii

Introduction · William C. Banks   1
Toward an Adaptive International Humanitarian Law: New Norms
    for New Battlefields

CRITICAL DEBATE I
Threshold Issues in Defining Twenty-first-Century Armed Conflicts

Chapter One · Geoffrey S. Corn   23
Extraterritorial Law Enforcement or Transnational Counterterrorist
    Military Operations: The Stakes of Two Legal Models

Chapter Two · Gregory Rose   45
Preventive Detention of Individuals Engaged in Transnational Hostilities:
    Do We Need a Fourth Protocol Additional to the 1949 Geneva Conventions?

CRITICAL DEBATE II
Status and Liabilities of Nonstate Actors Engaged in Hostilities

Chapter Three · David M. Crane and Daniel Reisner   67
"Jousting at Windmills": The Laws of Armed Conflict in an Age of Terror—State
    Actors and Nonstate Elements

Chapter Four · Eric Talbot Jensen   85
Direct Participation in Hostilities: A Concept Broad Enough for Today's
    Targeting Decisions

Chapter Five • Daphné Richemond-Barak   106
Nonstate Actors in Armed Conflicts: Issues of Distinction and Reciprocity

CRITICAL DEBATE III
Changing Twenty-first-Century Battlefields and Armed Forces

Chapter Six • Hilly Moodrick-Even Khen   133
Children as Direct Participants in Hostilities: New Challenges for International
    Humanitarian Law and International Criminal Law

Chapter Seven • Renée de Nevers   150
Private Military Contractors and Changing Norms for the Laws of
    Armed Conflict

CRITICAL DEBATE IV
Military Necessity and Humanitarian Priorities in International
    Humanitarian Law: Productive Tension or Irreconcilable Differences?

Chapter Eight • Robert P. Barnidge Jr.   171
The Principle of Proportionality Under International Humanitarian Law and
    Operation Cast Lead

Chapter Nine • Corri Zoli   190
Humanizing Irregular Warfare: Framing Compliance for Nonstate Armed
    Groups at the Intersection of Security and Legal Analyses

NOTES   213
CONTRIBUTOR BIOS   289
INDEX   293

Figures and Tables

FIGURE 2.1	Nonstate Entities in Armed Conflict	51
FIGURE 3.1	Military Necessity	70
TABLE 3.1	Participants in Modern Armed Conflict	82
TABLE 5.1	Reciprocity and the Application of the Laws of War to Nonstate Actors	127
TABLE 7.1	Which "Combatant" Rights or Dangers Accrue to Different Groups?	153

NEW BATTLEFIELDS/OLD LAWS

INTRODUCTION

Toward an Adaptive International Humanitarian Law

NEW NORMS FOR NEW BATTLEFIELDS

WILLIAM C. BANKS

Modern war is no longer characterized by "uniformed armies on a large plain, with civilians tucked away safely far behind the front-lines." Rather, military operations are now conducted in the contemporary operational environment, which assumes 360-degree operations against asymmetric opponents who strike at known weaknesses, including a nation's compliance with the law of war.[1]

One of the most troubling implications of modern asymmetric warfare is that a state's compliance with the *jus in bello*, the international treaties and other laws that define acceptable behavior for states engaged in armed conflict, may amount to an operational weakness in today's armed conflicts.[2] Consider two scenarios. Israeli military forces engage Hezbollah on the border of Lebanon only to find militants have employed human shields—a clear violation of the Fourth Geneva Convention—to undermine attempts of the Israel Defense Forces to dislodge gunmen at rocket launch pads in high-density residential neighborhoods.[3] Militants see the resulting civilian casualties as valuable for turning international opinion against their rival as they engage in "lawfare"— the use of law as a weapon by creating the impression, correct or not, that an opponent acts lawlessly.[4] The defending state's forces are thus faced with a dilemma: If they abide by the laws of armed conflict and curtail the attack to minimize civilian casualties, state forces compromise the military objective and leave their own civilians vulnerable. If they choose not to scale back an assault or do not realize that shielding is occurring, as when an adversary hides the practice in anticipating that such a misstep has political capital, the choice to proceed disregards the prohibition against targeting civilians, making a state appear derelict in its obligations under the law. In either case, the laws and customs of war have become a politicized weapon in asymmetric strategy. States that are committed to protecting civilians in the chaos of war face an operational and moral dilemma while they act to insulate state legitimacy in the eyes of their own populations and the world.

A second scenario demonstrates how asymmetric strategies have begun to challenge international humanitarian norms—on the battlefield and beyond. Well-intentioned international advocacy organizations have spent considerable time offering positive incentives to entice nonstate fighters to follow humanitarian law, such as by allowing some rights protections for their fighters in return for partial compliance with the all-or-nothing proposition of the laws of war. According to some, however, the wrong area of compliance has been relaxed—namely, the "fixed distinctive symbol" requirements of combatant status in Articles 43 and 44 of Protocol I to the Geneva Conventions. Without this standard, insurgents have no incentive to mark themselves off from the civilian population. The insignia rule is central to the principle of distinction and the very reason that combatants garner special privileges, because by differentiating themselves they make themselves available as targets. The incentives also wrongly presume common cultural objectives in war, namely, that soldiers do not want to die, that they are involved in traditional battlefield objectives and not religious or identity-defining experiences that convey submission to a divine authority or absolute faith by spilling one's (or an infidel's) blood.

Whether the parties to an asymmetric conflict are specialists in humanitarian law, or those least inclined to comport with secular law, both sets of participants are entangled in now prevalent challenges facing international humanitarian law. Existing laws are not well suited to take into account these asymmetries.[5] New circumstances require a fresh look at established core humanitarian law principles of distinction, proportionality, military necessity, and prevention of unnecessary suffering.

This volume synthesizes several critical insights from an interdisciplinary initiative at Syracuse University's Institute for National Security and Counterterrorism (INSCT), a research institute jointly sponsored by the Maxwell School of Citizenship and Public Affairs and the College of Law at Syracuse University, in partnership with the International Institute for Counter-Terrorism (ICT) at the Interdisciplinary Center (IDC) in Herzliya, Israel. The fruits of this dialogue have been encapsulated in our title, *New Battlefields/ Old Laws: Critical Debates on Asymmetric Warfare*. Our book addresses from an interdisciplinary legal and policy perspective the challenges posed to humanitarian law as weaker, nonstate combatants use forbidden tactics to offset their military disadvantage, and as irregular warfare becomes a common means for weaker parties to achieve political goals that they could not accomplish through established channels. Beginning with the premise that most of today's conflicts are low-intensity, asymmetric wars between militarily disparate forces, this volume focuses on the role of nonstate groups in many of the world's conflicts, how these conflicts increasingly involve irregular participants (paramilitaries, child soldiers, civilians participating in the hostilities, and private military firms), and the implications of these phenomena for international humanitarian law.[6] This volume debates what many have taken to be a foregone conclusion—that existing laws adequately govern current military conflicts. Our contributing authors believe that some regulations should be updated, revised slightly, or changed altogether (Corn, Crane, and Reisner), or that existing laws should be deployed differently or enlarged in their scope and application (Rose, Jensen). Still other contributors have given careful attention to how old laws are in the process of undergoing change under new conditions (Richemond-Barak, Moodrick Even-Khen, Barnidge, and Zoli).

We also explore the stakes in evolving conflict paradigms—for localized debates (such as whether nonstate actors can be belligerents, legally speaking), but also for the very legitimacy of this long-standing international legal corpus. We seek to untangle how legal instruments historically designed to humanize the anarchy of the battlefield have become politicized weapons in contemporary conflicts. Because the Hague and Geneva Conventions and Protocols do not account adequately for nonstate groups waging transnational attacks or prolonged campaigns of terrorism, for instance, today's new battlefields may be left unregulated so that parties in the conflict are without guidelines. When defending states find themselves without rules for dealing with tactics that blur the lines between soldiers and civilians for strategic ends, the most vulnerable feel the negative consequences.

These changes in warfare are, however, not only the product of gaps in or challenges for the law in new security environments, but also significant policy problems across the international community.[7] Without clear legal and normative understandings, terrorists or insurgent groups may be ever more emboldened to operate militarily from within civilian populations, instead of challenging states on political grounds. Most perniciously, humanitarian advocacy organizations pledged to protect the vulnerable and to help ameliorate the worst conditions in conflict may find themselves caught in the crossfire between those states unable or unwilling to exercise extreme restraint and highly organized transnational actors that flaunt their deviation from the laws of war. With these cross-cutting issues and dilemmas in mind this volume addresses the considerable challenges for the future of armed conflict.[8]

To structure our assessment, we have defined four overarching debates that provide perspective on the legal underpinnings and policy implications for humanitarian law as it contends with today's asymmetric challenges: *Threshold Issues in Defining Twenty-first-Century Armed Conflicts* identifies present vulnerabilities in the existing humanitarian law legal framework; *Status and Liabilities of Nonstate Actors Engaged in Hostilities* and *Changing Twenty-first-Century Battlefields and Armed Forces* address the legal, policy, and political issues raised when new actors that do not fit neatly into traditional legal status designations take active roles in armed conflicts and help to change the very nature of the battlefield; and *Military Necessity and Humanitarian Priorities in International Humanitarian Law: Productive Tension or Irreconcilable Differences?* revisits the fundamental question of humanitarian law as a compromise between sovereign states' national security interests and universal humanitarian principles and protections. The volume is not a comprehensive introduction to the laws of armed conflict in the twenty-first century; instead it presents key debates between a range of the most critical perspectives on the legal underpinnings and policy implications for international humanitarian law as it confronts new challenges, conflicts, actors, battlefields, and norms in the contemporary security environment.

The remainder of this introduction provides a primer on the problems of regulating new warfare within the international humanitarian law framework and the policy context for rethinking the law. The final section returns to a description of each contributor's analysis.

The State-Centric Paradigm of International Humanitarian Law

Following a signing ceremony in the Netherlands more than 100 years ago, on October 18, 1907, the Hague Conventions Respecting the Laws and Customs of War on Land required state parties to "issue instructions to their armed land forces in conformity with the present convention."[9] Another article in the same document made clear that the rules of the Convention apply only to wars between state parties, and yet another stipulation limited the Hague rules to state militaries, a subset of states' nationals defined as "lawful combatants"—a category evolved in customary law from the pre–Middle Ages practice of treating as enemies all inhabitants of another state.[10] Over time, the laws of war, or what is now referred to as international humanitarian law, developed from Clausewitz's Eurocentric conception of war based on symmetric conflicts between state armies of roughly equal military strength and of comparable organizational structures.[11]

The terms *"jus in bello,"* "humanitarian law," "law of armed conflict," and "laws and customs of war" are often used interchangeably in reference to the international legal instruments that prescribe rules for the conduct of military operations during armed conflict, including standards for the protection of civilians, civilian objects, and other protected entities. Such universally agreed-upon rules humanize war by setting criteria and limits on such issues as who and what may be targeted, how targeting may be executed, the weapons that may be used, how prisoners of war and other detainees must be treated, and the rights and obligations of occupying forces. The International Committee of the Red Cross (ICRC), the international organization founded to ensure humanitarian protection and assistance for victims of armed conflicts, defines international humanitarian law as "that body of rules which seek, for humanitarian reasons, to limit the effects of armed conflict, protecting persons who are not or are no longer participating in the hostilities, and restricting the means and methods of warfare."[12] As a *lex specialis*, a specific set of laws triggered by special circumstances, humanitarian law applies only during armed conflict.[13] Humanitarian law is also distinct from the *jus ad bellum*—the laws, such as the U.N. Charter, regulating when a state can justifiably enter into armed conflict. The *jus ad bellum* serve the interests of states as states, where the *jus in bello* are designed to protect the well-being of individuals, their property, and those who are *hors de combat* during armed conflicts. In this sense, "the *jus in bello* applies equally to belligerents, whether they are *jus ad bellum* aggressors or victims."[14] Although scholars have long maintained a bright-line distinction between these twin legal regimes, the fact that international law depends on the assent and compliance of states limits the humanitarian impulses codified in the *jus in bello* and attests to the delicate balance between humanitarian motivations and the dictates of military necessity. The difficulties will be examined in several applications throughout this volume.

It has been evident since at least the biblical story of David and Goliath that military conflicts may be unequal or asymmetric, involving attacks by nonstate entities against sovereign states. Yet the laws of war do little to accommodate the asymmetric form. Sixty years ago, following extensive revision to the Geneva Conventions, the decision makers and military leaders of the nations of the world agreed that the Common Articles codified in the revised 1949 Geneva Convention constituted the exclusive threshold criteria for triggering the laws of war. Under Geneva, there are two kinds of wars: interstate (or international) armed conflicts and intrastate (or internal) armed conflicts. The former invoke the full panoply of the laws of war, which in turn regulate the conduct of war (through the principles of distinction, proportionality, and military necessity); the latter do not trigger all the regulations for the conduct of war but provide limited humanitarian protections for civilians and those captured or detained.

The Geneva provisions deliberately exclude nonstate actors in two ways. First, they provide a regulatory scheme designed for wars between states, except for minimal protections for those involved in noninternational armed conflicts that may include nonstate belligerents. Second, they define, on the model of the state soldier, the criteria for earning the status of a lawful combatant. Requirements include putting in place a responsible command structure, wearing a fixed insignia recognizable at a distance, carrying arms openly, and conducting operations in accord with international humanitarian law. One byproduct is that only those meeting these criteria gain full prisoner-of-war (POW) protections under the Conventions. It is virtually impossible for nonstate actors to meet these criteria and thus to become lawful combatants under humanitarian law. Because humanitarian law includes a "combatant privilege," a form of legal immunity for acts that would be criminal if performed during peacetime, nonstate actors may neither engage in lawful combat nor be its deliberate target.

To invoke the laws of war and the humanitarian provisions that are part and parcel of them, there must be an armed conflict within the meaning of the Geneva Conventions—that is, either an international (between two or more states) or a noninternational (civil war) armed conflict. Although the Conventions do not define armed conflict, that part of the triggering mechanism traditionally has not been difficult to implement in state-vs.-state conflicts, because what constitutes armed conflict—the use of armed forces by opposing regular armed forces—is fairly clear. If the armed conflict threshold is not met (if the conflict is not state vs. state or an internal civil war), then the laws of war cannot apply. Determining the existence of a noninternational (or internal) armed conflict has, by contrast, not been easy. Many violent internal conflicts are civil disturbances that are amenable to and may be managed effectively by domestic laws. But others rise to the level of armed conflict and should be governed by the laws of war. The ICRC maintains that only if an internal conflict involves several criteria—identification of parties, protracted hostile acts, minimum level of organization of armed forces, for instance—do the laws of war clearly apply.[15] Yet the U.S. Supreme Court decided in 2006 that the U.S. conflict with al-Qaeda is a noninternational armed conflict, at least for the purposes of affording fair trial procedures to detainees accused of war crimes.[16] Likewise, international humanitarian law is not applicable to a war against "terrorism" because there is no state enemy; nor is it applicable to a conflict that involves a state and a transnational terrorist network. At the same time, many asymmetric conflicts, where relatively weaker nonstate belligerents attack a stronger state, are not "wars" either as defined under humanitarian law—there is no state-vs.-state or internal conflict. In these cases, the humanitarian law threshold criteria present definitional conundrums in addition to practical limitations. It may not be feasible, for instance, to implement the basic required humanitarian legal principles of distinction and proportionality in the case of transnational terrorism, because commanders and soldiers cannot readily distinguish civilians from combatants.

In the Cold War period after 1949 and before September 11, 2001, states came to realize that the dominant form of armed conflict was internal—civil wars or insurgencies—and that the failure to anticipate nonstate armies and incorporate them in some way into humanitarian law would disserve the humanitarian interests at the root of these policies and laws. In the mid-1970s, states therefore designed Protocol I, which sought to accommodate current national liberation movements, viewed by many observers as fighting just wars against colonial governments. The Protocol provided for National Liberation Movements to be included in Geneva criteria for international armed conflicts; it relaxed the criteria for obtaining POW status; and it permitted nonstate actors to join humanitarian law by formally declaring their intention to do so. Many states resisted these changes and declined to ratify the Protocol, for a variety of reasons, including the concern that the Protocol might have the effect of giving rights and privileges to terrorists. Over time, as decolonization slowed to a trickle, the Protocol debate became merely academic. No group has made the declaration allowed for by the Protocol, and no individual or nonstate group has sought or been afforded international humanitarian law treatment under the Protocol.[17]

Today asymmetric warfare is a central feature of twenty-first-century global affairs. The absence of rules to govern asymmetric warfare presents a serious problem both for states that benefit from guidance in conducting military operations and for those victimized by such conflicts. In the decades since 1949, a good deal of work has gone into attempting to modernize the status designation categories from the early Westphalian model to a post–World War II humanitarian-based legal regime. For example, within the ongoing discussions of the evolution of humanitarian law, one proposed approach has been to apply a principle of "protective parity" to all who participate in an armed conflict, regardless of their compliance with the criteria for lawful combatant status. However, the protective parity idea has not found political traction in the international community. Others have recommended that the test of combatant status should simply be functional: Is the person actively involved in planning or carrying out acts of violence? If so, protections would follow. Under traditional humanitarian law criteria, members of al-Qaeda, for instance (those who are not in some way affiliated with the armed forces of a state), cannot be "combatants" as that term is understood in international law. Nor could the term "armed conflict" be applied to the September 11, 2001, attacks by al-Qaeda operatives, although these heinous acts violated other international and domestic laws.

Shortly after the September 11, 2001, terrorist attacks, the Bush administration characterized its strategic response as a war. There was wide-ranging and bipartisan support for this view. Eventually, the policy that the United States was at war with a transnational, nonstate entity, wherever that enemy might be encountered, resulted in the concept of the "global war on terror." Although the phrase's emotional power reverberated powerfully in many parts of the world, calling U.S. counterterrorism policies a "global war on terror" sowed the seeds of legal and policy confusion that actually set back the cause of bringing legal regulation to asymmetric warfare. The problem is not that terrorists and insurgents are incapable of making war; we all know that they are. Indeed, whether we view terrorism as a crime or war or something else is in many cases simply a policy determination. To reiterate Michael Walzer's claim, war is "something people decide."[18]

This complicated legal picture was further obscured when in early 2002 White House Counsel Alberto Gonzales wrote that the "war against terrorism is a new kind of war" that "renders obsolete Geneva's strict limitations on questioning of enemy prisoners and renders quaint some of its provisions."[19] The Bush administration detained individuals at Guantanamo Bay and prepared to try them by military commission procedures, after applying new standards from the metaphorically powerful but legally boundless "global war on terror." Because some of the detainees were not seized on a traditional, legally recognized battlefield, their detention in military confinement was itself legally questionable. Matters were made worse when these detainees were labeled "unlawful combatants" by the Bush administration. With the exception of captured Taliban fighters, those detained at Guantanamo do not fall within the status designation of combatant of any type—enemy, lawful, or unlawful. They are unprivileged belligerents, amenable to prosecution in U.S. domestic or military courts for war crimes.

As the U.S. Supreme Court subsequently agreed in 2006, the armed conflict with al-Qaeda is a noninternational armed conflict, to which the humanitarian protections of Common Article 3 apply.[20] Beyond this minimal coverage, humanitarian law is of little or no guidance in asymmetric war involving nonstate actors. Because the use of military force will surely be a policy option for countering terrorism and other forms of asymmetric warfare in the foreseeable future, it is high time for humanitarian law to recognize and adapt to this reality.

Extending International Humanitarian Law to Asymmetric Warfare

Why bother attempting to extend the laws of war to conflicts with nonstate actors, whether terrorists, international criminals, insurgents, or some other variant? One reason is to provide notice to any state that finds itself in such a new conflict situation that the rules apply—including the human rights protections that would otherwise regulate traditional wars. But the more controversial issue is whether the laws of war should be made available in any respect to protect an enemy that is not deserving of protection. Why glorify an undeserving enemy and elevate his status to his own constituents?

Scholars have warned that affording a protected status to insurgents or terrorists, for example, may lend legal and moral legitimacy to their acts of violence against a state. Some have suggested that, rather than recognizing conflicts with nonstate groups as international armed conflicts, they be deemed, as the U.S. Supreme Court and some scholars have viewed them, a species of noninternational armed conflict, so that only the limited Common Article 3 protections would extend to the nonstate combatants. One significant problem with this approach is that Common Article 3 speaks only to the treatment of persons captured and does not regulate the combat operations themselves. Moreover, the text of the Article belies this interpretation (asymmetric conflicts are typically transnational). It would diminish the value of the Conventions to label a clearly transnational conflict noninternational.

Others have maintained that the existing humanitarian law framework works well enough and that it should not be adapted for asymmetric conflicts.[21] For these critics, the best solution is to leave international humanitarian law as it is and address terrorism and insurgents through the use of law enforcement mechanisms. In this view, terrorism is simply a crime, even if it is sometimes heinous and massive in scale. Therefore states should simply apply their domestic criminal laws to apprehend, arrest, and prosecute those who engage in terrorist acts against states. To the extent that states cannot enforce their own laws, an international force might be created to enforce domestic criminal laws.

The authors of this volume reject the view that domestic criminal laws should be the only means for countering and regulating terrorism and other forms of asymmetric warfare. We also, however, begin with the premise that the existing humanitarian law system is a good one and thus worth considerable effort and compromise to adapt it to include asymmetric warfare. With these considerations in mind, several questions remain: How can the convention-based laws of war be adapted to asymmetric warfare? How can the conventional be revised to account for the unconventional? At a more pragmatic level, if fighters on one side of a conflict lack the recognized structure of professional armies as well as their discipline and chain of command, how can a nonstate entity enforce the rules of war even if they were so extended? If a nonstate actor repudiates the core principle of humanitarian law—such as noncombatant immunity, as in the case of terrorist tactics—how can humanitarian law be in any way applied to their activities?

The problems are of varying magnitude and nature—including changing international norms and security contexts, new actors and tactics, evolving logistics in the conduct of hostilities, and new tests of political will. It is also worth noting that any such adaptive effort, at least in the beginning, must necessarily be one-sided, with states and humanitarian organizations in the lead. The prototypical nonstate actor—al-Qaeda, for instance—rejects the principles of noncombatant immunity and distinction. Bin Laden maintains that it is acceptable to kill noncombatants because they bear responsibility for harms suffered by Muslims at the hands of interlopers from the West. In this case, any adaptation of humanitarian law would need to proceed while one party to the conflict rejects its core principles. Moreover, al-Qaeda and like-minded organizations are loosely aligned in a networked fashion with no traditional command hierarchy to be held accountable for humanitarian law compliance, monitoring, or training, if they were so inclined; nor are there clear points of reference for negotiation. It is clear that any adaptive scheme for humanitarian law will thus need to be voluntary in the beginning, with incentives for complying. Even though it is unrealistic to expect nonstate entities invited to join an adapted humanitarian law to comply reciprocally with states, even modest gains in compliance by states and nonstate actors may be worth the effort made toward adaptation. It is in the service of laying the groundwork for such efforts that this volume provides analyses of the promises and pitfalls in proposed adaptations of humanitarian law to asymmetric warfare. A few issues are addressed throughout our chapters.

First, issues of moral authority and normative incentives for bringing nonstate actors into the humanitarian law system must be considered. In asymmetric conflicts between states and nonstate entities, when is it acceptable to go beyond law enforcement methods in combating asymmetric attacks and engage the attackers in armed conflict? Our view on these threshold questions is that one must consider the intensity, scale, and duration of conflict between a state and nonstate entity—in keeping with traditional approaches that define the existence of an armed conflict. But how to weigh each of these measures, considering that terrorist or insurgent activity is often sporadic, remains a matter of significant debate. A related threshold matter is determining possibilities for a middle ground between law enforcement and armed conflict regimes to guide states and to determine when a state is justified in using force. For states, we offer combatants POW status, which is difficult to apply to nonstate groups because of definitional difficulties. Likewise, the war crimes regime serves as a negative incentive, though it is not strong enough to deter fanatics. In creating incentives for nonstate entities to buy into the humanitarian law system, are there innovative ways to structure legal relationships in asymmetric war? Are there other incentives—to punish noncompliance and to reward compliance?

Second, international humanitarian law and accompanying policies should be clarified to take into account basic definitional dilemmas that arise in asymmetric conflicts. The most complex issue involves defining the terms "combatant" and "civilian." These status issues, in turn, lead to critical examination of what is meant by such related designations as "lawful combatant," "unlawful combatant," and "taking an active part in hostilities." Should humanitarian law classify terrorists as combatants, civilians, or neither? What about insurgents? If the law classifies these actors as combatants or some third category, is mere membership in a terrorist organization or insurgent group enough to identify an individual with an organization that acts in violent or destructive ways? Should we give terrorists POW privileges? These status designation issues call for a careful evaluation of the fundamental conceptual tools needed to adapt humanitarian law to the current multivariate conflict environment. How can we improve upon some of the open-ended, subjective, or historically outdated standards that underlie humanitarian law? For example, it is very likely that more concrete guidance can and should be provided on how to carry on a conflict in and around protected sites. Likewise, proportionality in asymmetric warfare could also be more clearly spelled out by establishing a set of criteria or preconditions for a proportionate military response. More controversially, should the threshold distinction between "international" and "noninternational" armed conflict be delinked from the question of state or party status?

Third, given the nature of new forms of conflict and new battlefields, critical thinking on the laws of war must consider the role of states in aiding and abetting nonstate actors, such as when states provide sanctuary for terrorists. Sanctuary, of course, includes a range of complex scenarios, including states that are culpable only by virtue of their inability to evict insurgent or terrorist organizations from state territory.

Fourth, we should all contemplate the roles and legal status of new nontraditional actors—private security companies, child soldiers, NGOs, among others—that increasingly play a prominent role on the battlefield in asymmetric conflicts and in postconflict settings. How the law (international and domestic) takes into account the role of private security contractors in the asymmetric setting has become a high-profile and controversial issue since at least the 2007 Baghdad Nisoor Square incident where Blackwater security personnel shot unarmed civilians. Military contractors in Iraq and Afghanistan are no longer playing merely support roles but are present in battle zones, especially as downsized militaries give them broader responsibilities. Likewise, military contractors have played a significant role in interrogation in ways that may skirt law-of-war provisions. What legal obligations and responsibilities do private contractors have? What protections do they deserve under humanitarian law? What are the obligations of states that hire them regarding their conduct? Because being inside or outside the strictures and protections of humanitarian law depends largely on these threshold determinations of armed conflict type and combatant status, working toward modifying or replacing traditional categories with ones that can reach some nonstate actors may also very well include contemplating the range of new actors on the battlefield.

Fifth, international humanitarian law requires that states engage in armed conflict based on reciprocal duties and obligations. Should reciprocity continue to be a requirement for all parties to a new protocol, for instance, and how might one account for whether a nonstate entity has an adequate internal disciplinary or command structure that can oversee its adherence to humanitarian law? In a similar vein, should groups fighting for self-determination be held to the same rules as other nonstate entities, and what about those who commit acts of sabotage against the state? Might there be legitimate and illegitimate nonstate entities for humanitarian law purposes?

What Might an Adaptive International Humanitarian Law Look Like?

If *New Battlefields/Old Laws: Critical Debates on Asymmetric Warfare* helps shape what may eventually be the building blocks for new guidelines for decision makers in the international laws of war, one sticking point in bringing asymmetric warfare to the table is that it upsets humanitarian law's state-centric universe of concepts, norms, and procedures—and their interdependence. In this respect, disrupting humanitarian law's fixed terminology may destabilize the existing paradigm.

Designating "combatant" and "civilian" status determines who may be targeted, detained, interrogated, and prosecuted in an overarching system of norms and procedures. In the future there may be reason to redefine combat status to focus on participants and nonparticipants in the conflict. Improving humanitarian law may very well require changing core terms to take into consideration such issues as who is a participant in combat and whether they are active or passive in a conflict. Likewise, it may be legally possible in the future to have an armed conflict between a nonstate entity, where the nonstate entity is defined by certain attributes identified by a revised humanitarian law. For instance, this nonstate actor might be a transnational group (based on ideology, politics, or religion) whose policies include the persistent use of force against a state to attain its objectives and where the nonstate entity cannot be effectively combated using traditional law enforcement means. Under a revised international humanitarian law, for example, members of the nonstate group may be targeted at any time during an armed conflict, whereas civilians could be targeted only when they are taking an active part in the hostilities. Implications from these changes for prosecution regimes will also need to be addressed. For instance, should the rules for detention, interrogation, and adjudication of combatants change in light of adapting humanitarian law to nonstate actors? Should the protections of human rights afforded by international law and treaties be extended to nonstate entities and, if so, which ones, and for which kinds of nonstate groups? In this way, modifying or replacing traditional humanitarian law categories with ones that reach some nonstate actors will invariably impact the legal regime and the development of new international norms.

Twenty-first-century forms of conflict, then, are fostering new questions about the legitimacy of the international humanitarian law corpus. The challenge is thus to balance reform with preserving these venerable international legal instruments to ensure their longevity, relevance, and continued success in humanizing the battlefield—including maintaining the balance at the heart of humanitarian law between states' security aims and the human rights community's commitments to minimize unnecessary suffering on the newest battlefields.

Perhaps the most difficult challenge will be dealing with how the contemporary battlefield itself has become a politicized space where legal regimes become a tool for tactical maneuvers. The law itself must be "recognized not as a neutral construct but as something much more complicated and dynamic," a product of a complex dance between military and humanitarian establishments' different perspectives on a common set of issues.[22] The politicization of law threatens the delicate balance between state security and human rights, and it can relegate reform efforts to the vagaries of power politics. The fact that we are focusing on a state-centric legal paradigm that must be applied to asymmetric disputes involving nonstate actors has created legal uncertainty and anxiety—in ways that may invite abuses of the law. The balance struck between international humanitarian law and other legal regimes is more critical than ever before, insofar as humanitarian law is a bulwark of human security in times of armed conflict, but only if invoked where it properly belongs and obeyed where properly invoked.[23] It is for these reasons that this volume is particularly timely and important.

Summary

The first critical debate, *Threshold Issues in Defining Twenty-first-Century Armed Conflicts,* identifies present vulnerabilities and uncertainties in the existing humanitarian law framework. The issues include identifying the nature of a conflict and the criteria for defining "armed conflict" for purposes of determining whether criminal law or the laws of armed conflict apply and, thereafter, which detention and prosecutorial systems are appropriate. Determining the legal regime applicable to a given conflict is critical for understanding the broad-scale shifts occurring in the nature of warfare and for seeing broad-scale historical changes in the function of war "as a means of law enforcement" in which war-waging parties can rationalize the use of force by weakening its prohibition.[24]

Geoffrey S. Corn's "Extraterritorial Law Enforcement or Transnational Counterterrorist Military Operations: The Stakes of Two Legal Models" and Gregory Rose's "Preventive Detention of Individuals Engaged in Transnational Hostilities: Do We Need a Fourth Protocol Additional to the 1949 Geneva Conventions?" probe from different perspectives key threshold problems in humanitarian law in light of new patterns of conflict—the triggering mechanisms that determine which legal framework (criminal law or the laws of armed conflict) is activated and states' obligations in light of this determination (including appropriate detention and prosecutorial systems). Corn critiques conventional opinion that military operations against transnational terrorism which do not fall neatly within the state-centric conflict categories derived from the Geneva Conventions should be treated as extraterritorial law enforcement activities. He makes the case for extending the humanitarian law framework to counterterrorist military operations by appealing to core historical principles of humanitarian law and to military protocol, namely, the decades-old mandate in the U.S. Department of Defense Law of War Program to "comply with the principles of the law of war during all military operations."[25] It is "invalid and disingenuous to characterize counterterror military operations employing combat power under a 'deadly force as a first resort' authority as extraterritorial law enforcement," Corn argues, and this understanding of this law-triggering paradigm actually weakens humanitarian law by contributing to the regulatory uncertainty of military operations against nonstate entities operating transnationally.

Gregory Rose, by contrast, argues for bridging the gap between military uses of force and civil law enforcement operations by developing a hybrid international protocol to combat insurgency that must be harmonized with domestic laws. Critical of what he sees as the anachronistic legality of insurgency in the 1977 Additional Protocol to the Geneva Conventions, Rose notes a tension in the fact that both terrorism and insurgency are outlawed under domestic laws, but not by international legal regimes. On the contrary, he argues, the Protocol's new rules for nonconventional armed conflict have aided the legality of insurgency because—unlike the 1949 Geneva Conventions, which obliged paramilitaries to wear a fixed distinctive sign and carry arms openly—combatant status has been made more widely available and afforded to fighters not in uniform. Such revisions encumber the laws of armed conflict with concepts that bear the stamp of decolonization and Cold War politics, he argues, a time when irregular forces were revolutionaries confronting dictatorial regimes, not networked cells skirting the obligations of humanitarian law. A better approach, Rose believes, is to realize that categorizing conflicts in the either/or terms of "armed conflict" or "not armed conflict" is "legalistic, simplistic, and misconceived" and that situations of political violence today are not binary but operate as a continuum in levels of intensity over time. When constabulary operations suffice, for instance, then domestic criminal law is sufficient to apply to a given conflict; but if military action is needed to respond to a sustained campaign of political violence, humanitarian law should apply. Both civil and military legal norms may therefore be brought to bear on a conflict and, if suitably harmonized, may be seamlessly applied in a single situation.

The second and third Critical Debates, *Status and Liabilities of Nonstate Actors Engaged in Hostilities* and *Changing Twenty-first-Century Battlefields and Armed Forces,* explore new kinds of actors that do not fit neatly into traditional status designations, as well as the range and volume of civilian and combatant positions involved in the hostilities. Addressing whether the traditional laws and norms of armed conflict provide sufficient guides for status determination, contributors define the parameters of this problem in more depth and address potential adaptations to humanitarian law to deal with the range of players. David Crane and Daniel Reisner, in "'Jousting at Windmills': The Laws of Armed Conflict in an Age of Terror—State Actors and Nonstate Elements," argue that two elemental humanitarian law precepts—the distinction between combatants and civilians and the link between combatant and POW status—create an impasse today for states dealing with such actors as Taliban fighters in Afghanistan or Hezbollah forces on Israel's borders. Designating these irregular forces as combatants, for instance, legitimizes their targeting during hostilities, but also grants them POW status, with its attendant privileges. By contrast, to define these fighters as "civilians taking a direct part in hostilities" avoids POW status privileges but entails more limited targeting options. Because no state dealing with transnational terrorism wishes to grant designated terror groups the legitimacy associated with POW status or impose upon themselves the targeting limitations of "civilians taking a direct part in hostilities," Crane and Reisner argue that a new category of combatant is necessary and that the contingent relationship between combatant and POW status should be reviewed in light of modern realities.

In contrast to Crane and Reisner, Eric T. Jensen, in "Direct Participation in Hostilities: A Concept Broad Enough for Today's Targeting Decisions," argues that no new status designation category is required. Jensen favors a broader interpretation of existing language in the 1977 Protocol Additional I to account for fighters who purposely attack from within civilian populations or use civilian status to frustrate targeting efforts. On the contemporary battlefield "actual harm" is too narrow when defining "direct participation in hostilities," Jensen argues, and criteria are necessary to address actions that may not cause "actual harm" but still make a person targetable, such as membership in organizations, proximity to the battlefield, or importance of actions in the chain of events leading to harm. This modernized view allows for the targeting of civilian fighters even after the actual attack if it is clear that they will return to the battlefield to do more harm, and it accounts for others who may not be actually pulling the trigger or setting off explosives but who still play key supporting roles, such as bomb makers or trainers. Allowing the targeting of members of armed wings of terrorist organizations, for instance, modernizes the definition "direct participation in hostilities" in a way that preserves the principle of distinction but still provides military commanders with the tools needed to conduct missions.

Crane and Reisner and Jensen deal with the legal dimensions of status designation under humanitarian law. Daphné Richemond-Barak's "Nonstate Actors in Armed Conflicts: Issues of Distinction and Reciprocity" adopts a historical perspective on the evolution of humanitarian law, showing how its provisions may change to meet each generation's new challenges, but that continuity in its principles should remain. Revisiting the historical purpose of the principles of distinction and reciprocity in humanitarian law, Richemond-Barak argues that the balance intrinsic to humanitarian law—between state equality and the protection of civilians—may be adapted to nonstate actors in today's armed conflicts through a broad interpretation of Article 44(3) of Additional Protocol I to the Geneva Conventions.

In the third debate, Hilly Moodrick-Even Khen's "Children as Direct Participants in Hostilities: New Challenges for International Humanitarian Law and International Criminal Law" and Renée de Nevers's "Private Military Contractors and Changing Norms for the Laws of Armed Conflict" analyze the implications for humanitarian law of the range and types of civilians and combatant positions now involved in armed conflicts. Using such examples as Hezbollah's recruitment of 2,000 children between the ages of 10 and 15 (known as "future suiciders") and informal reports of children as young as 16 years old detained at Guantanamo Bay, Khen identifies the problematic breaching of the two main protected-status positions (combatants and civilians) when children become involved in the hostilities. Khen also shows how child terrorists are creating legal status determination problems in the range of roles that they are being asked to play (e.g., as human shields and as direct participants in the hostilities). De Nevers also explores a new category of warrior, private security contractors, and how they fit within the Geneva Conventions and in any nation's domestic law. Since the nature of warfare and the warriors have changed since 1949, she argues, humanitarian law must address itself to a broader spectrum of warfare and seek greater international support for its regulatory role in the process of combating terrorism. Despite different emphases, each of these chapters provides careful analysis of the challenges of regulating warfare today when participants in the hostilities are not easily labeled to determine their status or treatment under the law.

The volume concludes with a fourth critical debate, *Military Necessity and Humanitarian Priorities in Humanitarian Law: Productive Tension or Irreconcilable Differences?* Here contributors revisit the foundational question of humanitarian law as a compromise between state sovereignty and humanitarian protections. Issues at stake in this final section include whether, at the broad level of international norms, present challenges to humanitarian law represent a shift in the balance between universal attempts to humanize war by protecting individuals in conflict settings and the kind of thinking that states do to meet their national security objectives—a core tension that forms the prescriptive force of the laws of war. If there is a shift in balance, the trend also has implications for a state's ability to project legitimacy to the broader international community. Robert P. Barnidge, in "The Principle of Proportionality under International Humanitarian Law and Operation Cast Lead," addresses the implications for this balance when warfare becomes not only a legal institution but a politicized one. Related to this question is whether the laws and customs of war are themselves being strategically manipulated by weaker adversaries who use tactics forbidden by international humanitarian law, such as human shielding, in order to win the public relations war against a militarily stronger adversary. In this case, if and when humanitarian law becomes part of the calculus of asymmetric strategy, these instruments become politicized weapons in a new breed of contemporary transnational conflict.

Corri Zoli, in "Humanizing Irregular Warfare: Framing Compliance for Nonstate Armed Groups at the Intersection of Security and Legal Analyses," differs with Barnidge's view that indeterminate elements of the law, particularly the principle of proportionality for assessing military necessity, enable asymmetric tactics. She suggests instead that lawfare plays a role in prompting once compliant states' overreactions and in creating the appearance of violations of humanitarian law. When Hamas, Hezbollah, and other armed groups use civilians and civilian sites to their military advantage, this routine asymmetric tactic, Zoli argues, comprises an essential strategic use of lawfare. Comingling fighters and weaponry with civilians in their living spaces is designed to protect insurgent forces (the asymmetric element) and heighten civilian casualties (the lawfare element), a direct reversal of humanitarian law norms and a savvy show of irregular forces' ability to hinge their own notion of military advantage on its political and legal implications (rather than on proportionality). Prompting stronger adversaries to violate—or appear to violate—principles of distinction and proportionality is part of this irregular political calculus. By far its most troubling implication is for humanitarian law itself, because when an overreaction does occur, the militarily weaker party succeeds in prompting the stronger party to play by their adversary's rule book. By understanding lawfare as a tool of asymmetric strategy it is possible to see how the changed security climate offers opportunities for adversaries to reframe the meaning of the law and, further, how gaps in humanitarian law emerge as much from new battlefield contexts as from internal tensions in the law itself.

In every chapter, readers are provided with a critical understanding of the potential shortcomings and challenges to international humanitarian law and policy in responding to new wars and asymmetric tactics mounted by nonstate groups. Far from offering a single voice or consensus on these issues, however, the structure of this volume is designed to guide readers through the most pressing debates and most cogently argued perspectives and to underscore the many stakeholders tackling the application of the law to new forms of warfare.

CRITICAL DEBATE I

Threshold Issues in Defining Twenty-first-Century Armed Conflicts

ONE

Extraterritorial Law Enforcement or Transnational Counterterrorist Military Operations

THE STAKES OF TWO LEGAL MODELS

GEOFFREY S. CORN

One of the most challenging issues in combating transnational terrorism has been determining the appropriate legal framework that covers counterterrorist military operations. Because the United States characterized its response to the terror attacks of September 11, 2001 as an "armed conflict,"[1] well-accepted standards for identifying when international humanitarian law (referred to also as the law of armed conflict or the law of war) applies have been thrown into disarray. In the years following, a variety of legal theories have competed to define the proper locus of counterterror military operations within the international legal regime. These include the U.S. position that counterterrorist operations are armed conflicts triggering humanitarian-law authorities, the International Committee of the Red Cross (ICRC) contention that such operations are international armed conflicts whenever a state conducts military operations in the territory of another,[2] and the view of human rights advocates that such operations fall under a human rights regulatory framework because armed conflict between states and transnational nonstate entities is a legal impossibility.[3]

Skepticism toward the U.S. claim for an armed conflict framework in fighting and prosecuting the "Global War on Terror" is unsurprising.[4] It is unjustifiably broad to argue that the struggle against terrorism invokes the full "authorities of war"[5] for all aspects of counterterrorism operations—from detaining terrorist "foot soldiers" on the conventional battlefield to capturing terrorist operatives with law enforcement assets in peaceful domestic environs.[6] But it is also wrong to claim that military operations launched for the primary purpose of using combat power against terrorist targets cannot trigger the humanitarian-law framework because they fail to satisfy a paradigm evolved from a different era in which interstate or intrastate armed conflicts were the norm.[7] Likewise, framing all counterterrorist operations within the state-centric conflict framework does not always produce helpful results. Treating the 2006 Israel and Hezbollah war as a subset of armed conflict between Israel and Lebanon, for instance, may result in an unjustified windfall for nonstate forces—namely, the opportunity to qualify for the privilege of combatant immunity.[8] Just as the military component of the international struggle against highly organized terrorist groups is bounded, specific, and rule driven, far more than the notion of a "global war" implies, so too must be the legal analysis to regulate these military operations.[9]

The issue that prompts the most intense debate with respect to the military role in combating international terrorism is whether an armed conflict can even exist outside the interstate/intrastate paradigm. Though the U.S. position has been an unequivocal "yes," there is no international consensus.[10] On the contrary, many experts in international law insist that such operations are not armed conflicts at all, but "extraterritorial law enforcement" operations.[11] Yoram Dinstein, one of the international community's most respected *jus belli* scholars, recently emphasized this point. During a symposium analyzing legal issues arising from combat operations in Afghanistan, Dinstein asserted clear and simple legal criteria for the conduct of transnational counterterror military operations.[12] Such operations qualify as armed conflict under only two conditions, both related to state-sponsored terrorism: first, when the operations are derived from an armed conflict with the state sponsor of a terrorist organization; and second, when the actions of the terrorist organization can be attributed to the sponsoring state as the result of terrorist authority over organs of the state.[13] All other uses of force against this threat must be regarded, according to Dinstein, as extraterritorial law enforcement and cannot amount to armed conflict.

This chapter challenges this dominant theory that military operations against transnational terrorist groups that do not fall neatly within state-centric conflict categories must be treated as extraterritorial law enforcement activities. This challenge is based on several grounds. First, it argues that characterizing counterterror military operations using combat power as extraterritorial law enforcement is disingenuous and inconsistent with the very nature of these operations. It argues, instead, that humanitarian law is the more appropriate and logical regulatory framework for military operations involving the use of combat power based on an inherent invocation of the principle of military objective, including those beset by regulatory uncertainty when they fall outside accepted law-triggering categories derived from Articles 2 and 3 of the Geneva Conventions. This is to suggest not that all uses of the military against transnational terrorism should trigger humanitarian-law principles, but that the nature of such use—and more specifically, whether it explicitly or implicitly involves the use of combat power reflecting the existence of armed conflict—should dictate whether the operation falls into the category of armed conflict or remains a matter of assistance to law enforcement.[14]

The second stage in the argument for extending the law-of-war framework to counterterror military operations invokes an important but little-known U.S. military policy based on an exemplary use of humanitarian-law principles—even when the enemy is a nonstate entity with no link to the state in which it operates. For more than three decades prior to 9/11, the Department of Defense Law of War Program imposed this simple mandate: "Comply with the principles of the law of war during all military operations," where "principles" reflect the fundamental balance between the dictates of military necessity and the obligation to mitigate suffering associated with armed conflict. Subjecting all military operations using combat power to the law-of-war regulatory framework aligns operational needs with the evolving nature of armed conflict, provides U.S. forces with a uniform regulatory standard, and offers a common standard of training and operational compliance during the range of military operations that advanced forces now see. Equally important, this policy helps to deal with the fact that such operations are often initiated prior to clear government determination of the legal applicability of the laws of war. Most critically, this regulation helps to preserve a disciplined force—an issue understood by earlier generations as one of the main reasons to legally regulate the battlefield.

The following discussion expands upon these arguments. It exposes the essential factors necessary to meaningfully analyze the legal framework for military operations against transnational terrorist operatives: the underlying nature and purpose of the existing law-triggering paradigm, the different nature of the authority derived from the law of armed conflict compared to the law enforcement framework, and the importance of maintaining a clear distinction between the *jus ad bellum*[15] and the *jus in bello*.[16] It concludes with the stakes involved in these issues. Though not easy, determining the most appropriate legal framework for the regulation of extraterritorial military operations directed against transnational terror operatives is critical given the prevalence of these operations globally and the U.S. role in them. This determination profoundly impacts the rights and liberties of individuals captured and detained in such operations, just as it fundamentally impacts states' authority to employ combat power—two sets of interests that may become positioned against one other in conflict settings.

Common Article 3 and "Armed Conflict Not of an International Character": Limitations of the Traditional LOAC Paradigm

All international humanitarian-law scholars and practitioners are versed in the "either/or" law-triggering paradigm created by Common Articles 2 and 3 of the four Geneva Conventions and the interpretation of these Articles that evolved since 1949. This paradigm may have proved generally sufficient to address armed conflict prior to 9/11, though its sufficiency does not justify the conclusion that no other triggering standard should be recognized to keep pace with the evolving nature of armed conflicts.[17] If the prospect of an unregulated battlefield is simply unacceptable to the international community—a premise evident in the response by the international community to the 2006 conflict in Lebanon—an important question is whether it is best to continue to fit a new breed of conflict into the international/noninternational paradigm or whether the time has come to endorse a new category of armed conflict.[18] It is the limited reach of Common Article 3 itself that compels the conclusion that recognizing a new category is now essential.[19]

The military role in the U.S. fight against al-Qaeda and the 2006 conflict between Israel and Hezbollah have strained the meaning of the traditional humanitarian-law-triggering paradigm,[20] creating uncertainty about the law that applies to transnational combat operations.[21] These operations employ armed force against nonstate actors operating outside the state's territory pursuant to what are essentially status-based rules of engagement.[22] An example of such an operation is the 2007 U.S. AC 130 gunship strike against an alleged al-Qaeda base camp in Somalia,[23] or the Israeli campaign against Hezbollah in southern Lebanon during the 1990s [24] and in 2006.[25] Although opposition to defining these operations as armed conflicts has been significant, this critique, in addition to the undeniable occurrence of these and other similar operations, may be stimulating a beneficial reassessment of the laws of war. One manifestation of this reassessment is the legal challenge brought by Salim Hamdan against the use of military commission to try him for war crimes. Before the U.S. Supreme Court ruled in *Hamdan* v. *Rumsfeld* that military tribunals convened to try detainees must comply with humanitarian law, as incorporated in the Uniform Code of Military Justice (UCMJ) and embodied in Common Article 3 of the Geneva Conventions, the Court of Appeals Judge Williams responded to the majority's conclusion that Common Article 3 did *not* apply to armed conflict with al-Qaeda because the president had determined that this conflict was one of international scope: [26]

> Nonstate actors cannot sign an international treaty. Nor is such an actor even a "Power" that would be eligible under Article 2 (¶3) to secure protection by complying with the Convention's requirements. Common Article 3 fills the gap, providing some minimal protection for such non-eligibles in an "armed conflict not of an international character occurring in the territory of one of the High Contracting Parties." The gap being filled is the non-eligible party's failure to be a nation. Thus the words "not of an international character" are sensibly understood to refer to a conflict between a signatory nation and a nonstate actor. The most obvious form of such a conflict is a civil war. But given the Convention's structure, the logical reading of "international character" is one that matches the basic derivation of the word "international," i.e., *between nations*. Thus, I think the context compels the view that a conflict between a signatory and a nonstate actor is a conflict "not of an international character."[27]

In a conflict "not of an international character," the signatory is bound to the modest requirements of Common Article 3 for "humane" treatment and "the judicial guarantees which are recognized as indispensable by civilized peoples."[28] Although Judge Williams did not sway his peers, the U.S. Supreme Court later adopted his view.

The *Hamdan* interpretation of Common Article 3 is particularly appealing: If the government invokes the authority of humanitarian law, it must abide by the modest obligations of humane treatment. Despite being embraced by a slim majority of the Supreme Court, this expansive interpretation of

Common Article 3 remains controversial because it defies the assumed "intrastate" limitation on the application of the Convention. This ambivalence reflects the inherent flaw in the humanitarian-law-triggering paradigm established by Common Articles 2 and 3 of the Geneva Conventions. As Judge Williams also realized, it is fundamentally inconsistent with the logic of humanitarian law to disconnect the threshold application of the regulation from its real-world necessity—conflict typing is not an adequate mechanism to determine when and how the laws of war should apply in complex cases involving nonstate actors. Williams, thus, looked beyond traditional interpretations of Common Articles 2 and 3 to produce a pragmatic reconciliation of these two considerations.

Ironically, it is the long-standing policy of the U.S. military that validates Williams's interpretation of the role of the laws of war in transnational conflicts.[29] That policy, as will be explored later, long ago rejected a formalistic interpretation for applying humanitarian-law principles to military operations in favor of a pragmatic approach based on the necessity of providing U.S. forces with a consistent regulatory framework. The pragmatic logic informing military policy on this subject for three decades prior to 9/11 should be regarded as a reflection of a general principle of humanitarian law—one that requires that all military operations involving the employment of combat power fall under the regulatory framework of international humanitarian law.[30]

Regulatory Gap: How Military Policies Reflect the Necessity of a "Principled" Approach to Military Operations

The need to provide a humanitarian-law-based regulatory framework for all combat operations—even those outside the accepted law-triggering categories derived from Common Articles 2 and 3—is not something only recently suggested by critics of Israeli operations against Hezbollah.[31] For more than three decades before this conflict, U.S. armed forces followed a clear and simple mandate codified in the Department of Defense Law of War Program: "Comply with the principles of the law of war during all military operations."[32] Although this policy mandate never articulated precisely what was meant by "principles"[33] (purportedly to provide operational flexibility by allowing each individual service to define the tactical scope of the mandate), the term is generally understood to refer to the concepts within humanitarian law that reflect a fundamental balance between the dictates of military necessity and the obligations to mitigate the suffering associated with armed conflict.[34] As Adam Roberts explains:

> Although some of the law is immensely detailed, its foundational principles are simple: the wounded and sick, POWs and civilians are to be protected; military targets must be attacked in such a manner as to keep civilian casualties and damage to a minimum; humanitarian and peacekeeping personnel must be respected; neutral or non-belligerent states have certain rights and duties; and the use of certain weapons (including chemical weapons) is prohibited, as also are other means and methods of warfare that cause unnecessary suffering.[35]

These concepts provide the foundation for the detailed rules of implementation.

If the U.S. Department of Defense has never defined what constitutes the "principles of the law of war" within the meaning of this policy, this is because a variety of U.S. military manuals and doctrine provide clarity about the content of the term, including all service branch manuals on the laws of war, and because venerable discussions of these now conventional principles are evident in texts that range from the 1863 U.S. Lieber Code to the Preamble to the Hague Rules of 1907. The "basic principles of the LOAC [laws of armed conflict] are beyond dispute," Dinstein notes, and include "the principle of distinction (between combatants and civilians), the principle of causing no unnecessary suffering to combatants, the principle of proportionality in attack."[36] These baseline norms "are elevated to the pinnacle of the law regulating the conduct of hostilities in international armed conflict" and provide the foundation for more extensive and comprehensive conventional regulation of armed conflicts. Yet, as Dinstein also notes, "as one descends from fundamentals to specifics, consensus shrinks."[37] Addressing how the laws of war encompass general principles and specific customary and treaty law, the recently revised *United Kingdom Ministry of Defense Manual for the Law of Armed Conflict* provides:

> Despite the codification of much customary law into treaty form during the last one hundred years, four fundamental principles still underlie the law of armed conflict. *These are military necessity, humanity, distinction, and proportionality.* The law of armed conflict is consistent with the economic and efficient use of force. It is intended to minimize the suffering caused by armed conflict rather than impede military efficiency.[38]

For U.S. forces and their operations, fulfilling the specifics of the mandate to comply with these principles during all military operations is left to operational documents and legal advisors, based on their discipline, training, and experience.

What is critical about this policy is therefore not the precise content of the term "principles," but the fact that the policy mandate requires that U.S. armed forces treat *any* military operation, especially those using combat power, as the trigger for applying the regulatory framework of humanitarian law.[39] As a result, this policy ensures that international humanitarian-law principles provide the basis for every phase of the military component of a counterterrorist operation, including those defined as part of what the United States characterized as the Global War on Terror.

The motive for this expansive policy is twofold. First, the policy provides a common standard of training and operational compliance during the range of military operations in today's complex operational environment.[40] Second, the policy responds to the reality that such operations are often initiated prior to a clear government determination of humanitarian-law applicability. Beyond policy considerations, however, U.S. armed forces (and their legal advisors) value this mandate because they recognize that operating within a well-defined regulatory framework during combat operations is essential to preserve a disciplined force.

A different, but important, purpose for battlefield regulation, though often overlooked today, was well known to prior generations—an emphasis evident in the *Oxford Manual of the Laws of War on Land*, a key precursor of the conventional laws of war:

> By [codifying the rules of war derived from state practice], it believes it is rendering a service to military men themselves. . . . A positive set of rules, on the contrary, if they are judicious, serves the interests of belligerents and is far from hindering them, since by preventing the unchaining of passion and savage instincts—which battle always awakens, as much as it awakens courage and many virtues—it strengthens the discipline which is the strength of armies; it also ennobles their patriotic mission in the eyes of the soldiers by keeping them within the limits of respect due to the rights of humanity.[41]

That battlefield regulation benefits both noncombatants and combatants on either side of the conflict is the motivation for imposing policy-based compliance with humanitarian-law principles. It also explains why other armed forces as well as multinational military commands have emulated this U.S. approach and, by their actions, filled the regulatory lacuna created by a restrictive humanitarian-law-triggering paradigm and new operational realities. For example, the *U.K. Law of Armed Conflict Manual* explains Britain's policies during what it defines as "Peace Support Operations"—military operations that do not trigger application of the law of armed conflict: "Nevertheless, such fighting does not take place in a legal vacuum. Quite apart from the fact that it is governed by national law and the relevant provisions of the rules of engagement, the principles and spirit of the law of armed conflict remain relevant."[42] The perceived need to resort to humanitarian-law principles to fill the regulatory void associated with contemporary military operations even transcends national policy through adoption by the United Nations. In recognition that forces operating under United Nations authority are habitually called upon to use military force in situations of uncertain legal classification, the Secretary-General issued a bulletin mandating compliance with foundational principles of humanitarian law during any armed conflict, with no qualification based on the nature of the armed conflict.[43]

No matter how helpful this mandate may be in terms of military efficiency and humanitarian protections, the existence of these policy prescriptions underscores the gap between the technical legal triggers for law-of-war application and the situations necessitating them.[44] Moreover, the issue of conflict typing, determining which conflict situations are categorically appropriate for triggering humanitarian law, has only recently become a major concern. Before the development of the legal triggering mechanisms for dictating application of this regulatory framework, armed forces did not consider conflict typing to be an essential predicate for compliance with regulatory codes. On the contrary, the recognition that combat is an endeavor that must be subject to an effective regulatory framework is derived from a history of self-imposed regulatory codes adopted by professional armed forces.[45] Although it is true that the framework established in these codes was self-imposed, they provided the seed for what are today regarded as foundational law-of-war principles.[46] In many respects, then, a pragmatic military logic deeply rooted in experiences from the history of warfare is reflected in the Department of Defense law-of-war policy.

In fact, combat operations conducted by regular armed forces against non-state armed groups prior to the development of Common Article 3 are not uncommon historically nor unaccounted for legally. Examples range from colonial expeditions to what we would call today "coalition operations," as in the multinational response to the Boxers in China. In *Savage Wars of Peace*, Max Boot notes several operations conducted by U.S. armed forces before World War II, including expeditions against the Barbary Pirates and Pancho Villa, where forces invoked an early version of these principles.[47] The principle of military necessity, for instance, was asserted in the authority to use all measures not forbidden by international law necessary to achieve the prompt submission of opponents, and an early form of the principle of humanity, as understood in historical context, was also invoked.[48] Although the nature of the constraints on the conduct of these operations was understood as matters of chivalry more than law, the basic premise from the early to the contemporary battlefield is similar: Combat operations trigger a framework of regulation needed for disciplined operations as the *sine qua non* of a professional armed force.[49] Today this framework is understood not as chivalric or honorable code but as compliance with legally defined principles of necessity, humanity, distinction, and prohibition against inflicting unnecessary suffering.[50]

It is clear that in 1949 international legal regulation was understood as being confined to hostilities between states—a point emphasized by Leslie Green's *The Contemporary Law of Armed Conflict*. Not only does Green reiterate that "[h]istorically, international law was concerned only with the relations between states," but he argues, "[a]s a result, the international law of armed conflict developed in relation to interstate conflicts was not in any way concerned with conflicts occurring within the territory of any state or with a conflict between an imperial power and a colonial territory."[51] Nonetheless, even early compliance with internal military codes reflects an understanding of the need to subject all combat operations to operational regulation. As international law evolved, this imperative gradually diluted the significance of the interstate/nonstate categories of armed conflict. In fact, the need to ensure effective regulation of all armed conflict was a critical motivation in extending law-of-war principles from international armed conflict to the realm of internal armed conflict by the *Tadic* ruling.[52] In that seminal opinion, the International Criminal Tribunal for the Former Yugoslavia confronted, and rejected, the assertion that rules of conduct developed for interstate hostilities had no role in the regulation of intrastate hostilities. Instead, the tribunal acknowledged that it was the fundamental nature of armed hostilities and not the international or noninternational character of those hostilities that created the imperative to extend the applicability of these norms of conduct to ensure both categories of hostilities were regulated by an effective balance between necessity and humanity. That contemporary international humanitarian law finds its origins in the pragmatic codes from which they evolved is also highlighted by Green: "[t]he law of armed conflict is still governed by those principles of international customary law which have developed virtually since feudal times."[53]

The historical underpinnings of humanitarian law and the contemporary application of its principles to a wide spectrum of military operations as a matter of national policy indicate that the dispositive factor in determining when this regulatory framework should apply is the nature of the military operation in question. When armed forces conduct operations employing combat power against a defined enemy with authority to kill as a measure of first resort, the operation must be regarded as armed conflict.[54] The underlying logic that has driven the historical application of humanitarian-law principles to combat operations provides compelling evidence in support of extending this framework to counterterror military operations that fall into this category, even when the enemy is a nonstate entity with no plausible link to the state in which it operates.[55] As will be discussed in the following section, an analytical focus on the fundamental nature of the authority invoked by the state to subdue a terrorist opponent indicates that characterizing such operations as law enforcement is not logically supported.

The Fundamental Distinction Between the Law of Armed Conflict Legal Framework and the Extraterritorial Law Enforcement Legal Framework

Thus far, I have shown why the most important consideration in determining the legal regulatory framework applicable to military operations directed against transnational nonstate entities must be the nature of the authority invoked and employed by state forces: that when a state authorizes its armed forces to employ combat power based implicitly on the principle of military objective (use of deadly force based on a determination of status), that use of force should be characterized as armed conflict.[56] I have also, however, explained why existing understandings of this law-triggering paradigm have at times operated very differently. As a result, military operations conducted by states against nonstate operatives who operate transnationally fall into a category of regulatory uncertainty.[57] In response to this uncertainty, scholars like Dinstein have argued that such operations are best understood as extraterritorial law enforcement activities and not as armed conflicts.[58] This view presumes that a law enforcement legal paradigm and not law-of-war principles is best suited to regulate such operations.

The most fundamental distinction between law enforcement and armed conflict is manifested in the scope of the use of deadly force authority—a distinction between using deadly force as a last or as a first resort.[59] Law enforcement activities, governed by domestic law and international human rights standards, limit authority to use deadly force as a measure of last resort.[60] In contrast, the use of deadly force against a military objective is a legitimate measure of first resort during armed conflict.[61]

This basic distinction reveals the fundamental fallacy of characterizing all transnational counterterror military operations as law enforcement based exclusively on incompatibility with the interstate/intrastate law-of-war triggering paradigm.[62] Consider the example of an air strike conducted against terrorist training facilities operating with impunity in the territory of another state.[63] It is inconceivable that the authority to employ deadly force by air assets will be determined on the basis of some provocation from the terrorist target. It is equally inconceivable that the pilots conducting the strike mission would be required to offer the potential targets an opportunity to submit to apprehension as a prior condition for employing combat power. Instead, the authority to employ that power will almost certainly be based on the principle of military objective, allowing the use of deadly combat power based solely on the identification of the target as one falling into the category of a defined terrorist enemy.

The use of military power under this type of authority is not law enforcement because it involves the authority to employ deadly force as a measure of first resort. Humanitarian law provides the most appropriate legal framework for operations using military force in such a manner.[64] Characterizing such operations as law enforcement creates an incongruity: the suggestion that the use of deadly force is limited to a measure of last resort and that less destructive means must be attempted prior to such use.[65]

Some scholars, including Gregory Rose in this volume, have responded to this friction between the fundamental operational nature of such operations and the existing humanitarian-law-triggering paradigm by proposing an alternative "hybrid" characterization: militarized law enforcement. According to Rose, this hybrid legal framework for the regulation of state response to transnational nonstate terrorist threats should be founded upon principles reflected in existing domestic laws related to the incapacitation of terrorists. This suggests that the overarching legal framework for extraterritorial counterterror operations must be derived from law enforcement authorities. However, under certain circumstances when the use of combat power to augment law enforcement capabilities is required, the presumptive law enforcement activity would be considered "militarized." This theory is consistent with the thesis of this essay to the extent that it suggests that *when* law enforcement activities become "militarized," enhancement of use of force capability results in a different legal framework, namely, humanitarian-law principles. If, however, the suggestion is that when a state "militarizes" law enforcement activities, the armed forces engaged in operations are bound to comply with a law enforcement legal framework, then the effectiveness of the "militarization" of the activity would be undermined.

One alternative middle ground is that armed forces would be regulated by humanitarian-law principles during the tactical phases of "militarized" law enforcement intended to subdue an opponent, but that individuals captured and detained, once removed from the area of immediate conflict, would be subject to a law enforcement legal regime. Such a hybrid approach responds to the primary objection leveled against the U.S. invocation of humanitarian-law authorities vis-à-vis captured terrorists —their indefinite detention without trial on the basis of military necessity. It also accommodates the needs of the armed forces engaged in such operations by providing them with the most logical legal framework during the application-of-force phases. One other potentially significant benefit of such a hybrid approach is that it eliminates any incentive for an unjustified invocation of humanitarian authority as a subterfuge for avoiding normal legal process related to detention.

The legitimacy of this "militarized" law enforcement theory rests on the assumption that existing domestic legal authority for the trial and incapacitation of such individuals will satisfy the necessity of preventing the return to belligerent activities. If this assumption is valid, then the hybrid approach holds great merit. If, however, the assumption is invalid, it seems inconsistent with a humanitarian-law-based authority that led to the capture of such individuals to require their release with full knowledge of their likely return to belligerent activities. Ultimately, however, even this approach to defining the applicable legal framework for counterterror military operations is based on an effort to reconcile operational reality with legal regulation.

No such incongruity would result from acknowledging that military operations with combat power targeting terrorist operatives are armed conflicts. Instead, such an acknowledgment achieves a critical effect: The authority invoked by the state is counterbalanced by the limiting humanitarian principles of the law.[66] In short, if such operations are categorized as armed conflicts, the law essentially creates a "package deal" for all participants, regardless of which "side" of the conflict they fall on. Although the principle of military necessity/military objective regulates the employment of deadly force as a measure of first resort, other principles limiting the methods and means of warfare and for establishing baseline standards of treatment for captured and detained personnel become triggered. Unless military operations conducted against terrorist operatives also trigger these complimentary humanitarian principles, states will continue to be free to employ force in a manner indicating a *de facto* armed conflict without being required to respect legally-mandated humanitarian limitations on the exercise of that power.

The Bright-Line Distinction Between the *Jus ad Bellum* and the *Jus in Bello*: Application of Humanitarian Law Must Not Be Influenced by Use of Force Legality

One significant objection to treating military operations against transnational terrorists as triggering law-of-war rights and obligations is that to do so would legitimize such uses of force. This argument, however, ignores what is known as the "bright-line distinction" between two separate legal regimes: the *jus ad bellum* and the *jus in bello*.[67] The *jus ad bellum* are a set of criteria, rules, and agreements in international law that regulate whether armed conflict is permitted. The *jus in bello* regulate the manner in which armed hostilities are to be conducted. One of the primary purposes of the use of the term "armed conflict" to trigger the 1949 Geneva Conventions was to ensure that applicability of the *jus in bello* would be determined irrespective of the legality of hostilities under the *jus ad bellum*, thereby preventing states from avoiding compliance with humanitarian obligations by asserting their opponents were engaged in illegal hostilities. Thus, the International Committee of the Red Cross Commentary to Common Article 2 indicates that:

> By its general character, this paragraph deprives belligerents, in advance, of the pretexts they might in theory put forward for evading their obligations. There is

no need for a formal declaration of war, or for the recognition of the existence of a state of war, as preliminaries to the application of the Convention. The occurrence of de facto hostilities is sufficient. It remains to ascertain what is meant by "armed conflict." The substitution of this much more general expression for the word "war" was deliberate. It is possible to argue almost endlessly about the legal definition of "war." A State which uses arms to commit a hostile act against another State can always maintain that it is not making war, but merely engaging in a police action, or acting in legitimate self-defence. The expression "armed conflict" makes such arguments less easy.[68]

This armed-conflict humanitarian-law trigger was perhaps the most important development in the 1949 revision of the Conventions and rapidly evolved into the dispositive standard for the applicability of the entire corpus of humanitarian law. This evolution reflects a categorical rejection of the pre-1949 practice of avoiding humanitarian obligations during armed conflict based on the illegality of an enemy's decision to engage in armed conflict. The justification for this rejection was clear: The people who are asked to fight war are almost never those responsible for the decision to do so. As a result, humanitarian law evolved to acknowledge that all participants in war—even warriors—are in this sense victims of war. From this recognition a clear distinction between the legality of resorting to war and the legality of conduct in war evolved. This distinction has long stood for the proposition that the legality of war must not be permitted to influence the application of the rules for conduct during war.[69]

This *ad bellum/in bello* distinction is a foundational principle of the Geneva Conventions and the de facto law-triggering provisions incorporated in them.[70] Accordingly, the "armed conflict" terminology included in the 1949 Conventions was intended to achieve this critical effect: to ensure that the legal regime protecting participants in armed conflict would never again be diluted or denied based on the choices of those who decide on armed conflict.[71] It is a reflection of the basic tenet of the Geneva Conventions that all individuals impacted by armed conflict, civilian and warrior alike, are in essence "victims of war," for they are not responsible for the decision to wage war.[72] The legal regime that operates to limit the harmful effects of war on both warrior and civilian must be triggered by a pure de facto standard: the existence of armed conflict.

In the intrastate context, the line between the use of state power for law enforcement purposes and armed conflict has been relatively well defined.[73] However, once states began to employ military power outside their territory for the purpose of combating terrorism, this line became blurred. I have addressed the problem of defining the line between law enforcement and armed conflict in the extraterritorial context in a prior article,[74] asserting that the nature of the use of force authority employed by armed forces is the most effective means of providing clarity and consistency in this increasingly common situation.[75] The salient point is that when a state authorizes the use of combat power based on an inherent invocation of the principle of military objective (in the form of status-based rules of engagement), a situation of de facto armed conflict exists.[76] This is so because the use of state military power based on this principle permits the employment of deadly force as a measure of first resort with no requirement to use that force proportionally vis-à-vis the object of attack. Such uses of force are simply not consistent with a law enforcement legal framework. This basic concept thus reveals why the *ad bellum/in bello* distinction is equally relevant in such a context. That is, even assuming that the use of force authorized by the state is in violation of the *jus ad bellum*, this in no way alters the basic reality that the state has implicitly invoked the laws of war for purposes of executing the operation. As a result, there is no justification whatsoever to deprive participants in the hostilities of the benefit of the fundamental principles of that law.

There is, however, an inversion of concerns about the *ad bellum/in bello* distinction for transnational armed conflicts. The primary concern when drafting the Geneva Conventions was preventing states from using the illegality of war as a justification for denying humanitarian protections.[77] By contrast, in applying the laws of war to military operations between a state and transnational nonstate entities, the concern is that acknowledging that such operations trigger the humanitarian-law framework bolsters the legal justification for the use of force by states. The underlying purpose of the *ad bellum/in bello* distinction is equally applicable in this context: The legal framework that regulates the conduct of military operations should in no way influence the assessment of the legality of those operations.

As I have written elsewhere,[78] this de facto standard is a core concept in the existing Geneva Conventions, and the focus of these law triggers is on the question of actual hostilities that rise above the level of law enforcement activities.[79] In such circumstances, the law of war is the appropriate legal framework to achieve the humanitarian objective of limiting unnecessary suffering. In the end, international humanitarian law should treat *ad bellum/in bello* issues as presenting independent legal questions. This analytical clarity would justify a conclusion that a state's use of military force to target a terrorist entity is in violation of the *jus ad bellum*, for instance, but, nonetheless, that the military operation qualifies as an armed conflict that must trigger fundamental humanitarian-law rights and obligations. This scenario is far more consistent with humanitarian precepts than asserting that the *jus ad bellum* violation requires, at once, denying participants in the hostilities the benefits of the legal framework best suited to regulate such activities.

On first glance, it appears that characterizing such operations as law enforcement avoids these issues entirely. But it is unlikely that states will escape accountability for armed intervention into another state's territory simply by asserting that they are exercising "extraterritorial law enforcement" authority. Regardless of the characterization adopted by a state, it is almost certain that the de facto nature of the action will be the focus of *jus ad bellum* judgment. As a result, the use of combat power under extraterritorial law enforcement authority may create a triple failure: It will be insufficient to avoid condemnation for a *jus ad bellum* violation, especially when combat force is obviously being used; it will deprive the forces engaged in the operation of the clarity afforded by the *jus in bello* legal framework; and it will leave combatants and noncombatants alike unprotected by humanitarian considerations.

If characterizing counterterror operations under the international humanitarian-law framework triggers more expansive authorities than treating these operations as law enforcement, requiring compliance with law-of-war principles will limit and constrain the scope of that authority. Other significant factors that will offset any tendency to treat such operations as armed conflict simply for the benefit of expanded authority include *jus in bello* considerations and domestic political and international relations considerations, and, perhaps most important, assessment of the most feasible means to achieve the neutralization objective. When a state, after considering all these factors, chooses to unleash combat power to achieve the national objective, the benefit of the humanitarian-law regulatory framework should not be denied simply because the enemy is a transnational organization without a traditional military structure. This standard will not increase the use of combat power by states for counterterrorist purposes.

The Law of Armed Conflict:
A Defined and Intuitive Regulatory Framework

One primary consideration for determining which legal framework is appropriate for regulating military operations is how effectively it achieves its purpose. It is here that applying humanitarian-law principles offers substantial advantages over the law enforcement framework. Two considerations support this view. First, fundamental law-of-war principles are well established and understood by professional armed forces. Indeed, these principles are so pervasive that they have formed the foundation for policy regulation of many military operations that are not technically subject to their regulation. Second, because of their pervasive use, armed forces conduct operations habitually, even intuitively, within this framework.

Organized militaries are not conversant with the law enforcement framework, and, as a general proposition, armed forces are not trained to conduct law enforcement operations.[80] Unlike their law enforcement counterparts, military personnel are trained to engage an enemy with deadly combat power on command, often using overwhelming, not graduated, force.[81] The law enforcement training, by contrast, demands a careful escalation of force suited to variable circumstances to ensure that the resort to deadly force is a measure of last resort.[82] Imposing a law enforcement framework on military personnel requires complex modifications to the role, responsibilities, and mindset of the combat professional, with all the training, planning, and execution challenges associated with it.

Nonetheless, one criticism of the prospect of applying humanitarian-law principles to military engagements with transnational terrorist groups arises from the purported uncertainty in developing specific rules that apply to such operations. For example, in responding to the transnational armed conflict theory, Dinstein challenged the validity of proposing a new theory of conflict regulation.[83] This criticism, however, is more appropriately leveled at the extraterritorial law enforcement paradigm. Though the rules for domestic law enforcement activities are well developed, there is no basis to assert that these can be transplanted to extraterritorial military operations. In fact, armed forces would be expected to comply with a regulatory framework that was never developed or intended to regulate armed hostilities, least of all the complexities of combat operations against terrorist operatives. In this sense, there is no need to substitute a new scheme for rules that work well. As

Dinstein has noted, the law of war is based on universal principles, including military necessity, military objective, proportionality, and humanity. Surely these rules amount to a starting point for developing the specifics for regulating this emerging category of armed conflict, and extending these principles to transnational armed conflicts is not a radical departure in the history of international law. A similar move was made in regulating internal armed conflicts by appealing to provisions developed in the context of interstate conflict.

Policy Application of the Law of Armed Conflict: Its Value and Limitations

The most compelling evidence in support of applying humanitarian law to these military operations is this framework's "default" standard, the fact that it is a validated solution to the legal uncertainties associated with contemporary military operations. The logic of this policy enhances the probability of disciplined operations by facilitating uniform training and planning criteria. As the only source of international law that evolved for the specific purpose of regulating military operations, the extension of the humanitarian-law framework to even nonconflict military operations was understood as pragmatically and operationally essential. These policies indicate that military operations are best regulated by law developed for this purpose and not for some other reason.

The past effectiveness of applying humanitarian law has led some to assert that there is no need to wade into the controversial legal waters of conflict characterization in counterterror military operations, but that compliance with these policies provides an effective solution to that regulatory dilemma.[84] This "policy is enough" argument is flawed for two reasons. First, it acknowledges that these operations require the regulatory framework that humanitarian law provides but avoids the difficult question of *why* it should be applied and what conditions trigger its application. Second, and more important, it underestimates the ultimate weakness in policy-based compliance: What policy makers giveth, policy makers may taketh away.

Until the U.S. response to the terror attacks of 9/11, the "policy is enough" argument held merit, because issues related to the regulation of these military operations, including the treatment of captured or detained individuals, were left almost exclusively to military decision makers.[85] This paradigm shifted dramatically after the 9/11 attacks, and the military was no longer free to "apply the principles of the law of war" with little or no interference from civilian decision makers. Yet this intervention proved important, for it exposed the limits of policy-based applications of humanitarian-law principles to new forms of armed conflict.[86]

In what are now regarded as notorious legal opinions, senior U.S. government lawyers advised Washington decision makers to adopt policies in treating captured and detained personnel that deviated from humanitarian-law principles. These new treatment standards were facilitated by the fact that compliance with humanitarian law was determined to be based on a policy mandate and thus was malleable. This process explains why simply asserting a policy-based application of humanitarian-law principles to counterterror military operations is insufficient to address regulatory issues. Participants in these counterterror military operations and the individuals engaged with combat power (whether they are subdued, captured, or detained) require a legally defined and mandated regulatory framework.[87] Only by acknowledging the legally mandated application of humanitarian-law principles to such operations will this essential certainty be achieved.

Conclusion: Case-by-Case Application and the Rejection of the Zero-Sum Game

This chapter has demonstrated that characterizing counterterror military operations employing combat power as extraterritorial law enforcement does not work. Instead, these operations should be regulated for what they are: armed conflicts that trigger a regulatory framework based on basic law-of-war principles. I am not suggesting, in a zero-sum analysis, that all uses of the military against transnational terrorism must be defined as triggering law-of-war principles. What I have proposed, instead, is that the essential nature of the use of force authority in any military operation must dictate whether that operation falls into the category of armed conflict or remains under the assistance of law enforcement.[88] This line may be difficult to decipher at times. But rejecting the application of law-of-war principles to operations, simply because to do so deviates from the traditional conflict-typing paradigm, defies the most significant advance of the 1949 Geneva Conventions: the recognition that only a de facto law-triggering standard will protect victims of war by ensuring that humanitarian-law authority is tempered by applying humanitarian-law-based obligations.[89] To illustrate this effect, one need only consider the initial U.S. decisions related to the treatment of captured and detained enemy combatants during the initial phases of the Global War on Terror. Their detention without charge or trial was justified based on an invocation of the principle of military necessity because, unlike the pre–September 11th security environment, they were captured in the context of an armed conflict. However, because that armed conflict did not fit within the existing common Articles 2 and 3 law-triggering paradigm, the United States disavowed any obligation to comply, as a matter of law, with humanitarian-law obligations.[90] Had the United States focused on the de facto nature of hostilities to determine the applicability of humanitarian-law-derived authority and obligations, this "authority without obligation" interpretation of the law would have been rejected.

Determining the most appropriate legal framework for regulating extraterritorial military operations against transnational terror operatives is no easy task, but an essential one. Since the United States began asserting its engagement in an "armed conflict" with al-Qaeda, scholars, legal advisors, policy makers, and courts have struggled with the question, producing a wide variety of outcomes. But two major theories have evolved. The first, epitomized by the U.S. position, asserts that these operations qualify as "armed conflicts" within the meaning of international law, thereby triggering a heretofore undefined package of legal authorities and obligations. The second, based on the premise that armed conflict can only occur within the interstate or intrastate law-triggering paradigm established by Common Articles 2 and 3, treats as armed conflict only those counterterror military operations that fit within this paradigm. In all other cases, including the use of combat power to target terrorist operatives in the territory of other states, military operations must be defined as extraterritorial law enforcement activities, presumably regulated by law enforcement authorities and human rights obligations.

This chapter has asserted that the law enforcement approach produces an outcome disconnected from the underlying purpose of international humanitarian law. It unjustifiably denies the armed forces and those whom they engage on that which is indisputably a battlefield the benefit of the regulatory framework developed specifically to limit the harmful consequences of combat. Although the overly broad assertion of law-of-war authority resulting from the Bush administration's Global War on Terror justifies a cautious approach, an underinclusive backlash is equally dangerous. What is needed is a case-by-case assessment of the fundamental nature of military operations:

When they are conducted pursuant to a "use of deadly force as a first resort" authority, there has been an invocation of humanitarian law.

Under such circumstances, armed forces must operate under the obligations established by that same body of law—principles that are generally well understood and that have formed the foundation for the operational regulation of virtually all military operations by many armed forces for decades. Whatever the uncertainty inherent in these principles, it is relatively insignificant compared with the far more uncertain content of the extraterritorial law enforcement legal framework. More significantly, military operations conducted pursuant to status-based rules of engagement are fundamentally inconsistent with a law enforcement legal framework because the forces are empowered to use deadly force as a measure of first resort. Acknowledging that under appropriate circumstances armed forces are bound to comply with law-of-war principles will not dilute operational effectiveness but will ensure, instead, a balance of authority and obligation. It will also limit uncertainty concerning which rules apply during these complex operations, thereby limiting the more extreme abuses that can occur in irregular warfare.

TWO

Preventive Detention of Individuals Engaged in Transnational Hostilities

DO WE NEED A FOURTH PROTOCOL ADDITIONAL TO THE 1949 GENEVA CONVENTIONS?

GREGORY ROSE

Contemporary battlefield conditions present new challenges for international law, which does not yet address nonstate entities engaged in transnational paramilitary attacks. The term "transnational" here refers to attacks across national borders by individual persons or private organizations, as compared with the term "international," which refers to interstate relations governed by public international law.[1] This chapter argues that renewed development of international legal norms is necessary to address transnational armed conflict with nonstate entities, and it tentatively explores the generative role of national laws in developing the basis for new international law. The chapter provides a comparative analysis of laws in Australia, Israel, and the United States, focusing on their legal processes for preventive detention relating to national security. Other emerging norms for detention, such as legal standards for the prosecution of nonstate fighters or the preconditions for lethal targeting of individual combatants, fall outside the scope of the investigation.

An explicit premise of this chapter is that transnational paramilitary attacks should no longer be considered legal under international law. Domestic insurgency and terrorism are both typically illegal under state domestic laws because of the state's traditional formal monopoly on the use of force. Yet states have not agreed to prohibitions in general on cross-border paramilitary attacks. Instead the wide-ranging "legitimacy of the struggle of peoples for independence, territorial integrity, national unity and liberation from colonial and foreign domination and foreign occupation by all available means, particularly armed struggle" is internationally endorsed.[2]

The broad generality of this legitimization of armed struggle is a legacy handed down from the period of twentieth-century decolonization struggles and the Cold War, when dictatorial state authority was often subject to paramilitary challenge by political revolutionaries. Decolonization was an explicit goal of the United Nations Charter in 1945.[3] By 1977, two Additional Protocols to the Geneva Conventions brought legal innovations in belated response to the changed battlefield in the era of decolonization, constraining governments within humanitarian limits when they use armed force against nonstate entities.[4]

However, there are at least three reasons that international legal inaction against nonstate entities conducting attacks across state borders was and is not good policy. First, inaction implies tolerance for breaches of the peace and interference in the internal affairs of other states in contravention of the motivating spirit of international law and of the UN Charter. Second, contemporary technologies afford nonstate entities greatly increased destructive power and a global reach that threatens not just subregions but all countries. Third, inaction debilitates efforts to confront globally networked terrorism through international cooperation. We should now urgently reconsider the wisdom of the international community's permissiveness toward transnational attacks by nonstate entities.

Nonstate Entities and New Battlefields

Replacing hierarchical and capital intensive paramilitary forces with networked cells that maximize impact at the least cost, the netwar appeared in the last decade of the twentieth century, succeeding the national liberation movements that had conducted decolonization struggles. The netwar connotes networks of nonstate entities, such as terrorists and irregular forces, engaged in a violent social conflict. It is a mode of conflict (and crime) at societal levels, involving measures short of traditional war, in which the protagonists use network forms of organization and related doctrines, strategies, and technologies attuned to the information age. These protagonists are likely to consist of dispersed small groups that communicate, coordinate, and conduct their campaigns in an internetted manner, without a precise central command.[5]

Such conflict is typically low level, sporadic, long term, and transnational. International humanitarian law is, however, not yet adapted for these non-state-initiated transnational hostilities.

OUTDATED INTERNATIONAL NORMS

Under the 1949 Geneva Conventions, which themselves responded to the military and humanitarian lessons of World War II, paramilitary or volunteer corps were obliged to wear a fixed distinctive sign recognizable at a distance and to carry arms openly.[6] These nontraditional forces were also required to conduct themselves in accordance with international humanitarian law and to be subject to a command ensuring their compliance.[7] Although that conduct was a precondition for their recognition as a legitimate armed force,[8] breaches by individual combatants did not negate the organization's armed forces status, which was based on indicators of organizational membership rather than activity.[9]

Under Additional Protocol I of 1977, combatant status affording privileges equivalent to those of traditional armed forces became more widely available, reaching fighters not in uniform and those concealing weapons until deployment before an enemy.[10] Fighters in national liberation movements became entitled to claim the status of international combatants and its incumbent Geneva Convention rights.[11] Such groups were still required to fight under a "command responsible . . . for the conduct of its subordinates" and "subject to an internal disciplinary system that shall, *inter alia*, enforce compliance with the rules of international law applicable in armed conflict."[12] But, again, breaches by individual combatants did not negate the organization's international status as armed forces.[13] An automatic right to judicial determination of whether combatant status should apply was awarded to persons taking part in hostilities,[14] whereas, conversely, any person not given combatant status was automatically afforded protected or "equivalent" civilian status under Geneva Convention IV.[15]

These changes, introduced by Additional Protocol I of 1977, marked a watershed in modern humanitarian law by adapting it to paramilitary revolutionary conflict. Daphné Richemond-Barak notes in this volume that combatant status thereby became a function of the individual's active engagement in hostilities. Yet by the twenty-first century the circumstances of armed conflict have changed again and those aspects of Protocol I of 1977 that imbue nonstate fighters with combatant status and its attendant rights might now be viewed as historical encumbrances, because they do not condition status on the fulfillment of definite responsibilities.

UNDEFINED RESPONSIBILITIES OF NONSTATE ENTITIES

In a wide range of circumstances, nonstate entities remain outside the obligations of contemporary international humanitarian law. Francis Lieber, a father of humanitarian law, observed more than a century ago that autonomous armed groups typically act outside ethical and legal constraints:

> we understand by guerrilla parties, self-constituted sets of armed men in times of war, who form no integrated part of the organized army, do not stand on a regular pay roll of the army, or are not paid at all, take up arms and lay them down at intervals, and carry on petty war (guerrillas) chiefly by raids, extortion, destruction, and massacre, and who cannot encumber themselves with many prisoners, and who will therefore generally give no quarter. They are peculiarly dangerous because they easily evade pursuit, and by laying down their arms become insidious enemies; because they cannot otherwise subsist than by rapine, and almost always degenerate into simply robbers or brigands.[16]

International law addresses the humanitarian responsibilities of these nonstate actors merely incidentally. The 1949 Geneva Conventions impose direct obligations only on their High Contracting Parties.[17] Combatants who are not regular armed forces are third parties and not obligated under the Conventions.[18] Liberation movements under Protocol Additional I of 1977 may choose to commit themselves by means of a unilateral declaration[19] to comply with the law,[20] but nonstate entities are otherwise not explicitly obligated by the Geneva Conventions. The reciprocal obligations inherent in its treaty structure were inapplicable to nonstate entities, as discussed by Richemond-Barak.

Beyond the Geneva Conventions, relevant norms are evolving in international criminal law and in international custom. The Statute of the International Criminal Court criminalizes certain acts of political violence by nonstate actors within a relatively narrow range of war crimes and crimes against humanity.[21] Its articulation of these crimes is a refinement of universal obligations upon individuals that have evolved in customary international law, but they address individual conduct post hoc, not nonstate entities as groups of fighters, and they do not constitute humanitarian law as such.

UNDEFINED RIGHTS OF NONSTATE ENTITIES

There is considerable controversy as to the circumstances in which nonstate fighters are afforded conventional rights by the High Contracting Parties to the Geneva Conventions, including prisoner-of-war or protected-person status,[22] a controversy that Additional Protocol I of 1977 only increased. These ambiguities have inhibited the acceptance of some elements of the Protocol as customary international law.[23]

Article 50 of Additional Protocol I provides that all persons who are not combatants are civilians,[24] yet Article 45(3) recognizes that a person might be regarded as neither a privileged combatant nor a protected civilian.[25] The official International Committee of the Red Cross commentary on this provision states that it "covers persons who not only cannot claim prisoner of war status, but are also not protected persons under the Fourth Convention."[26]

Common Article 3 of the four Geneva Conventions of 1949 is widely considered by judicial tribunals as a catch-all formula applicable to fighters engaged by nonstate actors. Article 3 refers to conflict *in the territory of one* of the High Contracting Parties. Murphy argues that a "fair reading" of the negotiated history of Common Article 3 indicates that it was "principally designed to address the situation of an armed conflict *internal* to a single State."[27] Yet the International Court of Justice, the International Criminal Tribunal for the Former Yugoslavia, and the U.S. Supreme Court have each considered Common Article 3 to be applicable also to transnational armed conflict engaged in by nonstate entities.[28] In particular, the U.S. Supreme Court decided in 2006 that Common Article 3 is to be interpreted broadly as meaning "in contradistinction to a conflict between nations."[29] These judicial decisions have been critiqued as legal policy innovation, effectively extending the coverage of Common Article 3 beyond its originally intended scope of application to internal armed conflict.[30]

Although the humanitarian sentiments motivating these judicial decisions to expand Common Article 3 to transnational armed conflicts are sound, the process of their formulation is worrying. The primary responsibility for the formulation of international rules governing armed conflict usually falls to national representatives advised by military experts in the context of international negotiations. The expansive judicial interpretation seems inconsistent with the position taken as recently as 1998 by states that negotiated the scope of application of the same phrase under the Statute of the International Criminal Court, which criminalizes serious violations of Geneva Protocol II in a protracted armed conflict *occurring in the territory of a State*.[31] In the absence of formulating urgently needed new norms by national representatives, international rules for the management of armed conflict are being made by judicial tribunals.[32]

Even when expansively interpreted, Common Article 3 provides only a limited framework for the rights of nonstate fighters and indicates the paucity of applicable rules. "As admitted by the diplomatic conferences that adopted them, Common Article 3 and Additional Protocol II of 1977 to the Geneva Conventions represent only the most rudimentary set of rules" for noninternational armed conflict.[33] In an era of transnational netwars, it is clear that the rules applicable to transnational armed conflict need further development.

CONFUSED CATEGORIES OF RULES FOR NONSTATE ENTITIES

Figure 2.1 sets forth the different categories in international law applicable to nonstate entities engaged in armed conflict. On the left, it indicates that where a foreign occupying force or a national liberation movement is engaged in an armed conflict with a state (an international armed conflict between states), the principal international rules governing the conflict are the 1949 Geneva Conventions, Additional Protocol I of 1977, and (to a limited and unsure extent) human rights treaties.[34] On the right, concerning armed conflict not of an international character, a distinction remains between internal and transnational armed conflicts governed by overlapping but not identical rules. In an internal armed conflict, Additional Protocol II, Common Article 3 of the four Geneva Conventions and human rights law govern. In a transnational armed conflict, the applicable law is Common Article 3 of the four Geneva Conventions and human rights law. There is no special protocol and only a very limited legal framework to address nonstate entities engaged in transnational armed conflict. The diagram also indicates that gaps exist in the categories of rules applicable to nonstate fighters. In addition, partly because

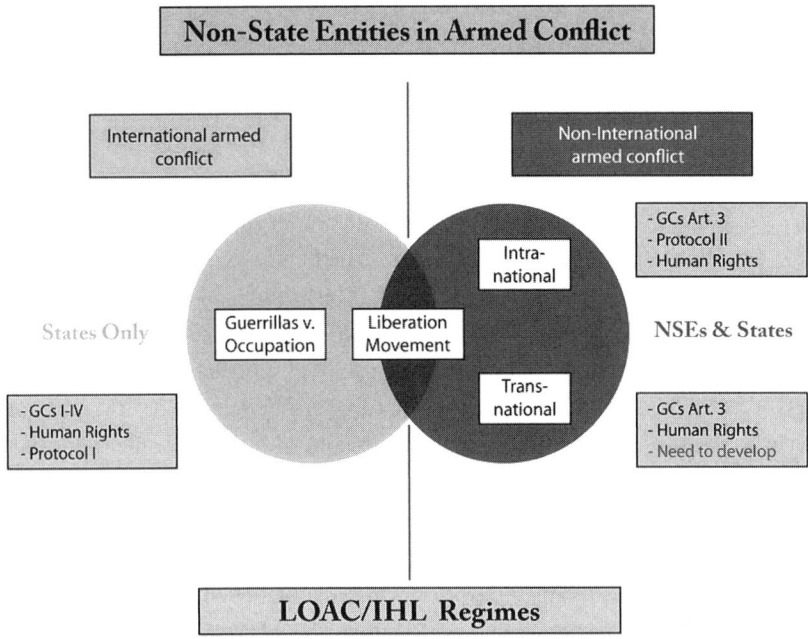

FIGURE 2.1   Nonstate entities in armed conflict.

of ambiguity in international law as to whether an "armed conflict not of an international character" is "internal," "transnational," or perhaps "internationalized" (in which nonstate entities operate from or are supported and supplied by foreign states), there is considerable confusion as to which category of rules apply to a nonstate entity.[35]

UNCERTAIN THRESHOLDS FOR DIFFERENT CATEGORIES OF ARMED CONFLICT

In cases of low-level hostilities that nonstate entities typically engage in, it is unclear what the threshold is for legal recognition of an armed conflict that would trigger the application of international humanitarian law.[36] Additional Protocol II of 1977 specifies that dissident armed forces or other organized armed groups must "exercise such control over a part of [a state's] territory as to enable them to carry out sustained and concerted military operations," if the conflict is "internal" to the territory of a state.[37] Thus, it does not apply to mere "situations of internal disturbances and tensions, such as riots, isolated and sporadic acts of violence and other acts of a similar nature."[38] These fall below the threshold of armed conflict.

Does a similar threshold apply to conflicts that are not merely internal but extend beyond borders to become transnational? Two categories of armed conflict not of an international character with arguably different thresholds are recognized in the establishment of war crimes subject matter jurisdiction in the International Criminal Court. The first is for "serious violations" of Common Article 3, which, expansively interpreted, applies to both internal and transnational armed conflicts.[39] That threshold requires that applicable conflicts are more than mere "situations of internal disturbances and tensions, such as riots, isolated and sporadic acts of violence or other acts of a similar nature." In contrast, a second category of "armed conflict not of an international character" is recognized for conflicts that take place in the territory of a state, i.e. internal conflicts. For this category, the threshold requires that armed conflict be protracted.[40] It makes sense that a state would regard political violence within its territory, normally subject to its own law enforcement jurisdiction as, instead, subject to international law when the violence is protracted and, thus, has reached a threshold higher than that for which it can exercise its law enforcement jurisdiction. Arguably, there is a lower threshold for transnational armed conflicts than for internal ones, as the Statute of the International Criminal Court does not require that the transnational conflict be protracted. This also makes sense, as states do not usually purport to exercise their domestic law enforcement powers in a foreign jurisdiction.[41] Nevertheless, there is no consensus on whether the two thresholds are different.[42] Unfortunately, the various formulations of the threshold do not provide a clear indication of whether merely sporadic acts of transnational violence, even though part of a concerted campaign, cross the threshold to qualify as armed conflict with nonstate actors.

FROM DYSFUNCTION TO COORDINATION

A better approach might be to recognize that the legalistic categorization of hostilities as either armed conflict or not armed conflict is simplistic and misconceived. In contemporary conflicts political violence modulates backward and forward across various levels of intensity over time. Just as the scale of violence might escalate from rioting to destruction of essential public infrastructure and back down again, the application of laws might be modulated across a range of legal responses dependent upon the circumstances in each particular situation (e.g., the intensity of organized violence confronted, relative capabilities of the opposing parties, cross-border cooperative relations, and the impacts on prospects for negotiated resolution).

The necessary implication is that, in some circumstances, organized political violence can be both a crime and a paramilitary attack. Both legal norms—civil and military—might be brought to bear on the one ongoing situation of political violence at different times and places. Police operations are appropriate where low-intensity violence is manifest, even while the constabulary might be inadequate to the task of protecting the domestic civilian population when violence achieves a high intensity or emanates from a foreign jurisdiction that does not cooperate effectively in providing law enforcement assistance. If there is no need to use military force because constabulary operations suffice, then the application of domestic criminal law is sufficient. In a sustained campaign of political violence requiring a military response, however, the norms established through international humanitarian law would apply.[43] If the two sets of legal norms are suitably harmonized, then they could apply to the one situation, modulating to address the realities of multifaceted political violence.

The dual character of political violence involving mass casualty terrorism, as both violent crime and as armed conflict, was recognized by United Nations Security Council Resolution 1373,[44] which described the September 11, 2001, attack in the United States as international terrorism and expressly connected it with both the right to self-defense (in the resolution preamble) and transnational organized crime (in para. 4). It can be asserted, therefore, that nonstate actors can perpetrate transnational violence on a scale sufficient to amount to an armed attack that triggers the target state's right of self-defense.[45] The Foreign Ministers of Security Council Member States made the connection once again in 2003 in Resolution 1456, by describing terrorism both as criminal action and as a serious threat to international peace and security.[46]

Comparable approaches were taken in the cases of the covert bombing under foreign state authority of Pan Am 103 over Lockerbie, Scotland, and of the Dutch-registered vessel *Rainbow Warrior* in New Zealand's Auckland Harbor. In relation to Pan Am 103, a criminal prosecution of Libyan government security service agents took place in Scottish domestic law in parallel with sanctions imposed upon Libya under the peace and security powers of the United Nations Security Council.[47] In the *Rainbow Warrior* case, security service operatives of the French Directorate-General of External Security were prosecuted in New Zealand under its domestic law and, even though the crime was not mass casualty, a parallel international legal settlement was negotiated between New Zealand and France under the auspices of the United Nations Secretary-General.[48]

Contrary to this international practice, the International Court of Justice has nevertheless held that states have no right to self-defense in the face of armed attack by nonstate actors across a national border.[49] Thus, international law remains unsettled on matters of transnational armed conflict with nonstate entities.

Geoffrey Corn argues in this volume that when law enforcement becomes militarized, international humanitarian law should apply, irrespective of an operation's uncertain basis in an established category of armed conflict. A central rationale for his position is that military operations employ lethal force and therefore need to be governed by a known and workable system of humanitarian restraints. The lack of reciprocity and abusive manipulation of those restraints by nonstate entities raise issues for further discussion elsewhere concerning current applications of some of these restraints and how they might be adapted. However, Corn suggests that, once detained, the combatants might be subject to the civil law enforcement rather than to military norms. His position recognizes a "hybrid" of law enforcement and armed conflict laws. Consistent with that approach, this chapter undertakes in the following sections an initial exploration of legal models for the detention of individual combatants in transnational armed conflict and argues that a modified law enforcement regime is suitable.

ADAPTING HUMANITARIAN LAW TO ADDRESS NONSTATE ENTITIES

Some have argued for the use of voluntary codes (agreed to by states with nonstate fighters) as a means to fill the lacunae in international legal standards of responsibility for nonstate entities.[50] As noted by Richemond-Barak, private military contractors do voluntarily conform to the general rules of international humanitarian law, although they are not legally bound by them. Yet the likelihood of insurgents or other fighters doing so is remote. In the case of

Additional Protocol I of 1977, for instance, only one national liberation organization ever purported (albeit ambiguously) to be bound by such codes and never subsequently modified its conduct to conform to Additional Protocol I obligations.[51] Another approach is needed to restrain their conduct of hostilities within humanitarian norms.

National legislatures have been far more innovative and agile than courts in confronting new national security challenges by devising legislation that forges a unique legal space to fill the gap between laws governing criminal procedure and armed conflict. Aspects of the national security law regimes of Australia, Israel, and the United States, all based within liberal democratic systems of government, demonstrate legal innovations in preventive detention of terrorists.[52] Broader and more detailed comparative examination of legal regimes in relation to national security detention in other countries is a pressing matter for further research.[53]

The U.S. Congress has been the most noted legislature to formulate internationally applicable domestic rules on armed conflict that describe a class of foreign combatants not entitled to prisoner-of-war protections under the Third Geneva Convention. Its efforts have faced a thicket of domestic objections, and the U.S. Supreme Court's recent rulings in relation to foreign detainees have been deeply divided.[54] Israel's efforts to suppress political violence against it by nonstate actors have driven domestic legal efforts that are complicated by the fact that two different legal regimes apply—civil law for Israeli territory and military law for disputed or occupied territory—though each legal regime enables preventive detention. Australia too has instituted laws that proscribe political violence by nonstate entities in situations described as terrorist crimes that enable emergency preventive detention and control orders.[55]

Preventive Detention of Transnational Nonstate Fighters

The essential purpose of preventive detention in a liberal democratic legal system is to prevent harm to society or to the detained individuals themselves. "Detention" refers here to holding individuals in custody without trial by the executive acting within constitutional, statutory, or other legal powers, whereas the term "preventive" indicates a specific purpose for detention in preempting prospective harm (rather than punitive action taken pursuant to past harm).[56] Thus, the premise upon which preventive detention for national security purposes rests is that persons detained threaten the state by reason of their intention and capability to perpetrate violent attacks upon its society. Detention without a criminal trial and conviction obviously creates public concern because of the threat it poses to the basic human right to liberty, as enshrined for common law countries at least since 1215 in the English Magna Carta: "No Freeman shall be taken or imprisoned . . . but by lawful judgment of his Peers, or by the Law of the Land."[57] Yet such detention is not unusual in times of armed conflict.

INTERNATIONAL HUMANITARIAN LAW

A clear limitation upon the application of the individual human right to liberty is embodied in the power of a state engaged in an armed conflict to detain enemy combatants. This power is recognized in Geneva Convention III, which provides that prisoners of war may be interned until the close of hostilities,[58] and in Geneva Convention IV, which provides that protected civilians may be interned for security reasons for as long as necessary.[59]

When armed conflict takes the form of long-term noninternational hostilities, as in the "war on terror," public acceptance of unlimited detention becomes attenuated. Unless it is obvious that the detainee will resume violence against the detaining state, it is politically difficult to justify indefinite detention until hostilities end, which may extend dozens of years in some cases. Instead, a transparent, publicly acceptable process is needed to demonstrate that ongoing detention is warranted in each case. Article 5 of Geneva Convention III provides that: in cases where the status of a person who has committed a belligerent act is in doubt, a state is to convene a "competent tribunal" to determine the detained person's status, but it does not elaborate requirements for the tribunal.[60] Available potential models for judicial oversight of preventive detention ordered by constabulary or military commanders range from civil court to military commission systems.[61] The following section examines Australian, Israeli, and U.S. judicial procedures for authorizing preventive detention.

AUSTRALIA

Legislation for Australian preventive detention for acts of political violence amounting to terrorism was introduced by the *Anti-terrorism Bill (No.2)*

2005.[62] It enables legal orders to permit the detention of terrorist suspects to prevent a terrorist attack from occurring or to protect evidence relating to a terrorist act, and to permit control of the movement and activity of persons threatening a terrorist risk.[63] Australian federal preventive detention orders are divided into two types: "initial preventive detention" orders (which must not exceed 48 hours), where the issuing authority is a senior Australian Federal Police (AFP) member,[64] and "continued preventive detention" orders.[65] Once an initial preventive detention order is in force, another issuing authority, an appointed official with legal expertise,[66] can issue a continued preventive detention order.[67] The standard of proof for obtaining an order is merely the civil standard. Preventive detention in Australia is a civil law process, and applications for the issue of preventive detention orders are not in themselves prosecutions for criminal offences.[68] The detainee may contact a lawyer for purposes of seeking a remedy in a federal court or for complaining to the Ombudsman.[69] That conversation with a lawyer is monitored,[70] although it is inadmissible for evidentiary purposes, and the laws of professional legal privilege are expressly preserved.[71]

A privative clause deprives a prospective detainee of opportunities to contest the application for an initial or continued preventive detention order, other than in the High Court, which has a judicial review jurisdiction guaranteed under the federal Constitution.[72] The Commonwealth Administrative Appeals Tribunal has no power to authorize or review preventive detention[73] but can award post hoc compensation to those wrongly detained,[74] as can a federal or state court—though neither can do so while an order under Commonwealth law is in force.[75] Complaints during detention can be made to the Commonwealth Ombudsman, who can make only recommendations to the relevant authorities.[76]

ISRAEL

In Israel the procedure for preventive detention for political violence threatening national security is initially and primarily military but is subject to review in the civil court system. For Israeli citizens detained within Israeli territory[77] preventive detention for national security purposes can be ordered by the chief of general staff for 48 hours or by the defense minister for up to six months, renewably. However, detainees must be brought before a judge within 48 hours; the detention is then reviewed quarterly by the president of a district court.[78] Thus, detention orders for citizens or residents by military authorities require the approval of civil court judges at an early stage and at regular intervals; furthermore, the issuance of detention orders is subject to appeal to the district court and to the Supreme Court.

In relation to the detention of foreign insurgents the Israeli Unlawful Combatants Law was enacted in 2002 to provide for the initial determination of combatant status by a high-ranking military officer immediately upon detention. Judicial review is required within fourteen days by a district court and biannually. Detainees can appeal to the Supreme Court. During detention, detainees have the right to meet with representatives of the International Committee of the Red Cross; to engage in such activities as religious practices, outdoor exercises, and correspondence; and to receive other specified benefits of humane treatment, such as access to food, clothing, and medicine. They may be held until the end of hostilities, but the court must rescind the detention order if a detainee no longer poses a threat to national security.[79]

UNITED STATES

In the U.S. military jurisdiction at Guantanamo Bay, preventive detention of noncitizens held as unlawful enemy combatants is within the jurisdiction of military legal system under the Detainee Treatment Act of 2005.[80] A Combatant Status Review Tribunal (CSRT) comprised of three military officers determines whether a person should be detained under military jurisdiction as an unlawful combatant.[81] Detainees appearing before the CSRT may have a "personal representative" to assist them, but that representative does not have the responsibilities of a defense counsel on behalf of the detainee, nor is the relationship bound by client confidentiality. Detainees have very limited opportunities to gather, present, or challenge evidence, can access only a limited summary of the evidence against them, and cannot obtain or cross-examine witnesses, or compel evidence.[82]

An appeal against detention can be made through the civil law system to the U.S. Court of Appeals for the District of Columbia.[83] However, the U.S. Supreme Court has repeatedly held that detainees have a broader constitutional right to judicial review within the civil court system based on the principle of habeas corpus. In *Hamdi* v. *Rumsfeld* the Supreme Court applied this protection to U.S. nationals.[84] In *Rasul* v. *Bush* foreign nationals held outside

U.S. territory at Guantanamo Bay were found to be entitled to an equivalent protection by reason of application of an existing statute (which was subsequently amended to remove the protection).[85] In *Boumediene v. Bush* the Supreme Court found that the constitutionally enshrined right to habeas corpus ensured rights of judicial review of detention even to persons held by the United States outside the country.[86] Thus, the Supreme Court has struggled successfully with Congress and the administration for a measure of control over some aspects of national military decision making on detainees.

JUDICIAL REVIEW OF DETENTION

Australian, Israeli, and American legal procedures each involve civil court review of detention, although the initial stage and subsequent degree of judicial engagement vary. The initial decision for detention is made by military authorities in Israel and in the United States, but by law enforcement authorities in Australia. The widest scope of military decision making is in the United States. In Benjamin Wittes's view, preventive detention should be determined by judicial decision supported by open, transparent, and robust review procedures in an open civilian court. Such detention requires creating for each detainee "a rigorous set of factual findings and a documentary record, available to the public and the press to the maximum extent possible and reviewed by an independent judicial body."[87] Wittes also urges the institution of a specialized national security court, rather than using either the relatively nontransparent military justice system for this purpose or a national civil court that would encounter difficulties in dealing with classified material in open judicial proceedings. A substantial advantage in using a special court located within the civil legal framework is that it removes the detainee from the military legal system. It also removes the controversy over unsupervised military fiat.[88]

National Security Jurisdiction

The notion of a national security court raises the specter of the mediaeval English Star Chamber and of the oppressive security courts currently used by some undemocratic regimes as tools of oppression. However, recent liberal democratic government's adaptation of civil courts for national security purposes can be seen in the Diplock courts established by the British government in Northern Ireland in 1973.[89] Diplock courts comprised a single judge who sat without a jury, so as to overcome the problem of jury intimidation by Northern Irish paramilitary groups. Although initially intended to try members of Northern Irish factions, an Al Qaeda–affiliated terrorist was also convicted in a Diplock court in 2005.[90] Aside from exceptional cases, Diplock courts were phased out in Northern Ireland in 2007 to normalize security arrangements in accordance with the country's peace agreements.[91] A comparable legal architecture for national security courts could be designed to ensure its effective functioning while remaining a transparent and politically accountable criminal procedure.

Such a conjectured legal architecture for national security courts, noting subject matter jurisdiction, admission of evidence, procedure and defendant rights, is considered later.

BASIS IN CIVIL JURISDICTION

Harding and Hatchard set out a model code of prescriptive standards for preventive detention requiring that a civil jurisdiction review its continuation within two months of detention.[92] Wittes considers that public perception of government legitimacy demands civil judicial control of review processes for preventive detention. He argues for the U.S. Foreign Intelligence Surveillance Court, which handles security data shielded from public scrutiny, as a model for adaptation to review preventive detention of detainees.[93]

HUMANITARIAN RIGHTS AND HUMAN RIGHTS PROTECTIONS

The Geneva Conventions, with the exception of Common Article 3, are not relevant to detention hearings in armed conflicts "not of an international character."[94] The basic guarantee in Common Article 3.1(d) is the prohibition on the "passing of sentences and the carrying out of executions without previous judgment pronounced by a regularly constituted court affording all the judicial guarantees which are recognized as indispensable by civilized peoples."[95] It does not prescribe detailed procedural and substantive standards for preventive detention hearings.

Nevertheless, international human rights instruments may bear upon the substantive and procedural rights accorded in a preventive detention hearing procedure. Although it can be argued that international humanitarian law forms a special law that suspends the application of human rights norms in the circumstances of armed conflict (e.g., the right to life in relation to an enemy combatant), U.N. bodies, including the bench of the International Court of Justice, have argued for the complementary application of human rights norms.[96] The U.K. House of Lords has decided that a person's human rights may be infringed lawfully in legitimate military operations where it is necessary for imperative reasons of security but that the human rights concerned are merely qualified to the extent necessary, not altogether suspended.[97] As yet, however, the (international) law has not crystallized. Not all states are bound by all the same relevant human rights provisions, and it is uncertain which human rights norms may be considered customary international law.

Therefore, the opportunity to craft adequate legal standards for preventive detention of nonstate entities engaged in armed conflict remains open. Legal innovation is needed if we are to address the uncertainties inherent in international humanitarian law and to clarify the application of human rights norms.

ADMISSION OF EVIDENCE

To protect sensitive intelligence and to make use of sources of available evidence, some derogation would be needed from the standards of evidence applied in a criminal court under the common law. In essence, evidence might be admitted if it is probative. Hearsay evidence is currently admissible in international criminal tribunals and in the criminal courts of civil law–system countries. It can be admitted in national security courts in common law countries too if it is considered by the judge, based on a standard of objective reasonableness, to be more probative than prejudicial. Similarly, breaches of procedure that could otherwise render evidence inadmissible, if strict adherence to technical requirements were required, can be tolerated. This tolerance would exclude breaches of procedure that "shock the conscience" of the court and should be applied at its discretion. In this connection, statutory guidelines for judicial consideration of evidence obtained through manipulation, inducement, or coercion would need to be elaborated. Legal representatives of the defendant could be required to have an appropriate classified-information security clearance as a condition of their appointment.

Wittes urges that the detainee be given sufficient information concerning the evidence against him/her to be able to rebut it.[98] Harding and Hatchard suggest that, although evidence might be withheld from a detainee when its production would be contrary to national security, the review body "must have power to scrutinize the evidence itself to verify the claim."[99] To protect sensitive evidence, parts of the proceedings could be held in the presence of the legal representatives but in the absence of the defendant. Further, parts of the proceedings could be held in camera.

DECISIONS AND APPEALS

Decisions in national security preventive detention cases should be chaired by a person of judicial standing, and they should have a statutorily prescribed code of procedure that complies with the requirements of natural justice.[100] Rather than empanel a jury and grapple with the consequent difficulties in dealing with sensitive information, prejudice, or intimidation, findings of fact and of guilt or innocence should be made by a bench of three or more senior judges. The judges would, of course, decide on the admissibility of evidence and on matters of procedure and of substantive law.[101] Some elements of the court's decisions might be required to be unanimous. For example, as with a jury, the bench might be expected to reach its final finding unanimously. In view of the pervasive difficulties accompanying the formulation of authoritative legal norms in humanitarian law, it seems appropriate that decisions on matters of law should be appealable to the jurisdiction's highest court on matters of law.

Conclusion: Toward Coherent Norms for Transnational Armed Conflict

International humanitarian legal norms currently do not define satisfactorily the circumstances or legal rights and responsibilities of parties engaged in transnational hostilities. In their stead, national legal approaches to the preventive detention of persons fighting on behalf of nonstate entities are emerging. Coherence in national approaches might be encouraged by international consultations to facilitate common understandings of appropriate practice. The Copenhagen Process on the Handling of Detainees in International Military Operations is such a consultation designed to clarify rights, responsibilities, and best legal practices in the handling and transfer of detainees in situations of noninternational armed conflict.[102] Initiated by the Kingdom of Denmark, it aims to come up with a formulation of rules that can be endorsed by the United Nations. It could help to resolve contemporary legal dilemmas concerning the treatment of persons engaged in transnational hostilities, including their preventive detention. This appears to be an alternative route to the major innovation needed in international humanitarian law, such as a Fourth Protocol to the Geneva Conventions, which seems a long-term or unlikely prospect, particularly because of its need for widespread ratification.

In the medium term, national security laws might converge sufficiently to provide the basis for an international consensus on procedures for detention of nonstate actors in such hostilities. This chapter's initial exploration of legal standards for preventive detention has compared legal approaches in Australia, Israel, and the United States. It found that in Australia the initial decisions to detain occur in a civil jurisdiction, whereas they are military in Israel and in the United States—although each jurisdiction subsequently uses civil jurisdiction for judicial review of detention. Rather than either a civil or military court, the creation of a specialist national security tribunal located within the civil jurisdiction might be the most appropriate way to craft credible procedures for review of preventive detentions. Much remains to be done to compare national legal models and to develop an adaptable best-practice template.

CRITICAL DEBATE II

Status and Liabilities of Nonstate Actors Engaged in Hostilities

THREE

"Jousting at Windmills"

THE LAWS OF ARMED CONFLICT IN AN AGE OF
TERROR—STATE ACTORS AND NONSTATE ELEMENTS

DAVID M. CRANE AND DANIEL REISNER

Don Quixote said to his squire, "Fortune is arranging matters for us better than we could have shaped our desires ourselves, for look there, friend Sancho Panza, where thirty or more monstrous giants present themselves, all of whom I mean to engage in battle and slay, and with whose spoils we shall begin to make our fortunes; for this is righteous warfare, and it is God's good service to sweep so evil a breed from off the face of the earth." . . .

"Look, your worship," said Sancho, "what we see there are not giants but windmills, and what seem to be their arms are the sails that turned by the wind make the millstone go."

"It is easy to see," replied Don Quixote, "that thou art not used to this business of adventures; those are giants; and if thou art afraid, away with thee out of this and betake thyself to prayer while I engage them in fierce and unequal combat."[1]

Introduction: New Problems for a New Era of Warfare

As the global community enters the twenty-first century, armed conflict and the consequential results threaten to erode peace and security. For almost a century, the international community has attempted to codify law, custom, and policy in a body of laws, treaties, and conventions referred to as international humanitarian law.[2] The cornerstone of this attempt to govern action on and off the battlefield was achieved in the course of the late nineteenth and twentieth centuries in the Hague and Geneva Conventions.[3] The question today remains whether modern international humanitarian law is viable in light of changing threats posed by terrorists locally, regionally, and internationally.

We pose to address this question in light of the many unresolved problems that now define our contemporary security environment:

- Can a civilian terrorist that is a threat to the national security of a state be considered a military target?
- Can actions by a nonstate actor be categorized as acts of war?
- Are such actions by this nonstate actor governed by the laws of armed conflict? If they are not, is the nation attacked held to the standards found in international humanitarian law, including the principles of military necessity, unnecessary suffering, proportionality, and discrimination?
- How should a state-versus-nonstate entity conflict be characterized? Is it a police action taken against criminals? What is the status of the law breakers under the Geneva Conventions of 1949? If they are unlawful combatants, how can they be fought?
- If countering nonstate actors constitutes a type of police action, what law controls it—domestic law or international law?
- Can the military be used in a police action or in a conflict that is not an international armed conflict? If so, does humanitarian law apply?
- What is the status of civilians when taking action against nonstate actors? Are actions taken that result in the loss of lives or property immune from legal action?
- What is the minimum standard for detention and treatment of persons caught up in the conflict with nonstate actors?
- Is a person who is part of the nonstate actors' organization entitled to any protections under humanitarian law or other international laws? Or is the controlling law domestic?
- Can a state ever justify targeting civilians or civilian property in an area controlled by a nonstate actor.

Today such challenges stress the rule of law and even potentially undermine the moral authority by which a nation conducts military operations under the principles of self-defense.

In this chapter we focus attention on the status, rights, and obligations of nonstate entities within the framework of international humanitarian law. More specifically, we describe the existing rules and paradigms of international law, including some recent examples of state practices in this regard, to present a new framework for the treatment of nonstate members within an armed conflict.

Military Necessity:
The Current Rules Under the Laws of Armed Conflict

Knights errant are exempt from the application of all laws and statutes, that for them law is their sword, statutes are their spirit, and edicts and proclamations are their will and desire.[4]

Under the Hague Conventions, the Geneva Conventions, their Protocols Additional, the various conventions and treaties related to weapons, and human rights declarations, the core limitation on the use of legal force remains military necessity. From this principle of military necessity flows the additional core concepts of humanitarian law: proportionality, prevention of unnecessary suffering, and discrimination.[5] These additional principles focus the kinetic energy of armed forces as precisely as technology allows, while keeping in mind the underlying bedrock principle that civilians can never be intentionally targeted.[6] Military necessity ensures that operational responses to hostile intent or actions focus on combatants and never civilians—a premise critical to concepts of proportionality and collateral damage. But military necessity also recognizes that the unintentional killing or injuring of civilians and their property is an accepted and justified corollary to a valid and legal military action.[7]

From a historical vantage point the need for Hague and Geneva rules protecting noncombatants became urgent in the growing industrial age, where weapons became more deadly, widespread, and indiscriminate, and collateral damage to surrounding civilian property and occupants in conflict situations increased accordingly. Moreover, the advent of the machine gun, larger artillery pieces, various gas munitions, combined with the ability to mass produce them, forced nations to come to grips with the terrible results of such developments at the end of the nineteenth century.[8] In response to this moment, the Hague Convention put forth the fundamental principle of military necessity, which required that all military operations be "indispensable for securing the complete submission of the enemy as soon as possible" using weapons that are not prohibited under the various customs, practices, and treaties.[9] Figure 3.1 demonstrates the process by which a conflict is determined to be lawful and delineates how military necessity is applied.

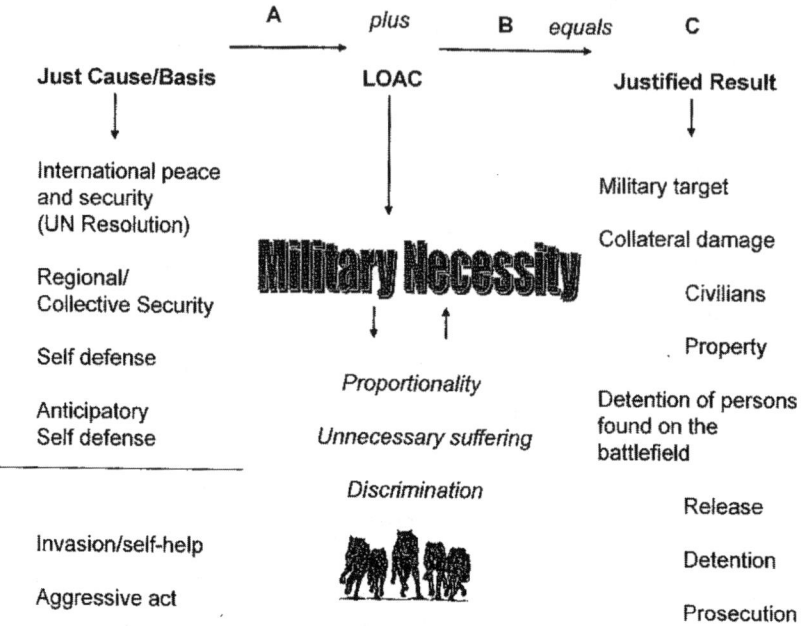

FIGURE 3.1 Military necessity.

Despite this century-long rule of military necessity codified in humanitarian law, the prevalence today of civilians on the battlefield and their increasing participation in conflicts presents one of the greatest challenges to armed forces. To address this development, our analysis focuses, first, on existing rules for combatant status and, second, on the role of civilians in the capacity in which we now find them on the contemporary battlefield space as protected persons, unlawful combatants, and *levée en masse*. We then return to possible revisions of the combatant status paradigm, reflected in current state practice, to address new battlefield conditions and tactics.

It is also true, however, that if it can be shown by a belligerent in an armed conflict that the target was necessary militarily, the possible and consequent collateral damage to property or protected persons, such as civilians, can be legally justified.[10] The concept of collateral damage, thus, recognizes that in the stress and strain of combat there will be damage—but this damage must be kept to a minimum. Moreover, the principles of military necessity, unnecessary suffering, proportionality, and discrimination are the bases by which collateral damage is minimized. Military necessity, however, has never been a defense to charges of violating the law of war as civilians cannot be intentionally targeted.

Combatant Status Rules: New Pressures on Current Law

We summarize below existing humanitarian rules for combatant status, according to the following six principles:

PRINCIPLE 1   Every individual on the battlefield is either a combatant or a civilian. When in doubt an individual should be assumed to be a civilian until indicated otherwise.

PRINCIPLE 2   Members of the armed forces of states (other than specific exceptions such as chaplains and medical personnel) are all combatants, irrespective of their role, function, or contribution or lack thereof with respect to the war effort.

PRINCIPLE 3   Combatants may legitimately be intentionally targeted unless they have surrendered or are *hors de combat*.

PRINCIPLE 4   Civilians may never be intentionally targeted unless, and for such time, as they are taking a direct part in hostilities. However, unintentional civilian casualties do not constitute a violation of the laws of war, provided that the attack complied with the requirement of proportionality.

PRINCIPLE 5   Captured combatants are generally entitled to prisoner-of-war (POW) status and may be held until the end of the conflict.

PRINCIPLE 6   Captured civilians may be detained only if and for as long as they pose a specific security threat. Captured civilians who take a direct part in hostilities may be prosecuted for their actions.

These principles are controversial, and some of them lack clarity. But, more important, over the last several decades, serious questions have emerged concerning their compatibility with contemporary warfare.

An example of current pressures with respect to Principle 1 includes the assumption of civilian status "when in doubt," a premise that grants nonstate entities potential advantages over regular armies on the battlefield when nonstate fighters choose not to wear uniforms or otherwise distinguish themselves from the civilian population. Under existing humanitarian law, a soldier encountering a nonuniformed individual on the battlefield is required to make a snap determination of status on the basis of available facts. When individuals are not wearing uniforms or carrying arms openly, the soldier is required to assess their status on the basis of supporting information, such as location, behavior, or intelligence. Such a process takes time, during which the soldier may be lawfully prohibited from taking action against the individual. Such nonstate fighters, however, are under no such limitations and may attack (using a concealed weapon) with the advantage of surprise.

With respect to Principle 2, the question of who exactly is a "member of an armed force" is complicated. In addition to the various forms of military service in use throughout the world, modern armies rely increasingly on civilian subcontractors to perform support activities, including combat support, as Renée de Nevers explores in this volume.[11] Thus, from a strictly military standpoint, it is arguable that the civilian responsible for supervising, analyzing, and transmitting to field commanders the real-time intelligence data-feed from a tactical reconnaissance satellite makes more of a contribution to the military effort than the conscripted military cook stationed at an administrative base and safely distant from any frontline. Yet, traditionally, the former, because of a lack of formal military status, would be classified as a civilian, whereas the latter, in spite of an obvious lack of military function, would be classified as a combatant.

Today throughout the world armed groups and bands, which do not meet the threshold requirements of humanitarian law for recognition as "organized armed forces," in practice look, act, and have capabilities indistinguishable from those of regular armed forces. Members of such groups would, however, still be classified as civilians, notwithstanding their uniforms, body armor, automatic weapons, and rocket launchers. In the event that such groups launch attacks they are designated as a special subset of civilians—civilians "taking a direct part in hostilities," who may be targeted only while they are actively or directly involved in attacks. As the privatization of military-related activities becomes ever more commonplace, the formerly strict differentiation between "soldier" and "civilian" appears simplistic and difficult to implement.

In today's security environment, the following difficult questions relating to the issue of surrender are raised by Principle 3: Must an opportunity to surrender be granted if it is possible to do so without endangering the attacking forces? Can someone surrender in the midst of an ongoing firefight? How should soldiers react to signs of surrender from only a part of an opposing force, if the rest continue to fight? Although none of these questions are new, their combination with the inherent difficulties of distinguishing between civilians and combatants on the modern battlefield makes them pressing today.

Two of the most difficult issues for the contemporary laws of war are raised with respect to Principle 4: the definition of the terms "taking a direct part in hostilities" and "proportionality."

Challenges with respect to Principle 5 include the difficulty of identifying the end of the conflict. In the past, conflicts ended when parties agreed that the conflict was over through a formal agreement or by other means, such as surrender. Obviously, given the realities of state-versus-nonstate conflicts, which exhibit less formal characteristics than state-versus-state conflicts, identifying the end of the conflict becomes more difficult.

With respect to Principle 6, two important new issues come to light. First, international law does not provide clear guidance on situations where civilians may legitimately be detained. Second, a civilian who takes an active part in hostilities and is prosecuted for this crime is entitled to be released at the conclusion of the sentence, irrespective of whether or not the conflict is ongoing. This creates the undesirable result in which captured soldiers may be detained for the duration of the conflict, but captured nonstate fighters may not.

Contemplating Flexible Combatant Status

Of the wide variety of issues that need to be addressed in relation to contemporary combatant status, we have chosen to focus on two critical humanitarian law premises that need reassessment in light of changing conflicts: (1) the seemingly clear-cut distinction between "combatants" and "civilians," addressed in Principle 1, and (2) the almost automatic linkage made between combatant status and POW status, addressed in Principle 5.

In distinguishing combatants and civilians, Article 43(2) of the 1977 First Additional Protocol defines the following as "combatants": "Members of the armed forces of a Party to a conflict (other than medical personnel and chaplains covered by Article 33 of the Third Convention) are combatants, that is to say, they have the right to participate directly in hostilities."[12] Article 43(1) further provides a more detailed definition of the term "armed forces" by providing that

> The armed forces of a Party to a conflict consist of all organized armed forces, groups and units which are under a command responsible to that Party for the conduct of its subordinates, even if that Party is represented by a government or an authority not recognized by an adverse Party. Such armed forces shall be

subject to an internal disciplinary system which, inter alia, shall enforce compliance with the rules of international law applicable in armed conflict.[13]

To be a "combatant" an individual must be a member of a force, group, or unit that meets the following conditions: It must be organized; it must be armed; it must be under a command responsible for the conduct of subordinates; it must be subject to an internal disciplinary system; and the internal disciplinary system must, *inter alia*, enforce the rules of humanitarian law.[14] As can be seen from the preceding definition, under current international law, combatant status is a question of membership and status, rather than one of function.

Civilian status, on the other hand, is defined in Article 50(1) of the First Additional Protocol as follows: "A civilian is any person who does not belong to one of the categories of persons referred to in Article 4 A (1), (2), (3) and (6) of the Third Convention and in Article 43 of this Protocol. In case of doubt whether a person is a civilian, that person shall be considered to be a civilian."[15] Civilian status is a mirror image of combatant status, whereby anyone who is not a combatant is automatically designated to be a civilian.[16] This stark differentiation, generally referred to as the "principle of distinction," is based upon several underlying moral, legal, and practical assumptions. These assumptions can be summarized as follows: First, membership in an organized armed force, as opposed to civilian status, implies informed consent to take an active part in hostilities; second, members of the armed forces contribute to the military effort, whereas civilians do not; third, organized armed forces will usually apply the rules of humanitarian law in their relations, as part of the reciprocity generally exhibited between states; and finally, both categories can be relatively easily distinguished on the battlefield. Modern realities indicate that these assumptions are no longer consistently valid, on both sides of combatant status.

Moreover, Article 44(1) of Additional Protocol I establishes a direct linkage between combatant status and POW status, by providing: "Any combatant, as defined in Article 43, who falls into the power of an adverse Party shall be a prisoner of war."[17] The common view is that, barring very specific exceptions, combatant status means (1) the right to participate in hostilities, (2) being a legitimate target during hostilities, and (3) the right to POW status if caught by the adversary.[18]

Conversely, the refusal to grant POW status (not on the basis of a specific individual's unlawful actions) will also prevent designating the individual as a combatant, and, thus, identifying him as a "civilian." This automatic link between "combatant" and POW status creates serious difficulties for states involved in state-versus-nonstate conflicts. On the one hand, no state wishes to grant terror groups the legitimacy associated with POW status. At the same time, states also do not believe it is logical to impose upon themselves targeting limitations associated with "civilians taking a direct part in hostilities," especially when combating nonstate armed groups. Israel faces two options, for instance, when confronting the quasi-military/guerilla/terror force Hezbollah under the current paradigm: (1) designating affiliates of Hezbollah as "combatants," thus legitimizing their targeting during combat and granting Hezbollah members, once caught, POW status; or (2) designating Hezbollah as "civilians taking a direct part in hostilities," entailing more limited targeting options, but avoiding the need to grant them POW status. Obviously, neither option is optimal from the state's perspective.

We believe that this "take-it-or-leave-it" package deal, enshrined in the existing paradigm of the laws of war, should be revisited and reviewed. Considerations should include whether the constantly changing realities of contemporary warfare may permit an equivalent willingness to accept increased levels of flexibility for states facing nonclassical military threats. It is time to consider whether all combatants should be granted the legitimacy of formal POW status and, in turn, whether all fighters refused POW status should automatically be viewed as civilians.

Adapting Combatant Status to New Conflicts: Recent State Practice

I tell you, when it comes to asking stupid questions and giving crazy answers, I don't need to go looking for help from my neighbors.[19]

Israel and the United States, both subjected to significant terror threats, have attempted to address these issues over the last decade. Israel developed two new approaches: First, in 2000 Israel adopted a policy of targeted killing that allowed its military forces to intentionally target active terrorists under certain conditions, even in non-life-threatening situations and when such terrorists were not actively engaged in hostilities at the time of the attack. As a justification, Israel argued for the recognition of a new category of "unlawful combatants" situated between combatants and civilians. Israel also argued that such a policy could be justified under the more conventional "civilians taking a direct part in hostilities" approach. As part of this discussion, Israel questioned the wisdom and relevance of the temporal limitation on the right to attack, as set out in Article 51(3) of Additional Protocol I.[20]

Second, in 2002 Israel issued a new Incarceration of Unlawful Combatants Law (IUCL).[21] Under this law the "unlawful combatant" was defined as

> a person who took part in hostilities against the State of Israel, whether directly or indirectly, or who is a member of a force carrying out hostilities against the State of Israel, who does not satisfy the conditions granting a prisoner of war status under international humanitarian law, as set out in article 4 of the Third Geneva Convention of 12 August 1949 relative to the Treatment of Prisoners of War.[22]

Under the IUCL, the Israeli chief of staff may detain any unlawful combatant indefinitely, until the hostilities between Israel and the relevant terror organization have ended.[23]

In combination, these two measures create, in effect, a new category of unlawful combatant that can be (1) legitimately targeted on the battlefield; (2) prosecuted for their crimes; and (3) irrespective of the status of their criminal proceedings, detained until the end of the conflict, like POWs. Unsurprisingly, these legal developments were challenged before the Israeli Supreme Court. Although the Court upheld both new measures and has allowed their continued use, it did not adopt the revolutionary new category, but preferred instead to fit the targeting and status changes into existing legal norms.

In fact, in its ruling on the issue of targeted killing, the Court refused to accept the Israeli government's contention that international law recognized a "third category" of unlawful combatant. In the words of the Court's president, Justice Barak:

> We shall take no stance regarding the question whether it is desirable to recognize this third category.... In our opinion, as far as existing law goes, the data before us are not sufficient to recognize this third category. That is the case according to the current state of international law, both international treaty law and customary international law.[24] It is difficult for us to see how a third category can be recognized in the framework of the Hague and Geneva Conventions. It does not appear to us that we were presented with data sufficient to allow us to say, at the present time, that such a third category has been recognized in customary international law. However, new reality at times requires new interpre-

tation. Rules developed against the background of a reality which has changed must take on a dynamic interpretation which adapts them, in the framework of accepted interpretational rules, to the new reality.[25]

The Court ruled that, in accordance with the current state of law, terrorists should be classified as "civilians taking a direct part in hostilities."

Nevertheless, recognizing that under a strict reading of the provisions of Article 51(3) of the First Additional Protocol of 1977 such a classification could severely hamper the capability of the security services to target terrorists, Justice Barak proposed an extremely wide definition of the Article's key phrases: "taking a direct part" and "for such time." In fact, the definitions proposed by Justice Barak were so wide that they convinced Vice-president Rivlin that, for all practical purposes, there was no difference between Barak's version of "civilians taking a direct part in hostilities" and the new unlawful combatants status sought by the state.[26]

> The interpretation proposed by our colleague President Barak, in fact, creates a new group, and rightly so. It can be derived from the combatant group ("unlawful combatants"), and it can be derived from the civilian group. President Barak takes the second path. If we go his way, we should derive a group of international-law-breaking civilians, whom I would call "uncivilized civilians." In any case, there is no difference between the two paths with respect to the result, since the interpretation of the provisions of international law proposed by President Barak adapts the rules to the new reality. That interpretation is acceptable to us. It is a dynamic interpretation which overcomes the limitations of a black letter reading of the laws of war.[27]

Regarding the IUCL, the Israel Supreme Court [28] also reiterated President Barak's position in the targeted killing case: "the term 'unlawful combatants' in the law under discussion does not create a separate category of treatment from the viewpoint of international humanitarian law, but constitutes a subgroup of the category of 'civilians.'"[29]

However, Justice Beinisch explained that the detention of terrorists under the IUCL accords with international law, as it is in reality just another form of administrative detention—a measure specifically allowed for civilians under the Fourth Geneva Convention of 1949. According to the Fourth Convention, civilians are to be especially protected and can be controlled for their own protection until it is appropriate to release and return them to their homes.

In the United States the issue of unlawful enemy combatants first arose in 1942 during World War II in the landmark case of *Ex parte Quirin.* before the U. S. Supreme Court.[30] As explained by Chief Justice Stone:

> Unlawful combatants are ... subject to capture and detention, but in addition they are subject to trial and punishment by military tribunals for acts which render their belligerency unlawful. The spy who secretly and without uniform passes the military lines of a belligerent in time of war, seeking to gather military information and communicate it to the enemy, or an enemy combatant who without uniform comes secretly through the lines for the purpose of waging war by destruction of life or property, are familiar examples of belligerents who are generally deemed not to be entitled to the status of prisoners of war, but to be offenders against the law of war subject to trial and punishment by military tribunals.[31]

More than half a century would pass before the United States revived this category of "unlawful enemy combatants."

A week after the terror attacks of September 11, 2001, Congress enacted the "Authorization for Use of Military Force against Terrorists" (AUMF),[32] and, on the basis of this authorization, on November 13, 2001, President Bush issued a Presidential Military Order, "Detention, Treatment, and Trial of Certain Non-citizens in the War Against Terrorism."[33] Although the Presidential Order did not specifically make use of the term, the Bush administration consistently referred to those who it detained within the context of the "war on terror" as "enemy combatants." Under subsequent U.S. legislation and practice, it soon became clear that such "enemy combatants" were viewed by the Bush administration as falling outside the scope of both U.S. and international humanitarian law. As combatants, the U.S. position was that they could and should be targeted on the battlefield. But given their "unlawful enemy" status, once caught, they were subject to unique and unprecedented rules and procedures that were extremely difficult to reconcile with accepted modern legal norms. In effect, the U.S. administration, similar to the Israeli government, had created a new status of "unlawful combatants."

The major difference between the two approaches, however, was that the Israeli government had made a significant effort to portray this new category as a reasonable and required development in international law, whereas the U.S. administration seemed to advocate the more extreme position that such individuals were in fact *ex lege*. In time, U.S. courts became more willing to address the legal issues raised by the U.S. administration's policies in waging the war on terror. The Obama administration, for instance, decided to disassociate itself from the "enemy combatants" term,[34] evident in a press release dated March 13, 2009 in which the Department of Justice clarified that

> The definition does not rely on the President's authority as Commander-in-Chief independent of Congress's specific authorization. It draws on the international laws of war to inform the statutory authority conferred by Congress. It provides that individuals who supported al Qaeda or the Taliban are detainable only if the support was substantial. And it does not employ the phrase "enemy combatant."[35]

Terminology aside, it still remains to be seen whether, in practice, the Obama administration will adopt a radically different approach to detained terrorists from its predecessor.

We believe that two important lessons can be learned from these Israeli and U.S. examples. First, both the international community and national legal systems are extremely hesitant to accept radical changes to existing international humanitarian legal structures, even in the wake of unprecedented terror attacks. Second, both Israel and the United States have identified deficiencies in the existing law that grant unreasonable advantages to non-law-abiding nonstate actors.

What are these deficiencies? We have identified four: First, modern conflicts between states and nonstate entities are not easily addressed within the structural framework of humanitarian law, which recognizes only two generic conflict types: international armed conflict and noninternational armed conflict taking place within the territory of one state. Cross-border conflicts between a state and a nonstate entity do not fall within the confines of the existing framework.

Second, all states are bound to comply with the principles of humanitarian law during armed conflict; as a result, the law assumes reciprocal compliance. Nonstate entities are not recognized as legal entities under international law, and they do not habitually comply with the rules. As compliance with humanitarian law is currently an element in the definition of combatants, nonstate entities that do not comply with the law are not currently entitled to combatant status. On the one hand, members of such nonstate entities executing attacks are committing a crime, for which they may be individually punished. On the other hand, under existing rules, members of such nonstate entities may not be attacked by virtue of their status, but only at such time as they are directly participating in an attack. These rules thus lead to a bizarre and unsatisfactory result: Nonstate entities refusing to comply with generally accepted principles of humanitarian law are more protected against attack than nonstate entities that (uncharacteristically) decide to fight "by the book" or even the state soldiers against whom they are fighting. As a result, the acceptance of the lack of reciprocity in compliance with the rules of humanitarian law creates a clear disincentive for nonstate actors to comply with the law.

Third, the total separation of combatant status from the role and function of the individual is not logically or practically workable. To be robust, combatant status should depend on a more developed combined test of formal membership and function.

Fourth, POW status has, over the course of many years, acquired an element of legitimacy. As a result, the linkage between combatant and POW status means that, to be able to target an enemy, states must recognize the legitimacy of that enemy's right to fight back. Although such a link is reasonable in the context of state-versus-state conflict, it may not be appropriate for state-versus-nonstate conflicts. It is therefore unsurprising that the United States and Israel have intentionally seen fit not to accept this linkage and have taken steps to disassociate combatant and POW status when facing various nonstate entities.

Redefining Combatant's Role and Function in Contemporary Conflict

I am in my right mind now, clear-headed and free of the murky darkness of ignorance brought upon me by my continual, bitter reading of those abominable books of chivalry.[36]

We argue for a new framework describing the status and rights of participants in modern conflict. At the core of this new framework is an attempt to inject two new elements into existing legal paradigms. First, we support a stronger correlation between the actual level of "combatancy" and an individual's resulting legal status. As a result, we argue for attaching greater importance to the actual and specific role played by individuals in the conflict (combat, support, or other), as opposed to their formal status classification (i.e., civilian or combatant). Second, we believe it is imperative to develop incentives for nonstate actors involved in armed conflicts to comply with humanitarian law requirements, especially because current paradigms create a disincentive for nonstate fighters to "play by the rules" as they appear to have nothing to gain. Our proposed framework takes this reality into account and attempts to create a linkage between the willingness of nonstate entities to comply with accepted international rules and their status. Under this linkage, the more a nonstate entity is willing to abide by international norms, the more we should be willing to grant its members a level of legitimacy usually reserved for state combatants.

Table 3.1 reflects these proposed relationships. Although this approach may not necessarily be adopted by international law in the near future, we view it as a useful heuristic tool to facilitate a more focused discussion on each of the elements of the problem. Participant roles in a conflict may include three functions: those who take a direct part in hostilities (i.e., "combatants" or "fighters"), those who provide combat-related support to combatants, and remaining fighters. In the case of regular armed forces, we do not suggest amending existing rules to reflect a different status for each subcategory (i.e., combat support), despite the fact that there may be grounds justifying such a development. However, these subcategories of direct participation and support become increasingly important in addressing nonstate categories of individuals present on the battlefield, as reflected in table 3.1.

Second, as previously noted, we believe that making a differentiation between nonstate fighters who comply with humanitarian law and those who refuse to do so and "rewarding" the former with POW status may create an incentive for irregular fighters to "play by the rules," thus partially addressing the "lack of reciprocity" dilemma. We are, however, aware that such a distinction raises difficult questions, including how to assess compliance. One approach would be to review the nonstate armed group's public acknowledgment of international norms; another could be to focus on the actual activities of fighters on the battlefield. However, this second approach could well be challenged in turn, as it may be argued that the compliance of the entity as a whole should be measured based upon the individual levels of compliance of each of its constituent members (an obviously very complicated test to implement in practice). We have intentionally chosen not to delve too deeply into this issue at this stage, with the understanding that, should the overall concept gain some support, it would be necessary to come up with a more robust test for compliance.

TABLE 3.1 *Participants in Modern Armed Conflict*

Party	Role of individual within Party	May attack?	May be attacked?	Status if caught?
1	ARMED FORCES OF STATES			
1.1	Direct part in hostilities	Yes	Yes	POW
1.2	Secondary/support	Yes	Yes	POW
1.3	Administrative/other	Yes	Yes	POW
2	NSES COMPLYING WITH IHL			
2.1	Direct part in hostilities	Yes	Yes	POW
2.2	Secondary/support	No	No	POW
2.3	Inactive/member	No	No	POW
3	NSES NOT COMPLYING WITH IHL			
3.1	Direct part in hostilities	No	Yes	Criminal
3.2	Secondary/support	No	No	Criminal
3.3	Inactive/member	No	No	Criminal/ protected
4	CIVILIANS			
4.1	Direct part in hostilities	No	Yes	Criminal
4.2	Secondary/support	No	No	Criminal
4.3	Inactive	No	No	Protected

Third, in the case of nonstate fighters who comply with the law, we clearly break the link between combat and POW status, thus enabling members of such forces to be entitled to POW status, without designating them as combatants.

Fourth, our use of the language "taking a direct part in hostilities" is an attempt to merge our proposal with existing humanitarian law principles, even though the exact scope and interpretation of this formula is still unclear. Recent attempts to better codify and interpret this principle by the ICRC may still fall short of meeting the requirements of modern-day state-versus-nonstate conflicts.[37]

Fifth, the term "criminal" is intended to denote a civilian who may be prosecuted for his involvement in illegal combat activities. The term "protected" is intended to describe a "normal" civilian, who should be protected under law.

Sixth, specifically in relation to subcategories 3.1 and 4.1, in which we believe states should be granted the right to target such individuals without granting them a reciprocal right to attack and without granting them POW status, it should be noted that a similar result can be inferred from the provisions of the second Additional Protocol to the Geneva Conventions of 1977 in relation to noninternational armed conflicts.[38] As a result, the application of a similar concept to state-versus-nonstate conflict appears to be a reasonable development.

Finally, we have intentionally chosen not to identify the various subcategories as "lawful," "unlawful," or "unprivileged" combatants. We focus our attention on the practical characteristics of the status of each subcategory, as opposed to their formal title. We nevertheless acknowledge that, in relation to nonstate entities, many elements of our proposed Table 3.1 coincide with ideas put forward throughout the last decade concerning a possible third category of "unlawful combatants."

Conclusion

Open thine arms and receive, too, thy son Don Quixote, who, if he comes vanquished by the arm of another, comes victor over himself, which, as he himself has told me, is the greatest victory anyone can desire.[39]

The authors recognize that attempts to develop a new "bottom-up" approach to modern armed conflicts, addressing specific subcategories of actors not yet recognized in international law, may be overly ambitious. Nonetheless, we believe that it is doubtful that humanitarian law with respect to nonstate fighters will be adequately developed on the basis of restating existing laws. Having said that, however, we also wish to emphasize that despite current strains described in this chapter the laws of armed conflict are generally sound, and scholars and practitioners should exercise caution in opening up for change that which does not need revision. Just because it may be difficult to place an operational circumstance in a precise area of the law does not mean that wholesale change is necessary.

The laws of armed conflict are one of the more important contributions of humanity. They symbolize the difference between the human rights focus of the twenty-first century and the "might-is-right" emphasis of previous eras. As a result, all efforts to combat contemporary terrorism must exert extreme care to preserve and support humanitarian law, for these rules grant the moral justification for our actions. Kinetic energy and the use of force will not defeat terrorism—the rule of law ultimately will. In the words of the Israel Supreme Court:

> [H]ow is the manner in which the State wages war different from that of its enemies, in that the former fights while respecting the laws, while the latter fight while breaking them. The moral strength and substantive justification of the authorities' fight are both dependent on compliance with the State's laws: by relinquishing such strength and justification, the authorities serve the purposes of the enemy. The moral weapon is no less important than any other weapon, and may even outweigh them—and there is no more moral and effective weapon than the rule of law.[40]

FOUR

Direct Participation in Hostilities
A CONCEPT BROAD ENOUGH FOR TODAY'S
TARGETING DECISIONS

ERIC TALBOT JENSEN

Long before the post-9/11 advent of the war on terror, civilians began to suffer increasing costs, both in lives and property, from the conduct of modern hostilities.[1] In response, the international community has created conventional law designed to protect civilians from the effects of hostilities. These laws provided restraints on how war fighters may use military force when it might be expected to harm civilians. However, scholars and military practitioners have called into question the validity of these rules—particularly as a result of the war on terror—because many of those who engage in hostilities against organized armed forces exploit these laws to their advantage.[2] These fighters, who do not fit into the traditional definition of lawful combatants, purposely blend in with the civilian population during military operations in order to increase their effectiveness and survivability due to their opponent's desire to protect civilians.[3] They rely on the respect for law by military forces who, in an effort not to harm innocent civilians, refrain from attacking fighters who operate within the civilian population.

These tactics and their resultant dilemmas are part of the basis for Crane and Reisner's assertion that the traditional law of war should be amended to allow fighters from nonstate entities (NSEs) who would not otherwise meet the requirements for combatant status to gain that status if they comply with the law-of-war requirements for combatants. They argue that this would provide nonstate fighters with an incentive to comply with the law of war by granting prisoner-of-war status (POW) upon capture.[4] This is certainly a potential method of motivating these fighters and, if embraced by nonstate groups, would do much to protect civilians in modern armed conflict. However, Crane and Reisner choose to not address the fundamental issue under what conditions these NSEs can be attacked other than to refer to the principle of "direct participation in hostilities." Rather, they say that "the exact scope and interpretation of [direct participation in hostilities] is still unclear, and that recent attempts to better codify and interpret this principle by the [International Committee of the Red Cross] may still fall short of meeting the requirements of modern day state vs. nonstate entities."[5]

In contrast to Crane and Reisner, this chapter argues that although motivating fighters to comply with the law of armed conflict is important, those fighters must themselves accept the idea. The concept provides a paradigm for fighters to gain POW status but does not provide any help to armed forces who are currently battling these fighters, if the fighters decide not to be motivated and continue to fight from inside the civilian population. Instead, what is necessary is a modernized view of "unlawful combatants" and "direct participation in hostilities" that accounts for the modern battlefield where fighters are members of armed groups analogous to modern state militaries and where civilians purposely attack from within civilian populations and hide behind their protected status to frustrate legitimate targeting efforts. This modernized view must allow for the targeting of members of organized groups engaged in hostilities with military forces, including those who may not be actually pulling the trigger or setting off the explosive but still play an intricate supporting role, such as bomb makers and trainers. For targeting purposes, the distinction between unlawful and lawful combatants becomes unnecessary. Every member of an organized force that is participating in the armed conflict can be targeted based solely on their membership, not on the actions they perform.

This modernized view must further allow for a broader understanding of the elements of "direct participation in hostilities" to authorize targeting of civilians who, by their actions, are not refraining from hostilities. When civilians choose to become involved in the armed conflict, they correspondingly decide to surrender their immunity from attack so long as their involvement continues. By either conducting harmful actions or directly supporting those who do, civilians are directly participating in hostilities.

By allowing the targeting of these and other civilians who become members of armed groups or who are involving themselves directly in hostilities, the definitions of "unlawful combatants" and "direct participation in hostilities" takes on a modern character that will preserve the principle of distinction but still provide the military commander with the tools needed to bring opponents to submission.

The first section offers a brief history of the development of the applicable standards for combatants, lawful and unlawful, and civilians, those who take a direct part in hostilities and those who do not. The second section analyzes how these standards apply to targeting during military operations and the potential results for civilians. It further describes how these standards and their effect on targeting operations have come under severe criticism in the current war against transnational terrorist organizations, leading some to call for a revision of the law. The third section explains why such a revision is unnecessary and proposes a contemporary understanding of the definition of direct participation in hostilities that reconciles necessity and humanity.

Combatants and Civilians During Armed Conflict

One of the most fundamental principles of warfare is distinction—the requirement to differentiate on the battlefield between those in the fight and those not in the fight.[6] The law of war generally divides persons on the battlefield into two broad categories, combatants and civilians, and limits hostilities to combatants.[7] This bifurcation between civilians and combatants is born out of the balance between necessity and humanity. During hostilities, military necessity allows for those actions necessary to bring about the complete submission of the enemy.[8] However, military operations are tempered by the principle of humanity and the desire to limit the effects of warfare to those who participate in the fight.[9]

The codified statement of this principle is found in Additional Protocol I (hereinafter "GPI") to the Geneva Conventions. It requires militaries to "distinguish between the civilian population and combatants and between civilian objects and military objectives and accordingly [to] direct their operations only against military objectives."[10] The standard is easily applied on a sterile battlefield where the civilians and combatants are neatly separated and can be easily distinguished. However, in modern war, where fighters purposely dress and live as civilians but fight as combatants, such a distinction is much more complex. Determining who falls into the category of combatants and who is a civilian is worthy of a closer look.

COMBATANTS

There is no consensus definition of "combatant" in international law. As Crane and Reisner point out, GPI has created a definition in Articles 43 and 44,[11] but this definition is disputed by a number of nations, including the United States.[12] Despite the lack of a codified definition, most international law scholars agree that there are both lawful and unlawful combatants (sometimes called unprivileged belligerents) and that at least the class of persons who are lawful combatants is fairly clear.

LAWFUL COMBATANTS

The idea of a "lawful combatant" stems from the fact that a person is taking part in hostilities on behalf of some state or other armed group authorized to engage in hostilities. In most cases, that grant of authority comes from a sovereign state and constitutes the basis for a combatant's immunity from prosecution for otherwise unlawful acts.[13] When acting as the agent of the sovereign, the combatant is not personally liable for his authorized acts.[14] Where a combatant is not acting on behalf of a sovereign, combatant immunity does not attach except by the grant of opposing forces.[15]

The benefits of combatant immunity accrue in the postcapture status of a prisoner of war. It is only as a prisoner that lawful combatants receive their greatest protections and privileges, including the dispensation of combatant immunity. As reinforcement for the idea that lawful combatants are acting on behalf of a sovereign, they are only held as prisoners of war as long as hostilities continue and may be punished only for acts that violate the laws of war. Once hostilities conclude, lawful combatants are returned to their own country, free to continue life unimpeded by their lawful hostile acts.[16] Crane and Reisner's proposed grant of combatant status to NSE fighters would untether this connection between the grant of combatant immunity and its basis in the grant of agency from the sovereign.

Given these and other benefits, qualifying as a lawful combatant is of utmost importance for a fighter on the battlefield. As mentioned, although this status is undefined in practice, a combatant is someone who qualifies for prisoner-of-war status as described in Geneva Convention (III) Relative to the Treatment of Prisoners of War (hereinafter "GPW").[17] Based on Article 3 and earlier conventional and customary law, Yoram Dinstein has distilled the requirements of a lawful combatant to seven "general—and cumulative—conditions for lawful combatancy: (i) subordination to a responsible command, (ii) a fixed and distinctive emblem, (iii) carrying arms openly, (iv) conduct in accordance with the *jus in bello*, . . . (v) organization, (vi) belonging to a party to the conflict, . . . [and] (vii) lack of duty of allegiance to the Detaining Power."[18] These requirements pose no problem for a nation's armed forces or even many other historical groups that have fought as organized parties to the conflict.

UNLAWFUL COMBATANTS

Unlawful combatants are members of a group that would otherwise qualify for combatant status but, as a matter of course, choose not to comply with all of the seven criteria outlined above. As Crane and Reisner rightly note, in this age of terrorism irregular forces seldom meet the requirements of combatant status. The requirements of carrying their arms openly and wearing a fixed and distinctive emblem, as noted by Dinstein with regard to the Taliban and al Qaeda,[19] often prove either too difficult to accomplish or too hazardous to be fully accepted. Additionally, some irregular forces may not meet the requirement of belonging to a party to the conflict or complying with the laws of war. They generally belong to an organization, which is one of the key distinguishing characteristics separating them from civilians who are directly participating in hostilities, as will be discussed later. Examples of unlawful combatants include members of the armed wing of a political organization, members of an armed insurgent group, and, likely, members of the armed portion of transnational organizations such as terror groups. It would not include members of the political wing of such organizations or groups, as these individuals are civilians who may be classified as direct participants in hostilities, depending on their actions.

It is necessary to differentiate unlawful combatants at the organizational and individual levels. Lawful combatants that disregard one of the seven criteria or violate the laws of war do not become unlawful combatants because of these individual actions. They retain their status as a combatant but may be punished (through judicial or administrative means) for unlawful conduct—

though an exception may include combatants working as spies or saboteurs, as in the *Quirin* case.[20] Likewise, a member of an organization that individually complies with the seven criteria, even though his organization routinely violates these standards, should have the opportunity to establish his record of compliance when determining his postcapture status. Crane and Reisner would do this as a matter of law, while it is best done on an individual basis.

Unlawful combatants are groups or forces that would otherwise be lawful combatants if they met the seven criteria—they are not civilians and should not be considered to have the same civilian protections that will be discussed next.

CIVILIANS

NONPARTICIPANT   Armed conflict has never been detached from the civilian populace. But in many respects the history of the modern laws of war is one of greater concern with civilian protection. With the rise of professional armies, military practice began to avoid civilian death and destruction to the extent possible. Beginning with the American Civil War, the "Instructions for the Government of Armies of the United States in the Field" (written by Francis Lieber, otherwise known as the Lieber Code) received wide acclaim across Europe as an accurate description of the laws and customs of war at the time and provides insight into the evolution of the doctrine of civilian protection.[21]

Between the American Civil War and World War II, although the law of war advanced significantly, little was done by way of specific protections for civilians from the effects of war. The dramatic civilian death tolls in World War II horrified the world and resulted in the first international law convention designed specifically to protect those not fighting in the conflict. The fourth of the four 1949 Geneva Conventions, titled the Convention for the Protection of Civilians in Times of Armed Conflict (hereinafter "GCC"),[22] dealt broadly with the plight of civilians and granted protections to broad categories of civilians who might find themselves on the battlefield, as well as providing special protections for those "in the hands of a Party to the conflict or Occupying Power of which they are not nationals."[23] Although the annunciation of civilian protections was revolutionary in conventional international law, it did not specifically provide any protection from enemy targeting.

The civil wars and wars of liberation of the 1960s and 1970s were marked by a desire by many in the international community, headed by the International Committee of the Red Cross (ICRC), to revise and update the laws of war, including the protections for civilians during times of armed conflict. The results of these efforts were the 1977 Protocols to the Geneva Conventions,[24] each in turn dealing with international and noninternational armed conflict and providing an even more extensive set of protections for civilians.[25] From these Protocols the international community draws the current legal framework for the protection of civilians from targeting in times of armed conflict.

A simple statement provides the modern standard for civilians. Article 50, GPI defines civilians as "any person who does not belong to one of the categories of persons referred to in Article 4 A (1), (2), (3) and (6) of the Third Geneva Convention and in Article 43 of this Protocol,"[26] which was discussed earlier. It further states that "[i]n case of doubt whether a person is a civilian, that person shall be considered to be a civilian."[27] Civilians are those who are not combatants and who are not taking actions normally reserved for combatants. There are, however, a potential group of civilians who are not combatants but still involve themselves in the hostilities. These are known as direct participants.

DIRECT PARTICIPANTS   The issue of civilians participating in hostilities is not new. In 1793 a Spanish general sent his French opponent a letter confirming that civilians who directly participate in hostilities without being part of the "company of which he is wearing the uniform" could be summarily hanged, though as long as the civilian is not participating in hostilities he or she is protected from hostilities.[28] As stated in GPI, Article 51:

> 1. The civilian population and individual civilians shall enjoy general protection against dangers arising from military operations. To give effect to this protection, the following rules, which are additional to other applicable rules of international law, shall be observed in all circumstances.
>
> 2. The civilian population as such, as well as individual civilians, shall not be the object of attack. Acts or threats of violence the primary purpose of which is to spread terror among the civilian population are prohibited.
>
> 3. Civilians shall enjoy the protection afforded by this Section, unless and for such time as they take a direct part in hostilities.

There is virtually no dispute that GPI, Article 51, states the current customary international law standard for the protection of civilians during hostilities.[29]

It is well recognized that civilians are protected from attack unless their conduct removes that immunity. The pertinent question is, "What level of action on the part of a civilian removes that immunity and for how long?" In today's transnational armed conflicts where fighters choose to fight while dressed as civilians,[30] militaries that are committed to apply the principle of distinction may be unable to effectively draw this distinction without placing themselves or compliant civilians at dramatically increased risk.

At the time that the GPI standard was adopted, the ICRC Commentary sought to illuminate the meaning of the language of Article 51.3:

> The immunity afforded individual civilians is subject to an overriding condition, namely, on their abstaining from all hostile acts. Hostile acts should be understood to be acts which by their nature and purpose are intended to cause actual harm to the personnel and equipment of the armed forces. Thus a civilian who takes part in armed combat, either individually or as part of a group, thereby becomes a legitimate target, though only for as long as he takes part in hostilities.[31]

This clarification sets up a two-pronged analysis when considering civilian actions on the battlefield: first, the specific actions taken by the civilian that may remove his or her immunity; second, the length of time for which that immunity is removed.

Dealing with the first consideration, the Commentary takes a narrow interpretation of the phrase "direct participation in hostilities," requiring an act that causes "actual harm" to the equipment or personnel of the opposing military forces. The second consideration for the loss of immunity is the temporal element of "for such time." The ICRC Commentary allows that this would include "preparations for combat and the return from combat,"[32] but then adds "once he ceases to participate, the civilian regains his right to the protection under this Section, i.e., against the effects of hostilities, and he may no longer be attacked."[33] This interpretation creates the controversial "farmer by day, fighter by night" scenario, where a civilian can work and move among the civilian populace during the day with complete immunity and under the cloak of darkness actively engage in hostile acts, only to return to his farmer occupation in the morning.

Although not universally accepted even at the time it was written, the GPI framework has come under even more scrutiny in modern military operations. By taking a direct part in hostilities and engaging in hostile acts against combatants, these "participants" have brought the standard under fire from militaries and nations engaged in combat operations on the modern asymmetrical battlefield.

"Direct Participation" Standard Under Fire

With categories of persons on the battlefield now described, this section reviews the targeting standard for each category and details how these standards and their effect on targeting operations have come under severe criticism in the context of current operations against transnational terrorist organizations.[34] The focus of this criticism has revolved around the categories of unlawful combatants and civilians who directly participate in hostilities.

If one envisions targeting standards as a spectrum, on one end are lawful combatants and on the other are civilians who take no part in hostilities. Lawful combatants, as discussed, carry combatant immunity with them in battle because they represent the sovereign. In exchange for that immunity, they accept the risks associated with identifying themselves openly as members of a party to the conflict, allowing them to be targeted at all times. Whether eating, washing, watching television, or even sleeping, a lawful combatant is targetable by an opposing force at any time, regardless of his actions. Once an opposing force determines that an individual is a lawful combatant of the opposing forces, they may target him or her at their discretion.

In contrast to lawful combatants at the opposite end of the spectrum, civilians who take no part in hostilities, as stated in GPI, "shall enjoy the protection afforded by this section, unless and for such time as they take a direct part in hostilities."[35] That protection includes immunity from attack. This does not prevent civilian deaths, even as a result of direct attack. But it does require targeters to never target civilians and to attack targets only where civilian death or damage is not excessive to the concrete military advantage anticipated.[36] This standard is noncontroversial. But between the two ends of the spectrum the clear lines begin to blur.

DIRECT PARTICIPANTS

The standard in GPI is that civilians who take a direct part in hostilities forfeit their protection from targeting but only "for such time" as they are involved in those actions.[37] Though Crane and Reisner leave this definition unclarified, it is here that the most clarity is needed. The difficulty comes in trying to determine which activities, particularly in the current fight against transnational terrorists, equate to direct participation and thus make civilians targetable, and the meaning of the application of "for such time" in the often protracted and episodic fighting that characterizes irregular warfare and terrorism.

When this standard is applied narrowly, critics argue that it has simply proven insufficient to address the realities of contemporary warfare.[38] It allows fighters to take advantage of civilian immunity from attack while picking and choosing when to act as fighters, returning immediately to a nontargetable status if not killed or captured in the act of hostilities. In the age when civilians engaged in conflict was the exception not the rule, this standard may have been adequate.[39] On today's battlefield, terrorists purposely refuse to make themselves noticeable and actively blend into civilian populations to increase their protection. Such actions make it nearly impossible for lawful combatants to target them or distinguish when the preparation for the attack actually begins.

Furthermore, a restrictive definition of "direct participation" does not allow sufficient coverage of the range of activities involved in fighting transnational terrorist organizations. It preserves immunity for those building explosives such as improved explosive devices (IEDs) (unless they meet the definition of unlawful combatants as will be discussed later) because their actions do not result in actual harm. It also preserves the civilian immunity of those importing and distributing weapons, organizing attacks, and training insurgents in both the tactical and technical aspects of warfare. Crane and Reisner's proposal would appear to leave these fighters immune to attack if their actions were considered a "secondary" or "support" role.[40]

This narrow interpretation justifiably results in calls for reform of the definition of "combatancy." If civilians can engage in conduct that includes actively producing IEDs, training others to do so, operating training camps, and openly distributing weapons and munitions without fear of targeting, the standard does not adequately address the needs of state armed forces in striking the balance between necessity and humanity. It is true that these individuals could be detained at some later time when military forces can find them,[41] but in many cases detention is impractical because of the geographic location or the tactical situation. Moreover, a military's ability to monitor activities such as weapons distribution may allow the identification of that action without providing the means for individual identification, making current targeting possible but future detention unlikely.[42]

Even the ICRC has recognized that this interpretation of direct participation in hostilities has come under increasing pressure since the terrorist attacks of September 11, 2001. Over the past several years, the ICRC has engaged in a comprehensive review of the concept, including seeking input from experts in the field (though many of those experts were not participants in the final report).[43] The result was the recently released *Interpretive Guidance on the Notion of Direct Participation in Hostilities* (DPH Guidance). Although it shows some flexibility, the DPH Guidance fails to sufficiently address core issues in the targeting debate.

For example, in discussing the definition of "direct participation" the ICRC continues to argue that "[t]he revolving door of civilian protection is an integral part, not a malfunction, of IHL" that "prevents attacks on civilians who do not, at the time, represent a military threat."[44] In a conflict where those directly participating in hostilities use car bombs and IEDs to specifically target civilians, the revolving-door principle and its limitation on targeting likely produces an inverse effect—greater civilian deaths than would occur with a more relaxed application of targeting principles. Nevertheless, the DPH Guidance insists that:

> A deployment amounting to direct participation in hostilities begins only once the deploying individual undertakes a physical displacement with a view to carrying out a specific operation. The return from the execution of a specific hostile act ends once the individual in question has physically separated from the operation, for example by laying down, storing or hiding the weapons or other equipment used and resuming activities distinct from that operation.[45]

The inflexibility of this position encourages fighters to maintain their status of civilians to reap the benefits of civilian protections while being able to commit acts normally reserved for combatants. What incentive does the law give to fighters to distinguish themselves at all if they can attack from among the civilian population and only be targetable during an attack window? In instances where individual identification sufficient to support detention (as opposed to identifying generally that an individual is taking a direct part in hostilities without having to be able to specifically know his identity for later detention) is the requirement, such a standard will encourage civilians to disdain distinction and embrace direct participation.

The ICRC's DPH Guidance lays out "constitutive elements" of a civilian's direct participation in hostilities. To qualify as direct participation in hostilities, a specific act must meet the following cumulative criteria:

1 The act must be likely to adversely affect the military operations of military capacity of a party to an armed conflict or, alternatively, to inflict death, injury, or destruction on persons or objects protected against direct attack (threshold of harm), and
2 There must be a direct causal link between the act and the harm likely to result either from the act or from a coordinated military operation of which the act constitutes an integral part (direct causation), and
3 The act must be specifically designed to directly cause the required threshold of harm in support of a party to the conflict and to the detriment of another (belligerent nexus).[46]

In practice, this means that "[t]he assembly and storing of an [IED] in a workshop, or the purchase or smuggling of its components, may be connected with the resulting harm through an uninterrupted causal chain of events, but, unlike the planting and detonation of that device, do not cause that harm directly."[47] Despite the fact that IEDs are known to be used to target civilians and that their use clearly constitutes direct participation, under this standard only their use (or the immediate events leading up to their use, such as moving to the emplacement site) would allow targeting of the participating individual.

Supporters of this view see such actions as analogous to the munitions factory worker involved in a conventional confrontation between two states. In that context, the law still protects such workers though they are contributing to the general war effort. This analogy is misleading. The civilian factory worker functions under the auspices of the sovereign, making munitions to be employed in sanctioned warfare. The IED supplier, maker, and storer have no such approval. Just as the sovereign can grant combatant immunity to its forces, it can expect its general population (though considered the enemy, as Lieber stated earlier) to be protected from the general ravages of war. A civilian choosing to act on his own against a sovereign's forces has and deserves no such protections.

Another area where the DPH Guidance appears inflexible with respect to the contemporary battle space is in its treatment of continued intent and its repercussions.

Where civilians engage in hostile acts on a persistently recurrent basis, it may be tempting to regard not only each hostile act as direct participation in hostilities, but even their continued intent to carry out unspecified hostile acts in the future. However, any extension of the concept of direct participation in hostilities beyond specific acts would blur the distinction made in IHL between temporary activity-based loss of protection (due to direct participation in hostilities) and continuous, status- or function-based loss of protection (due to combatant status or continuous combat function).[48]

Although few would argue that direct participation in hostilities changes an individual's status from civilian to combatant, it seems equally incongruous to argue that a civilian who has directly participated in hostilities and shown continuing intent to do so should be immune from targeting. For example, assume that a local civilian population has been harassed by an individual who randomly launches mortars.[49] Even if that individual is not personally identifiable (perhaps he was spotted by an unmanned aerial vehicle that did not provide clear enough resolution for individual identification), if his truck can be identified and is later seen moving to an area from which mortars have been fired, is it necessary to delay targeting until another mortar is launched and more civilian casualties are incurred? This example highlights why current standards for targeting civilians that directly participate in hostilities may lead to more civilian deaths and foster greater anxiety about the rules on today's modern battlefield. The same consternation exists concerning unlawful combatants.

UNLAWFUL COMBATANTS

The DPH Guidance also serves as a useful template for discussing the dissatisfaction with the current standard with respect to unlawful combatants. Although there is still discussion of the status of irregular forces under international law,[50] it seems clear that irregular armed forces do not deserve the protection from targeting granted to civilians. In the DPH Guidance, the ICRC states that "it would contradict the logic of the principle of distinction to place irregular armed forces under the more protective legal regime afforded to the civilian population merely because they fail to distinguish themselves from the population, to carry their arms openly, or to conduct their operations in accordance with the laws and customs of war."[51]

Yet the ICRC takes a very narrow view of "party to the conflict," assuming that even organized fighting groups would not be considered unlawful combatants unless they are directly tied to a pre-existing party to the conflict.[52] It is unclear how one becomes a party to a conflict once the conflict has started. For example, when members of al Qaeda began fighting in Iraq, they were still not technically a party to that conflict. Under the DPH Guidance, the forces in Iraq would have to afford al-Qaeda members full civilian protections until they formally allied themselves with the insurgency.

Further, the DPH Guidance would not allow targeting of all members of a fighting group, but only those serving in a continuous combat function.[53] This includes those who have "repeatedly directly participated in hostilities in support of an organized armed group in circumstances indicating that such conduct constitutes a continuous function rather than a spontaneous, sporadic, or temporary role assumed for the duration of a particular operation."[54] It would not include recruiters, trainers, financiers, propagandists, or those who purchase, smuggle, store, manufacture, or maintain weapons and other military equipment.[55] The DPH Guidance goes so far as to define membership by function: "[m]embership must depend on whether the continuous function assumed by an individual corresponds to that collectively executed by the group as a whole, namely the conduct of hostilities on behalf of a non-State party to the conflict."[56]

The incongruities from this position open the DPH Guidance to severe criticism from states and others engaged in armed conflict in Iraq and Afghanistan and similar conflict situations throughout the world. By contrast, groups who are fighting in these areas purposefully advocate the ICRC position, as it allows them to protect the vast majority of their members that provide vital support and logistics—a benefit never enjoyed by lawful combatants. A financier, mechanic, recruiter, and trainer are all equally targetable on the front lines or miles away from the conventional fight. The inequity of this position and the incentive it provides for armed groups not to distinguish themselves on new battlefields or even comply with law-of-war requirements, begs for adaptation of current targeting rules. The United States has initiated attempts to begin this process of adapting the rules.

In the Military Commissions Act of 2006, which dealt largely with treatment and prosecution of detainees, the United States defines unlawful enemy combatants as

(i) a person who has engaged in hostilities or who has purposefully and materially supported hostilities against the United States or its co-belligerents who is not a lawful enemy combatant (including a person who is part of the Taliban, al Qaeda, or associated forces); or

(ii) a person who, before, on, or after the date of the enactment of the Military Commissions Act of 2006, has been determined to be an unlawful enemy combatant by a Combatant Status Review Tribunal or another competent tribunal established under the authority of the President or the Secretary of Defense.[57]

When modifying the Military Commissions Act in 2009, the new administration under President Obama changed the name from "unlawful enemy combatant" to "unprivileged enemy belligerent" but left the key phrase "purposefully and materially supported hostilities" in the statute.[58] This general definition can be read broadly to include persons who merely supply financial support to an organization involved in hostilities against the United States—though in practice it has not been used in that manner. As a reflection of state practice, the statute illustrates that not only those pulling a trigger within their armed group are acting unlawfully. The statute provides no time limit for automatic expiration of the designation of unlawful enemy combatant status, making it presumably a permanent status.

In practice, President Obama appears to have backed away from this definition to some degree,[59] but it is also clear that the United States still intends to take a more expansive view of the unlawful combatant beyond those who just pull the trigger. This move in the right direction applies equally to the targeting of individuals on the battlefield. To limit targeting to only those who perform a fighting function within a fighting force does not account for the workings of a modern fighting organization that requires funding, supplies, training, and a host of other logistical support.

A Modern View of Direct Participation in Hostilities

The problems highlighted in the previous section do not necessitate a revolutionary approach to the laws of war or even their fundamental revision, as Crane and Reisner suggest.[60] What is needed is simply a contemporized understanding of the time-honored definition of "combatant" and "civilian." Just as the ICRC has begun to modernize ever so slightly these definitions in its DPH Guidance, this process needs to move forward at a more accelerated pace.

Several distinctions must be made. In the DPH Guidance, the ICRC conducted its analysis using a clear line of demarcation between international armed conflict and noninternational armed conflict. In the case of targeting, this distinction is no longer meaningful or necessary. Instead the conflicts between transnational armed terror groups and state militaries are better categorized as transnational armed conflicts (TAC)[61] and fall somewhere between the two traditional categories of armed conflict. Moreover, targeting principles generally apply to every type of armed conflict.[62] This means that the important threshold question for the application of targeting principles applies not to the type of conflict but to the nature of the actors. If a state military is conducting military operations in an armed conflict, the targeting principles apply.

Given the universal application of the targeting principles to state military action in any armed conflict, it is important to revisit the definitions of unlawful combatants and civilians that directly participate in hostilities. As noted, the application of targeting principles warrants a broader scope of targeting authority than currently understood under international law and, more specifically, requires some methodology to distinguish those individuals who remain immune from attack by their abstention from any participation in hostilities and those who, on their own initiative or by their connection with and conduct in support of an armed hostile group, are justifiably characterized as lawful objects of attack. This contemporized methodology must be consistent with the underlying purposes of international humanitarian law.

Humanitarian law mandates that everyone on the battlefield may be divided into two categories: combatants and civilians. Targeting in any armed conflict must therefore remain true to the principle of distinction that underlies this division. However, the principle of distinction is a double-edged sword: While requiring protection for those who do not take part in hostilities, it authorizes attacks on those who do. In other words, although humanitarian law embraces the principle of humanity and protecting those not involved in hostilities, it also confirms that military necessity allows the targeting of everyone who is involved in hostilities—some based on their status as combatants and others based on their conduct as direct participants in hostilities.[63]

Direct participation is a conduct-based authorization, inherently linked to an individual's conduct. If a civilian does not participate in some kind of hostile conduct, his immunity from attack remains. But the law-of-war principle of necessity does not allow for a purely cause-based framework, because such a framework would not be inclusive of those who take part in hostilities during armed conflict. For example, the premise that soldiers could traverse the battlefield without fear of being attacked so long as they did not act in a way openly harmful to the enemy has no basis in humanitarian law. Once an individual joins a nation's armed forces, even as a cook or court reporter, he or she immediately becomes targetable by the enemy. The significant characteristic is not the actions or conduct of the cook or court reporter, but the fact that he or she is now a member of the armed forces. It is membership that makes the difference.

Thus, humanitarian law accepts some overbreadth on targeting based on individual affiliation and organizational membership. It may not be necessary to kill the court reporter to accomplish the complete submission of the enemy, but humanitarian law takes into account the fact that the court reporter is part of the enemy fighting organization and may transform into an infantry fighter at any time. His or her organizational identification provides the military necessity that allows unrestrained targeting on the battlefield.[64] Historically, this identification came through meeting the qualifications of GPW, Article 4.[65]

But humanitarian law also accepts some significant underinclusiveness. As confirmed by GPI, anyone who does not meet the criteria of Article 4 is a civilian.[66] Yet many meet the definition of "civilian" who do not refrain from participation in the armed conflict. Although humanity should and does protect those who refrain from hostile actions, military necessity ought to have equal claim on those who do not so refrain. Civilians who choose to involve themselves in hostilities also choose to accept the natural consequences that should come with that choice, including surrendering their immunity.

DIRECT PARTICIPANTS

It is clear that civilians who directly participate in hostilities lose their immunity from being made the lawful object of attack. Dispute arises, however, over what it means to take a *direct* part in hostilities. Given the propensity of armed civilians to participate in hostilities while hiding among the protected and innocent civilian populace, a modern definition of "direct participation," as well as clarity on the temporal limitation of "for such time," is now essential.

The starting point for this contemporary definition must be the recognition that the definition of direct participation, the "actual harm" standard from the ICRC Commentary,[67] is too restrictive in that it fails to address individuals who, although they are not members of an armed group that is a party to the conflict, still openly support hostilities by constructing, financing, or storing weapons and materials of warfare. These individuals do not deserve the same protections as civilians who disdain hostilities and comply with their status. Accordingly, direct participation should be understood to include not only those who cause actual harm, but those who directly support those who cause actual harm. In addition to those who construct, finance, or store weapons, this would include those who gather intelligence or act as observers and supply information to fighters, those who solicit others to participate in hostilities, and those who train them on military tactics. In short, individuals who choose to involve themselves in the process of fighting surrender their immunity from attack.

This standard would overcome the problem presented by individuals who construct improvised explosive devices to be used on the streets of Baghdad but do not place or trigger the device. On a strict reading of "actual harm," the individual who merely builds the device is not causing actual harm even though it is clear that the individual is participating in terrorist activities and the fight against Iraq and coalition forces. Similarly, those who recruit and compensate others to act as suicide bombers are certainly participating in the hostilities but are not targetable under a strict requirement of causing actual harm. How long is individual civilian immunity divested once the choice is made to participate in hostilities? When does someone who constantly stores weapons in his home stop participating? The current narrow reading of "for such time" is inadequate to support the principle of distinction and to sufficiently demotivate potential fighters, and it does not adequately account for the current involvement of civilians in hostilities requiring a broader understanding of direct participation. A modern view of "for such time" must include the full time that an individual is directly participating, not just the time that results in actual harm. So the financier who, as part of his business operation, organizes finances to be used to take part in armed conflict is targetable until he ceases his role as a financier. The civilian who acts as a weapons storage site is targetable until he stops serving that function. The individual who conducts training for individuals to take part in hostilities is targetable until he ceases all training activities. As long as persons function in roles that directly support hostilities, they are targetable until they cease to function in those roles.

Critics will no doubt argue that this broadened definition of "direct participation" opens up a much greater number of civilians to the effects of hostilities when the purpose of the principle of distinction is to protect civilians. Yet the best way to truly protect civilians and implement the principle of distinction is not to be lenient on the hostile activities that civilians may participate in, but to strictly enforce civilian nonparticipation and sanction civilian participation with loss of protection. A broadened definition of "direct participation" would still support the principle of proportionality. Because these fighters are civilians who are taking part in hostilities, the proportionality analysis must reflect the reality of the situation. By participating in hostilities, these fighting civilians have surrendered the immunity they would otherwise be granted. Therefore, when a commander conducts his proportionality analysis, he need not account for civilians who are fighters, but must still apply the principle as he would under the Protocol to any other civilians and civilian property that will be affected by his attack. In applying this proportionality analysis, the commander must still determine that the danger of death or injury to nontargetable civilians is not excessive to the concrete and direct military advantage anticipated from the attack. However, in doing so, he must balance that against the military advantage gained from the death of the targetable civilians. Doing so would fully account for those who have not forfeited their protections while authorizing the attack of those who willfully violate their responsibility as civilians.

UNLAWFUL COMBATANTS

It is already clear that fighters who are part of organized groups that are parties to the armed conflict but that do not meet the stipulated requirements discussed earlier[68] are unlawful combatants. But this standard is underinclusive of those who the principle of military necessity allows to be targeted as combatants. All individuals who are members of the armed group, including those who only provide logistical or other necessary services but do not directly fight, still meet the definition of "unlawful combatants" for targeting purposes and should be targetable at all times, regardless of their actions. In other words, membership is the key. Once individuals join the armed wing of an organization, they have surrendered their immunity from attack and become targetable until such time as they affirmatively opt out of the organization and permanently eschew all hostile acts. If they are members of the irregular force, even if they merely supply logistics, such as maintaining the weapons systems, they are targetable. This standard is analogous to organized state military forces that meet the definition of "combatant." For targeting purposes, the distinction between unlawful and lawful combatants is illusory and should be discarded. For the purposes of targeting, members of organized fighting groups, whether they meet the criteria of Article 4, GPW, can be targeted for the duration of the hostilities unless they become *hors de combat* or openly discard their membership and refrain from any further affiliation or activities in support of that armed group.

Each military throughout the world has people who do not normally serve a combat role, such as cooks, paymasters, clerks, and legal personnel. However, each of these, as members of the military, is targetable as infantrymen, artillerymen, and aircraft pilots. Because they have joined the military, they are no longer civilians and have opened themselves up for targeting by opposing forces.[69] Until that individual affirmatively renounces that membership and ceases ties to the armed group, he or she remains targetable. This same pattern should apply to all members of armed groups on the battlefield, whether lawful or not.

Conclusion

Modern warfare creates difficulties in targeting people and property and preserving the foundational humanitarian law principle of distinction. The complexity of the situations that commanders face is a daunting task. Crane and Reisner's suggestion of motivating NSE fighters to comply with the law of war by offering combatant/POW status if they do will not solve the current problem. Rather, a modernized view of "unlawful combatants" and "direct participation in hostilities" is required to protect civilians from the ravages of armed conflict. This view must allow for targeting civilians who directly support militant operations that result in actual harm to others, including those who may not be actually pulling the trigger or setting off the explosive but still function in a role that supports actual fighters (such as making or storing weapons or training fighters).

This modern view must also authorize targeting all members of the armed wings of irregular organizations, whether or not they perform a combat function. Mere membership is sufficient to allow targeting and remains sufficient until the individual openly renounces his membership and ceases his affiliation with the armed group.

By allowing the targeting of these individuals, the definitions of "unlawful combatants" and "direct participation in hostilities" take on a modern character that will preserve the principle of distinction but still provide military commanders with necessary and lawful tools required to conduct military missions.

FIVE

Nonstate Actors in Armed Conflicts

ISSUES OF DISTINCTION AND RECIPROCITY

DAPHNÉ RICHEMOND-BARAK

This chapter considers how concepts designed to regulate state-to-state interaction apply to conflicts involving nonstate actors—be they guerilla groups, terrorist organizations, or private military contractors. The "principle of distinction" holds that civilians and combatants are clearly distinguishable protagonists on or near the battlefield. "Reciprocity" in international law refers to the expectation by a belligerent state that other state parties to a conflict will respect similar legal and behavioral norms—nonuse of prohibited weaponry, minimization of collateral damage, and humane treatment of prisoners of war. The focus in this chapter is on reciprocity and distinction because they constitute meta-issues whose resolution determines the applicability of accepted legal principles to virtually all modern conflicts. A close examination of these topics suggests that reciprocity and the principle of distinction are of central importance in conflicts involving nonstate actors.

This chapter follows an unconventional approach to reading the Geneva Conventions and their Protocols—the main vehicles of international humanitarian law today—by drawing on an expanded body of sources to inform our understanding of the principle of distinction. The chapter reviews the historical evolution of the principle, how it became so fundamental to the laws of war, and how the concept of "combatant" evolved over time from an activity-based to a membership-based designation. The substance of the law, as stated in the Geneva Conventions, is then examined. The Conventions diverge from earlier and subsequent formulations of the principle of distinction in the manner in which they characterize combatants. Although this is explicable in the context of the purpose and history of the Geneva Conventions, a more expansive understanding of the combatant is in order—a reading that allows for the greater application of international humanitarian law to nonstate actors, an easier implementation of the principle of distinction, and improved protection of civilian populations.

On the issue of reciprocity, this chapter argues that the involvement of nonstate actors in warfare does not, in and of itself, affect the applicability of the laws of war. True, states are encouraged to comply with the laws of war under the expectation that other states will too; and in conflicts involving nonstate entities this incentive is usually ineffective. A nonstate entity may not feel bound by the laws of war—and even if it does, it may not be able to reap the benefits of the law for the reasons described in the discussion of the principle of distinction.[1] Does the fact that one party to the conflict (the state) cannot build on the expectation that the other party (the nonstate entity) will operate "reciprocally" mean that the system as a whole breaks down? Or put differently, is the primary objective of the laws of war to establish norms of state-to-state interaction or humanitarian safeguards? *Most* of international humanitarian law is binding in *most* conflicts on *most* actors (whether or not the parties behave reciprocally). The only situation in which a state may *not* be bound by all of humanitarian law is when an opposing nonstate party repeatedly violates international humanitarian law in an international armed conflict. This chapter does not seek to identify the rules, if any, that might be "relaxed" in those limited circumstances; it merely highlights the (limited) role of reciprocity in conflicts involving both states and nonstates.

Distinction

The laws of war rest on the fundamental assumption that a distinction can (and should) be made between civilians and combatants.[2] Many of the rules governing the conduct of war stem from this absolute principle, such as the types of targets that are legitimate. The principle of distinction also underpins the rights and obligations of individuals in times of war—civilian immunity, prisoner-of-war status, or the protected status of religious and medical personnel.

As Eric Jensen appropriately writes in chapter 4, the distinction between combatants and civilians "is easily applied on a sterile battlefield where the civilians and combatants are neatly separated and can be easily distinguished" but "in modern war, where fighters purposefully dress and live as civilians but fight as combatants, such distinction is much more complex."[3] Undoubtedly, the principle of distinction worked well enough when war was a state-to-state affair, with dueling sovereigns or empires battling for territory or treasure on clearly delineated battlefields. Adopted in 1949 in the wake of World Wars I and II, the Geneva Conventions crystallized this view of warfare—regulating war by clearly defining the rights and obligations of civilians and combatants, which they treat as separate and identifiable groups. The assumption that civilians and combatants are easily distinguishable in war resulted from the recent experience of the state parties with conflicts between large, standing armies at the service of sovereign states. Generally speaking, and setting aside the case of partisans (also a product of World War II experiences), the Geneva Conventions envisage the active involvement of nonstate actors in warfare only to deny them the legal benefits afforded to ordinary soldiers.[4]

But the modern battlefield is different from that contemplated by the Geneva Conventions and earlier international instruments—as all contributors to this book agree. Modern warfare features an array of nonstate participants playing central roles in hostilities, often with substantial resources and firepower at their disposal. From guerilla and terrorist groups in South Asia to American military contractors in Iraq to human shields in Gaza, the legal status of the varied participants in modern conflict is less clear-cut than it was in the past. This is particularly the case in fluid urban battle zones, where combatants can easily find shelter among, hide behind, or blend into civilian populations. Distinguishing between civilians and combatants in these situations—even at the level of theory—is increasingly difficult. Nonstate actors find themselves somewhere along the spectrum of the traditional "black-and-white" civilian/combatant divide, though the laws of war contemplate not a spectrum but rather clear-cut criteria.

Consider, for example, the case of private military contractors, tens of thousands of whom support U.S. forces in Iraq, Afghanistan, and elsewhere. The range of tasks entrusted to these actors illustrates the problems inherent in the distinctions set forth in international legal instruments. Although not part of a standing army, private military contractors are a far cry from ordinary civilians. Contractors perform activities ranging from preparing food and building bases to delivering armaments and fuel, planning combat operations alongside ordinary troops, gathering intelligence, providing personal security for senior military and civilian officials, and training soldiers in the use of military hardware. By virtue of the environment they operate in, the activities they perform, and their close relationship with armed forces, military contractors are in practice more akin to combatants than they are to civilians. Yet the Geneva Conventions generally regard them as civilians because they do not meet the formal requirements of combatant status. Only in limited circumstances are they treated as "civilians directly participating in hostilities," a status that does not allow for any predictability but that at least recognizes that they constitute legitimate targets.[5]

Their legal status is in stark contrast to the reality on the ground: In the eyes of the "enemy," contractors are clearly allied with the armed forces they are hired to support.[6] However deliberate their attempts to steer clear of combat, private contractors do take part in military activities on or near the battlefield. Telling examples include the involvement of Vinnell Corporation employees in repelling Saudi rebels in 1979,[7] or the 2003 capture of employees of California Microwave Systems by the Revolutionary Armed Forces of Colombia (known as FARC) while the company's employees were conducting a surveillance mission on behalf of the Colombian government.[8] In such cases, it is extremely difficult for friendly or enemy forces (or, for that matter, outside observers) to determine whether the contractors are civilians or combatants. The application of the current laws of war to these actors often leads to absurd or inconsistent outcomes.

The situation with terrorist organizations is even more complex because they tend to be well integrated into and make extensive use of civilian populations. They might even view themselves as civilians and engage in combat activities only episodically. Terrorist groups make tactical use of civilians to hide from their enemies; they target civilian populations to achieve political and military objectives; and they sometimes draw fire upon civilians to arouse public sentiment. They often "rejoin" the civilian population immediately after engaging in hostile acts by simply putting down a weapon and walking home. It is difficult to identify terrorists-to-be before attacks are actually carried out, and any attempt at stopping them may lead to civilian casualties.[9]

Today's accepted legal tools, formulated as they are, do not allow for a straightforward, before-the-fact, or consistent determination of a nonstate actor's legal status. The Geneva Conventions set forth a view of combatant status that is highly formalistic, membership based, and excludes a number of nonstate entities from the definition. In a provision widely held as defining the meaning of "combatant," the Third Geneva Convention, Article 4, enumerates the categories of those entitled to prisoner-of-war status as including "Members of the armed forces of a Party to the conflict, as well as members of militias or volunteer corps forming part of such armed forces" and

> Members of other militias and members of other volunteer corps, including those of organized resistance movements, belonging to a Party to the conflict and operating in or outside their own territory, even if this territory is occupied, provided that such militias or volunteer corps, including such organized resistance movements, fulfill the following conditions:(a) that of being commanded by a person responsible for his subordinates;(b) that of having a fixed distinctive sign recognizable at a distance;(c) that of carrying arms openly;(d) that of conducting their operations in accordance with the laws and customs of war.[10]

Though widely embraced, this definition is problematic, if not anachronistic. Together with many of this book's contributors, I am tempted to ask: What nonstate actors would fulfill such rigid conditions? Why should the wearing of a uniform or recognizable sign be required? What logic is there for excluding from the definition of "combatant" those who do not act in accordance with the laws of war? A more reasonable position would be for the law to bring all armed actors within the ambit of its obligations and protections and create incentives for such actors to comply. The requirements set forth by Article 4 of the Third Geneva Convention are difficult to apply in practice. To take only one example, it is arguable whether contractors meet the "recognizable-at-a-distance" test. Most contractors do wear company hats or polo shirts with the company logo, but is this sufficient to be recognizable "at a distance" as required by Article 4?

As we shall see, one of the difficulties with the Geneva Conventions—and the Third Geneva Convention in particular—is that they focus on membership in identifiable and organized armed formations as the touchstone of combatant status. In other words, the Geneva Conventions, as commonly understood, focus not on a person's activity but on his or her membership status: Only soldiers and their like are considered combatants.

A contemporary reading of the Geneva Conventions requires us to place the four conditions set forth by the Third Geneva Convention in context, and a substantial amount of history and moral tradition must be read into the text. Recent additions to the Geneva Conventions, in particular Additional Protocol I of 1977, should inform our understanding of the Geneva Conventions (particularly the Third Geneva Convention). Nonstate actors should fall within an expansive understanding of combatant status if we are to "ensure respect for and protection of the civilian population,"[11] as the principle of distinction requires.

EARLY FORMULATIONS OF THE PRINCIPLE OF DISTINCTION

The principle of distinction is an age-old principle. As Geoffrey Best notes,

> From as far back as there is written evidence of the laws of peoples and the decrees of kings come examples of injunctions to distinguish in combat between warriors and the rest: between the arms-bearing, "combatant" part of society, the part which alone made it able to conduct war, and the other "noncombatant" parts whose contribution to war-making could be at most indirect and, in the case of those old men, women, and children who have always figured as the essential noncombatants, probably not even that.[12]

This passage captures well the nature of warfare in past centuries, when large standing armies met on battlefields removed from population centers and the bulk of an army's troops wielded muskets, cannons, and swords.[13] The laws of war derive from this traditional view of warfare, establishing a clear distinction between civilians and combatants in order to protect the former based on their nonparticipation in the war effort.

A number of ancient and widely embraced codes already required that belligerents exercise care not to kill civilians. Although each civilization expressed this requirement slightly differently, the motivation remained the same: to spare civilians from the brutality of warfare. Although the injunction to avoid harming civilians was sometimes couched in legal terms, often it was no more than the expression of a moral or ethical duty on the part of the warring parties. The origins of noncombatant immunity, in other words, are not exclusively legal.

As Best points out, most deserving of protection against hostilities were women and children.[14] From the earliest times, women and children have been regarded as a protected category. The Old Testament provides a valuable illustration of this special status in the chapter of Deuteronomy setting out the rules applicable "when you go out to battle against your enemy."[15] Although fighters were allowed to "smite all the males by the edge of the sword," they were told that "women, the small children, the animals, and everything that will be in the city—all its booty—may you plunder for yourself."[16] Similarly placing an emphasis on the treatment of women and children, Mohamed's successor, Caliph Abu-Bakhr, urged the Muslim Arab army invading Christian Syria in 634 AD not to mutilate or kill a child, man, or woman.[17] These examples are not meant to suggest that the Abrahamic religions only advocated peace and protection. They did, however, establish a distinction between who ought to be killed or spared as part of a divinely justified war.

Only later did early just war theorists give a legal dimension to what divine law and morality had identified as the limits of warfare. In its effort to establish rules governing the conduct of war, early legal scholarship focused on the elaboration of specific guidelines on who could be killed in war. This long process—which eventually led to the codification of the principle of distinction—began in the fifth century with the prominent philosopher and theologian Augustine. Although Augustine did not distinguish between soldiers and noncombatants, he developed the concepts (and terminology) that others after him used to shape noncombatant immunity.[18] Following in Augustine's footsteps, in the thirteenth century Saint Thomas Aquinas took two important steps when he proclaimed that "it is no way lawful to slay the innocent."[19] First, he set forth the notion that certain acts ought to be prohibited in *all* wars, whether just or unjust. Second, he established categories among enemy nationals, distinguishing between those who are innocent (and can never be killed) and those who are guilty (and can be killed).

Progressively, innocence and the bearing of arms became the yardsticks for noncombatant immunity.[20] In the period spanning from the late tenth to thirteenth centuries, the Church strengthened adopted regulations granting immunity from violence to the clergy, peasants, merchants, children, women, and, more generally, anyone not bearing arms.[21] As for the concept of innocence, although it remained at the heart of noncombatant immunity, it became understood independently of the notion of punitive war. Instead of conceiving war as a way to punish the enemy—both combatants and civilians—Hugo Grotius promoted the laws of war as a set of rules founded in custom and natural justice applicable even to those on the unjust side of war.[22] Although some of his predecessors had touched on the subject, Grotius was the first to give strong and sustained force to the argument that restraint, moderation, and compassion should apply to all belligerents in times of war.[23]

Whereas immunity had been conceived as an attribute of those waging a just war, Grotius argued that restraint should also be exercised toward innocent enemy civilians—i.e., those who are not armed or immediately harmful.

Jean-Jacques Rousseau's formulation of the principle of distinction in the eighteenth century further highlighted the importance of bearing arms when distinguishing between civilians and combatants. Rousseau's formulation of noncombatant immunity was couched in universal, nonlegal, and nonreligious terms, and it distinguished the soldier who carries his weapon, on the one hand, and the "man" who has laid it down, on the other: "Since the purpose of war is to destroy the enemy State, it is legitimate to kill the latter's defenders *so long as they are carrying arms*; but as soon as they lay them down and surrender, they cease to be enemies or agents of the enemy, and again become mere men, and it is no longer legitimate to take their lives."[24]

Moving beyond just-war theory, Rousseau established (and durably so) that there are two categories of enemy nationals: whereas those "who are carrying arms" deserve to die, others deserve to be protected. Protection from attack, in other words, is to be granted to civilians on both sides of a conflict. With Rousseau the principle of distinction—and the importance of bearing arms at its core—was firmly established.

A century later the principle of distinction was finally formulated in legal terms with the drafting of the Lieber Code—a pamphlet prepared by the jurist Francis Lieber at the request of General Henry Wager Halleck, General-in-Chief of the Union Armies, during the American Civil War.[25] It is the first document that can be said to have codified the laws of war. The Lieber Code could not have phrased the principle of distinction in clearer terms: "All enemies in regular war are divided into two general classes—that is to say, into combatants and noncombatants, or unarmed citizens of the hostile government."[26]

Building on Grotius, the Lieber Code emphasized that restraint should be exercised even vis-à-vis enemy noncombatants. Building on Rousseau, it defined noncombatants as "unarmed citizens of the hostile government." All subsequent legal pronouncements governing the conduct of war reiterate the essential distinction established by the Lieber Code between civilians and combatants.[27] Most remarkable is the definition of armed forces provided by the Hague Regulations of 1907 as consisting of both combatants *and* noncombatants. This definition implies that only members of the armed forces actually involved in combat constitute legitimate targets.[28] The Hague Regulations provide that the activity performed by the soldier matters, at least for purposes of targeting. (Note that even under the Hague Regulations all members of the armed forces—irrespective of the type of activity they perform—are entitled to prisoner-of-war status.) Subsequent legal instruments abandoned this activity-based approach to combatant status in favor of one based upon membership.[29]

THE PRINCIPLE OF DISTINCTION AS FORMULATED IN THE GENEVA CONVENTIONS AND ADDITIONAL PROTOCOL I

The Hague Regulations—and early formulations of the principle of distinction—took into consideration the nature of the activity in which individuals were engaged, in particular whether they bore arms and were involved in combat. But in the wake of two world wars fought largely by opposing conventional forces, with millions dead in indiscriminate attacks on civilian infrastructure, and following the detention of hundreds of thousands of uniformed soldiers, the Geneva Conventions of 1949 shifted the focus from an actor's activity to membership.[30] The Third Geneva Convention views combatant status through the prism of large-scale conventional warfare: All members of the armed forces are combatants, regardless of what their function within the armed forces might be.

What is more, the Geneva Conventions define combatants in an inconvenient place: The conditions of accession to combatant status are set forth in the Third Geneva Convention, which deals with prisoners of war.[31] I agree with Eric Jensen that, in practice, a combatant is someone who qualifies for prisoner-of-war status under the Third Geneva Convention.[32] This less than ideal confusion between the concept of combatant and the protection of prisoner of war—also criticized by Reisner and Crane in their chapter—is at the heart of the Geneva Conventions. The Geneva Convention's drafters, mindful that the new treaties conferred benefits upon captured combatants, were reluctant to extend the benefits of prisoner-of-war status to any but the most legitimate, well-trained, and accountable parties. It is for this reason that under Article 4 only "members of the armed forces of a Party to the conflict" (and similar actors operating under similar conditions) qualify as combatants.[33] The only exception (i.e., a nonstate actor *not* operating under such strict conditions but nevertheless entitled to prisoner-of-war status) is based on the model of partisans—allied, it should be recalled, with the victors of World War II.[34]

The development of the laws of war, however, did not end in 1949. With awareness of the narrowness of the Third Geneva Convention and, given the backdrop of the wars of liberation and guerilla movements of the 1960s and 1970s, the Additional Protocols to the Geneva Conventions were adopted in 1977 with a far more expansive view of both armed conflict and combatant status. Placing a greater emphasis on activity, Article 43(1) of Additional Protocol I declares, "The armed forces of a Party to a conflict consist of *all organized armed forces, groups and units which are under a command responsible to that Party for the conduct of its subordinates,* even if that Party is represented by a government or an authority not recognized by an adverse Party. Such armed forces shall be subject to an internal disciplinary system which, inter alia, shall enforce compliance with the rules of international law applicable in armed conflict" (emphasis mine). This definition of "armed forces" widens the scope of actors brought within combatant status. Under Article 43's expanded definition, an indirect or implicit relationship between a nonstate entity and the state party can establish combatant status. In place of the four conditions required by the Geneva Conventions, Additional Protocol I requires that two conditions be met: (1) responsible command under a Party to the conflict and (2) behavior in accordance with the laws of war. Gone are the requirements to wear uniforms or carry weapons openly. Such requirements are no longer relevant to identify combatants; they only matter "with respect to a combatant's entitlement to prisoner of war status."[35]

This shift in the direction of a more-activity-based definition of "combatant" is gaining ground. Setting aside continuing disagreement over the benefits afforded to nonstate combatants (e.g., Hezbollah or al-Qaeda) or the status of Article 43 of Additional Protocol I as customary international law,[36] Additional Protocol I certainly marks a return to the traditional meaning of "combatant" as characterizing harmful individuals, bearing arms, and posing a threat. The practice of certain states also shows a renewed emphasis on activity as opposed to membership or status. Military manuals of Germany and the United States (importantly, not a party to Additional Protocol I), for example, point out that there can be noncombatant members of the armed forces besides medical and religious personnel (i.e., members of the armed forces who do *not* have any combat mission).[37]

We should therefore be circumspect about using the formal, membership-based standards of Article 4 of the Third Geneva Convention to define who is a combatant and who is a civilian generally, and keep in mind the historical context surrounding the adoption of the Geneva Conventions. The Third Geneva Convention is substantially focused on who is entitled to benefit from prisoner of war status; it became the touchstone of combatant status only because combatant and noncombatant are not defined elsewhere in the Conventions. But the rationale that guided the crystallization of the principle of distinction and underlies the Geneva Conventions—protecting innocent, harmless, individuals—can be instructive in characterizing battlefield protagonists. Similarly, definitions of combatant status adopted after 1949 (whether or not accepted by all states) can shed light on the meaning of Article 4 of the Third Geneva Convention.[38]

In particular, it is helpful to turn to Additional Protocol I when interpreting the phrase "belonging to a Party to the conflict" contained in Article 4 of the Third Geneva Convention. Article 4 provides that combatants, in addition to all members of the armed forces, are "members of other militias and members of other volunteer corps, including those of organized resistance movements, *belonging to a Party to the conflict* and operating in or outside their own territory, even if this territory is occupied," provided that such groups meet the required four conditions (being commanded by a person responsible for his subordinates, having a fixed distinctive sign recognizable at a distance, carrying arms openly, and conducting their operations in accordance with the laws of war).[39] Depending on the interpretation of the phrase "belonging to a Party to the conflict," certain nonstate actors on today's battlefields might qualify as combatants.[40]

Even before Additional Protocol I was adopted, it was accepted that neither a formal incorporation into the state's forces nor the authorization of all the armed group's activities by the state was required for an armed group to "belong to a Party to the conflict" in the meaning of Article 4. A de facto relationship between the armed group and a party to the conflict was already deemed sufficient to meet such requirements.[41] With Additional Protocol I, the type of relationship required between the armed group and the state became even looser. Under Article 43 of Additional Protocol I, the definition of "combatants" encompasses all organized forces, groups and units *that are under a command responsible to that party for the conduct of its subordinates*, have an internal discipline, and respect international humanitarian law. By conferring combatant status on armed groups under a command responsible to a party to the conflict, Article 43(1) retroactively sheds light on the meaning of the phrase "belonging to a party to the conflict" of Article 4 of the Third

Geneva Convention: "Belonging to a party to the conflict" essentially means being in relationship of subordination with a belligerent state (i.e., receiving orders from such state, including through contract, or fighting alongside the state's armed forces). As a result, Additional Protocol I is commonly understood as conferring combatant status on the members of a nonstate group fighting *on behalf* of a party to the conflict.[42]

Private military contractors, such as those operating on behalf of the United States in Iraq, are a particularly good example of why the interpretation of "belonging to a Party to the conflict" matters. There is little doubt that employees of Xe (formerly Blackwater), Aegis, or DynCorp operating alongside American forces in Iraq might be considered as "belonging to a Party to the conflict," especially when such a phrase is interpreted in light of Article 43 of Additional Protocol I. Similarly, the relaxed standards of Additional Protocol I (which require only that they operate under a party to the conflict and that their behavior be in accordance with the laws of war) might call for a broader interpretation of Article 4's requirements with respect to their command structure, their obedience to the laws of war, or their dress (as noted earlier, they might not, strictly speaking, display "a fixed, distinctive sign recognizable at a distance").

The status of guerillas and terrorists under the Geneva Conventions is more problematic, even if they were to fall within more inclusive definitions of "combatant." Except in the most unusual cases (a uniformed, disciplined, openly armed and legally compliant guerilla army reporting to a state), guerillas and terrorists would not meet the conditions of Article 4. They would also have difficulty meeting the more relaxed definition of Additional Protocol I, though one can imagine a terrorist organization or guerilla group operating on behalf of a Party to the conflict that acts generally in accordance with the laws of war (i.e., targeting exclusively military forces and infrastructure). As the laws are formulated and interpreted today, any attempt at making such actors fit within the civilian/combatant divide requires convoluted legal exercises.

In the case of guerillas, terrorists, and private military contractors alike we should look beyond the letter of the law, to the principles underpinning the Geneva Conventions and earlier formulations of the principle of distinction, for guidance. As the battlefield has evolved, as nonstate actors have proliferated, and as the destructive capacity of irregulars has exponentially increased, we should endeavor to subject *all* nonstate actors to the laws of war. This does not necessarily entail extending to them prisoner-of-war status. It does, however, suggest we step back from the purely status-based definition of Article 4 of the Third Geneva Convention in favor of one that also takes into account a long line of religious, historical, and legal tradition; is informed by subsequent formulations of combatant status; and upholds the ultimate goal of the laws of war to enhance protection to all actors.[43]

NOTE ON NONINTERNATIONAL ARMED CONFLICT

To this point I have dealt with the application of the principle of distinction in international armed conflicts.[44] The principle of distinction also applies in noninternational conflicts, defined as conflicts "not of an international character" occurring on the territory of a signatory state.[45] Such conflicts deserve separate treatment. The category of noninternational armed conflict includes (1) conflicts between government forces and nonstate actors and (2) conflicts between two nonstate actors on the territory of a single state (in these conflicts, state participation is generally not required).[46] Examples include the recently concluded conflict pitting the Sri Lankan government against the Liberation Tigers of Tamil Eelam, the ethnic conflict in Rwanda, and the conflict involving the United States in Afghanistan.

For purposes of the principle of distinction, the involvement of nonstate actors in noninternational armed conflicts raises one important question. Given the technical nature of humanitarian law, there are no combatants *stricto sensu* in noninternational armed conflicts, as combatants are defined in the context of the Third Geneva Convention and Additional Protocol I, both of which apply to international armed conflict. If there are no combatants in noninternational armed conflicts, how can there be a duty to distinguish between civilians and combatants?

Noting this important feature of noninternational armed conflicts, the *Customary International Humanitarian Law* study explains that in noninternational armed conflicts the term "combatant" is used in the generic sense to refer to "persons who do not enjoy the protection against attack accorded to civilians, but does not imply a right to combatant status or prisoner of war status."[47] Similarly, the International Committee of the Red Cross' *Interpretative Guidance on the Notion of Direct Participation in Hostilities* considers that "for the purposes of the principle of distinction in noninternational armed conflict" civilians are those individuals who are neither members of the state's armed forces nor members of the armed force of a nonstate party.[48] These statements underscore the continued relevance of the principle of distinction, even in noninternational armed conflicts. In such conflicts, the obligation to distinguish between protected and unprotected individuals holds, and for such limited purposes unprotected individuals are actually comparable to combatants in international armed conflicts.[49]

Reciprocity

Borrowing from general international law, international humanitarian law builds on the notion that a state is generally willing to grant another state's citizens certain protections it wishes guaranteed to its own.[50] In times of war, the laws of war seek to provide an incentive for states to limit inhumane treatment of enemies. Reciprocity, however, is much less of a concern for nonstate actors. For a variety of reasons, the idea of reciprocal rights and duties simply does not translate well to entities that generally do no feel bound by international law. Absent reciprocity, do the laws of war apply to these nonstate actors?

This section analyzes the implications of the breakdown of the reciprocal relationship between states and nonstates. In Iraq, where both state and nonstate actors are engaged in hostilities, there is no real expectation of reciprocity by any party. Does the absence of reciprocity, on which the laws of war are based, imply that the laws of war cease to be applicable to the conflict? At the heart of the issue is the question of whether the laws of war should be regarded as a set of interdependent obligations or as unilateral and unconditional undertakings.[51]

Discussions of the importance of reciprocity on the laws of war abound, often in the context of terrorist organizations or guerilla groups.[52] But the question is also relevant to other nonstate entities found on the modern battlefield, such as private military contractors. Taking into account the prominence of nonstate actors today, reciprocity constitutes a threshold issue in the applicability of the laws of war to an increasing number of conflicts.

In the vast majority of cases reciprocity has minimal relevance. Despite the conflicting messages provided by the laws of war on the role of reciprocity, such laws envisage only one situation in which a state is no longer required to comply with humanitarian law: When, in an international armed conflict, the state fights against a nonstate actor that neither accepts nor applies the law.

And even in such a situation, certain principles continue to apply. Thus only *part of* humanitarian law would cease to apply in the limited circumstances where a state is fighting a noncompliant nonstate entity as part of an international armed conflict. In all other situations and conflicts, the absence of reciprocity would have no effect on the applicability of the laws of war. This conclusion, which acknowledges the limited role of reciprocity, echoes the humanitarian concerns embedded in the laws of war.

RECIPROCITY IN INTERNATIONAL HUMANITARIAN LAW: AN AMBIVALENT AND EVOLVING POSITION

Determining whether the absence of reciprocity is fatal to the application of international humanitarian law comes down to establishing what the true objective of the law is: Is it meant to advance the interests of states in certain limited circumstances, or is it meant to protect civilians in *all* armed conflicts? Each of these positions embodies an essential purpose of the laws of war. The Geneva Conventions were drafted by states for states, creating a set of expectations and reassurances on which states can rely in times of war. The underlying assumption is that a state party will comply with the laws of war in the hope that the other party will too.[53] Under this logic, the entire purpose of the laws of war is that they are agreed to and observed by both sides.[54] Translated into legal terms, this would mean that the obligations set forth by international humanitarian law are interdependent, namely, when a party violates its side of the bargain, the other party ceases to be bound: "[r]eciprocity refers to the interdependence of obligations assumed by participants within the schemes created by a legal system."[55] Or, as Michael Walzer puts it, "one side must do, or thinks it must do, whatever the other side does."[56]

But what happens when, to paraphrase Walzer, one side does not do what the other side does? In such cases, those who regard international humanitarian law exclusively as a state–state legal vehicle and consider that the obligations it sets forth are interdependent will view the absence of reciprocity as fatal to the applicability of the laws of war.[57]

An opposing line of thinking shifts the focus of the law from the state to the individual and holds that the purpose of humanitarian law is primarily humanitarian.[58] Protecting civilians in times of war was without question among the most significant factors driving the elaboration of the Geneva Conventions. The focus on the individual, as opposed to the state, is often regarded as the raison d'être of the Geneva Conventions.[59] In this context, suspending the application of the laws of war in cases of nonreciprocity would negate its humanitarian character and would be damaging to the protection of civilians.[60] Even when one party does not respect its side of the bargain, the other party must be bound by its own.

This latter view is ascendant, even though the Geneva Conventions and the Additional Protocols may have been understood differently (and as more reciprocal in nature) by their drafters. During the drafting sessions of the Geneva Conventions of 1949, the question arose whether the conventions would apply to conflicts between a signatory state and an entity (state or otherwise) that had not ratified the Geneva Conventions.[61] The U.S. delegation had suggested to "draft the reciprocity clause by saying that [the Conventions] would apply if the insurgent civil authority declared it would observe it."[62] The Special Committee entrusted with the task of resolving this question concluded that a contracting state is *not* bound to apply the Convention in its relations with an entity that neither recognizes itself as bound by the Geneva Conventions nor abides by it in practice.[63]

The present formulation of Article 2, common to all four Geneva Conventions ("Common Article 2"), reflects these considerations: "Although one of the Powers in conflict may not be a party to the present Convention, the Powers who are parties thereto shall remain bound by it in their mutual relations. They shall furthermore be bound by the Convention in relation to the said Power, *if the latter accepts and applies* the provisions thereof" (emphasis mine).

Common Article 2 embodies one of the few instances in which the laws of war contemplate situations where reciprocity is lacking—in this case, between a belligerent state that has ratified the Geneva Conventions and another entity, also involved in the conflict, but not a party to them. Common Article 2 enjoins state parties to continue to apply the Geneva Conventions "in their mutual relations" (i.e., among themselves). As for their relationship vis-à-vis a nonsignatory (referred to as a "Power" to distinguish nonsignatory states from "Contracting Parties"), a signatory is bound to comply only if the nonsignatory "accepts and applies the provisions" of the Geneva Conventions. Common Article 2 thus provides valuable insight by (1) providing for "bilateral reciprocity even within a multilateral, interstate war"[64] and (2) subjecting the Geneva Conventions' application to a minimum amount of reciprocity on the part of a nonsignatory party.

Although the letter of Article 2 requires a certain degree of reciprocity as a prerequisite to the applicability of the Geneva Conventions, since 1949 views have shifted toward a nonreciprocal conception of compliance. In the well-respected Commentary of Jean Pictet ("Pictet Commentary") to the Geneva Conventions, for example, the case is made that obligations arising under the conventions are independent and that the Geneva Conventions "are coming to be regarded less and less as contracts concluded on a basis of reciprocity in the national interests of the parties and more and more as a solemn affirmation of principles respected for their own sake, a series of unconditional engagements on the part of each of the Contracting Parties' vis-à-vis the others."[65]

That a state must at all times comply with the laws of war—even when an opposing party does not—has become the prevailing view. In recent forays by the U.N. Human Rights Council into the field of international humanitarian law, the Human Rights Council has placed absolute obligations on states to comply with international law even in the clear absence of reciprocity. When addressing the ongoing conflict in Sri Lanka, the Human Rights Council emphasized the obligation for all parties—including the Liberation Tigers of Tamil Eelam—to respect norms of international humanitarian law regardless of reciprocity. The Human Rights Council condemned the use of human shields by the nonstate group but did not consider how this might affect the obligations of the government forces in Sri Lanka.[66] Further illustrating the declining role of reciprocity is the report of the mission led by Judge Richard Goldstone on Operation Cast Lead.[67] The report does not consider that the conduct of a belligerent (in that case, Israel) should be analyzed differently in light of the other party's (Hamas) disregard for humanitarian law. The lack of reciprocity has no apparent bearing on the scope of Israel's obligations under the law. Setting aside jurisdictional questions regarding the Human Rights Council's authority to opine on matters squarely within the realm of humanitarian law, the Human Rights Council's findings only strengthen the growing belief that humanitarian obligations are not interdependent.

Also minimizing the legal relevance of reciprocity in war are the so-called grave-breaches provisions common to all four Geneva Conventions (the "Grave Breaches Provisions"): "No High Contracting Party shall be allowed to absolve itself or any other High Contracting Party of any liability incurred by itself or by another High Contracting Party in respect of *breaches* referred to in the preceding Article."[68] These breaches are defined by the Geneva Conventions as "willful killing, torture or inhuman treatment, including biological experiments, willfully causing great suffering or serious injury to body or health, and extensive destruction and appropriation of property, not justified by military necessity and carried out unlawfully and wantonly" committed against persons or property protected by the relevant convention. The Grave Breaches Provisions are, to a large extent, reciprocity neutralizers. Reciprocity no longer has any role to play when it comes to grave breaches of humanitarian law. As Mark Osiel explains, "[i]t is immaterial, when one's own violations are judged, that one's military opponent committed the same breaches."[69] Echoing this view, René Provost writes that "the fact that High Contracting Parties cannot absolve each other of responsibility for grave breaches of the 1949 Geneva Conventions underscores the nonbilateral, *erga omnes* character of *some* obligations under humanitarian law."[70]

Article 1 of the Geneva Conventions ("Common Article 1") lends further support to the view that the obligations imposed by the laws of war are unilateral and nonreciprocal. It provides that "[t]he High Contracting Parties undertake to respect and to ensure respect for the present Convention in all circumstances." This undertaking, René Provost notes, "is not based on any consideration in the form of the creation of similar obligation on behalf of other state parties to the Conventions and Protocol."[71]

Taken together, Common Article 1, the Grave Breaches Provisions, and recent statements by the Human Rights Council support the application of humanitarian law even in the absence of a reciprocal relationships between belligerents. But what can be made of the letter of Common Article 2 itself, which, as noted earlier, exempts states from their obligations vis-à-vis nonstates that neither accept nor apply humanitarian law?

A distinction must thus be made, in international armed conflicts, between nonsignatory parties that operate in disregard of the Geneva Conventions and those that adhere to the Geneva Conventions. Private security and military companies provide a good example of entities that have expressed a wish to abide and be bound by the laws of war. Some companies have adopted internal policies that refer explicitly to the Geneva Conventions or to the laws of war more generally.[72] Others have publicly expressed their commitment to international law and/or become involved in efforts undertaken at the international level to regulate the private security and military industry.[73] Members of the main industry association, for example, are "encouraged to follow all rules of international humanitarian law and human rights law that are applicable as well as all relevant international protocols and conventions," including the Geneva Conventions and their Protocols.[74] While such self-regulation is not devoid of weaknesses, the efforts and declared intention of military contractors should generally be taken as meeting the requirement of Common Article 2 with respect to reciprocity. In other words, military contractors may fall within the category of nonsignatories who are not parties to the Geneva Conventions but "accept and apply" the provisions thereof. In international armed conflicts involving such companies, states are certainly under an obligation to apply all of international humanitarian law.

In contrast to private military companies, which generally embrace the laws of war, transnational terror networks neither accept nor apply international humanitarian law. The very modus operandi of such networks contradicts the spirit of the laws of war. (Their declared targets are often civilians or civilian infrastructure.) In an armed conflict against a terrorist organization that neither accepts nor applies the laws of war, Common Article 2 implies that the state is not bound to respect such laws. Ignoring, for the sake of argument, the countervailing view of Common Article 1 and the Grave Breaches Provisions, the question arises whether, under Common Article 2 itself, a state may cease to be bound by all or part of humanitarian law. Do the laws of war continue to apply *at all* in an international armed conflict pitting a state against a noncompliant nonstate entity such as al Qaeda?

In recent years, a consensus has emerged that certain humanitarian norms apply to all actors in all armed conflicts. Defining these minimum standards goes beyond the scope of this chapter, but it should be noted that the "Minimum Humanitarian Standards" defined by Judge Meron and the Turku Declaration of 1990 constitute pertinent examples of this trend.[75] The "minimum humanitarian standards" applicable to all actors in all conflicts would echo and expand Article 75 of Additional Protocol I, which provides that captives in international armed conflicts who are not entitled to prisoner-of-war status "shall be treated humanely in all circumstances and shall enjoy, at a minimum, the protection provided by this Article without any adverse distinction based upon race, color, sex, language, religion or belief, political or other opinion, national or social origin, wealth, birth or other status, or on any other similar criteria."[76] Article 75 further provides that "[e]ach Party shall respect the person, honor, convictions and religious practices of all such persons,"[77] and prohibits "at any time and at any place" the threat and infliction of violence, murder, torture, corporal punishment, mutilation, the taking of hostages, and collective punishment. It also provides guarantees in cases of arrest or detention, and criminal convictions. The commitment of Additional Protocol I to the concept of minimal protection for all is most apparent in Article 75(7)(b), which provides that persons accused of war crimes or crimes against humanity shall be protected "whether or not the crimes of which they are accused constitute grave breaches of the Conventions or of this Protocol." This provision illustrates the broad scope of application of Article 75—even individuals who have committed grave violations of humanitarian law benefit from its protections.[78]

That a set of minimum protections is available to all actors in all armed conflicts also transpires from Article 3 common to the four Geneva Conventions ("Common Article 3") applicable to noninternational armed conflicts: "Persons taking no active part in the hostilities, including members of armed forces who have laid down their arms and those placed *hors de combat* by sickness, wounds, detention, or any other cause, shall in all circumstances be treated humanely." These obligations apply to states even when they fight against noncompliant nonstate entities.

To conclude, although the Geneva Conventions communicate apparently contradictory messages on the reciprocity of obligations under the law, by their own terms they contemplate the suspension of the laws of war only in the most limited of circumstances—namely, in the case of international armed conflicts involving states and nonstate entities that neither accept nor apply humanitarian law. And even in these limited circumstances, the "suspension" of the laws of war is only partial: The core obligations to distinguish between civilian and military objectives and avoid causing unnecessary harm and suffering, for example, continue to apply. That a minimal set of unilateral obligations apply to states in all conflicts, involving all types of actors, is supported by the letter and spirit of Common Article 1 ("High Contracting Parties undertake to respect and to ensure respect for the present Convention in all circumstances"), the reasoning of the Pictet Commentary (regarding the Geneva Conventions as a "series of unconditional engagements"), the declarations of the U.N.'s Human Rights Council (not taking into account the disregard by a nonstate entity of its obligations when analyzing the obligations of the opposing state), Article 75 of Additional Protocol I (affording human treatment to all in international armed conflicts), Common Article 3 (affording human treatment to all in noninternational armed conflicts), and a growing amount of state practice.[79] In other words, the conflicting messages given by the laws of war themselves as to the role of reciprocity can be resolved by saying that in the vast majority of conflicts, all (or at least part) of humanitarian law applies without any condition of reciprocity.

NOTE ON NONINTERNATIONAL ARMED CONFLICT

In noninternational armed conflicts, the role of reciprocity must be assessed by reference to the specific norms governing such conflicts. Norms applicable to noninternational armed conflicts are contained in Common Article 3 and Additional Protocol II to the Geneva Conventions ("Additional Protocol II").[80] Unlike Common Article 2, Common Article 3 includes no reference to cases in which one party to the conflict may not behave in accordance with the laws of war. Why did the drafters not include a reference to reciprocity in cases of noninternational armed conflict as they did in Common Article 2? In noninternational armed conflicts, by definition, a state is fighting against an entity that is *not* party to the Geneva Conventions (or two nonstate groups are fighting each other). The existence of a noninternational armed conflict inherently suggests a nonreciprocal relationship between the warring parties. Yet the purpose of Common Article 3—and Additional Protocol II—is precisely to extend the application of the laws of war to such conflicts. There was no reason to indicate that humanitarian law applies to nonstate entities or to states that are not party to the Geneva Conventions, because the objective of these instruments was precisely to subject this type of nonreciprocal, nonsymmetrical conflict to the laws of war—without any condition of reciprocity.

In noninternational armed conflicts, therefore, there is no need to distinguish between entities that comply with the law and those that do not. Whether terrorist organizations or private military companies or some other kind of actor are involved, and whether or not they respect the law, Common Article 3 (and, when appropriate, Additional Protocol II) apply. Because noninternational armed conflict takes into account the lack of reciprocity *ab initio*, the applicability of the laws of war is *never* conditioned upon reciprocity between the parties to such conflicts.[81]

Table 5.I summarizes how reciprocity or the lack thereof affects the application of the laws of war to armed conflicts involving nonstate actors. As the table shows, the absence of reciprocity affects the application of humanitarian law rules *only* in international armed conflicts involving entities that openly disregard the laws of war. Although Common Article 2 suggests that

TABLE 5.1 *Reciprocity and the Application of the Laws of War to Nonstate Actors*

	International Armed Conflict State v. State (including occupation and wars of national liberation)	Noninternational Armed Conflict State v. Nonstate Nonstate v. Nonstate
Abiding Nonstate actor *Ex*: Private Military Company	All of IHL applies	All of Common Article 3/AP II rules apply
Nonabiding Nonstate actor *Ex*: Terrorist network	Part of IHL applies	All of Common Article 3/AP II rules apply

the Geneva Conventions do *not* apply to such situations, other provisions of the Geneva Conventions (the Grave Breaches Provisions, for example) and subsequent developments in the field of humanitarian law indicate that its core norms still apply.[82] To paraphrase Louis Henkin, it might therefore be said that almost all international humanitarian law applies to almost all armed conflicts involving nonstate actors, almost all the time.[83] The only conflicts in which part of international humanitarian law (and not all of it) might be suspended or relaxed are international armed conflicts involving states and noncompliant nonstate entities. Even in these conflicts, the absence of reciprocity does not render the laws of war wholly inapplicable. At the very least, humanitarian law provides minimum protections and obligations to all actors in all armed conflicts. In other words, the absence of reciprocity among the parties should not, in the overwhelming majority of cases, constitute an obstacle to the application of the laws of war in conflicts involving nonstate actors. What remains to be determined is how certain rules (such as proportionality and targeting) might be relaxed in light of the provisions (and limited circumstances) envisaged by Common Article 2.

Conclusion

This chapter has focused on two meta-issues that arise whenever a nonstate actor—*any* nonstate actor—is involved in hostilities: distinction and reciprocity. Whether a private military company, a well-organized guerilla army, or a loose band of terror activists, nonstate actors raise important yet legally unsettled issues under the laws of war.

The chapter first examined the challenges posed by nonstate entities to the principle of distinction. From this basic principle, which calls on combatants to distinguish themselves from the civilian population and on commanders to distinguish between civilian and military objectives, most norms of international humanitarian law have evolved—whether customary, treaty based, or judicially mandated. The hybrid nature of nonstate entities (they fall somewhere along the continuum separating civilians and combatants) makes any application of the principle of distinction to these entities extremely difficult. Nonstate actors do not fall neatly within the categories of actors entitled to the guarantees and protections (as well as the obligations) contemplated by the laws of war as crystallized in the Geneva Conventions. This situation not only is adverse to the interests of nonstate participants in warfare, but also (and perhaps most important) hurts the civilian population, whose protection cannot be properly ensured.[84]

This chapter proposes a way to overcome issues of distinction in conflicts involving nonstate entities. The formal and technical requirements of the contemporary laws of war should be interpreted to allow nonstate actors to accede to combatant status—a more practical view that is squarely in line with centuries of moral, religious, and legal tradition. The definition of combatant status contained in Article 4 of the Third Geneva Convention should be understood within its proper context, historical and legal, as setting forth the requirements for prisoner-of-war status under the Geneva Conventions. It was not meant to govern the more straightforward assessment of who is a combatant and who is a civilian, and continued reliance on Article 4 for this purpose is misplaced. Our understanding of combatant status should instead be informed by a long line of formulations of the principle of distinction that preceded (and to some extent followed) the adoption of the Geneva Conventions.

The second issue dealt with in this chapter is reciprocity. Here I have considered whether the absence of reciprocity among the parties to a conflict is fatal to the application of the laws of war. In conflicts involving nonstate actors, this issue often arises. In contemporary terms, do al-Qaeda militants deserve the benefits of the laws of war? Are there minimum unilateral standards that constrain states? The laws of war themselves provide a confusing answer to these questions.

I have argued that although the role of reciprocity in international humanitarian law should not be undermined, the laws of war should continue to apply even when reciprocity is lacking. This conclusion is warranted both by a technical analysis of the intention of the Geneva Conventions and by an evolving consensus regarding minimum humanitarian obligations applicable to all. By the Geneva Conventions' own somewhat convoluted terms, reciprocity was never made a prerequisite to the application of the laws of war, except in the case of international armed conflicts involving entities that do *not* apply or respect the laws of war. In such conflicts, and in such conflicts only, a state may be absolved of some of its obligations in light of the refusal of the nonstate to comply with the laws of war.

Although Common Article 2 would set aside the Geneva Conventions in those circumstances, it is well accepted today that certain core norms of humanitarian law apply to all actors in all armed conflicts, at a minimum. In light of the growing consensus on the constant applicability of minimum humanitarian standards, in most conflicts (whether international or noninternational) the absence of reciprocity will not affect the applicability of the laws of war. The only case in which part of humanitarian law—and not all of it—may be relaxed is an international armed conflict involving a state and a noncompliant nonstate entity, such as a transnational terrorist network. Further analysis is required to examine what rules, in substance, may be set aside or relaxed in such conflicts.

CRITICAL DEBATE III

Changing Twenty-first-Century Battlefields and Armed Forces

SIX

Children as Direct Participants in Hostilities
NEW CHALLENGES FOR INTERNATIONAL HUMANITARIAN
LAW AND INTERNATIONAL CRIMINAL LAW

HILLY MOODRICK-EVEN KHEN

The phenomenon of child terrorists, a subcategory of child soldiers, represents a significant new chapter in the field of contemporary conflict.[1] These nontraditional actors exemplify the challenges that modern battlefields have created for policy makers, lawyers, scholars, and governments. More specifically, they illustrate the complex balance, central to humanitarian law, that must be achieved between military advantage and refraining from harming those not directly participating in hostilities. Children (defined here as minors under the age of fifteen) who are involved in terrorist activities pose a real danger to counterterrorist forces. At the same time, children are used by terrorist groups and irregular armies as human shields and in other exploitative ways, and counterterrorist forces must try to avoid harming them.[2]

This chapter addresses two major challenges arising from the issue of child terrorists. The first is how contemporary humanitarian law deals with incidents of children participating in terrorist activities. Included within the overarching problem of child terrorists are issues of regulating the direct participation of children in hostilities and controlling the use of children as human shields. This chapter elucidates rules available within the scope of humanitarian law that (1) provide maximum protection to children who do not participate directly in hostilities and (2) regulate their use as human shields. Admittedly, though, in certain circumstances humanitarian law regards children who participate directly in terrorist activities as legitimate targets.

The second issue addressed here is the criminalization of acts of terrorism carried out by children. The discussion in this chapter relies on the assumption that offenses committed by child terrorists on the battlefield can in most cases be treated as acts committed without criminal *mens rea* (criminal intent). The second section will thus focus on the prosecution of recruiters of child terrorists and leaders of terrorist organizations to prove that these persons are, in fact, the actual perpetrators of the offenses children have committed.

New Battlefields and Actors: Can Children Participate Directly in Hostilities?

The treatment of children on the battlefield is regulated in international humanitarian law mainly by the first Protocol Additional to the Geneva Conventions (API). Protocol I prohibits the recruitment of children under the age of fifteen into armed forces and calls on parties to the conflict to refrain from incorporating children under this age in armed activities.[3] Protocol I also addresses issues of protection and care of children on the battlefield and demands that children who fall into the power of the adverse party enjoy special protections (such as being held in separate quarters from adults) and that children under the age of eighteen shall not be subject to the death penalty.[4]

In addition to Protocol I, various humanitarian organizations have begun to tackle this problem over the last decade—a period in which children's incorporation into armed forces and terrorist groups has increased globally.[5] The frequency of the phenomenon and the increasing recognition of the variety of severe social and psychological implications for children[6] has generated efforts that range from the resolution confirming the appointment of a U.N. Special Representative for Children and Armed Conflict at the General Assembly[7] to several U.N. Security Council resolutions dealing with the recruitment of child soldiers both by states and by nonstate actors.[8] Most efforts are aimed at reducing the number of children recruited into armed forces and criminalizing their recruiters, whereas relatively less attention has been directed at reconsidering the legal status of children participating directly in hostilities and the rules for their targeting.

The emphasis on reducing recruitment and punishing recruiters results from the presupposition that children do not generally participate in hostilities; hence, international law concentrates on protecting them and only indirectly considers their incorporation into armed forces (i.e., by determining the age under which their participation in hostilities is forbidden). International law does not refer to the question of whether the use or abuse of children on new battlefields should result in specific standards regulating the targeting of children who *do* participate directly in hostilities. This lacuna in international humanitarian law is especially relevant for regulating child terrorism because one of the major changes effected by terrorism for modern warfare is the incorporation of new irregular actors, such as children, into the battlefield, thus challenging the concept of direct participation in hostilities.

It is worth noting that both terrorism research and the operational branches of government (such as the military and other national security institutions) have recognized the increasing changes that terrorism has wrought on modern battlefields: the blurring of distinctions between combatants and civilians, the use of civilians for military missions, the elimination of uniforms or identifying emblems in military operations, the hiding of armed forces among civilians not involved in hostilities, and the use of civilians as human shields. All these practices refute the core tenant of humanitarian law that civilians must be kept outside the scope of the battlefield. Terrorists shatter the very basic distinction between civilians and combatants spelled out in the sections of the Additional Protocols to the Geneva Conventions that discuss the civilian population.[9] These distinctions are expressed in such Protocol instructions as to protect the civilian population against dangers arising from military operations,[10] to refrain from attacking and terrorizing the civilian population,[11] to avoid indiscriminate attacks,[12] and to refrain from directing the movement of the civilian population or individual civilians with the intent of shielding military operations or military objectives from attacks.[13]

One tactic of terrorist organizations that disregards all these rules and tenets of international humanitarian law is to use children in various exploitative ways—for example, as active participants in hostilities or as human shields. Their success in this depends on several conditions influencing a child's leanings toward terrorist organizations. Recent research on why and how children come to participate in terrorist and other military groups suggests that poverty, a harsh environment, the lack of access to education, family and social/political motivations, and the desire for revenge are factors that attract children to terrorist groups.[14]

The two most crucial of these factors are poverty and political or ideological motivations. Recruiters offer generous financial rewards to families of potential child candidates, especially those who are designated for suicide bombing missions.[15] Political or ideological motivation strengthens the appeal of terrorist organizations for the children, as it is sometimes built upon the concept of martyrdom that emerges in one radical conception of Jihad— or the personal battle to improve one's faith.[16] Martyrdom is a significant pull factor when talented propagandists present it as an ideal to inexperienced teenagers whose lives are miserable and hopeless.

One result of this tactical use of children by terrorist groups is the emergence of a sophisticated chain of recruiters, trainers, and charismatic leaders. The focus with regard to criminal liability should not be on the children, but on prosecuting these other functionaries in terrorist organizations. Before addressing prosecution issues, however, it is necessary to define direct participation in hostilities, which is an essential step in light of the changes that terrorism has generated for new battlefields. Several methods will then be developed for determining the status of direct participants in hostilities, including children. This discussion also raises the issue of using children as human shields and considers how the proportionality rule can address this problem.[17]

DISTINGUISHING BETWEEN COMBATANTS AND CIVILIANS

One effect of terrorism is the blurring of the distinction between combatants and civilians. As a result, it is becoming increasingly difficult to identify direct participants in hostilities. Regular members of armies and even militias adhering to the Geneva Conventions[18] can be easily distinguished from civilians because of their identifying emblems (usually a uniform). But terrorists conduct their activities intentionally disguised as civilians, which poses great challenges for counterterrorism forces.[19] A question that arises from this core change in the modern battlefield—and one that has been recognized by both academic and practical researchers since the events of 9/11—is how direct participants can be distinguished from the civilian population.[20]

Direct participation in hostilities can refer to a variety of activities performed in the battlefield and attached to the military effort—from manufacturing warfare and training potential fighters to supplying real-time intelligence during a military operation.[21] Yet the extensive research on direct participation in hostilities seems to have produced more controversies than solutions. Several issues that are fundamental to the definition of the nature and scope of direct participation in hostilities are not settled in international law. For example, controversy still exists over the scope of activities forming direct participation in hostilities and the span of time over which they take place.[22] Hence, these matters are often decided on a case-by-case basis,[23] and no clear definition of the concept of direct participation in hostilities can be extrapolated.[24] Notwithstanding the uncertain definition of direct participation in hostilities, however, those participating directly in the hostilities are removed from Geneva protections evident in Article 3 common to the four Geneva Conventions of August 12, 1949 (CA 3), API,[25] and the Second Protocol Additional to the Geneva Conventions of August 12, 1949, and Relating to the Protection of Victims of Non-international Armed Conflicts, of June 8, 1977 (APII).[26]

Although the question of what can be defined as direct participation is legally fraught, one unconventional legal method for deciding this issue can be extrapolated from AP(I) article 52(2), "General protection of civilian objects": "Attacks shall be limited strictly to military objectives. Insofar as objects are concerned, military objectives are limited to those objects which by their nature, location, purpose or use make an effective contribution to military action and whose total or partial destruction, capture or neutralization, in the circumstances ruling at the time, offers a definite military advantage." The decision on what can be deemed a legitimate inanimate target is based on two criteria: First, the objective must contribute to military action; and second, the target must pose a risk to the other party and be destroyed to thwart this risk (the "risk test"). Although this article refers to objects and not to persons, its underlying rationale may prove useful in defining rules for the acts of persons posing a risk to troop forces and civilians and whose killing may result in a (definite) military advantage. However, using this article as a means of interpretation requires defining what constitutes a definite military advantage: Does it refer to a single military action, to several operations, or to the whole battle?[27] Once this question is answered, specific criteria could be formulated to define direct participation in hostilities.

The risk test is also applicable in determining the span of time that an actor can be considered to be participating directly in hostilities. According to the test, terrorists should be considered direct participants in hostilities—and therefore may be targeted—from the moment they pose a risk to the counterterrorist forces or to civilians. The application of this general test requires answering a number of questions: At which stage of the terrorist act is the risk to the counterterrorist forces created? Is the planning stage part of this danger zone? Does the mere participation in a terrorist group constitute a threat to the counterterrorist force?[28] To address these questions, one must analyze the immediate danger parameter, evaluate its relevance in the context of international humanitarian law,[29] and compare it to the anticipated military advantage from the killing of the terrorist. Some scholars refer to an immediate danger parameter and conclude that the response should be determined according to the need rather than according to the danger. In other words, the threats posed by terrorism are different from those understood by the prevailing concept of self-defense (i.e., threats that constitute an immediate and tangible danger to the victim of the attack). Hence, terrorist acts should be frustrated before immediate danger arises.[30]

DISTINGUISHING BETWEEN LEADERS AND ORDINARY PARTICIPANTS

Another important distinction that should be made is between leaders and ordinary participants. Identifying and classifying the various groups of persons in terrorist organizations and understanding their roles in carrying out the terrorist act could assist in determining a general definition of direct participation. First of all, political leaders who are not directly in charge of carrying out military acts could be distinguished from those who directly influence these acts and from operational leaders who are integrated in the chain of command. Following this, the functional role of those who seem to be directly involved in military activities should be analyzed in light of two basic doctrines: the *doctrine of command responsibility*[31] and the *doctrine of organizational and functional control*. Although the latter function is applied mainly in criminal law,[32] it could, by way of analogy, be applied to international humanitarian law categories of combatants and participants in combat. Through this analytical methodology, then, we could characterize the functions of a direct participant, thereby forming a definition of direct participation.[33]

The difficulty of distinguishing between regular activists and leaders of terrorist organizations is related to the problem of identifying members of terrorist organizations: Because members have recourse to renouncement and relinquishment, executive authorities cannot easily determine who took a direct part in hostilities and at what point in time they did so. Because members of terrorist organizations do not wear uniforms or carry a distinguishing emblem, identifying them or the role that they play in their organization is difficult. This lack of an identifying emblem also makes it more difficult for them to surrender in a way perceptible to the other party to the conflict. Regular soldiers can cut themselves off from the military framework simply by taking off their uniforms and laying down their arms, but the members of a terrorist organization do not have such obvious options. As a result, they might mistakenly be considered to be members of the organization even after they have renounced affiliation with it.

It can be argued that the difficulties considered above place the right to life of the terrorist or the ex-terrorist over the right of the state to defend its residents. Distinguishing between leaders of terrorist organizations and ordinary members may help to resolve this dilemma. It will likely be easier to identify well-known leaders (for both the public and security branches), and it is reasonable to presume that these leaders do not regularly renounce their roles in their organization. Therefore, it is legitimate to refer to them as direct participants in hostilities and even to assume that their participation is unquestionable throughout the entire period of their leadership.[34]

In the case of ordinary members of terrorist organizations, however, the difficulties in identifying them and ensuring that they have a significant and realistic opportunity to abandon their participation in hostilities creates a situation in which it is impossible to identify the duration of their participation in hostilities. These ordinary members should thus not be targeted during the planning stage of an operation, but rather only when they set out to or engage in the performance of a terror act.[35]

PROPORTIONALITY

The final issue connected to the question of direct participation is that of proportionality. The standard of proportionality mandated by international humanitarian law rules determines that an indiscriminate, and therefore forbidden, attack is one "which may be expected to cause incidental loss of civilian life, injury to civilians, damage to civilian objects, or a combination thereof, which would be excessive in relation to the concrete and direct military advantage anticipated."[36] This criterion for estimating unavoidable collateral damage to civilians in the neighborhood of legitimate targets is one of the most fraught norms of international law. Not only does it demand the evaluation of abstract values that cannot be quantified, but it requires one to balance these values. The difficulties in working out and applying this formula have been discussed by numerous scholars but to no satisfactory conclusion.[37]

Nevertheless, one can extrapolate some guidelines for carrying out the process of balancing the competing values. For example, the army's respect for the human dignity of enemy civilians should impose upon soldiers a positive duty to take precautions to reduce the degree of harm and to use more discriminating weapons even if they are more expensive or take longer to take effect. Nevertheless, this duty will only reduce harm to enemy civilians, and it does not require that the soldiers risk their own lives to protect these civilians.[38] Another proposal focuses on estimating the probability of the competing values. The more significant and clear the anticipated military advantage is, the greater the precedence it should be given over the anticipated collateral damage.

Thus, in a case where the anticipated military advantage is significant and relatively certain, the operation should be authorized even when the estimated damage to civilian population is more than negligible. But when the anticipated military advantage is not clear, greater weight should be accorded to the anticipated collateral damage. In effect, there should be an inverse proportion between the significance and certainty of the anticipated military advantage and the anticipated collateral damage to the civilian population.[39]

The key question is, "What constitutes a concrete and direct military advantage?" Based on my discussion earlier of the possible parameters of this advantage in the context of Article 52, AP(I), the answer to this question lies in weighing all the preceding factors to determine the special characteristics of combating terrorism. These include the significant contribution of leaders to the activity of terrorist organizations, the difficulty of identifying regular activists in terrorist organizations, the potential for these activists to abandon these organizations, and the influence of human rights law discourse on the application of international humanitarian law rules. Deciding the question of what constitutes a concrete and direct military advantage will render the balancing process more tangible and less casuistic.

The question of proportionality is crucial when considering the use of children as human shields. Should children who are sent to areas in Gaza from which *Kassam* missiles have been deployed in order to thwart the military's response be protected from targeting? In the targeted killings case, the Israeli Supreme Court suggested that people who serve as human shields could be considered legitimate targets if they carry out this role of their own free choice.[40] But because the Court failed to present a general theory of direct participation, it does not and cannot explain how acting on such free will changes the status of these persons from civilians to direct participants in hostilities.[41] However, if we use the preceding criteria to determine direct participation in hostilities—namely, focusing on leaders of terrorist organizations as prime targets and otherwise looking for people who present a clear and direct danger to the counterterrorism force—children should not be regarded as legitimate targets.

Nevertheless, the use of children as human shields clearly prevents the army from fulfilling its role of protecting other civilians from terrorist activities. Therefore, the principle of proportionality should be applied. Even if the children are not to be regarded as legitimate targets, the army should—according to the principle of proportionality—be allowed to target the place where the children are located. A certain amount of damage to the children may be justified in accordance with the principle of proportionality.

Having revisited some international humanitarian law rules with respect to children as direct participants in hostilities, I shall now examine how international criminal law should deal with criminal offenses committed by them. Whereas the battlefield sometimes leaves the counterterrorist force with no other option than to target children when they pose an immediate and clear danger to those fighting them, international criminal law (ICL) has mechanisms that can take into account the special characteristics of children's participation in hostilities, thereby protecting both them and society from the evils of terrorism.

Child Terrorists and Leaders of Terrorist Organizations: Who Is the Actual Perpetrator of Criminal Offenses?

This section addresses the option of exempting child terrorists from criminal liability for criminal offenses and focuses on the possibility of prosecuting their recruiters and the leaders of terrorist organizations. Although concentrating on leaders and overlooking the deeds of rank-and-file activists could be difficult to apply on the battlefield (because the dangers posed by the latter can sometimes be as crucial as those created by the former), this proposal seems more feasible in the case of ICL procedures. This conclusion is based on the argument that the criminalization of children's acts on the battlefield should be weighed against the sociological factors that influence children's joining up with terrorist groups and obeying their leaders.

The phenomenon of child soldiers and child terrorists has recently become one of great interest for sociologists, psychologists, and practitioners. Much research has been devoted to the question of why and how children come to participate in terrorist and other military groups.[42] Most researchers agree, as mentioned, that several major factors influence participation, including poverty, a harsh environment, lack of access to education, family and social/political motivations, and the desire for revenge.[43] The presence of these factors raises the questions of whether criminal *mens rea* can and should be attributed to child terrorists and whether pressing charges against them under these circumstances is appropriate.[44]

One alternative, therefore, is to suggest that the actual perpetrators of the criminal offenses committed by these children are their recruiters and the leaders of terrorist organizations. The focus should be on *their* prosecution instead of on the children's. Indeed, in the ICC—as well as in special criminal courts such as that of Sierra Leone—efforts in this vein are currently being made.[45] In the remaining part of this chapter, I shall discuss the doctrinal justifications for such a course of action.

Like other criminal offenses, those committed by child terrorists are not perpetrated as isolated actions. Rather, they are acts committed in partnership with others—such as the recruiters, the leaders, the suppliers of explosives, and the providers of intelligence.[46] The question is, "Which actors play the most important part in—and thus are the perpetrators of—the joint criminal act, and which actors only count as aiders, abettors, or solicitors?" Although it is most common to refer to the actual perpetrator of an act as the one who should bear the highest criminal liability, some legal doctrines support the idea that cases exist where partners who did not actually execute the act should count as the main perpetrators and bear criminal liability accordingly.

The first of these is the *doctrine of solitary responsibility of conspirators*.[47] According to this doctrine, "a person engaged in the commission of an unlawful act is legally responsible for all the consequences which may naturally or necessarily flow from it and ... if he combines and confederates with others to accomplish an illegal purpose, he is liable... for everything done by his confederates."[48]

Two other doctrines—both of organizational or functional control—also justify attributing criminal liability to partners of the criminal offense other than to the actual perpetrator, focusing mainly on the leaders of the criminal group. The first of these, the German law *doctrine of organizational control*, suggests that leaders of large criminal organizations should be considered as the perpetrators of every crime committed by their subordinates. This principle follows because their almost absolute control over the organization guarantees that every order will be executed. The actual perpetrators of the order hence become irrelevant, since if they refuse to act upon the leader's orders, they will simply be replaced. This doctrine was accepted by the Statute of the ICC, which regards the "commissioner through another"(i.e., the one who has organizational control) as the actual perpetrator of the criminal offense.[49] The second of these doctrines, the *functional control doctrine*, attributes criminal responsibility to either (1) the leader of a criminal group (even those not defined as criminal organizations) whose leadership is expressed by planning and guiding the operation or (2) anyone else who controls the commission of the offense. This control is manifested by the partner either allocating functions to the group members or influencing the models of operation to such an extent that if he or she had not participated in the joint operation, the offense might have been committed in a completely different manner—or not committed at all. In other words, what defines criminal offense partners as the main perpetrators is the dominant nature of their contribution to the act, which may be expressed either in the actual execution of the act or in designing its commission.

The doctrine of solidarity responsibility is sometimes criticized for too broadly attributing criminal liability to those who are too remote from the actual commission of the act to bear such responsibility. However, even the critics of this doctrine agree on its importance in tackling organized crime and confirm its success in preventing the leaders of criminal organizations from escaping justice:[50]

> The ever-increasing sophistication of organized crime presents a compelling reason against abandonment of Pinkerton ... [i.e., the Pinkerton rule, which sets the doctrine of the responsibility of confederates to all the consequences of the

conspiracy]. Empirical evidence has repeatedly demonstrated that those who form and control illegal enterprises are generally well insulated from prosecutions, with the exception of prosecutions predicated upon the theory of conspiracy. To preclude uniformly their exposure to additional sanctions, regardless of the circumstances, for the very crimes which sustain their illegal ventures, would have the most unfortunate and inequitable consequences.[51]

It is widely accepted that criminal liability should be attributed to the leaders of criminal groups, who are seen as the primary perpetrators of the orders they give, even when they do not actually execute these orders. However, there remains the question of why they should be counted as primary perpetrators and not as mere solicitors.

Most criminal law systems support the *differential participation model*, which assumes that when a criminal offense is executed by a group of persons, not all of the group members should be regarded as perpetrators. Different functions can be attributed to different members (i.e., the aiders, abettors, and solicitors). The perpetrators who contributed most to the execution of the offense should bear the highest level of criminal responsibility; those whose contribution was indirect and sometimes secondary should bear a lower level of criminal liability.[52] Nevertheless, it is not always easy to distinguish among the perpetrator, the aider, and the solicitor, because the boundaries between mere inducement and actual commission are often not clear. Nor is it easy to decide whether a certain act is merely aiding or is part of the actual perpetration of the offense.

It is now necessary to focus on the difference between acts of solicitation and perpetration. This distinction is required, given the assumption that terrorist leaders have a strong persuasive influence over the acts of terrorist activists; hence, their acts resemble acts of solicitation more than acts of mere assistance.

In one definition of "solicitor," a person may be guilty of solicitation to commit a crime "if with the purpose of promoting or facilitating its commission he commands, encourages or requests another person to engage in specific conduct that would constitute such crime...."[53] The solicitor is the intellectual perpetrator of the crime—the one who "plants" the criminal intent in the heart of the perpetrators and encourages them to commit the crime when they hesitate. Sometimes a solicitor, "working his will through one or more agents, manifests an approach to crime more intelligent and masterful than the efforts of his hireling."[54]

The International Criminal Court for the Former Yugoslavia (ICTY) described the importance of the supporting character of acts of aiding and abetting: "The aider and abettor carries out acts specifically directed to assist, encourage or lend moral support to the perpetration of a certain specific crime... and this support has a substantial effect upon the perpetration of the crime."[55] According to this, a solicitor's acts do not generally count as acts of perpetration. However, some characteristics of solicitation do blur the boundaries between solicitation and perpetration. In certain cases, the solicitor not only persuades someone to commit a crime but also plans and designs the commission of the crime. Should we consider such a person a perpetrator of the act?

The reason for broadening the boundaries of perpetration at the expense of mere solicitation lies in the goal of preventing the "big fish" from escaping criminal responsibility—or at least of reducing the instances of this happening. The aim is to prevent the leaders of criminal and terrorist organizations from imposing the highest level of criminal liability on the rank-and-file activists (such as children) while they, the "brains" behind the actual perpetration, escape it. [56] Israeli Supreme Court former Justice Heshin described this problem:

> Can we accept that the "brain" will be secondary to the soldiers who act by his words? Indeed, if the "brain'" is in fact the one without whom the octopus of the criminal participation model could not move its arms, it will be hard to accept that his responsibility will be lower than that of the actual perpetrator. The evil spirit of the leader lies above the whole criminal operation... and when the offence is committed the leader "is there" with the perpetrators. He will be there with them throughout the whole perpetration and will leave them only if he positively acts to prevent the perpetration.[57]

The analytic doctrinal justification for the preceding conclusions lies in the *hegemonic control* or *organizational control doctrine*,[58] which suggests that control is the main characteristic of perpetration. In criminal organizations, where leaders are so confident of their control that they know that any order they give will be executed (no matter by whom), it is possible to say that the leader is "committing the offense through another."[59] Therefore, it is with the leader, the one who gives the orders, that the central part of the offense lies.

The special nature of the leader's status is expressed through the others' blind obedience in following orders. Leaders not only are the "spiritual" parents who ask that their words be implemented by another,[60] but are the actual perpetrators who have full control over the offense: They can order to withdraw from perpetration,[61] to modify it, or to commit it as was first ordered. From the moment the order is given, leaders can be sure that if someone refuses to act upon their words, another will step forward as a replacement. Hence, the offense will be committed even if the leader does not know the actual perpetrator. It is for these reasons that the leader—the central force determining the nature of the offense—is the actor responsible for its execution and not the rank-and-file activist who actually commits it.[62]

It is important to note that the organizational control doctrine was accepted into the ICC Statute. Abiding by the German doctrine of commission through another, this statute follows the idea that indirect perpetrators can use their control to commit a crime through the direct, physical perpetrator. This doctrine allows imposing criminal liability on the indirect perpetrator, but it remains indifferent to the question of whether the direct perpetrators can be ascribed criminal liability or whether they are incapable of bearing such a liability (for instance, if they are minors or are not mentally competent).[63]

Another doctrinal justification for extending criminal responsibility lies in the functional control doctrine. This is a test that was developed by Israeli jurisprudence and is suitable both for large organizations (such as large criminal organizations) and for small ones that follow one charismatic leader. According to this doctrine, the leader's control is expressed through planning the operation, directing it, and ensuring its execution. These acts make the leader a perpetrator rather than a mere solicitor. Hence, leaders who give the orders and direct the operation, even from a remote location, should count as perpetrators because their acts exceed the mental sphere of solicitation and cross the boundaries of actual perpetration.[64]

According to the functional doctrine control, the leaders can count as actually participating in the commission of the act even when planning and directing it from a distant location or when they are not present at the actual location of the act. Such was the verdict in the case in which a fragmentation grenade was thrown into a butchers' market in the Old City of Jerusalem: The Israeli Supreme Court decided that being present was not an indispensable condition for perpetration. The leader of the group that intended to throw the grenade canceled his participation at the last moment, authorizing the others to commit the offense without him. However, because he directed the act until its very last phases, the Supreme Court decided to regard to him as a perpetrator:

> He took a central part in each and every act that was needed to implement the offence.... He was the head of the group. The fact that he was not present when the fragmentation grenade was thrown... does not detach him from the multi-participants criminal operation. He climbed the "carriage of perpetration" and moved it until its purpose was fulfilled without doing anything to stop it. Under these circumstances he should be counted as a perpetrator. He is not a mere solicitor since he was not satisfied with inducing [the others] but did actual acts of perpetration. He is not a mere aider since he is an insider person and a leader.[65]

Hence, the distinction between perpetrator and solicitor derives a particular type of perpetration—"perpetration through control"—which is based on the leader's control over the occurrences. In a high-tech era, where people can connect through technological means, the leader does not even have to be present at the location where the offense is committed for this control to be proven. Therefore, when it is proven that leaders' acts exceed the mental contribution of perpetration and become an actual part of it, they should count as perpetrators who must bear the highest level of responsibility.

The preceding theoretical analysis has important implications with regard to the question of whether it is worthwhile for the executive branches, such as the police and the prosecution, to focus on incriminating terrorist leaders who have had a major influence over the acts of children in terrorist organizations. In many cases terrorist leaders—who are not the physical perpetrators of criminal acts but possess all the characteristics of organizational or functional control—should be prosecuted as main perpetrators of the offenses they order others to commit.[66] Indeed, when leaders of terrorist organizations are absolutely certain that their orders will be fulfilled regardless of by whom (when they direct the perpetration, have the ultimate veto over it, or are the only ones who can call a halt to the offense), they are undoubtedly the perpetrators of the offense, whether they are present in the actual location of the commission or not.

The doctrine of control thus not only leads to the conclusion that the acts of terrorist leaders usually exceed the mental sphere of solicitation and reach the level of perpetration, but also supplies the executive branch with the justification to focus on the "big fish." Because concentrating on the leaders is undoubtedly much more efficient for the prevention of terrorist crimes, it is worthwhile for the prosecution to collect evidence against terrorist leaders that proves their control so that they can be charged with being actual perpetrators of criminal offenses.

Conclusion

The participation of children in terrorist activities is perhaps one of the most cynical abuses by terrorist organizations of the principle of distinction. In this chapter, I suggested several tools and mechanisms for the international community both to protect itself from terrorist activities in which children may participate and to defend the children from the abuse of cynical and cruel terrorist leaders by concentrating on the prosecution of leaders rather than the children.

The first part of the chapter dealt with the dualism of encountering children on the battlefield. On the one hand, children on modern battlefields can serve as "fighters" and may hence pose real danger to the counterterrorist force. On the other hand, they may sometimes be unwillingly participating directly in hostilities and being used as human shields.

The second part of the chapter discussed the question of whether it is legally possible to incriminate the leaders of terrorist organizations for crimes committed by children under their command. Many children are driven into committing criminal offenses in terrorist organizations under circumstances that negate their criminal intent and that may lead to an effort to incriminate the leaders at the expense of prosecuting the children.

In the final analysis, these two parts can be tied together by focusing more on the targeting and the punishment of the leaders of terrorist organizations than on the punishment and targeting of rank-and-file activists. As we have seen, on the battlefield this course of action can prevent harm to civilian targets, thereby ensuring better protection of IHL principles of distinction and proportionality. In the legal field, concentrating on leaders instead of children, whose criminal *mens rea* may be subject to doubt, leads to better protection of society from crimes of terrorism because it means tackling the roots of terrorism and not merely dealing with its surface effects.

This chapter introduces one of the most difficult challenges that modern battlefields pose for states that tackle terrorism. The phenomenon of child terrorism exemplifies the delicate balance that needs to be kept between the protection of human rights and ensuring the right of life to all people under the ongoing threat of terrorism in this era. Therefore, carrying out the means and procedures suggested here should go hand in hand with the international community's mission to address special attention to the situation of child terrorists in order to diminish the harm they inevitably suffer in the course of the community's confrontation with modern terrorism.

SEVEN

Private Military Contractors and Changing Norms for the Laws of Armed Conflict

RENÉE DE NEVERS

On September 16, 2007, a U.S. State Department security detail consisting of employees of Blackwater U.S.A., a private security company (PSC) working for the Department of State as part of its Worldwide Personal Protective Services (WPPS) contract, was traveling through Nisoor Square in Baghdad when Blackwater guards engaged in a firefight. Seventeen people were killed and more were injured. Although Blackwater spokesmen claimed that its guards responded to an attack by insurgents following a car bomb explosion nearby, Iraqi witnesses insisted, and U.S. and Iraqi investigations confirmed, that Blackwater guards fired without provocation on a slow-moving civilian car that failed to stop, killing its occupants, and they continued firing in response to the panic and confusion of civilians and Iraqi security forces in the square.[1]

The turmoil caused by the Blackwater incident led to greater scrutiny of the legal and regulatory bases for PSCs operating in Iraq, and in particular, the immunity from Iraqi law that contractors working for the U.S. government were granted at the end of the U.S. occupation.[2] Equally important, this incident illustrates the dilemmas created under humanitarian law by greater reliance on PSCs, whose status in combat zones is both problematic and often ambiguous. Regardless of their immunity from Iraqi law, Blackwater employees appear to have violated humanitarian law guidelines for civilians in war zones during the September 16th shooting incident, and under humanitarian law and U.S. domestic law, they could be subject to prosecution for war crimes. The U.S. government indicted five Blackwater employees on manslaughter charges in December 2008 for the 2007 Nisoor Square incident. The charges were dismissed in December 2009, however, because of errors on the part of prosecutors in making their case.[3]

The explosive growth in the use of PSC employees to carry out tasks formerly reserved for states' armed forces has outpaced efforts to assess the consequences of this increased reliance on PSCs for humanitarian law. This matters both for the states that hire them and for the employees of PSCs on or near battlefields. Moreover, many of the conflicts in which PSCs are playing a role are asymmetric, in that they are fought between parties with very different military capabilities and often between states and nonstate actors.[4] This increases the challenge of determining what PSC actions are appropriate within the laws of war. This chapter examines the legal and policy status of PSCs under the existing humanitarian-law framework, and it explores whether the law should be revised to more fully account for the roles of PSCs. It focuses specifically on activities where PSC employees carry weapons in conflict zones so that we may evaluate their status under international humanitarian law.

In most cases PSC employees cannot be accorded combatant status under humanitarian law because they do not meet the criteria for combatancy. Whether resort to force is allowed without jeopardizing their civilian protection from attack depends on the activities they are undertaking at the time, as well as how they use force. If they act in self-defense while protecting nonmilitary targets, their protections are secure, but resort to force related to military targets puts their protections at risk. PSC employees today are often in situations where their actions put their civilian protections under humanitarian law at risk, and this is particularly true in asymmetric conflicts. Changing PSCs' status on the battlefield to take into account the tasks they currently are performing is not the answer, and the costs of doing so could outweigh the benefits on the battlefield. This is particularly pertinent as evidence emerges about the sweeping scope of activities that have been outsourced to private actors.[5] Rather, states need to rethink the tasks that PSCs conduct on their behalf with humanitarian law in mind, even if it means reducing reliance on PSCs or limiting state military activities. Notably, the United States should reevaluate its reliance on private security contractors to conduct tasks where they are likely to be involved in military-like engagements. This is particularly important with regard to protecting diplomats who are treated as targets by insurgents in conflict zones. If they are likely to be attacked, then surely their protection should be considered a critical mission for the military and not one relegated to private contractors. This may well have implications for the U.S. military's force structure in current and future wars.

This chapter proceeds as follows. First, I lay out humanitarian law's classifications of different actors and discuss how PSCs fit within this framework by examining how their status, who they work for, and the jobs they do affect PSC employees' standing under humanitarian law. I then examine the implications of reliance on PSCs given the increased likelihood of asymmetric conflicts and conclude with a discussion of the similarities and differences in the challenges for law and policy presented by contractors and children on the battlefield.

Status Questions under Humanitarian Law

Under humanitarian law, two categories of persons are recognized in conflicts: combatants, and civilians/noncombatants. This distinction matters for two main reasons: first, the distinction ensures protections for noncombatants as far as possible; second, status determines who can fight without fear of prosecution. The "combatant's privilege" gives soldiers the right to kill, and it is accompanied by responsibilities for conduct in battles. This status also accords combatants the protections of prisoner of war (POW) status if they are captured, assuming they have conducted themselves in battle according to humanitarian law. This protection is intended to give soldiers an incentive to follow humanitarian law's rules, which have as their core goal mitigating the brutality of war. The differences in status are also meant to keep others out of combat. Those who engage in combat in violation of the distinctions between the two recognized groups are unprivileged belligerents who do not receive POW protections.[6]

Combatant status and the protections it accords do not apply in noninternational armed conflicts. The combatant–civilian distinction remains critical, however, because civilians are protected from direct attacks in noninternational as well as international armed conflicts—so long as they do not fight.[7] In noninternational armed conflicts, the targeting distinction turns on who

TABLE 7.1 Which "Combatant" Rights or Dangers Accrue to Different Groups?

	Right to Fight	POW Status	Lawful Target of Attack
Armed Forces	Yes	Yes	Yes
Militias*	Yes	Yes	Yes
"Civilians Accompanying The Force"	No	Yes	No**
Civilians/Noncombatants	No	No	No
Unprivileged Belligerents	No	No	Yes

*   Members of the armed forces and militias are accorded combatant status under humanitarian law.

** Both CAFs and civilians cannot be deliberately targeted, but if they are at or near legitimate military targets, then they may be victims of attack as "collateral damage." If they participate in hostilities directly, such as by protecting military targets, then they may be direct targets of attack.

is involved directly in fighting. Who may lawfully participate in hostilities is dependent on the domestic laws of the state involved.[8]

Although humanitarian law delineates two stark classifications, combatant and civilian, it must fit a range of actors within them. Combatant status is reserved for members of armed forces and for militias and similar groups affiliated with the state. The militia category was established to ensure protections and obligations for resistance fighters, with World War II in mind.[9]

All those who are not combatants are civilians. Civilian status is intended to ensure that those whose lives are affected by conflicts are protected from hostilities and in particular from direct attack. As long as they do not take part in hostilities, civilians cannot legitimately be targeted by attackers. It is important to keep in mind that humanitarian law does not prohibit civilian participation in combat; instead, it provides protections for civilians if they stay out of combat.

"Civilians accompanying the force" (CAFs) can gain some of the protections associated with combatant status, notably POW status, so long as they are properly identified as civilians working for the armed forces. They cannot be targeted deliberately, although if they are co-located with legitimate military targets, attacks against those locations are nonetheless legitimate. While their direct contribution to the war effort means that CAFs risk their protection against attack, they are not combatants; and if they participate directly in hostilities by taking up arms (as opposed to conducting intelligence or targeting weapons systems), then they also lose the right to POW status.[10] Moreover, as Michael Guillory has noted, "If they do [participate], they are considered unlawful combatants or belligerents and may be prosecuted as criminals" if captured.[11] Table 7.1 breaks down the rights and dangers that accompany status under humanitarian law.

Private Security Companies Within the Humanitarian Law Paradigm

Private security companies have been defined as "private companies that sell military services."[12] Current conceptions of the industry are broad, incorporating companies that provide offensive military services, and those offering security, protection, and intelligence services. Many terms have been used to describe companies offering military and security services internationally, including "the private security industry" and "the global security industry." "Private military and security companies" has become the accepted shorthand for those seeking to develop international standards for companies in this realm.[13]

There is little certainty about the industry's size, but this is a growing and global industry. The majority of PSCs working internationally are based in either the U.S. or the U.K.[14] The well-established companies claim a worldwide clientele for services ranging from protection to risk management, and they maintain offices around the globe.[15] Ninety companies were estimated to be working in Afghanistan in 2007, and at least 310 PSCs based in a range of countries had contracted or subcontracted with the U.S. government to provide services in Iraq between 2003 and late 2008.[16] These companies employed over 50,000 armed contractors in Iraq and Afghanistan in mid-2009.[17]

No international conventions directly govern the activities of PSCs, and international efforts to regulate PSCs have been "spectacularly unsuccessful."[18] Mercenaries are banned by the International Convention against the Recruitment, Use, Financing and Training of Mercenaries, signed in 1989 and in force since October 2001. Many observers have argued that PSCs closely resemble mercenaries, and in 2006, the UN General Assembly supported a resolution prohibiting "private companies offering international military consultancy and security services" from intervening in conflicts or being used against governments.[19] Those states relying on PSCs have not signed the 1989

Convention, however, limiting its effectiveness. Moreover, the heavy reliance on PSCs by the United States and Britain has led other observers to argue that it simply is too late to seek to ban PSCs; the goal instead should be to make PSCs accountable.[20]

I explore the middle ground between banning and blessing PSCs.[21] Humanitarian law's stipulations cover all individuals in conflict zones. Therefore, the activities of PSC employees can be evaluated within this framework.

Where do PSCs fall in humanitarian law's categories of persons? Three issues matter: 1) their classification as combatant or civilian, 2) who they work for, and 3) what they do. The combatant/noncombatant distinction is related to the differences between recognized members of a state's armed forces and PSCs. Who the PSC works for may matter because it creates distinctions regarding how near or far from the "battlefield" and the armed forces PSC employees are, and what authority the military has over them. And what PSC employees do in fulfilling their contracts determines whether they merit protection or potential prosecution under humanitarian law.

COMBATANTS OR NONCOMBATANTS?

First, there is general agreement that PSCs, both the companies and their employees, are civilians and cannot be considered combatants under humanitarian law.[22] Although they share some characteristics with militias—at least if they are working for their own government—international legal scholars agree that it is too great a stretch to conclude that PSCs fit this model.[23]

Due to the ways that PSCs operate, they generally do not meet all the criteria required for nonstate armed groups or militias to merit combatant status: operating under a clear command, having a distinctive sign or uniform that can be recognized from a distance, carrying weapons openly, and abiding by the laws of war.[24] First, PSCs are unlikely to meet the "clear command" criteria. Most PSC teams in places like Iraq and Afghanistan work on the basis of a "leader" or "agent in charge" who directs the other "operators" who work with him on a particular mission. It is not clear if outsiders can distinguish between the leader and operators and how much authority the leader has over others on his team.[25] Moreover, although most major PSCs adopt hierarchical procedures similar to military operations because many of their employees are ex-military, it is unclear if this implies a stable, fixed hierarchy within the company.[26] The industry's rapid expansion may also have diluted military discipline, particularly as more companies hire contractors of different backgrounds and nationalities.

Additionally, many contractors work for third parties—the company that has the government contract—not directly for the government whose combat they may be supporting. This means the country's government and military do not have command over the subcontracting companies, a point underscored in the U.S. Army's guidelines for working with contractors.[27] As one military lawyer points out, this makes their consideration as combatants "a nonstarter."[28] Simply being under contract to the government is insufficient to merit combatant status.[29] Moreover, many PSC employees are third-country nationals, which further erodes the government's command authority over them.

Second, many U.S. PSC employees tend to have a similar "look" that makes them distinguishable from civilians—and they have been caricatured as trying to look like "badasses" or "tough guys"—but they do not wear uniforms. A key issue is that the employees of PSCs are often indistinguishable from *each other*.[30] This makes monitoring their actions and ensuring accountability difficult. Notably, Iraq has tried to address this problem through its licensing requirements. Those companies registered with the government are issued distinctive numbered decals for their vehicles that would allow a bystander to identify them from at least a short distance. The Iraqi government also requires companies to register their weapons and personnel with the Interior Ministry.[31] Following the Blackwater incident in September 2007, the State Department adopted similar vehicle identification requirements, along with stricter audio and video recording requirements to improve the ability to evaluate incidents.[32] Before 2008, few PSCs formally registered in Iraq due to the frequent changes in guidelines, along with requests for bribes.[33] The Status of Forces agreement (SOFA) reached by the United States and Iraq in November 2008 reinforced the licensing requirement and made contractors liable under Iraqi law. Third, most PSC employees carry their weapons openly, as required by humanitarian law. Whether they abide by humanitarian law will be discussed in detail later.

A further hindrance to combatant status is that many contractors are hired on the basis of individual short-term contracts.[34] This may be appropriate for the companies and employees, but it suggests that allegiance to a state is not what guides employees' actions. Indeed, the first group of contractors assigned to protect Afghanistan's new president, Hamid Karzai, resigned en masse at the end of its first rotation due to disputes over their promised vacation pay with the parent company that had won the U.S. government contract to provide Karzai's security detail.[35]

Many American contractors working in Iraq and Afghanistan strongly support the U.S. government's overall mission. It is equally true, however, that PSC contractors are there for the money, and U.S. contractors in Iraq are surrounded–indeed, outnumbered by compatriots from around thirty countries who may have different motivations. In Afghanistan, the bulk of PSC employees are Afghan nationals, working for both locally owned and foreign companies that contract with a range of U.S. and international agencies.[36] Mercenaries are generally thought of as individuals who are willing to fight for money, either to attack other forces or to defend against them.[37] The increasing use of third-country nationals by PSCs working in conflict zones such as Iraq and Afghanistan is problematic because of the appearance of mercenarism this creates. Hiring locals raises a different concern: the institutionalization of security forces not under the state's authority.

WHO THEY WORK FOR: EMPLOYERS

PSCs contracting with the military are generally classified as civilians accompanying the force. This is the case in the U.S. Department of Defense's (DoD) 2003 instructions governing contractors, and it builds on earlier U.S. policy regarding contractor employees.[38]

However, the fact that many PSCs operating in war zones today are working under contracts signed by other government agencies [e.g., the Department of State, Interior, or CIA, or in the case of the United Kingdom, the Department for International Development (DFID) limits whether these contractors can also be considered CAFs. DoD contractors are CAFs, because they are "accompanying" the armed forces and clearly support the military mission, whereas PSCs working for other branches of government do not warrant that status. Blackwater was working for the State Department as part of its WPPS contract when the 2007 Nisoor Square incident occurred, for example. Moreover, Blackwater employees appear to have participated actively in CIA missions in Iraq, including possibly killing suspected insurgents.[39] U.S. legislation expanded the reach of the Uniform Code of Military Justice (UCMJ), which guides the behavior of the armed forces, to include the DoD's contractors on the battlefield as well in 2006. The DoD's guidance stresses that the UCMJ shall apply to civilian contractors who are not otherwise amenable to criminal prosecution under U.S. law, or whose conduct is "adverse to a significant military interest of the United States."[40] Other civilians working on overseas military bases can be prosecuted under the Military Extraterritorial Jurisdiction Act (MEJA), which was amended in 2004 after the Abu Ghraib scandal, to cover contractors hired by agencies other than the DoD. The issues of status and accountability under national law deserve greater clarification by governments, because the examples of Iraq and Afghanistan suggest that PSCs working for multiple government agencies are likely to be the norm where military operations coincide with reconstruction and development activities.

The practice of subcontracting also raises questions about which companies can be considered employed by the government as opposed to other private companies, and which deserve CAF status, if the initial contract is with a country's military forces.[41] At least 135 companies have subcontracted on U.S. government contracts in Iraq since 2003, for example, so the number of employees affected is significant.[42]

PSCs work not only for states, but also for international and private actors, by providing security to corporations, nongovernmental organizations, and international organizations. Employees working for these actors are clearly civilians under humanitarian law.[43] Use of force by these employees puts their civilian protections at risk.

WHAT THEY DO: PSC ACTIVITIES IN CONFLICT ZONES

Assuming they are civilians or CAFs, what are the potential consequences under humanitarian law for PSC employees who use force? To address this question, we must examine the general activities undertaken by PSC employees and discuss the implications of their activities under humanitarian law. Here the focus is on activities that could involve the use of force by PSC employees carrying weapons. What counts as "direct participation in hostilities" is subject to extensive debate, as treated in this volume, but many scholars concur that at least some tasks conducted by PSC employees who do not carry weapons, such as intelligence gathering, qualify as "direct participation" under some circumstances.[44] These also deserve attention but are beyond the scope of this discussion.[45]

COMBAT (OFFENSIVE USE OF FORCE)   Under humanitarian law, civilians cannot lawfully take part in combat. In general, PSCs do not openly engage in combat activities. During the 1990s, there were some notable examples of private military companies such as Executive Outcomes or Sandline International contracting to fight wars for the governments of Sierra Leone and Angola.[46] The widespread condemnation of these activities has led to rejection of an explicit combat role by most PSCs, and some scholars argue that a norm against offensive missions is emerging in practice.[47] British industry officials argue this point in particular, stressing that British companies are "purely defensive," and U.S. industry representatives, in discussing offensive actions, insist that "none of the companies do it."[48] Other scholars suggest that companies engaging in offensive activities have simply learned to avoid public view.[49] Although many firms argue that they work only for governments or "reputable" clients, the market for the services they provide is broader than this, so that companies willing to work for disreputable governments or non-state actors, including criminal groups, will find willing buyers.[50] The industry's argument that companies will avoid such work because it would damage their reputation is belied by the fact that few if any companies have paid a financial price in terms of lost business by working with illicit groups.[51]

PSCs continue to engage in offensive activities in parts of Africa and elsewhere, often with the sanction of the governments they support. At least in some cases companies have been deputized as parts of the state's armed forces.[52] If PSC employees are incorporated into a country's armed forces, then they likely hold combatant status if they are involved in fighting an international armed conflict, assuming they meet the legal tests for combatant status noted earlier.[53] If they are not incorporated into the armed forces, then PSC engagement in direct combat would be unlawful under humanitarian law, even in the service of the state.

PROTECTION (SECURITY SERVICES)   Many PSCs and their representatives describe their business as the protection of people, places, and things. This protective, defensive mission is important to the industry's claim that PSCs are not mercenaries. Humanitarian law makes no distinction between offensive and defensive uses of force, however; it focuses on whether the actor has the right to use force or not.[54] Moreover, what they are protecting and its status as a potential military target matters immensely to whether PSC employees can lawfully use force, even defensively, without endangering their status and protections under humanitarian law.

The key to what PSCs can do while providing security services without risking their civilian status and claim to POW protection rests on two factors: (1) whether they are protecting people, places, and things that could be considered military targets or to be contributing to the war effort, and (2) who is doing the attacking. Attacks by enemy forces against military targets are legitimate under humanitarian law, whereas attacks by nonstate actors, insurgents, and criminals are not, because *they* are not lawful combatants.[55]

Who do PSCs protect and how does this affect their status? If PSC employees are protecting people who cannot legitimately be viewed as military targets, then arguably they have more leeway to respond with force than if they are protecting valid military targets. Under the laws of armed conflict such attacks are not "hostilities" but criminal acts.[56] This means that PSCs may lawfully defend themselves and those they are protecting without putting their own civilian status at risk and without being viewed as taking direct part in hostilities.[57] A key issue is what constitutes self-defense in furtherance of the security function. Many common PSC security tactics in Iraq, such as "clearing by fire" and indiscriminate shooting, go beyond self-defense.

The Blackwater employees protecting U.S. State Department officials in Iraq need not worry about becoming unprivileged belligerents by using force defensively to protect their "clients" against attacks, because these diplomats cannot lawfully be attacked. This does not give PSC employees the right to use indiscriminate force to carry out their missions; however, if they do so, then they have committed a war crime, criminal acts, or both. Many of the reports that have gained attention since the 2007 Blackwater incident suggest that Blackwater employees in Iraq frequently used force without provocation and thus in excess of self-defense.[58]

Because military officers are legitimate military targets, PSC employees risk coming under attack when protecting them. But because they are not combatants but CAFs, PSC employees' use of weapons in hostilities is unprivileged under humanitarian law.[59] Moreover, although their presence at a military target puts them at risk of harm, if they use force to defend such targets from lawful attacks, they become legitimate targets of attack themselves. Because their participation is unprivileged, they could be prosecuted as criminals if captured. PSCs' use of force is legal under U.S. domestic law if it accords with their contract terms and they abide by their employer's rules of engagement, but the U.S. legal authority does not change individuals' status under humanitarian law. This awkward predicament calls into question the reliance on private contractors to protect people who are legitimate targets of military attack.

If the places and things PSC employees are protecting are considered military targets, then attacks on these sites by opposing forces are legitimate. In turn, contractors' use of force to defend these sites would constitute direct participation in hostilities.[60] Scholars disagree about how the right to use force in self-defense fits in such cases. Some note that "civilians [also] may always defend themselves,"[61] but other scholars argue that if contractors do use force, even in self-defense, they become unprivileged belligerents. Michael Guillory has stated this bluntly: "No matter the level of danger [civilians] face because of their location, participation in combat activities is forbidden."[62]

In at least one case in Iraq, in April 2004, Blackwater employees engaged in a protracted firefight against the Mahdi army that is loyal to cleric Moqtada al Sadr, while they were in local Coalition Provisional Authority (CPA) headquarters in Najaf. Employees of two other PSCs, Control Risks Group and Triple Canopy, who were providing protection for other contractors and the CPA compound in Al Kut, Iraq, engaged in a day-long battle against the Mahdi Army a few days later.[63] Under humanitarian law, their direct participation in hostilities caused them to lose their civilian protection against attack, and their use of force was thereby unlawful.

If the places and things PSC employees guard are not military or related to the war effort, then attacks against those guarding them are illegal. This makes the use of force in defense acceptable and not direct participation in hostilities.[64]

The more difficult problem is drawing lines in the gray areas; it is virtually impossible to determine with precision what sites might be deemed to contribute to a war effort, thus making them legitimate targets. For example, pipelines, radio towers, and electricity stations could be seen to help a war effort because of their role in supporting the state and its armed forces. Other locations, such as museums and hospitals, clearly are not military targets.

PSCs in Asymmetric Conflicts

As states shift focus to train for asymmetric warfare, they should think hard about how PSCs fit in these campaigns. This is especially important given the variability in PSC status under humanitarian law. One of the keys to success in fighting insurgent groups is "hearts and minds," winning the trust of the civilian population in order to gain their support and cooperation against rebel groups. This is also critical in efforts to combat terrorism. The fact that the opposing group tends to blend in with the population complicates efforts to fight it. How such conflicts are evaluated under international law can be unclear, because governments generally do not want to legitimize their opponents by categorizing internal struggles as "armed conflicts." Nor do they want to concede that their rule may be under threat.[65] Nonetheless, there is general agreement that Common Article 3 of the Geneva Conventions applies to all armed conflicts, and some armed forces, such as that of the United States, assume as a matter of course that humanitarian law applies in all armed conflicts.

Asymmetric conflicts have several implications for PSCs. First, the unequal capabilities of the opponents in an asymmetric war mean that insurgents are likely to look for "softer" targets. Those in "protective" roles are thus more likely to be drawn into hostilities because their clients will be targeted. Second, the danger that PSC employees, as well as soldiers, will hurt civilians is greater, because of the difficulties in distinguishing between enemy opponents and innocent civilians. But the fact that the opponent is hiding among the civilian population does not lessen the legal requirement to avoid civilian casualties as far as possible. Third, this suggests that developing mechanisms for control and accountability as part of humanitarian law are if anything more important in an asymmetric conflict and that this set of challenges applies to PSCs as much as it does to armed forces.

Should PSCs be given a lawful combatant role in asymmetric conflicts? With an increasingly global industry, some observers worry that employees of firms from different states might find themselves in conflict against each other, and it is important to ensure that all PSC employees comply with humanitarian law.[66] According PSCs combatant privileges, however, could directly affect their overall contribution to the military mission in irregular conflicts. A core concern of humanitarian law is to ensure the universality of the laws governing conflict. This suggests a need to recognize the similarities of condition and action, and either to sanction or proscribe nonstate groups involved in conflicts on the basis of regularized criteria. As legal scholars have noted, the goal of recognizing the "equality of belligerents" requires an effort to be consistent in how the laws are applied;[67] indeed, this is at the heart of a legal framework in general. Singling out PSCs by granting them some form of lawful status could be a step in the wrong direction, if similar recognition is not considered for other nonstate groups. To begin with, such a policy appears to privilege the nonstate actors preferred by strong states, thereby enhancing strong state capabilities against nonstate opponents. But cherry-picking nonstate groups will not help ensure broader respect for humanitarian law, if locals perceive that companies they equate with mercenaries are getting special treatment. In many places where PSCs work, a negative view of mercenaries endures.

To be sure, a fundamental concern is to ensure that PSC employees do not fall outside the law. Whether the correct solution is to change humanitarian law, however, is debatable. Rather, states relying on contractors must remember their own responsibility for those in their employ. Not only are states required to prevent civilian participation in hostilities, but they are also required to ensure that civilians in their employ are aware of their obligations under humanitarian law. The state or its representatives may be liable if its employees commit violations.[68] This suggests that states must remove the limits on prosecution and regulation that currently exist in domestic law so that they can regulate the companies and prosecute PSC contractors who commit crimes.[69] Notably, states must keep in mind that using force to fulfill contractual obligations may be legal under domestic law, but contract terms do not change what PSC employees can legitimately do under humanitarian law without risking their civilian protections.

A second problem with according PSCs legitimate status to undertake tasks that put them in combat is that such a change could damage the broader mission. The U.S. experience in Iraq highlights the pitfalls of relying on PSCs, which touch directly on the battle for hearts and minds. Local populations do not distinguish between soldiers and civilian PSC employees but see them all as "Americans," and if Americans behave badly this feeds anti-American sentiment—and, often, insurgencies.[70] Additionally, PSCs working to fill contract goals without attention to the bigger picture can be detrimental to the military's mission. This has been acknowledged bluntly by U.S. military commanders, and U.S. Secretary of Defense Robert Gates noted that although PSCs conducting security details have a simple mission of ensuring that those they protect are transported safely, the way PSCs achieve this goal "work(s) at cross purposes to our larger mission in Iraq."[71] Indeed, both military leaders and independent observers have argued that contractor behavior can be detrimental to the mission because PSC employees are more likely than military troops to commit abuses.[72]

Third, to the degree that the United States and the international community support strengthening, not weakening, humanitarian law and seek to encourage nonstate groups to abide by humanitarian law, reliance on PSCs needs to be managed carefully. In Iraq and elsewhere, PSCs are carrying out tasks that could both alienate the locals and make them unprivileged belligerents. Several observers have stressed the need to consider the appropriate balance between public and private roles with regard to the use of force.[73] One clear solution is to rethink the missions that it is appropriate to delegate to PSC employees in international as well as in asymmetric conflicts on the basis of humanitarian law.

One way to determine appropriate "lines" would be to demarcate, as far as possible, those tasks in which PSC employees could put their civilian protections at risk by engaging directly in hostilities. This approach would depart from current U.S. policy, which relies on PSC employees to guard military commanders and "static" sites that might be considered legitimate military objectives, along with other traditional support functions. The Iraq example suggests, however, that the use of PSCs to guard diplomats in the middle of an insurgency is highly problematic. To be sure, diplomats are not legitimate targets under humanitarian law, but they are frequently targeted. Not only does resort to PSCs potentially damage the counterinsurgency effort itself, but it is likely to put PSC employees squarely in the middle of hostilities.

U.S. military spokesmen generally argue that the DoD needs to rely on contractors for defensive tasks in order to "free up" the armed forces to go after the enemy.[74] But humanitarian law does not recognize a distinction between offensive and defensive uses of force; contractors acting in either capacity risk their protections. Moreover, if "soft targets" are more likely to be targeted in an insurgent conflict—legally or not—then obvious soft targets like diplomats should be protected by the military. This policy change would lessen PSCs' danger of becoming unprivileged belligerents, it would reduce frictions with the local population, and it would place military troops in engagements with the insurgents they seek to defeat.

Finally, how PSCs do their jobs on battlefields matters. Notably, states are responsible for the actions of their soldiers and others working for them in conflict situations. The recent Montreux Document agreed to by the Swiss government, the International Committee of the Red Cross (ICRC), and several states that rely on PSCs seeks to remind states of their obligations in hiring PSCs to ensure that these companies comply with humanitarian law. If they fail to do so, then the states themselves are in violation of international law.[75]

Both the U.S. military and PSCs have learned that they can reduce their reliance on force if pressed. The U.S. army successfully reduced civilian casualties at checkpoints in Iraq, for example.[76] Following the Nisoor Square incident of September 2007, the DoD and the State Department established greater coordination in both guidelines and oversight of PSCs operating in Iraq, with the result that between December 2007 and June 2008, incidents in which PSCs fired weapons decreased by 67 percent.[77] This experience suggests that stricter accountability can positively affect the behavior of companies.

Certainly, its current missions and capabilities suggest that the U.S. military would be hard pressed to take on protective missions in the short run. Moreover, some analyses suggest that both the military and the State Department previously rejected reliance on the military for diplomatic security.[78] But although diplomatic security may be an appropriate civilian function in general, it is not when providing security regularly requires resort to military force. Particularly in asymmetric conflicts, the resort to force in conflict zones must be measured and consistent, and privatization of security tasks may not be appropriate. The military may have to rethink its force structures to ensure that it can carry out what are appropriately military missions with uniformed personnel.

Contractors and Children on the Battlefield

Children and contractors represent different means that actors fighting asymmetric conflicts employ to bolster their position relative to their opponents in asymmetric armed conflicts. Their use complicates the task of state actors in asymmetric conflicts for several reasons. State armies seek to abide by humanitarian law and face serious challenges in responding to child terrorists or soldiers. Such children present a real threat to soldiers trained not to kill innocents, and killing or wounding children even when it is clear that they present a real threat has negative repercussions in eroding local support for insurgents or terrorists.

The actions of PSCs working for states can also obstruct the battle for hearts and minds. Events in Iraq and Afghanistan have led to the paradox that law-abiding behavior by PSCs receives little attention, whereas incidents of poor behavior or perceived excesses resonates widely and damages state military efforts. Notably, the negative image PSCs gained in the Iraq conflict has reverberated globally and is now being exploited by terrorist groups. For example, some Pakistani groups believed to be responsible for the rash of suicide bombings in Pakistan in the fall of 2009 disavowed responsibility for specific attacks that led to strong public condemnation and blamed these attacks on Blackwater.[79] The fact that the CIA hired Blackwater for some covert operations in Afghanistan and Pakistan, and the general tendency to believe conspiracy theories in Pakistan make this claim potentially very damaging to U.S. efforts in South Asia. Indeed, Afghan president Hamid Karzai announced that private security companies would have to leave Afghanistan in two years during his second inaugural speech in November 2009.[80]

A critical difference between these two groups is their motivation for participation in hostilities. PSC employees find themselves on or near battlefields by choice; the same cannot be said for children recruited by insurgents or terrorists. Both the companies' and PSC employees' central motivation is monetary; most contractors receive salaries significantly higher than their home militaries offer. Some may be driven as well by patriotism and a desire to support government missions, but money is clearly paramount for the majority.[81] As Hilly Moodrick-Even Khen notes, children become involved in conflicts for a range of reasons, including poverty, the harsh environments they are in, and revenge. But the key point about children's participation in conflicts is that it is not voluntary; it is on this point that Moodrick-Even Khen's argument for holding the leaders who recruit them responsible resonates powerfully. Children are often driven to insurgents by the need to survive, and they are also frequently abducted or coerced into participation. Children are ideal pawns for these leaders because of their immaturity, obedience, and incomprehension of the risks they may face; in contrast to contractors, they are "low-cost"—and expendable.[82]

Is the use of children by terrorists distinct from the problem of child soldiers? The question is worth raising because it may be a mistake to focus too closely on holding terrorist leaders responsible for exploiting children. Why not hold the leaders of all groups that do so equally culpable? As Moodrick-Even Khen notes, enlisting children under fifteen in combat is a war crime under the statutes of the International Criminal Court. Both boys and girls have been recruited, sometimes forcibly, to participate in conflicts or military forces in eighty-six countries, with governments, paramilitary groups, and insurgents relying on them.[83] The main difference between child terrorists and child soldiers may be that Western militaries participating in contingency operations are more likely to encounter children as terrorists than as soldiers, which causes moral dilemmas as well as questions of appropriate conduct.

Although the focus here has primarily been on the question of how the activities undertaken by PSC employees may affect their status under humanitarian law, Moodrick-Even Khen's discussion of the culpability of leaders for the actions of child soldiers points to the need to examine the responsibility of states that hire PSCs, as well as the culpability of private security companies for the actions of their employees.

States are responsible for ensuring respect of humanitarian law generally, and this creates an obligation to ensure that those who are delegated tasks by the state are trained in their rights and obligations under humanitarian law. States are responsible for actions undertaken by PSCs that fall outside humanitarian law's guidelines, if they had failed to provide such training.[84] Yet those states that have relied most heavily on PSCs in recent years, notably the United States, have done little to maintain oversight of the activities of the PSCs and other contractors in their employ. Moreover, the government acknowledged in 2007 that it did not know how many PSCs it employed.[85] An additional dilemma raised by the question of state responsibility is how to evaluate responsibility for violations of humanitarian law if a state acts on the advice of a PSC in its employ.[86]

As to the responsibility of private security companies, these corporations are legal "persons" and thus can be sued in state courts.[87] As it is with states, it is difficult to assign criminal responsibility for those running a company, because of the challenges of determining who gave orders and how much control was exercised by corporate leaders.[88] This has led us to resort to civil lawsuits by the victims of abuses by PSC contractors.

If warfare is too important to be left to the generals, it is certainly too important to be delegated to the contractors. Nor should the pace of outsourcing be allowed to determine whether humanitarian law's guidelines are eroded or reinforced. U.S. resort to PSCs is largely driven by domestic politics. Many scholars of the private security industry have highlighted the problem of determining appropriate public and private functions with regard to the use of force. They have noted the danger that outsourcing may go too far in this particularly critical area; indeed, some argue that privatization has already gone too far.[89] The problem has been to establish clear dividing lines. Humanitarian law may help provide such guidelines. Governments have a responsibility to evaluate whether they should scale back their reliance on PSCs, to ensure that they don't put the contractors' status in jeopardy, and to reaffirm their own commitment to humanitarian law. Particularly if more countries are going to add their own PSCs to the market, it is critically important to ensure that their employees adhere to the laws of war. Alternately, if fundamentally military activities cannot be undertaken by the state, perhaps they should not be done at all.

CRITICAL DEBATE IV

Military Necessity and Humanitarian Priorities in International Humanitarian Law: Productive Tension or Irreconcilable Differences?

EIGHT

The Principle of Proportionality Under International Humanitarian Law and Operation Cast Lead

ROBERT P. BARNIDGE JR.

International law straddles an ever-changing world of theory and practice, and it always has. It has before it the heady task of remaining relevant in the face of both widespread compliance and widespread violation, and in doing so, it must adapt to present predicaments while retaining an integrity that can command compliance. It is one of international law's great paradoxes, furthermore, that even as it insists that it is "above" politics, it is quintessentially "of" politics. It is, after all, the by-product of the complex machinations of states and other actors jockeying for advantage in a crowded landscape of disparate interests and limited resources.

International humanitarian law—a set of rules and standards that seeks to legally determine who "matters" and who does not, and how, in situations of armed conflict—necessarily operates within this reality. As President of the Supreme Court of Israel Aharon Barak put it in the 2002 *Ajuri v. IDF Commander* case, "[e]ven when the cannons speak and the Muses are silent, law exists and operates, determining what is permitted and what forbidden, what is lawful and what unlawful."[1] The law in this context fundamentally roots itself in a commitment to distinction, and from this principle springs the balance of international humanitarian law, including the principle of proportionality. Indeed, without this commitment to distinguish, according to the

Commentaries to the 1977 Additional Protocol I to the 1949 Geneva Conventions (AP I), international humanitarian law would collapse, so crucial is this "foundation on which the codification of the laws and customs of war rests."[2]

This chapter critically examines the principle of proportionality under international humanitarian law and contextualizes its vulnerabilities by looking at Israel's actions during Operation Cast Lead in the Gaza Strip between December 27, 2008, and January 18, 2009. It begins by providing a black-letter law overview of the principle. Although widely accepted, the proportionality principle suffers from significant shortcomings that impact its usefulness as a predictable tool for distinguishing between the lawful and the unlawful, particularly in the context of asymmetrical warfare.[3] These shortcomings exist at both a theoretical level, in the abstract, and at a practical level. To focus these discussions, the second half of this chapter looks at the largely negative international reaction to Israel's actions during Operation Cast Lead. This reaction, which was and has been typically couched with a feigned certainty that belies and leaves unanswered the theoretical shortcomings of the principle of proportionality, suggests that, more often than not proportionality acts as the ultimate exemplar of law used instrumentally as a tool to further a particular politics and paradigm of power.

The Principle of Proportionality Under International Humanitarian Law

As alluded to earlier and as the International Court of Justice (ICJ) stated in the 1996 *Legality of the Threat or Use of Nuclear Weapons (Nuclear Weapons)* case, the principle of distinction acts as one of international humanitarian law's "cardinal principles."[4] Indeed, it is a "first principle." Article 48 of AP I, which Dinstein describes as embodying the "kernel of LOIAC [i.e., law of international armed conflict] as it currently stands,"[5] gives the clearest statement of this principle. Calculated to "ensure respect for and protection of the civilian population and civilian objects," it juxtaposes the "civilian population" with "combatants" and "civilian objects" with "military objectives" and only permits of operations directed against military objectives.[6] Operations that are directed against anything other than military objectives, which is to say, operations that are directed against civilian objects, will by definition violate the principle of distinction.[7]

Assuming that a party to a conflict has complied with the principle of distinction, it will also need to satisfy the related yet distinct principle of proportionality. In AP I, this latter principle appears in Articles 51(5)(b), 57(2)(a)(iii), and 57(2)(b). The first of these articles frames proportionality within the context of discrimination or the prohibition of indiscriminate attacks, whereas the latter two articles operate within the context of precautionary measures that must be taken to ensure compliance with international humanitarian law. These two sets of understandings of proportionality, although not substantially different as a matter of law, are best considered separately.[8]

As just stated, Article 51(5)(b) couches the principle of proportionality within the context of indiscriminate attacks and the prohibition of them. Specifically, it gives as an example of an indiscriminate attack one that "may be expected to cause incidental loss of civilian life, injury to civilians, damage to civilian objects, or a combination thereof, which would be excessive in relation to the concrete and direct military advantage anticipated." Attacks that fall foul of this provision will be both disproportionate and a type of indiscriminate attack.

The two provisions of AP I that require a proportionality assessment but that do so within the context of precautionary measures are Articles 57(2)(a)(iii) and 57(2)(b). The balancing language in these two articles exactly replicates the language in Article 51(5)(b), an attack that may be "expected to cause incidental loss of civilian life, injury to civilians, damage to civilian objects, or a combination thereof, which would be excessive in relation to the concrete and direct military advantage anticipated." The implications here are unsurprising: planners and decision makers cannot authorize the launching of disproportionate attacks[9] and must cancel or suspend attacks if their disproportionate nature "becomes apparent."[10] Put differently, Article 57(2)(a)(iii) upholds the principle of proportionality at the authorization stage whereas Article 57(2)(b) acts at the stage during which an attack that was determined to have been proportionate but that is later determined to be disproportionate has already been authorized or may be under way. Clearly, these precautionary measures are meant to lessen the likelihood of indiscriminate and other types of unlawful attacks.

By definition, of course, AP I only creates legally binding rights and obligations for states that are parties to it,[11] and the fact that it does not apply to non-state parties implies the nonapplicability of all its provisions, including those that specifically prohibit disproportionate attacks, namely, Articles 51(5)(b), 57(2)(a)(iii), and 57(2)(b). This means that parties to an armed conflict that are not also parties to AP I will, as a matter of international treaty law, be completely free to disregard all of its provisions for the simple reason that they have not consented to be bound by them. Such states will, however, remain bound by those principles of international humanitarian law that exist under customary international law in addition to and alongside AP I.[12]

To what extent, then, does the principle of proportionality also exist under customary international humanitarian law? As the ICJ put it in the *Nuclear Weapons* case, international humanitarian law's "fundamental rules ... constitute intransgressible principles of international customary law,"[13] and according to the International Committee of the Red Cross' (ICRC) Customary International Humanitarian Law (CIHL), much, if not all, of what AP I understands by proportionality is also binding as a matter of customary international law, both with regard to the prohibition of indiscriminate attacks and within the context of precautionary measures. Specifically, CIHL exactly replicates Article 51(5)(b)'s proportionality language and holds that this obligation reflects customary international law in both international and noninternational armed conflicts.[14] Rules 18 and 19 of CIHL, furthermore, effectively recognize as being binding as a matter of customary international law in both international and noninternational armed conflicts Articles 57(2)(a)(iii) and 57(2)(b) of AP I.[15]

The Problem with Proportionality: Theory and Practice, with Specific Reference to Operation Cast Lead

The principle of proportionality is firmly entrenched in international humanitarian law discourse, and it applies in both international and noninternational armed conflicts as a matter of both international treaty law and customary international law. The language of the proportionality balancing test, furthermore, is consistent both with regard to the prohibition of indiscriminate attacks and within the context of precautionary measures: The attacks at issue are those that "may be expected to cause incidental loss of civilian life, injury to civilians, damage to civilian objects, or a combination thereof, which would be excessive in relation to the concrete and direct military advantage anticipated."

Although simply stated, however, the proportionality balancing test suffers from a number of significant shortcomings, and these must be addressed and admitted, frankly and honestly. The following sections explore some of these problems as a matter of both theory and practice, with an examination of Operation Cast Lead to contextualize the latter.

THEORY

Clearly, the language of the proportionality balancing test involves trade-offs. It requires the identification of expectation and balancing based on a vague notion of what can be considered "excessive," with considerations of the civilian and a forward-looking anticipation of "concrete and direct military advantage" on opposite sides of the scale. Given the death and destruction that are inherent in armed conflict, one might think, or perhaps even hope, that these trade-offs would be taken seriously by all those concerned and that this would engender a certain hesitancy to "pull the trigger." At the same time, however, it should be acknowledged that war is meant to be fought and to be fought effectively. As U.S. General George S. Patton bluntly put it in 1944, "[w]ar is a bloody, killing business. You've got to spill their blood, or they will spill yours."[16]

Bearing such tensions in mind, to what extent can it be said that the language of the proportionality balancing test as such provides a tangible clarity to the proportionality principle? Put differently, to what extent does it actually assist in being able to interpret the principle, to apply it, and to do so in a predictable way as a matter of law? It is helpful to begin this inquiry by looking at the *Commentaries* to AP I.

Section I of part IV of AP I, which contains both Articles 51 and 57, deals with the general protection of civilians from the effects of hostilities and provides a general picture. According to its *Commentary,* the adopted text is "not always as clear as one might have wished, but [according to it] it seemed necessary to leave some margin of appreciation to those who will have to apply the rules."[17] The *Commentary* continues by stating that the effectiveness of the protection provisions depends upon the desire of the parties to the conflict to act humanely and in good faith.[18] Of course, this latter variable, good faith, adds very little to the discussion because the 1969 Vienna Convention on the Law of Treaties already requires states parties to perform their treaty obligations in good faith[19] and to interpret treaties "in good faith in accordance with the ordinary meaning to be given to the terms of the treaty in their context and in the light of its object and purpose."[20]

The *Commentaries* to the articles in AP I that specifically contain the proportionality balancing test, namely, Articles 51(5)(b), 57(2)(a)(iii), and 57(2)(b), add to this unsettling sense of ambiguity. Article 51's *Commentary*, for example, notes that its paragraph 5 had been criticized for its "imprecise wording and terminology"[21] and, while recognizing an at least partial justification for these concerns, again stresses the importance of good faith and a "desire to conform with the general principle of respect for the civilian population."[22] Article 57's *Commentary*, unsurprisingly, echoes these concerns. Acknowledging that the terms of Article 57 are "relatively imprecise and are open to a fairly broad margin of judgment."[23] It puts great trust in both good faith and common sense as interpretative tools, although it fails to define the substance of either of these concepts as a matter of law.[24]

The academic literature is largely in agreement with this acknowledgment of the question-begging nature of the proportionality balancing test under international humanitarian law. Schmitt, for example, states about the principle of proportionality that "there is no question that [it] . . . is among the most difficult of LOIAC norms to apply."[25] Rogers, noting that proportionality is "more easily stated than applied in practice,"[26] stresses that greater care to minimize potential risks to civilians may actually expose attacking forces to increased risks of harm.[27] How is balancing to be done in this context and to be done within the law, predictably? Does the proportionality balancing test lead to singular, incontrovertible conclusions as a matter of law? Should it? Or, rather, to quote Sloane, is the "problem . . . not that international law provides the wrong answers . . . ; it is that often it provides *no* answer or only a very abstract one[?]"[28]

Consider one side of the scale in the proportionality balancing test, the concept of the "concrete and direct military advantage anticipated." How does international law as such distinguish between the concrete and direct natures of anticipated military advantages? Does "concrete" mean definite? Tangible? Reasonably definite? Reasonably tangible? Should "direct" be understood in contradistinction to indirect? Whose direct? Whose indirect? Is the fact that the *Commentary* to Article 57 concludes that the phrase "concrete and direct" was "intended to show that the advantage concerned should be substantial and relatively close, and that advantages which are hardly perceptible and those which would only appear in the long term should be disregarded"[29] a source of comfort, or is it redundant? What about the concept of anticipation? Does it leave the law hopelessly mired in the "sphere of expectation rather than arithmetic[,] ... never ... a job for one's pocket calculator[?]"[30] And as to "military advantage anticipated," is this to be broadly interpreted, as the Eritrea–Ethiopia Claims Commission did in a 2005 partial award[31] and as seems to be indicated by the analogous international criminal law provision in the 1998 Rome Statute of the International Criminal Court (ICC)?[32] Other questions, of course, could also be asked, but like these, they do not admit of easy answers.[33]

The *Final Report to the Prosecutor by the Committee Established to Review the NATO Bombing Campaign Against the Federal Republic of Yugoslavia (Final Report)*, which was released in 2000, attempted to provide some general parameters to these and other questions related to the proportionality balancing test.[34] It did this by collapsing the heavy burden of decision making on the shoulders of the "reasonable military commander."[35] At the same time, however, it acknowledged that the decision maker's values, background, education, and combat experience will likely influence what might be considered excessive, less than excessive, or perhaps even just not quite excessive.[36] As Dinstein notes, particular facts and circumstances will also play an important role in these determinations.[37]

It is precisely the absence of what Schmitt calls a "common currency of evaluation"[38] that makes the task of the "reasonable military commander" so difficult and so legally inconclusive. As Kalshoven suggests, what is at issue is an "agonizing dilemma in which the law cannot provide a clear-cut answer."[39] A committed pacifist and an "ends justifies the means" militarist may both argue their cases using the language of the proportionality balancing test, referring to good faith and other interpretative tools in so doing, but it is scarcely believable that they will reach the same legal conclusions. To contend otherwise is to wish for an objectivity, certainty, and integrity in the law related to proportionality that simply does not exist.[40]

PRACTICE: OPERATION CAST LEAD

If the language of the proportionality balancing test as such, assisted by whatever interpretative tools one might wish to bring to bear on the matter (e.g., a sense of humanity, good faith, common sense, or a combination of these interpretative tools or perhaps others), does not of itself bring a tangible clarity to the proportionality principle as a matter of law, then an examination that shifts the discussion from theory to practice may be more satisfying. Perhaps the lawyerly tendency to analyze to excess, to argue for argument's sake, renders proportionality in theory problematic but does not hold up in practice where there might exist a common understanding of the principle. A look at the largely negative international reaction to Israel's actions in Gaza during Operation Cast Lead, however, suggests that the proportionality principle's theoretical shortcomings are only exacerbated in practice.

This section exposes some of these practical shortcomings by separately looking at how different actors, both state and nonstate, have grappled with the substance of proportionality in the context of Operation Cast Lead and, just as important, at the process through which these discussions have taken place. As regards the latter, particular attention is given to the U.N. Fact-Finding Mission on the Gaza Conflict (Fact-Finding Mission).

The Substance of Proportionality

Israel launched Operation Cast Lead in a particular context. That context involved *hudnas,* or ceasefires, with Hamas that had given the group tactical advantages when it had been militarily weak and opportunities to regroup, opportunities that had effectively allowed it to fight and to fight more effectively another day.[41] The years immediately prior to Operation Cast Lead, of course, had seen Israel's disengagement from Gaza; the election of Hamas and the routing of Fatah in Gaza; an increasingly bellicose and apocalyptic posture by Iran with its support for Hamas ever-present and central, and thousands of rockets being launched into southern Israel from Gaza.[42] These years had also seen international pressure of a diplomatic nature, an Israeli blockade of Gaza, and indirect negotiations.[43] The *génocidaires* of Hamas, however, buttressed by their constitutional and religious commitments to "kill the Jews,"[44] had strengthened their position, and Israel responded with Operation Cast Lead. As Israeli President Shimon Peres put it at the beginning of Operation Cast Lead, "We cannot permit that Gaza will become a permanent base of threatening and even killing children and innocent people in Israel for God knows why."[45]

Given that the proportionality principle has become what Walzer refers to as the "favorite critical term in current discussions of the morality of war,"[46] it is unsurprising that the international reaction to Operation Cast Lead seized upon this legal term of art and its close kin, "excessive," in condemning Israel. International organizations figured prominently in this regard. U.N.

Secretary-General Ban Ki-Moon, for example, who had been "saddened... profoundly,"[47] condemned the "excessive use of force by Israel."[48] For President of the U.N. General Assembly Miguel d'Escoto Brockmann, Operation Cast Lead was "wanton aggression [and] ... [a] disproportionate military response."[49] Asma Jahangir, chairperson of the coordinating body for independent U.N. human rights experts, criticized Israel in the following terms: "[t]he use of disproportionate force by Israel and the lack of regard for the life of civilians on both sides cannot be justified by the actions of the other party. They constitute clear violations of international human rights and international humanitarian law."[50] U.N. Special Rapporteur on the Situation of Human Rights in Palestinian Territories Occupied Since 1967 Richard Falk issued a statement on the first day of the operations, December 27, 2008, condemning Israel's "disproportionate military response."[51] Similar criticisms came from the presidency of the Council of the European Union[52] and many states.[53] The League of Arab States–commissioned *Report of the Independent Fact-Finding Committee on Gaza: No Safe Place (No Safe Place),* released in April 2009, concluded that there was "no evidence that any military advantage was served by the killing and wounding of civilians or the destruction of property"[54] and that "buildings were destroyed not for any military advantage or for reasons of military necessity but in order to punish the people of Gaza for tolerating a Hamas regime."[55]

Across the globe, demonstrations by members of civil society "in defense of peace" also criticized Operation Cast Lead. Admittedly, some of these protests devolved into blatant expressions of anti-Semitism,[56] expressions that only seemed to confirm Israeli Prime Minister Ariel Sharon's concerns, voiced before the Knesset in January 2005, that "[t]his phenomenon of Jews defending themselves and fighting back is anathema to the new anti-Semes."[57] Words such as "proportionality" and "excessive" were frequently bandied about as emotional crutches, and one did not get the sense that the legal nature of these terms was either known or appreciated."[58] The title of an opinion piece published on January 11, 2009, in London's *Sunday Times,* authored by more than two dozen prominent, mostly United Kingdom–based international lawyers typified the mood: "Israel's Bombardment of Gaza Is Not Self-defence—It's a War Crime" ("Israel's Bombardment").[59]

In their seeming adjudications of the law *proprio motu,* however, it is unclear exactly how these international organizations, states, and members of civil society arrived at their apparently conclusive judgments that Israel's actions during Operation Cast Lead had obviously violated the substance of proportionality. Even when they seemed cognizant of the fact that the legal balancing test for proportionality applies in both international and noninternational armed conflicts and that it does so as a matter of both international treaty law and customary international law, these actors hardly hesitated to conclude that the attacks at issue were disproportionate rather than, for example, less than disproportionate, or perhaps even just not quite disproportionate. In other words, there was little qualification and more than a hint of what Kennedy calls "self-confident outrage."[60] Where had proportionality's inherent flexibility and ambiguity gone? Had they been concealed for the sake of more convincing and powerful argument, for the sake of "the cause"?

A cynical, though perhaps not inaccurate, explanation might be that "disproportionate attacks" are simply those that emanate from parties to conflicts that particular "namers" and "shamers" do not want to "win," regardless of the largely indeterminate and complex balancing between civilian and military considerations that the proportionality principle formally requires as a matter of law.[61] As Walzer notes, Operation Cast Lead "was called 'disproportionate' on day one, before anyone knew very much about how many people had been killed or who they were."[62]

Although the use of legal language for political purposes cannot, and should not, be discounted and undoubtedly explains some of the largely negative international reactions to Operation Cast Lead, as does the fact that it was a Jewish state (indeed, *the* Jewish state) that was in the dock in the court of world public opinion, another explanation seems to be a fundamental misunderstanding of the substance of the proportionality principle itself, the idea that it somehow prohibits "extensive" collateral damage as a matter of law.[63] In fact, many of the criticisms of Operation Cast Lead that based themselves in (dis)proportionality expressly made their claims in ways that seemed to have assimilated, in error, "excessive" with "extensive."[64]

To give a few examples, consider that Chairperson Jahangir "call[ed] on all parties to immediately cease all actions that result in civilian casualties, or put them at great risk."[65] Special Rapporteur Falk lamented "extensive" civilian casualties and "extensive" damage to both public and private property in Gaza.[66] In its discussion of indiscriminate and disproportionate attacks in the context of war crimes, *No Safe Place* decried, and thus presumably sought to make of legal relevance, "massive destruction" that had taken place to Gazan hospitals, mosques, private homes, schools, government buildings, businesses and factories, U.N. facilities, and farmland.[67] These discussions seem to imply that international humanitarian law gives dispositive weight to "extensive" damage, particularly to civilian objects and to civilians themselves but perhaps not even exclusively to them, in assessments of proportionality.

The legal test for (dis)proportionate attacks, however, focuses *only* on those attacks that "may be expected to cause incidental loss of civilian life, injury to civilians, damage to civilian objects, or a combination thereof, which would be *excessive* in relation to the concrete and direct military advantage anticipated." What may be "excessive" need not be, though it may be "extensive," and what may be "extensive" may be, though it need not be "excessive." In fact, to suggest that proportionate attacks must necessarily avoid extensive damage *in addition to* the already-existing positive law obligation to avoid excessive damage risks effectively subjecting parties to an armed conflict to tying not one but both of their hands behind their backs.[68] Indeed, as Chief Prosecutor of the ICC Luis Moreno-Ocampo put it in his February 9, 2006, response to communications that he had received concerning Iraq, "under international humanitarian law and the Rome Statute, the death of civilians during an armed conflict, no matter how grave and regrettable, does not in itself constitute a war crime."[69]

Indeed, international humanitarian law in general and the principle of proportionality in particular are the great facilitators of death and destruction in armed conflict, "extensive" or otherwise. Put differently, as long as the casualties at issue can "fit" and be "argued within" the formal constraints of law, there will be no violation of law. What is at issue is a discourse of blood sacrifice, since "the rule opens latitude for nonexcessive civilian casualties and merely prohibits attacks that are likely to exceed its imagined limit. This latitude is where sacrifice occurs—beyond this, it is murder."[70] As Kennedy notes, "law enables, frames, channels and legitimates the practice of war,"[71] and there is no need to pretend otherwise.

If the largely negative international reaction to Operation Cast Lead generally failed to rigorously parse and apply to the facts identified expectation and a balancing based on a vague notion of what can be considered "excessive," with considerations of the civilian and a forward-looking anticipation of "concrete and direct military advantage" on opposite sides of the scale, and if it confused "excessive" with "extensive," it also reflected a fundamental confusion as to the actual extent of the collateral damage in Gaza.

Consider the following accounts, arranged chronologically, of collateral damage during the December 27, 2008–January 18, 2009, conflict:

January 3, 2009: In the preamble to its Final Communiqué on the Ongoing Israeli Assault on Gaza, the Expanded Extraordinary Meeting of the Executive Committee at the Level of Foreign Ministers of the Organization of the Islamic Conference stated that Operation Cast Lead had "claimed hundreds of civilian victims, including children, women and the elderly."[72] Paragraph 1 of the same Communiqué nuanced this damage upwards.[73]

January 8, 2009: In a statement in the U.N. Security Council immediately after adoption of Security Council Resolution 1860,[74] Palestinian National Authority Minister for Foreign Affairs Riyad al-Malki asserted that "more than 760 Palestinian martyrs have fallen, 40 per cent of them women and children. More than 3,000 persons have been wounded, and vast damage has been done to the basic infrastructure in the district, including United Nations installations... the brutal Israeli war machine has destroyed Gaza."[75]

January 11, 2009: "Israel's Bombardment" identified the "killing of almost 800 Palestinians, mostly civilians, and more than 3,000 injuries, accompanied by the destruction of schools, mosques, houses, UN compounds and government buildings."[76]

February 11, 2009: In his Report to the U.N. Human Rights Council, Special Rapporteur Falk concluded as follows: as regards deaths, a "total of 1,434 Palestinians were killed, of whom 235 were combatants. Some 960 civilians reportedly lost their lives, including 288 children and 121 women; 239 police officers were also killed, 235 in air strikes carried out on the first day"[77]; as regards injuries, a "total of 5,303 Palestinians were injured, including 1,606 children and 828 women (namely, 1 in every 225 Gazans was killed or injured, not counting mental injury, which must be assumed to be extensive)"[78]; and figures were also cited as regards the number of damaged homes and internally displaced persons.[79]

February 15, 2009: According to an article published in the *Jerusalem Post*, the preliminary findings of a study by the Israel Defense Force (IDF)'s Gaza Coordination and Liaison Administration (CLA) concluded that there were 1,338 Palestinian fatalities during Operation Cast Lead, and of the more than 1,200 of these whose identities had been positively identified, 880 had been classified as either combatants or noncombatants.[80] Of these 880 Palestinian fatalities, furthermore, there were approximately two combatants killed for every noncombatant killed, the "reverse of the impression created by Palestinian officials during the conflict, and a world away from the Hamas claim that just 48 of its fighters were killed."[81]

March 26, 2009: Citing Israel Defense Intelligence's Research Department, the IDF stated that 709 of the 1,166 Palestinians killed during Operation Cast Lead were terrorist operatives; 49 of the 295 uninvolved Palestinians killed were women, 89 of these uninvolved Palestinians were children under 16 years of age; and the organizational affiliation, if any, of 162 Palestinian men killed during the conflict remained unclear, at least as of then.[82]

April 2009: No Safe Place cited disparate figures from a variety of sources, as to the precise number of Israeli and Palestinian casualties, both military and civilian.[83]

April 2009: The International Institute for Counterterrorism at the Interdisciplinary Center Herzliya, Israel, issued a series of reports on casualties in Gaza during Operation Cast Lead.[84] These methodically combed through various Palestinian websites and cross-referenced casualties with organizational affiliations. Through a statistical analysis, it was concluded that "at least 63% to 75% of the Palestinians killed in Operation Cast Lead appear to have been specifically targeted, combat-aged males."[85]

July 2, 2009: According to Amnesty International's *Israel/Gaza: Operation "Cast Lead": 22 Days of Death and Destruction,* by the end of Operation Cast Lead, "some 1,400 Palestinians had been killed, including some 300 children and hundreds of other unarmed civilians, and large areas of Gaza had been razed to the ground, leaving many thousands homeless and the already dire economy in ruins."[86]

September 25, 2009: Like *No Safe Place,* the *Report of the United Nations Fact-Finding Mission on the Gaza Conflict (Gaza Report)* arrived at only a "ballpark figure," between 1,166 and 1,444 Gazan fatalities.[87]

The disparate nature of these figures reminds one of a point that U.N. Secretary-General Kofi Annan made about the ratio of civilian to combatant casualties in armed conflict situations in his March 2001 *Report to the Security Council on the Protection of Civilians in Armed Conflict:* "the truth is that no one really knows . . . The victims of today's atrocious conflicts are not merely anonymous, but literally countless."[88]

How is international law to respond in this uncertain environment? Indeed, how should it? Given the "fog of war" and the fact that accusations have been made against Israel for its actions during Operation Cast Lead that were later proven to be false, the most famous of these being that the IDF had attacked a U.N. Relief and Works Agency for Palestine Refugees in the Near East school in the Jabaliya refugee camp in Gaza,[89] prudence might suggest taking all these figures with a "grain of salt." This is particularly the case given what Dershowitz calls the "continuum of civilianality," the fact that "'civilianality' is often a matter of degree, rather than a bright line."[90]

These disparate figures also reveal two of the great complexities of asymmetrical warfare in general, namely, distinguishing between civilians and combatants and applying the proportionality balancing test alongside this and in "real time," complexities to which many of the contributors to this volume allude. Put bluntly, Hamas has used civilians to their military advantage as human shields, launched attacks from urban centers, and stored weapons in mosques and in buildings with civilian living quarters.[91] During Operation Cast Lead, the urban spaces of Gaza became its fighting spaces, with the attendant intermingling of civilians and combatants in close quarters.[92] Civilian residences were taken over and used by Palestinian forces for tactical military advantage, for attacking the IDF and as weapons depots,[93] and mosques were used for military purposes that included the storage of Kalashnikov assault rifles, improvised explosive devices, Qassam rockets, an antiaircraft gun, and ammunition.[94] Even a zoo in Gaza was found to have been used during Operation Cast Lead to store a rocket-propelled grenade and light arms.[95] It is this strategy that Dershowitz has called the "Hamas 'dead baby' strategy—to cause as many civilian casualties as possible by firing its deadly rockets from schools and densely populated areas."[96]

Clarity in this environment, if there is to be found any, surely cannot be located in the legal language of the proportionality balancing test. Rather, essentially unconstrained by the language of law, what is at issue here is an inherently moral calculus, with different actors interacting with and understanding the variables differently, the "question of whether or not the positive consequences of actions on one front morally justify the negative consequences of another."[97] The *Final Report* seemed content to collapse this heavy burden on the shoulders of the "reasonable military commander," but does the "reasonable military commander" also have a "reasonable morality," and if so, what is it?

Processing Proportionality

In a recent article dealing with the proportionality of countermeasures under international law, Franck makes the point that a vaguely phrased principle such as proportionality has "created a large space for third-party decision making and has become a staple in second-opinion discourse, whether in judicial or quasi-judicial proceedings, or in the forums of politics and public opinion."[98] He goes on to argue that the ability of these discussions to actually affect the actions or omissions of relevant actors will partly depend upon the credibility of the process through which these discussions take place.[99] Related to this is the oft-cited legal maxim that "justice not only must be done but also must be seen to be done."

Unfortunately, the most high-profile international investigation of Operation Cast Lead from the standpoint of international humanitarian law, the Fact-Finding Mission, suffered from a number of significant "process" flaws, and these flaws seriously cut against its credibility. Established by U.N. Human Rights Council Resolution S-9/1 to "investigate all violations of international human rights law and international humanitarian law by the occupying Power, Israel, against the Palestinian people throughout the Occupied Palestinian Territory, particularly in the occupied Gaza Strip, due to the current aggression,"[100] the Fact-Finding Mission's underlying terms of reference had clearly already presumed that Israel had violated its international legal obligations during Operation Cast Lead.[101] This leads one to wonder exactly what "facts" Resolution S-9/1 had been charging the Fact-Finding Mission with "finding," because any process that can even pretend to credibility surely requires ascertaining facts *before* reaching conclusions of law. When and through the agency of who or what, furthermore, had Israel's "alleged violations" of international law morphed into categorical "violations," as Resolution S-9/1 states? And what of the fact that Resolution S-11/1, which the Human Rights Council adopted in late May of 2009 in response to the major Sri Lankan offensive against the Tamil Tigers, neither established a fact-finding mission nor inquired into possible illegalities associated with Sri Lanka's counterterrorism operations, all of this despite serious concerns from human rights observers?[102]

It is true that there were some attempts to "massage away" Resolution S-9/1's unfortunate underlying terms of reference. Human Rights Council

President Ambassador Martin Ihoeghian Uhomoibhi of Nigeria, for example, who was charged with appointing the members of the Fact-Finding Mission, stated on April 3, 2009, that he had understood as the Fact-Finding Mission's mandate the independent and impartial assessment of "human rights and humanitarian law violations committed in the context of the conflict which took place between 27 December 2008 and 18 January 2009 and ... [the provision of] much needed clarity about the legality of the thousands of deaths and injuries and the widespread destruction that occurred."[103] This understanding would seem to have permitted the investigation of possible international law violations that took place by Palestinian factions, though, like Resolution S-9/1, it also couched the Fact-Finding Mission's mandate in terms of "violations" rather than "alleged violations." Ambassador Uhomoibhi's statement of June 15th reflected a different assertion, a mandate understood as an investigation of "international human rights and humanitarian law violations that *may have been* committed between 27 December 2008 and 18 January 2009 in relation to the conflict in the Gaza Strip."[104]

Contradicting both Ambassador Uhomoibhi's confused signals and Resolution S-9/1 as to the actions of which parties to the conflict in Gaza could be investigated and whether these were to be understood as prima facie "violations" or simply "alleged violations," the head of the Fact-Finding Mission, South African Justice Richard Goldstone, stated on April 3rd that the Fact-Finding Mission's mandate was the investigation of "substantial allegations of war crimes and serious violations of international human rights law having been committed before, during and after the military operations in Gaza between 27 December 2008 and 18 January 2009."[105] Adding further confusion, an official U.N. press release from May 8th completely contradicted Resolution S-9/1, stating that the Fact-Finding Mission's terms of reference were the investigation of "all violations of international human rights law and international humanitarian law that might have been committed at any time in the context of the military operations that were conducted in Gaza during the period from 27 December 2008 and 18 January 2009, whether before, during or after."[106] Clearly, these attempts to "massage away" Resolution S-9/1's unfortunate underlying terms of reference were inconsistent and convoluted, as well as perhaps *ultra vires*.[107] In any event, they ultimately ended up being beside the point, because the Human Rights Council Resolution that endorsed the *Gaza Report,* Resolution S-12/1, expressly "recalled" Resolution S-9/1.[108]

The 2009 *Guidelines on International Human Rights Fact-Finding Visits and Reports (The Lund-London Guidelines)(Guidelines)*[109] provide a useful rubric for approaching some of these questions of "process" integrity as regards the Fact-Finding Mission. Although they would counsel against underlying terms of reference such as those contained in Resolution S-9/1 because they "reflect . . . predetermined conclusions about the situation under investigation,"[110] the *Guidelines* are also useful in evaluating the question of potential bias and particularly focus on this issue. For example, they state that the "mission's delegation must comprise individuals who are and are seen to be unbiased."[111] The members of fact-finding missions, furthermore, must be aware that "they must, at all times, act in an independent, unbiased, objective, lawful and ethical manner"[112] and "understand the need to be unbiased and not prejudge any issues during the mission."[113] Of course, the question of potential bias is crucial to the credibility of fact-finding missions or, for that matter, any attempted ad hoc adjudication of law. The words of ICJ Judge Manfred H. Lachs in his separate opinion in the 1986 *Case Concerning Military and Paramilitary Activities in and Against Nicaragua* are particularly worth bearing in mind in this context: "[a] judge—as needs no emphasis—is bound to be impartial, objective, detached, disinterested and unbiased."[114]

If the terms of reference of Resolution S-9/1 reflected unfortunate "predetermined conclusions," a perception that the members of the Fact-Finding Mission were at least potentially biased was even more regrettable and problematic from a credibility standpoint. Reasonable cases can be made that each of the delegates—Goldstone, Irish Colonel Desmond Travers, Professor of International Law at the London School of Economics and Political Science Christine Chinkin, and Pakistani Supreme Court Advocate Hina Jilani—could not reasonably have been or have been seen to be unbiased.

Consider that Justice Goldstone had in the past sat on the board of directors of Human Rights Watch, a human rights nongovernmental organization that has itself "thrown its hat in the ring" on Operation Cast Lead.[115] Goldstone had also, along with Colonel Travers, Jilani, and others, signed a letter, "Find the Truth About the Gaza War," in which they had advocated an "international investigation of gross violations of the laws of war, committed by all parties to the Gaza conflict."[116] Chinkin, as a signatory to "Israel's Bombardment," had effectively argued and legally concluded, as early as January 11, 2009, that Operation Cast Lead had violated the law related to the use of force and that Israel had committed an act of aggression in Gaza.[117] The full title of that opinion piece, to repeat, is revealing: "Israel's Bombardment of Gaza Is Not Self-defence—It's a War Crime." Admittedly, some of these cases are stronger than others, but taken together they are very troubling indeed.[118]

Given these and other serious "process" flaws associated with the Fact-Finding Mission, it is difficult to lend much credibility to the *Gaza Report*. Although a critical evaluation of its substance lies outside the scope of this chapter, suffice it to say that its hostile conclusions as regards Israel were as wholly to be expected as its findings that Israel had violated the principle of proportionality under international humanitarian law were unsurprising.[119] The *Gaza Report* was rocket fuel for the Hamas propaganda machine.[120] As with the ICJ's failure to recuse Judge Nabil Elaraby from participating in the 2004 *Legal Consequences of the Construction of a Wall in the Occupied Palestinian Territory* case, despite an evident bias against Israel,[121] double standards and a priori condemnations of Israel are hardly new.

Conclusion

Asymmetrical warfare poses perhaps the greatest challenge to international humanitarian law since the establishment of the United Nations at the end of World War II and the adoption of the Geneva Conventions in 1949. Partly in response to this, new rules and standards have proliferated in recent years, but these developments should not lead one to conclude that adjudications of law in this area are necessarily more predictable, much less that they are less fraught with political bias or problems in applying abstract legal theories to particular facts and circumstances. To use Schmitt's phrase, the "fault lines" are vast and varied.[122]

The case of Operation Cast Lead reveals these very real and complex problems in the context of a specific asymmetrical conflict. Unsurprisingly, given what British Colonel Richard Kemp refers to as the "automatic, Pavlovian presumption by many in the international media, and international human rights groups, that the IDF are in the wrong, that they are abusing human rights,"[123] the international reaction to Operation Cast Lead was largely negative. But it is easier to criticize, to simply "speak truth to power," than it is to suggest what one would have done differently.

Those who would seek to legally condemn the IDF for particular attacks that it undertook during Operation Cast Lead should be asked before casting stones, "How would a 'reasonable military commander' have acted 'more proportionately' during Operation Cast Lead, in a way that would not have been excessive and that would have been both available and effective on the battlefield?"[124]

NINE

Humanizing Irregular Warfare

FRAMING COMPLIANCE FOR NONSTATE
ARMED GROUPS AT THE INTERSECTION
OF SECURITY AND LEGAL ANALYSES

CORRI ZOLI

Violations may be frequent—even rampant—but the burden remains on those who challenge the wisdom and sufficiency of existing norms to prove their obsolescence... [I]t is the shift from opprobrium to acceptance that places prohibitions at risk.[1]

This chapter combines legal and security analyses to bring the traditional law of war balance between humanitarian and security values back into new paradigms of warfare. The chapter begins by showing how new challenges of regulating nonstate armed groups in armed conflict has eroded the original balance at the core of humanitarian law between states' national security interests and humanitarian priorities to reduce unnecessary suffering for all victims of conflict.[2] The chapter then explores how nonstate armed groups, by adopting an asymmetric strategy calculus that treats compliance with the law as a tactical vulnerability, have succeeded in leveraging compliance in their favor and, in turn, co-opted conventional incentives for increasing compliance, such as relaxed combatant status criteria in Additional Protocol I. Such resulting unintended consequences from attempts to change the law are constitutive: They not only create loopholes or disincentives for nonstate compliance, but enable the legal recognition of modern nonstate actors and their signature noncompliant practices on contemporary battlefields. I then return to the controversial history of the Martens Clause to provide perspective on the problem of the nonstate actor, showing that although this actor has never been entirely absent from the state-centric *jus in bello*, its marginal appearance in the law was a product of states' early authority in regulating conflict—an authority now eroding as other international actors enter conflict regulation.

The result is a "practicality gap," a vacuum of *ex ante* formal spaces for habituating actors into the laws of war and its rules of engagement and the rise of *ex post facto* solutions, namely, the prevalence of prosecutorial measures and criminal law in humanitarian law. The chapter ends by recommending a policy approach for enlisting disparate and often recalcitrant armed groups into engagement with the law that targets their asymmetric calculus and maximizes the sources of resilience internal to humanitarian law.

State Sovereignty and Humanitarian Norms: Balance or Tension?

One of the most beguiling aspects of international humanitarian law, informing each of its core principles—distinction, military necessity, proportionality, and prohibition of undue suffering—is the requirement to balance states' national security needs with humanitarian obligations by regulating the conduct of hostilities and treatment of those in the power of the enemy. "Humanitarian law is a compromise," human rights lawyer Gabor Rona explains. In return for minimizing unnecessary suffering by regulating the battlefield, "humanitarian law elevates the essence of war—killing and detaining people without trial—into a right," if only for those designated as "privileged combatants," such as soldiers in an army.[3] Those "who take part in hostilities without such a privilege are criminals subject to prosecution and punishment, but they do not thereby forfeit the rights" they may accrue under humanitarian, human rights, or criminal law.[4] Though cited frequently enough, this pivotal balance between the duty to preserve state security and that of protecting especially vulnerable populations in war is not clearly understood, despite the fact that it has enormous ramifications.

The compromise between states' perception of their rights and obligations and universal humanitarian values, values that aim to protect all human beings equally (not as citizens of states), goes a long way in explaining enigmatic, even counterintuitive, elements of the *jus in bello*. Why, for instance, do we distinguish between international (state-vs.-state) and noninternational (internal) armed conflicts in Common Articles 2 and 3 of the four Geneva Conventions of 1949? Why do Common Article 3 protections for detainees appear less robust than those of Common Article 2?[5] Although it is easy to imbue these rules with loftier, more cogent aims, the simple explanation is that states were unwilling to concede to more meddling in their own internal affairs than they were in their involvement in international conflicts. "The reason there are two separate strands of humanitarian law is sovereignty," as Rona notes, as "[s]tates are more willing to accept greater international controls on their [foreign] affairs than on their internal ones."[6] This realization demystifies the law. Like other foundational texts, it is partly a product of pragmatic melding of conflicting interests made under historically specific pressures.

The compromise also reveals an upside to sovereignty in the practical bias of states' contributions to humanitarian law.[7] It is well known that the *jus in bello* are state-centric. First, as Geoffrey Corn and Eric Jensen explain, the "criterion for determining when the law of war applies to any given military operation is based on an assumption that armed conflicts will occur either between the armed forces of states or between state armed forces and internal dissident groups."[8] Established law-triggering mechanisms, derived from Common Articles 2 and 3 of the four Geneva Conventions of 1949, thus hinge the scope of the law on state parties to the conflict. These mechanisms ensure that humanitarian law only applies in armed conflicts that by definition involve states. Second, humanitarian law applies to only two conflict types, both defined by reference to states: international (two or more state parties clashing, including occupation) and noninternational armed confrontations in the territory of a state (with no other state forces involved).[9] But a practical rationale lies at the heart of what otherwise may appear to be a simple state-centric bias in the *jus in bello*: "[t]here can be no humanitarian law conflict without identifiable parties," whereby the very concept of a party "suggests a minimum level of organization required to enable the entity to carry out the obligations of law."[10]

It is not only that conflicts at their most elemental need sides or parties, both for their existence and regulation, but that there can "be no assessment of rights and responsibilities under humanitarian law in a war without identifiable parties."[11] The requirement of parties does not rule out organized nonstate actors per se. Yet it does explain why their role is fraught in this legal regime. This practical recognition also goes a long way in explaining why, for instance, disparate nonstate armed groups (most obviously, transnational terrorist organizations) will always frustrate the paradigm's need for identifiable and functional parties to a conflict to deliver the law, and why the war on terror will always be the proverbial square peg in the round hole of the laws of war. This practical bias also reveals why nonstate actors have the ability to throw off the core balance between state security and humanitarian aims, once taken for granted in humanitarian law.

The following sections explain in more detail why these different interests of security and humanity comprising the law might now be better described as in tension when it comes to regulating nonstate parties in new conflicts. It is also important to note that this compromise was rarely constant over time, especially in functional systems where players acted in concert or provided checks and balances to each other's different aims. The trick is to distinguish between helpful and hurtful changes, between variations that update the law for new contexts, and concerning trends that may amount to derogating the law's effectiveness or protections. The overarching claim here is that undermining the balance between state security interests and humanitarian aims, especially in regulating nonstate actors in armed conflicts, undermines the law itself. Moreover, the stakes involved in this issue go beyond whether nonstate actors can be belligerents under the law, who has a right to participate in hostilities, or the legal status of new tactics. At issue is the very legitimacy of the laws and customs of war themselves. In many respects, Barnidge's analysis of the Goldstone Report provides a cautionary tale about this crisis of confidence in the laws of war and a concerning trend that might characterize our future: the intrusion of politics more forcefully into the process of regulating warfare with negative results for all sides, including once compliant states.[12]

Lawfare: Symptom of Changing Equilibrium Between Security and Humanitarian Goals

Although asymmetry is as old as warfare itself, it constitutes a troubling new aspect of it.[13] As Charles Dunlap explains in an early essay, the "use of law as a weapon of war" is "the newest feature of 21st century combat" and includes, among its several dimensions, "hijack[ing]" the rule of law for "another way of fighting" to the "detriment of humanitarian values as well as to the law itself."[14] Contrary to "seeking battlefield victories, *per se*," Dunlap writes, this "method of warfare" uses the law "as a means of realizing a military objective."[15] Practitioners of lawfare try to destroy an opponent's "*will* to fight" by "undermining the public support that is indispensable when democracies like the U.S. conduct military interventions."[16] This approach includes making it appear that the United States is waging war in violation of the letter or spirit of the laws of armed conflict.[17] In doing this, in deliberately preying upon legal standards integrated into international norms, adversaries focus on turning public opinion against law-abiding nations by creating the impression, true or not, that the opponent acts lawlessly. In fact, the potential inaccuracy of the image is part of the utility of the practice.

Lawfare itself stems from the now prevalent role of the law and lawyers in planning and executing military operations, from NATO's Kosovo campaign forward.[18] It arises when "international law has become so important in military interventions" and when "hyperlegalism" characterizes all military campaigns—to the point, according to some critics, that "lawyers" have become de facto "tactical commanders."[19] Some critics have asked whether international law itself is "undercutting the ability of the U.S. to conduct effective military interventions," or if it has become a "vehicle to exploit American values in ways that actually increase risks to civilians?"[20]

If lawfare is a reminder of Clausewitz's dictum that war is politics by other means, it is also an indication that asymmetric tactics are part of a larger coherent strategy that counts the law as one of its nonconventional targets. In countries defined by a strong rule-of-law political culture "as a cornerstone of their legitimacy" this technique is "as effective as a weapon in undermining [the] public support" necessary to conduct and win wars.[21] But weaker parties also leverage underexamined political advantages from lawfare by developing signature military tactics predicated upon its impacts: systematically targeting civilians as well as fostering civilian casualties as "valuable" for turning regional or international opinion against rivals.

In a later essay, Dunlap defended a neutral assessment of the ability to use lawfare, "like any other weapon, for good or bad purposes," including that of "reducing the destructiveness of war."[22] He detailed positive instances of lawfare by the United States, such as the U.S.-built Rule of Law Complex in the Baghdad Green Zone to help "Iraqis to solve Iraqi problems in relative safety for themselves and their families" with support from the Law and Order Task Force and judge advocate attorneys.[23] U.S. Senator and reserve officer Colonel Lindsey Graham (after a tour with the Law and Order Task Force) explained the U.S. government's rationale in lawfare terms: building a fair legal system for holding all segments of the population accountable is "[o]ne way to kill the insurgency beyond [using] military force."[24] However, Dunlap's neutral and depoliticized approach to lawfare, including his recommendation that law-abiding states engage in "positive lawfare" to garner respect for the law, reveals very different rationales used by irregular forces targeting prohibited persons or sites to gain advantages against militarily superior adversaries.[25]

It is true in both cases that the deliberate use or misuse of the law "as a substitute for traditional military means to achieve an operational objective" is an example of asymmetric warfare, the ability to exploit an opponent's weaknesses.[26] Yet, though lawfare is used by both powerful states and irregular nonstate entities, there is a clear difference of intention. Militarily weaker opponents adopt asymmetric means to target a state's compliance with the law, a practice that assumes that they themselves are not compliant (otherwise there is no asymmetry) and that abiding by humanitarian law is a military weakness. Militarily stronger states need not target the rule of law, of course, if they are themselves compliant. But violations by traditionally compliant states are increasingly the product of overreactions in which irregular forces have successfully baited a stronger party into violating the law or, equally impactful, appearing as if they have. This distinction is worth preserving in refining lawfare: Lawfare covers strategic intentions and capabilities, not simply tactical ones, and it defines that capacity of an adversary to link military advantage not to proportionality, as in the case of humanitarian law-abiding states, but to lawfare's political value, especially to an international audience.

Interpreting recent examples of this dynamic, such as the Israel–Lebanese War of 2006 and Israel's 2008–2009 Gaza Strip incursion (and the international community's response in the Goldstone Report), I differ with Barnidge's view that indeterminate elements of the law, particularly the principle of proportionality for assessing military necessity, enable asymmetric tactics.[27] I suggest instead that the success of lawfare lies in prompting states' overreactions and creating the appearance of violations of humanitarian law principles, particularly to the international community. Barnidge is certainly right to note that in humanitarian law theory and practice proportionality standards are notoriously vague and some of the most difficult to apply, and that contemporary modes of warfare tax the inherent difficulty of the proportionality balancing test in situations where irregular forces remain neither bound by nor interested in the same rules.[28] But lawfare serves to distort the legal assessment of actual battlefield contests such that routine tests of the proportional and, thus, the legal use of force become politicized. When Hamas, Hezbollah, and other armed groups use civilians and civilian sites to their military advantage, either as direct participants, as human shields, or as a means of launching attacks from population centers, this routine asymmetric tactic comprises an essential strategic use of lawfare. Comingling fighters and weaponry with civilians in their living spaces is designed to protect forces (the asymmetric element) and heighten civilian casualties (the lawfare element), a direct reversal of humanitarian law norms, and, by extension, a savvy indication of irregular forces' ability to hinge military advantage on its political implications (rather than proportionality).[29] Prompting stronger adversaries to violate—or appear to violate—principles of distinction and proportionality is part of this irregular political calculus. By far its most troubling implication is for humanitarian law itself, because when an overreaction does occur, the militarily weaker party succeeds in prompting the stronger party to play by their adversary's rule book, which amounts to abandoning the law. In this context, the law itself becomes the target as lawfare-style strategic victory helps to set international terms for its re-evaluation and debate.

By understanding lawfare as a tool of asymmetric *strategy* it is possible to see how the changed security climate offers opportunities for adversaries to reframe the meaning of the law and, further, how gaps in humanitarian law emerge as much from battlefield contexts as from internal tensions in the law itself. In the service of this distinction the next section looks at modifications to the law that have provided opportunities for such strategic manipulation.

Unintended Consequences of Modified Combatant Status Criteria in Additional Protocol I: Enabling a New Actor

This section considers how the law may play a constitutive role in shaping new battlefields and how its loopholes unwittingly provide legal status for nonstate actors who are now a prevalent part of contemporary global conflict patterns.

Legal scholars have often criticized changes in traditional combatant status criteria in the relaxed provisions of Additional Protocol I.[30] W. M. Reisman has argued, for instance, that the relaxation of combatant status criteria threatens to undermine the principle of distinction, arguably the most fundamental principle of international humanitarian law.[31] Some uses of force, he explains, may be "rendered lawful by the contextual factors of military necessity, proportionality, and distinction—though this use of force requires often complicated legal assessments" in ways that Daphné Richemond-Barak and Robert Barnidge describe in this volume.[32]

Traditionally, however, the principle of distinction—the standard that differentiates combatant from civilian in myriad ways—is not open to such contingent use or manipulation.[33] Resiman goes on to draw out the implications for traditional prohibitions of perfidy in Article 3(1) of Additional Protocol I resulting from changes to the once "venerable requirement imposed on combatants that, to be lawful, they must wear uniforms and bear arms openly" (Article 4 of the Third Geneva Convention).[34] The API combatant status criteria no longer require a uniform when "owing to the nature of hostilities an armed combatant cannot so distinguish himself."[35] Moreover, Article 44(4) API also provides that a combatant who fails to meet the "requirements set forth" in paragraph 3 "shall forfeit his right to be a prisoner of war," but "shall, nevertheless, be given protections equivalent in all respects to those accorded to prisoners of war by the Third Convention and by this Protocol," which include "protections equivalent to those accorded to prisoners of war by the Third Convention in the case where such a person is tried and punished for any offences he has committed."[36]

Relaxing the combatant requirement confuses the sanctions that have historically "functioned as an enforcement mechanism" and degrades "indispensable and easily implemented and policed means for protecting noncombatants,"[37] which reiterate humanitarian law's core protection of noncombatants by insisting on their difference from combatants. Without distinctive insignia, Reisman argues, "belligerents cannot distinguish adversaries from civilians, with predictable results," and in not having to distinguish themselves, belligerents glean certain advantages that "feigning to be a civilian" offers which are unavailable to traditional uniformed personnel. Moreover, Article 44 of API undermines the traditional mechanism for enforcing the principle of distinction that had historically been the "denial of the protections of the law of war to those violating it," as well as the customary punishment for unprivileged belligerency, which had once been, unapologetically, death.[38]

Most troubling, this change from absolutely prohibited use of perfidious force to its permitted use under certain conditions suggests a "disturbing correlation between the increasing failure to comply with this . . . prohibition, the installation in its stead of new rules allowing its converse, and the appalling increase in death and injury to noncombatants relative to those of combatants."[39] It is self-evident, Jensen concurs, that noncombatants are "most at risk when combatants hide among them, wearing civilian clothes and using civilians as human shields," and further, that this very approach embodied in API is counterproductive because, rather than "giv[ing] battlefield fighters an incentive to strive for complete compliance," it "lowers the requirement for combatant status to bring more people into the ambit of the Convention's coverage" and thus does not support "promoting the protection of the civilian population from the effects of hostilities."[40] Such a change "solves the problem of combatant status by relaxing standards, which thereby gives insurgents a *disincentive* to distinguish themselves."[41]

Yet another implication is evident in the shift from traditional Geneva to API combatant status criteria: the problematic correlation between modifying the law in relaxed combatant status criteria and the rise of nonstate actors in conflict situations. Conflict research over the last decade has shown that civilian causalities have far outpaced combatant causalities and that the vast majority of wars today are internal, civil conflicts fought by nonstate actors.[42] This coincidence between changes in the law and new battlefield phenomena suggests an uncomfortable conclusion: Nonstate actors are no simple lacunae in the laws of armed conflict but are, instead, one unintended consequence of legislated changes to gain greater compliance with the law. Instead of proving helpful, then, changes designed to expand coverage for nontraditional actors have produced at the very least ambivalent results, a marked increase in deliberately noncompliant groups in conflict situations and the brazen sense among them that the law itself is a strategic target. Moreover, the correlation between modifications in the law and the newly prominent feature of the contemporary battlefield—nonstate actors hiding among, recruiting from, and/or targeting civilian populations—raises serious concerns about how the law becomes a site of political contention, whether those changes (and the process of debate to arrive at them) are informed by well-intentioned arguments that generate unexpected results or by the success of new asymmetric strategies, such as lawfare, that intentionally create doubt about fundamental distinctions in the law in new security settings.

That the law may play a constitutive role in shaping new battlefields deserves further study. It also offers potential fruitful lessons about the law itself, how it not only reflects (well or badly) a changing security climate, but has a role in constituting it. But insofar as changes occur as a result of partisan interventions, an even greater lesson is at stake. Reisman criticizes the advocacy efforts of the International Committee of the Red Cross (ICRC) as sponsor of Additional Protocol I in their desire to "favor the so-called national liberation combatants" and "help them win" at all costs—despite the unethical and illogical arguments used for relaxing combatant status criteria.[43] Even "if irregulars did henceforth comply" with API standards, he explains, the fact that they now could "lawfully fight without uniforms and without bearing arms openly" means that their adversaries would be placed at a new level of disadvantage but that they would also "be unable to distinguish [fighters] as foes and as a result could not help but kill or injure more noncombatants."[44] Moreover, if such reduced criteria did actually prompt more compliance with the law such a "gain would be purchased with the lives of noncombatants," an unethical proposition incompatible with humanitarian precepts, notably distinction. Beyond these important bases for concern (ethics, logic), it is important to identify the partisan role in changing the law and its potential to shift the core balance of humanitarian law from that of compromise between state and humanitarian interests to a conflict between them, in this case, between state-based definitions of the combatant and broader international humanitarian ideals.[45]

Given the role of the law in influencing the place of nonstate actors in armed conflict, the following section considers the Martens Clause as one area in the law that explicitly admits of the conundrum of irregular fighters in the state-centric *jus in bello*. In the Martens Clause one can see both the past and the future: states' early authority in regulating conflict and an early invocation of alternative norms beyond strong security needs, which now define the present.

The Martens Clause, *Francs-Tireurs*, and Legal Vehicles for Changing Norms

Legal scholarship has from an early time highlighted the complex position of irregular forces, even pointing out, as Lester Nurick and Roger W. Barrett noted in 1946, that the "problems of the status of guerillas under the laws of war" constitute a perennial and unsolved issue that has "arisen during almost every war in modern history."[46] One area in humanitarian law developed to address this dilemma is the Martens Clause of the 1899 Hague Convention II.

At the early Peace Conference in the Netherlands, Russian delegate Fyodor Fyodorovich Martens made a lasting intervention into the resonant problem of this fighter at a time when the debate over his legal status promised to devolve into an impasse along predicable power lines. Leading military powers (Russia, Germany) sought to treat so-called *francs-tireurs* (literally, free shooters) as unprivileged belligerents subject to execution upon capture, whereas less powerful states (e.g., Belgium) viewed them as lawful combatants rightfully resisting or throwing off colonial oppression.

Martens introduced a compromise into the drafting debate that was subsequently included in the 1899 Hague Convention Preamble, the first formal international statement of the laws of war:

> Until a more complete code of the laws of war is issued, the High Contracting Parties think it right to declare that in cases not included in the Regulations adopted by them, populations and belligerents remain under the protection and empire of the principles of international law, as they result from the usages established between civilized nations, from the laws of humanity and the requirements of the public conscience.[47]

In the aftermath, the Martens Clause reappeared in a range of places, in many treaties and international agreements, and was seen "as a significant turning point in the history of international humanitarian law."[48] But it also achieved the status of "legal myth," according to Antonio Cassese, in large part because its "evasive yet appealing contents" enabled "a multiplicity of often conflicting interpretations," thus making room for certain grand designs attributed to it.[49]

The most important and expansive of these attributions was that the Martens Clause "upgrades to the rank of sources of international law" two of its featured rationales: "the laws of humanity" and the "dictates of public conscience."[50] Supporters argue that it was the "first time in which the notion that there exists international legal rules embodying humanitarian considerations" that are "no less binding" than "those motivated by other (e.g., military or political) concerns were set forth."[51] In this view, the clause is assigned a norm-creating character, either directly as a "norm establishing two new sources of law" or indirectly as a "norm which raises to the rank of principles of international law standards of conduct perceived by states as required by, or at least consistent with, the laws of humanity or the dictates of public conscience."[52] In either case, the state's traditional authority over defining and regulating warfare receives serious competition on this view of the Martens Clause.[53]

Against this position, Cassese posits Martens's contribution as a diplomatic gimmick deployed by a savvy jurist eager to break deadlocked negotiations between small and powerful states at a peace conference that could easily have gone the way of the previous one, the 1874 Brussels Peace Conference, which failed to produce a set of international rules.[54] Martens's interjected compromise was seen to limit the extensive powers accorded to occupying forces and to identify, if not resolve, the lack of provisions made for citizens in occupied territories to forcibly resist occupation, as part of the fundamental right of self-defense. In fact, the British delegate's proposal that lost out to Martens had argued for conferring lawful combatant status on some fighters in occupied territories—a provision that did not find its way into humanitarian law until 1949.

That the marginal *francs-tireurs* mattered at all in the birth of the Hague Conventions, particularly to strong states that might otherwise simply dominate the process of inventing this early legal architecture, reveals the strong imprint of nineteenth-century war, particularly European counterinsurgency doctrine, on the developing international laws of war—at least on one side of the debate. Ian F. W. Beckett and John Pimlott explain that European experience was decidedly slim on the subject of irregular warfare—despite the fact that Clausewitz and other lions of conventional warfare produced equally impressive thinking on partisans attached to conventional wars (if not guerilla warfare per se).[55] There were two exceptions to this gap in experience and both involved the *francs-tireurs*. The first example made such an impression on European consciousness that it found its way into the *Oxford English Dictionary*'s very definition of *francs-tireurs*: "[o]ne of a corps of light infantry, originating in the wars of the French Revolution, and having an organization distinct from that of the regular army."[56] The term's popularity in 1870 coincided with the Franco-Prussian War, in which French armed civilians harried German technologically superior forces, most memorably at the fateful Siege of Paris. Resolute in their efforts to stave off France's defeat (at which they failed), these savvy French fighters disrupted German supply lines to such a degree that German commanders two generations later authorized severe retaliatory measures against them and French guerilla hotspots in World War I.[57]

In fact, British social critic G. K. Chesterton later offered a scathing critique of such retaliation (in his review of German strategist General Erich Ludendorff's memoir) by defending the *franc-tireur*: "A *franc-tireur* is emphatically not a person whose warfare is bound to disgust any soldier," nor a "type about which a general soldierly spirit feels any bitterness," and certainly "not a perfidious or barbarous or fantastically fiendish foe."[58] Instead, a *"franc-tireur* is a free man, who fights to defend his own farm or family against foreign aggressors, but who does not happen to possess certain badges and articles of clothing catalogued by Prussia in 1870," which means, he is "you or I or any other healthy man who found himself, when attacked, in accidental possession of a gun or pistol, and not in accidental possession of a particular cap or a particular pair of trousers."[59] Chesterton even compares this irregular fighter to an "honourable prisoner of war," adding that demeaning this fighter "is not a moral distinction at all, but a crude and recent official distinction made by the militarism of Potsdam."[60] This position represents the other side in the earlier Hague debate that produced the Martens Clause.

The second instance in which Europeans encountered *franc-tireurs* involved a non-European fighter and occurred outside Europe in their expanding colonial empires, the conflicts from which Europe's most "coherent counter-guerilla doctrine originated."[61] In fact, the core problem for European irregular warfare doctrine in the colonial setting—the difficulty of defining nonstate actors under the law, given their diversity—is also evident in the debate over and need for the Martens Clause. As Beckett and Pimlott explain, the "kind of enemies encountered and usually (but not invariably) defeated" by Europeans abroad were "widely diverse in characteristics and (tactical) methods."[62] They continue:

> It is perhaps an illustration of the diversity of circumstances encountered that the British Army had no standard manual until the publication of C. E. Callwell's celebrated Small Wars in 1896 . . . [which] represents [not] much more than a synthesis of individual commanders' approaches to specific campaigns of the past. . . . Similarly, the campaigns [by] the United States Army against Indians, or latterly, Filipino guerillas, were too diverse to suggest the need for a coherent doctrine of counter-insurgency. . . . In reality a fairly similar response developed to the different military threats posed by Indians, Mexicans or Filipinos, while the US Army's operations against irregulars continued to be governed throughout the latter nineteenth century by General Order 100 of April 1863, which sought to lay down a basic code on the treatment of irregulars in warfare.[63]

Given such diversity, Beckett and Pimlott conclude that "there was always tension between the conflicting demands for humanity and severity with regard to a hostile subject population in the American experience" though such a battle of conscience rarely touched European armies.[64] "It cannot be said that any of the European armies of the late nineteenth century had any real concern for what a later generation would call 'winning hearts and minds,'" and the "Imperial German Army in particular had a notoriously casual regard for the niceties of the admittedly ill-defined laws of war, insisting on 'military necessity' and the 'rights' of invaders."[65] Both experiences with the *francs-tireurs* reveal an established European approach to these fighters, which was the source and impetus for their arguments in the 1899 Hague debate: They "were shot out of hand during the Franco-Prussian War while the unfortunate Herreror and Hottentots of German South West Africa were ruthlessly slaughtered when they rose in revolt (1905–7)."[66]

Such sentiments were replayed in the debate between, on the one side, Russian and German delegates, and delegates from Britain, Belgium, Switzerland, and elsewhere, on the other. They are also evident in the final compromise that won the day and represents the high-water mark in hegemonic state security interests. The Belgian delegate, rightfully realizing that he had a steep challenge in establishing the *francs-tireurs* status as lawful combatants in resisting occupation, argued that their status be simply left unregulated. Rebutting him and the British proposal, Martens argued against "leaving matters unregulated by treaty" and up to the vague "body of principles and the law of nations," because to do so would leave large powers uncertain about their rights and small states unsure about which obligations bound powerful states.[67] Martens also claimed that the Hague Conference did not in any way wish to remain "blind to the heroism of the inhabitants of countries occupied by the enemy," but it was also not fit to "codify all the cases that might arise."[68] His Russian compatriot more bluntly deferred to operational matters in making his case, saying that it would be "impossible to grant to the population of an occupied territory the right to attack lines of communication, for without such lines the foreign occupying army could not survive."[69] The German delegate reiterated these "interests of large armies," noting that they "imperatively required security for their lines of communication and their areas of occupation," which were irreconcilable with the "concerns of occupation populations."[70] If representatives of states' militaries weighed in heavily, it was, after all, a tactical era in the history of warfare: even irregular guerrilla warfare, note Beckett and Pimlott, "prior to the Second World War represented primarily a tactical method" in contrast to modern insurgency, which "implied a politico-military campaign waged by guerillas with the object of overthrowing the government of a state."[71]

Nonstate actors are not outside the laws of war—they belong, at a minimum, to this resonant treatment of *francs-tireurs* in the Martens Clause. But if they exist within the law's norms, the history of the Martens Clause also indicates that their privileges are circumscribed in significant part so that states (and their militaries) may maintain their authority in determining regulation regimes with respect to armed conflicts. It is this authority that is now eroding. Equally important, as Rupert Ticehurst reminds us, although there is no accepted interpretation of the Martens Clause and it is subject to a "variety of interpretations, both narrow and expansive," at its broadest interpretation the Martens Clause allows that "conduct in armed conflicts is not only judged according to treaties and custom but also to the principles of international law referred to by the Clause."[72] As Judge Shahabuddeen in the International Court of Justice (ICJ) Advisory Opinion on Nuclear Weapons explained, it reflects evolving concepts, providing "authority for treating the principles of humanity and the dictates of public conscience as principles of international law," even while "leaving the precise content of the standard implied by these principles of international law to be ascertained in the light of changing conditions."[73] The Martens compromise did not found new norms in any legal sense, but it did provide a space to anchor a shift in balance in the law, itself made possible by the increasing influence of international norms among the international community. As such, the Martens Clause is bound up with especially modern contemplations of new bases for legal authority beyond positivist conceptions of the law as state power and humanitarian aims.

The following section probes this shift in balance from states' influence over the law and increasingly important international humanitarian rationales as a product of blurred boundaries between international legal and policy norms, the latter of which bring new kinds of nonstate actors and the role of international consensus to bear on the process of humanizing irregular warfare.

International Norm Creation and Critical Compliance Tools

One principal instrument through which any constitutive relationship between international law and the security climate occurs is norm creation—a process that scholars concede is not well understood. Part of the difficulty arises from different uses and meanings of the term "norm" in law and international relations. If norms in general are prescriptive statements that set parameters for human conduct, in legal application norms are statutes—rules for behavior with a coercive component derived from the power, integrity, and legitimacy of the legal system itself as well as its effective structure of authority.[74] Though traditions in legal positivism, natural law, and normative jurisprudence have addressed how norms develop and identified processes of change in a given legal regime, scholars have less often probed the differences between law and policy norms, despite the fact that "norm discourse" now informs key schools of thought at the intersection of international law and international relations theory. As Martha Finnemore writes, "during the past two decades research agendas in international relations and international law have converged around the issues of norm creation and norm compliance."[75]

Norms in contemporary international relations theory signify a broad, even amorphous area of institutional and organizational conduct that brings another category of nonstate actor to bear on international affairs: international and nongovernmental organizations (IOs and NGOs). Audie Klotz defines norms in this context as "shared (thus social) understandings of standards for behavior"[76] and suggests that the increased authority of such actors as the United Nations, the World Bank, or Human Rights First depends in large part on their ability to create political influence through international norms—though, again, how this occurs is subject to debate and diverse opinions.[77] Nonetheless, social scientists have emphasized the importance of norm creation processes as part of a dissatisfaction with "approaches that focus entirely on formal state action" or ignore "the amount of cooperation that seems to arise by other means (than coercion) and from other sources (than states)."[78] This emphasis, what Keohane calls the "normative optic,"[79] also informs changing priorities in security studies, though a difference between constructivist and security approaches to norms, for instance, is visible in Steven Ratner's research which examines how nonstate actors "promote peaceful change, not by coercion or enforcement of state-sponsored rules" but by focusing on "creating new rules or understandings and persuading actors to comply with them."[80]

Though norms are at once seen as embedded in legal and other bureaucratic regimes and as playing an increasing and influential role in foreign, defense, and security policy, this relationship between international norms and the law is neither clear nor consistent. Reisman, for instance, puts forth the strange status of foreign policy doctrine (whether Bush-era preemptive self-defense or earlier doctrines from the Breshnev, Carter, or Reagan eras) as an obvious exception to universal modern international law.[81] A doctrine is a "formal and credible statement by a significant international actor of a firm policy and the resolve to implement it upon certain contingencies," Reisman explains.[82] But doctrines are "positioned at the interface of law and power," not based on "a general right that is theoretically available to other states" consistent with the rule of law, and, for this reason, they constitute "a demand for an exception."[83] In the case of American preemptive self-defense as a single state doctrine reserved for the "global superpower for its episodic forays as international policeman," its danger of rampant use by other states may be limited—though its abuse by an "uncontrolled superpower is not."[84]

Another example of the blurred boundary between legal and policy norms and, perhaps because of that erosion, the increasing role of international norms in exercising a constraining influence on traditional power politics, is evident in the controversy over the Bybee Memo, written to provide the Central Intelligence Agency (CIA) with a legal opinion on permissible interrogation tactics for al-Qaeda detainees in and outside the United States.[85] At issue in the Memo was the meaning of the statutory term "torture," as defined in 18 U.S.C. §2340, a section of federal law that obligates the United States under the international Convention Against Torture and Other Cruel, Inhuman, and Degrading Treatment or Punishment.[86] The purpose of the Memo confronts us squarely with the institutional tensions undergirding legal and policy norms in the United States, as well as an inside view of the organizational process involved in such shifts between legal and policy bureaucracies.[87] In this case, Department of Justice attorneys approached issues involving the laws of war as a private attorney might, an opportunity to protect their client from the potential negative effects of existing laws, whereas Judge Advocate General's (JAG) attorneys (less visibly involved in this case) played an unheralded role—defending the Constitution and the international laws of war as an alibi for protecting soldiers' humanity. The Bybee Memo, thus, offers a road map of a policy norm in the midst of transformative change and how that change operates in tension with established legal norms, namely, instigating separation of powers confusion in which the "political branches may switch the Constitution on or off at will," a presupposition if it were to hold that "would lead to a regime in which they, not this Court, say what the law is."[88] That the Office of Legal Counsel felt such license reiterates the potential breadth of policy norms, that they may circumscribe, eclipse, even supersede legal norms—at the domestic and international level.

If policy is what governments do (not necessarily what they say that they do), invariably public policy in modern democracies is informed by regulatory measures and established laws, including international laws, as well as legal bureaucracies. In this sense, policy norms are anchored by legal standards.[89] But what is clear from the Bybee Memo and its repeal is that legal opinion was utilized for policy norm creation in such a politicized manner that policymakers were forced to reevaluate and reverse its conclusions because it was so out of step with prevailing laws, as well as international norms. On the one hand, the give and take between legal and policy norms reveals legal authority operating in a more circumscribed arena than policymaking. It also shows the dangers of policy norms untethered to courts and to the rule of law and how easily legal opinion may be conscripted for executive authority. But more surprisingly, the Bybee Memo controversy highlights, on the other hand, the influential role that international organizations and contestation over (even domestic) policy norms are now playing as mechanisms for critical debate and spurring change. In the timeless debate between realists and idealists over that which exercises more influence on international affairs and state behavior, in this case, international norms scored a significant point over the power politics of states in U.S. asymmetric warfare detention policies.[90]

This analysis is also to suggest that humanitarian law compliance initiatives today may also benefit from similar paths and approaches—provided, as suggested, one distinguishes asymmetric warfare from asymmetric strategy. This is precisely what has been missing. Consider one baseline point of reference for promoting compliance with humanitarian law in the work of the ICRC, well known in its permanent mandate status for field operations to aid victims of armed conflict worldwide, but less often recognized as the guardian of international humanitarian law and as statutorily responsible for disseminating "knowledge of its applicability in armed conflicts."[91] In

Increasing Respect for International Humanitarian Law in Non-international Armed Conflicts (2008), the ICRC addresses familiar challenges in the effort to get noncompliant states and nonstate belligerents to abide by the laws of war: ignorance about the law, denial of its application to a given conflict, lack of training in the law, security threats that prevent access to parties, the diversity of conflicts and parties, and lack of political will in implementing the law.[92] The ICRC recommends as solutions to these problems training programs for armed groups; pushing for special agreements between parties to make an "explicit commitment to comply with humanitarian law" (provided for in Common Article 3); fostering "strategic" engagement with parties adapted to the concrete, operational contexts of a given conflict; and explaining why compliance may be in their best interests. But the authors also warn that although experience has shown that "where the requisite conditions exist, certain legal tools and policy arguments may help" in getting conflicting parties to better comply with the rules, "[o]ne should have no illusions that there are any legal tools or policy arguments that can avail in those instances when the law is being systematically flouted, if the political will to abide by it is lacking."[93]

Given the specific purpose of asymmetric uses of lawfare to target the legitimacy of humanitarian law, it is an understatement to say that political will for compliance is simply lacking. In such cases, departures from the law are not a lapse or oversight, but reflect a core contestation with the laws governing warfare by a strategy that deliberately leverages weaknesses in the legal architecture. This tack is no more obvious than in the now voluminous extremist literatures theorizing suiciders in situations of occupation, defensive or armed forms of jihad, the complicity and targetability of all noncombatants in certain conflict settings, and appeals to specific jurists or schools of jurisprudence to develop alternate doctrines of warfare, including a recent circulated Taliban rule of war book.

In this very different asymmetric context, effective international instruments to promote compliance with international norms are those that impact, curtail, or constrain the rudimentary functioning of such armed groups as organizations, including the group's ability to sustain and reproduce itself. Such approaches along these very different lines include international terrorist financing laws, for instance, which use other laws and multiple levels (state, international coordination, IOs, private financial institutions) to undermine the infrastructure of support for noncompliant groups' capabilities.

This approach would also include pressure points from another angle, professional associations, for instance, such as the Arab Center for the Development of the Rule of Law and Integrity (ACRLI), which creates a network of competent legal professionals to develop and reinforce the rule of law, integrity, and good governance in Arab countries.[94] Voluntary regulatory guidelines in ancillary areas, such as the Department of Justice Voluntary Guidelines for Muslim Charities, for instance, which were applied widely beyond their intended target audience, are particularly interesting case studies in defining the parameters for success in approaching problems of humanitarian law compliance in asymmetric settings. Such nonconventional approaches to legal compliance have more potential because they are not reliant on persuading armed groups to adopt norms or rules that are antithetical to their organizational missions. Instead, they target the numerous, practical ways that even nonstate armed groups are, practically speaking, behaving as parties to a conflict: They must recruit committed fighters, train and plan for and finance military campaigns and engagements, conduct intelligence, cultivate and enlist a community of support from local populations and sympathizers at large. Part of the virtue of this approach to compliance is that it does not succeed or fail on the basis of the either/or state precept, or define the application of humanitarian law protocols through a state-centric worldview.

This is to say that humanitarian law is not only a legal paradigm that balances states security interests and humanitarian protections but an international norm that helps us make sense of new conditions of conflict and warfare. In many respects, the law-of-war paradigm is framing our approach to new belligerents, tactics, strategies, and outcomes. In this way it is worth thinking about international norms informed by humanitarian law as functioning, if not as a specific critical compliance instrument, then as a normative framework for making compliance meaningful, especially when compliance is severely hampered, as in asymmetric contexts.

Resilience in International Humanitarian Law

Dunlap raised an overlooked observation about the *jus in bello* as seen through the lens of military practitioners, particularly JAG's, which revealed a functionally different perspective on the laws of war that turns out to be one of the most important guarantees of its resilience:

> Military lawyers seem to conceive of the rule of law differently [from civilian government lawyers]. Instead of seeing law as a barrier to the exercise of the[ir] client's power, these attorneys understand the law as a prerequisite to the meaningful exercise of power.... Law makes just wars possible by creating a well-defined legal space within which individual soldiers can act without resorting to their own personal moral codes.[95]

It may not take a lot of imagination to recognize that in the chaos of armed conflict, discipline—rather than reactivity or vengeance—is a significant asset. This view of the *jus in bello* as enabling a disciplined and accountable battle space, and not just as a regime that constrains actors (by threat of prosecution), is part of what accounts for the depoliticized nature of the *jus in bello*.

That is, in framing humane approaches to irregular warfare, there are several intrinsic features of humanitarian law, particularly the *jus in bello*, that makes this *lex specialis* resilient in the face of contemporary challenges. Most interestingly, humanitarian law covers insurgents and liberation movements as subjects of international law, making the laws of armed conflict somewhat unique and indispensible in light of new realities. Likewise, in contrast to the *jus ad bellum*, which comprises very few documents (e.g., the U.N. Charter) for regulating when states may employ force as an instrument of their national policy, the *jus in bello* encompasses many and varied sources for achieving humanitarian protections: international conventions and treaties, international custom and general practice, general principles recognized by civilized nations, "judicial decisions and the teachings of the most highly qualified publicists of the various nations, as subsidiary means for the determination of rules of law."[96] This wealth of resources to draw upon lends itself to an exceedingly robust set of sources for elucidating and developing humanitarian norms, as well as providing "fail-safe" redundancy measures. Many have also remarked upon the unique and unusual aspect of this law in its universal application in that the Geneva Conventions are accepted by all states, as well as core *jus in bello* stipulations that reside in universal customary law. Part and parcel of this universal status is the significant commitment in the outlay of resources by states to integrate this law into domestic law and professional military operations.

But arguably the most crucial reason for humanitarian law's resilience stems from the depoliticizing impulse at the core of the *jus in bello*, a premise inseparable from the role of this law in delineating the legal battlefield. Unlike the *jus ad bellum*, which is contingent upon a body of state decision makers (the U.N. Security Council) to determine its application, the *jus in bello* apply equally on all sides in a designated armed conflict, regardless of right or wrong, victim or aggressor, just or unjust cause. Such a premise arose in part from the realization that the justness of a war could not be neutrally adjudicated and, further, that wars were often conducted with more brutality when belligerents felt imbued with moral cause. The *jus in bello* thus humanize war by not allowing the definition of what constitutes humane treatment during the exigencies of armed conflict to be based on politics. Instead, these rules preemptively define how military operations must take place, who and what may be targeted, how targeting may be executed, the weapons that may be used, how prisoners of war and other detainees must be treated, and the rights and obligations of occupying forces. In focusing on common rules for conducting hostilities for all parties, the *jus in bello* eschew partisan determinations for a regulated battlefield—a battlefield coterminous with the law.

As a norm paradigm the "constraining actors" approach to this law now predominates, in part because asymmetric adversaries have expanded the battle space beyond that which has been and can be regulated. At the most elemental level this difference reiterates the importance of retaining the balance between states security interests and broader humanitarian norms to preserve together the humanity of soldiers and victims of conflict.

Notes

Introduction

1. Eric Jensen, "Combatant Status: It Is Time for Intermediate Levels of Recognition for Partial Compliance," *Virginia Journal of International Law* 46, no. 1 (2005): 209–49: 210–11 (quotation source and internal notes omitted).

2. Asymmetry has been defined as "[a]cting, organizing, and thinking differently than opponents in order to maximize one's own advantages, exploit an opponent's weaknesses, attain the initiative, or gain greater freedom of action. It can be political-strategic, military-strategic, or a combination of these. It can entail different methods, technologies, values, organizations, time perspectives, or some combination of these. It can be short-term or long-term. It can be deliberate or by default. It can be discrete or pursued in conjunction with symmetric approaches. It can have both psychological and physical dimensions." See Steven Metz and Douglas V. Johnson II, "Asymmetry and US Military Strategy: Definition, Background, and Strategic Concepts," *Strategic Studies Institute of the US War Army College Report* (January 2001): 5–6. See also Stephen J. Blank, "Rethinking Asymmetric Threats," *Strategic Studies Institute of the US War Army College Report* (September 2003); Steven J. Lambakis, "Reconsidering Asymmetric Warfare," *Joint Force Quarterly* 36 (2004): 102–108; Montgomery Meigs, "Unorthodox Thoughts about Asymmetric Warfare," *Parameters* 33, no. 2 (2003): 4–18; Emanuel Gross, "The Laws of War Waged Between Democratic States and Terrorist Organizations: Real or Illusive?" *Florida Journal of International Law* 15 (2003): 389–480.

3. Israel Ministry of Foreign Affairs, "Preserving Humanitarian Principles While Combating Terrorism: Israel's Struggle with Hizbullah in the Lebanon War," *Diplomatic Note 1* (April 2007): 7; UN Human Rights Council, Special Rapporteur, Mission to Lebanon and Israel, "Report of Investigation sent to UN General Assembly" (October 2, 2006): 14.

4. Charles J. Dunlap, Jr., "Law and Military Interventions: Preserving Humanitarian Values in 21st Century Conflicts" (working paper, Carr Center for Human Rights Policy Kennedy School of Government, Harvard University, Cambridge, MA, 2001), www.ksg.harvard.edu/cchrp/Web%20Working%20Papers/Use%20of%20Force/Dunlap2001.pdf.
5. The literature on both sides of the debate, post 9/11, is enormous. For some examples see John B. Bellinger, U.S. Department of State Legal Advisor, speech at Oxford University, "Prisoners in War: Contemporary Challenges to the Geneva Conventions" (December 10, 2007), http://london.usembassy.gov/ukpapress72.html; Michael N. Schmitt and Jelena Pejic, eds., *International Law and Armed Conflict: Exploring the Faultlines: Essays in Honour of Yoram Dinstein* (Leiden, Netherlands: Martinus Nijoff/Brill, 2007); David H. Wippman and Matthew Evangelista eds., *New Wars, New Laws? Applying the Laws of War in 21st Century Conflicts* (Ardsley, NY: Transnational Publishers, 2005); Wolff Heintschel von Heinegg and Volker Epping, eds., *International Humanitarian Law Facing New Challenges: Symposium in Honour of Knut Ipsen* (New York: Springer, 2007); Jordan J. Paust, "Post-9/11 Overreaction and Fallacies Regarding War and Defense, Guantanamo, the Status of Persons, Treatment, Judicial Review of Detention, and Due Process in Military Commissions," *Notre Dame Law Review* 79, no. 4 (2004): 1335-64; Steven R. Ratner, "*Jus ad Bellum* and *Jus in Bello* after September 11," *The American Journal of International Law* 96, no. 4 (2002): 905-21; W. Michael Reisman, "Assessing Claims to Revise the Laws of War," *The American Journal of International Law* 97, no. 1 (2003): 82-90; Robert D. Sloane, "Prologue to a Voluntarist War Convention," *Michigan Law Review* 106 (2007): 443-86; Gabor Rona, "Legal Frameworks to Combat Terrorism: An Abundant Inventory of Existing Tools," *Chicago Journal of International Law* 5, no. 2 (2005): 499-509; Knut Dörmann, "The Legal Situation of 'Unlawful/Unprivileged Combatants,'" *International Review of the Red Cross* 85, no. 849 (2003): 45-74.
6. See Richard Burchill et al., *International Conflict and Security Law: Essays in Memory of Hilaire McCoubrey* (Cambridge: Cambridge University Press, 2005); Helen Duffy, *The "War on Terror" and the Framework of International Law* (Cambridge: Cambridge University Press, 2005); Dieter Fleck and Michael Bothe, *The Handbook of Humanitarian Law in Armed Conflicts* (Oxford: Oxford University Press, 1999).
7. Sir Lawrence Freedman, "A Theory of Battle or a Theory of War?" *The Journal of Strategic Studies* 28, no. 3 (2005): 425-35.
8. See Judith Gail Gardam, *Necessity, Proportionality and the Use of Force by States* (Cambridge: Cambridge University Press, 2004); Wolff Heintschel von Heinegg and Volker Epping, eds., *International Humanitarian Law Facing New Challenges: Symposium in Honour of Knut Ipsen* (Berlin: Springer, 2007); Howard M. Hensel,

INTRODUCTION

The Law of Armed Conflict: Constraints on the Contemporary Use of Military Force (Aldershot and Burlington: Ashgate, 2007).

9. Article 1, Convention (IV) respecting the Laws and Customs of War on Land and its annex: Regulations concerning the Laws and Customs of War on Land, The Hague, October 18, 1907, http://www.icrc.org/ihl.nsf/FULL/195.

10. Article 2, Convention (IV) respecting the Laws and Customs of War on Land and Article 1, Annex to the Convention: Regulations concerning the Laws and Customs of War on Land, The Hague, October 18, 1907, http://www.icrc.org/ihl.nsf/FULL/195.

11. Carl von Clausewitz, *On War* (1832), trans. Michael Howard and Peter Paret (Princeton: Princeton University Press, 1976).

12. International Committee of Red Cross, "International Humanitarian Law: Answers to Your Questions," http://icrc.org/Web/Eng/siteeng0.nsf/htmlall/p0703/$File/ICRC_002_0703.PDF!Open

13. The term "war" is considered archaic in international law and has been replaced by "armed conflict." According to Gabor Rona, this distinction reflects a change from when wars were "declared, to the present, in which facts on the ground are rightfully given greater emphasis over the declarations of parties to conflict." The rationale for not confusing or conflating "declared war" with actually occurring "armed conflict" is to prevent politics from infiltrating battlefield rules because when they do, more persons implicated in the hostilities will be left unprotected. See Gabor Rona, "Interesting Times for International Humanitarian Law: Challenges from the 'War on Terror,'" *Fletcher Forum of World Affairs* 27, no. 2 (2003): 55–74, p. 70.

14. Michael N. Schmitt, "21st Century Conflict: Can the Law Survive?" *Melbourne Journal of International Law* 8, no. 2 (2007): 443–76, p. 444.

15. See J. S. Pictet, *Commentary of the First Geneva Convention for the Amelioration of the Condition of the Wounded and Sick in Armed Forces in the Field* (Geneva: International Committee of the Red Cross, 1952), 49. See also Marco Sassoli, "Transnational Armed Groups and International Humanitarian Law," Program on Humanitarian Policy and Conflict Research, Harvard University, Occasional Paper Series, no. 6 (Winter 2006): 8–9. But see S. Boelaert-Suominen, "Humanitarian Law Applicable to All Armed Conflicts," *Journal of International Law* 13 (2000): 619, "In light of the ICTY jurisprudence since 1995, it can be safely concluded that the threshold suggested by the ICRC Commentary has failed to crystallise into customary law."

16. *Hamdan v. Rumsfeld*, 126 S. Ct. 2749 (2006).

17. Andrew Clapham, "Human Rights Obligations of Non-state Actors in Conflict Situations," *International Review of the Red Cross* 88, no. 863 (2006): 491–523, p. 494.

18. Michael Walzer, *Just and Unjust Wars: A Moral Argument with Historical Illustrations,* 3rd ed. (New York: Basic Books, 2000), 24–25.

19. Draft Memorandum from White House Counsel Alberto R. Gonzales to President George W. Bush (January 25, 2002): "Decision re Application of the Geneva Convention on Prisoners of War to the Conflict with al Qaeda and the Taliban."
20. *Hamdan v. Rumsfeld*, 126 S. Ct. 2749 (2006).
21. For this view see Gabor Rona and Yoram Dinstein's work generally, but especially, Dinstein, *The Conduct of Hostilities Under the Law of International Armed Conflict* (Cambridge: Cambridge University Press, 2004) and Rona, "Legal Frameworks to Combat Terrorism: An Abundant Inventory of Existing Tools," *Chicago Journal of International Law* 5, no. 2 (2005): 499–509, as well as analysis from ICRC reports on the subject, and the Harvard University Program on Humanitarian Policy and Conflict Research (HPRC) Informal High-Level Expert Meeting on the Reaffirmation and Development of International Humanitarian Law (January 27–29, 2003) recommendation: "no development of humanitarian law."
22. Geoffrey S. Corn and Eric T. Jensen, "Untying the Gordian Knot: A Proposal for Determining Applicability of the Laws of War to the War on Terror," *Temple Law Review* 81, no. 3 (2008): 787.
23. Rona, "Interesting Times," 70.
24. Volker Epping and Gottfried Wilhelm Leibniz, "Confronting New Challenges: Knut Ibsen and International Humanitarian Law," eds. Wolff Heintschel von Heinegg and Volker Epping, *International Humanitarian Law Facing New Challenges: Symposium in Honour of Knut Ipsen* (Berlin: Springer, 2007). See also Liesbeth Zegveld, *Accountability of Armed Opposition Groups in International Law* (Cambridge: Cambridge University Press, 2002).
25. U.S. Department of Defense (DoD) Directive 2311.01E, DoD Law of War Program (2006), 4.1: "Members of the DoD Components comply with the law of war during all armed conflicts, however such conflicts are characterized, and in all other military operations," http://www.dtic.mil/whs/directives/corres/html/231101.htm.

1. Extraterritorial Law Enforcement

1. *Authorization for the Use of Military Force*, Public Law 107–40, *U.S. Statutes at Large* 115 (2001): 224.
2. Gabor Rona, When Is a War Not a War?—The Proper Role of the Law of Armed Conflict in the 'Global War on Terror' (paper presented at workshop on the Protection of Human Rights while Countering Terrorism, Copenhagen, Denmark, March 15–16, 2004), http://www.icrc.org/Web/eng/siteeng0.nsf/html5XCMNJ.
3. Capt. Brian C. Baldrate, review of *Imperial Hubris: Why the West Is Losing the War on Terror*, by Michael Scheuer, *Army Law* (2005): 29.
4. David E. Graham, "The Treatment and Interrogation of War and Detainees," *Georgetown Journal of International Law* 37 (2005): 61.

5. *Hamdi v. Rumsfeld*, 542 U.S. 507 (2004).
6. *Rumsfeld v. Padilla*, 542 U.S. 426 (2004).
7. Geoffrey S. Corn, "Hamdan, Lebanon, and the Regulation of Armed Hostilities: The Need to Recognize a Hybrid Category of Armed Conflict," *Vanderbilt Journal of Transnational Law* 40 (2007): 295.
8. Catherine Bloom, "The Classification of Hezbollah in Both International and Non-international Armed Conflicts," *Annual Survey of American Law* 14 (2008): 61.
9. Andras Sajo, "Terrorism, Globalization and the Rule of Law: From Militant Democracy to the Preventive State?" *Cardozo Law Review* 27 (2006): 2255.
10. *Authorization for the Use of Military Force*, Public Law 107-40, *U.S. Statutes at Large* 115 (2001): 224.
11. Yoram Dinstein, *The Conduct of Hostilities under the Law of International Armed Conflict* (Cambridge: Cambridge University Press, 2004), 1.
12. Ibid. at 5.
13. Dinstein, *The Conduct of Hostilities*, 1.
14. Geoffrey S. Corn and Eric Talbot Jensen, "Untying the Gordian Knot: A Proposal for Determining Applicability of the Laws of War to the War on Terror," *Temple Law Review* 81 (2008): 787.
15. International & Operational Law Department, *The Law of War Deskbook* (Charlottesville, VA: The Judge Advocate General's Legal Center and School, 2000), at Chapter 1.
16. Ibid.
17. Geoffrey S. Corn, *Hamdan, Lebanon, and the Regulation of Armed Conflict: The Need to Recognize a Hybrid Category of Armed Conflict*, 40 *Vanderbilt Transnational Law Journal* 295 (2006).
18. See Louise Arbour, "Lebanon/Israel: U.N. Rights Body Squanders Chance to Help Civilians" (paper presented at Human Rights Watch, August 11, 2006), http://hrw.org/english/docs/2006/08/11/lebano13969_txt.htm; Kofi Annan, "U.N.: Open Independent Inquiry into Civilian Deaths" (paper presented at Human Rights Watch, August 8, 2006), http://hrw.org/english/docs/2006/08/08/lebano13939.htm.
19. See supra, n. 8.
20. Kenneth Watkin, "Controlling the Use of Force: A Role for Human Rights Norms in Contemporary Armed Conflict," *American Journal of International Law* 98 (January, 2004): 1 (discussing the complex challenge of conflict categorization related to military operations conducted against highly organized nonstate groups with transnational reach); Kirby Abbott, "Terrorists: Combatants, Criminals, or . . . ?" (published in *The Measures of International Law: Effectiveness, Fairness, and Validity*, Proceedings of the 31st Annual Conference of the Canadian Council on International Law, Ottawa, Canada, October 24–26, 2002) [hereinafter Abbott]; CRS

Report for Congress, "Terrorism and the Laws of War: Trying Terrorists as War Criminals Before Military Commissions," Order Code RL31191, December 11, 2001 (analyzing whether the attacks of September 11, 2001 triggered the law of war).
21. Report of the Commission on Human Rights on its fifty-third session, UN Doc. E/CN.4/1997/150; letter dated 14 April 2003 from the Chief of Section, Political and Specialized Agencies of the Permanent Mission of the United States of America to the United Nations Office at Geneva, addressed to the Secretariat of the Commission on Human Rights, UN Doc. E/CN.4/2003/G/80, at 2–3 (22 Apr. 2003).
22. See supra, n. 17.
23. Lloyd de Vries, "U.S. Strikes in Somalia Reportedly Kill 31," CBS News, January 9, 2007, http://www.cbsnews.com/stories/2007/01/08/world/main2335451.shtml (accessed Feb. 13, 2009).
24. Michael N. Schmitt, "'Change Direction' 2006: Israeli Operations in Lebanon and the International Law of Self-defense," *Michigan Journal of International Law* 29 (2008): 127.
25. Sarah Leah Whitson, "Hezbollah Needs to Answer," *Human Rights Watch*, http://hrw.org/english/docs/2006/10/05/lebano14336.htm (2006).
26. *Hamdan v. Rumsfeld,* 548 U.S. 557 (2006).
27. *Hamdan v. Rumsfeld,* 415 F.3d 33 (D.C. Cir. 2005).
28. Ibid. (Williams, Sr. Judge, concurring).
29. U.S. Department of Defense, Dir. 2311.01E, DoD Law of War Program (May 9, 2006); Geoffrey S. Corn, "Hamdan, Lebanon, and the Regulation of Armed Hostilities: The Need to Recognize a Hybrid Category of Armed Conflict," *Vanderbilt Journal of Transnational Law* 40 (2007): 295.
30. Corn, "Hamdan, Lebanon, and the Regulation of Armed Hostilities," 295; Corn and Jensen, "Untying the Gordian Knot," 787.
31. Sarah Leah Whitson, "Hezbollah Needs to Answer," *Human Rights Watch*, http://hrw.org/english/docs/2006/10/05/lebano14336.htm (2006).
32. U.S. Department of Defense, DIR. 2311.01E, DoD Law of War Program (May 9, 2006) (cancelling Dep't of Defense Directive 5100.77, DoD Law of War Program (December 9, 1998).
33. For examples of U.S. Service implementation of these principles, see Joint Chiefs of Staff, Instr. 5810.01C, Implementation of the DoD Law of War Program (31 January 2007); U.S. Department of the Navy, Marine Corps Order 3300.4, *Marine Corps Law of War Program* (20 October 2003); and U.S. Department of the Navy, Secretary of the Navy, SECNAV Instruction 3300.1B, *Law of Armed Conflict (Law of War) Program to Ensure Compliance by the Naval Establishment* (27 December 2005).
34. Major Geoffrey S. Corn, *The Principle of Military Necessity,* Department of the Army Pamphlet 27–50–308 (The Army Lawyer), TJAGSA Practice Note (July 1998) at 72.

1. EXTRATERRITORIAL LAW ENFORCEMENT   219

35. Adam Roberts, "Counter-terrorism, Armed Force and the Laws of War," *Survival*, 44(1) 7-32, p. 8. Also see Roberts' revised version of the essay, "The Laws of War in the War on Terror," in Fred L. Borch and Paul S. Wilson, *International Law and the War on Terror* (U.S. Naval War College, International Law Studies, Vol. 79, 2003), 175–230.
36. Dinstein, *The Conduct of Hostilities*, 255.
37. Ibid.
38. U.K. Ministry of Defense, *The Manual for the Law of Armed Conflict* (New York: Oxford University Press, 2005), at par. 2.1 (emphasis added). *The Manual* also provides an extensive definition of these principles.
39. U.S. Department of Defense, Dir. 2311.01E, DoD Law of War Program (May 9, 2006); Major Timothy E. Bullman, "A Dangerous Guessing Game Disguised as an Enlightened Policy: United States Laws of War Obligations During Military Operations Other Than War," *Military Law Review* 159 (1999): 152 (analyzing the potential that the U.S. law of war policy could be asserted as evidence of a customary norm of international law). Other armed forces have implemented similar policies. For example, the German policy to apply the principles of the law of war to any armed conflict, no matter how characterized, was cited by the ICTY in the *Tadic* jurisdictional appeal as evidence of a general principle of law extending application of the law-of-war principles derived from treaties governing international armed conflict to the realm of internal armed conflict.; *Prosecutor v. Tadic*, Case No. IT-94-1-AR72, Appeal on Jurisdiction (Oct. 2, 1995), at par. 118 (citing the German Military Manual of 1992), reprinted in *I.L.M.* 35 (1996): 32.
40. U.S. Department of Defense, Dir. 2311.01E, DoD Law of War Program (May 9, 2006), par. 5.7.2. (The Directive requires that the head of each military service "Institute and implement effective programs to prevent violations of the law of war, including law of war training and dissemination, as required by [the Geneva Conventions].")
41. *The Laws of War on Land* (Oxford, September 9, 1880), http://www.icrc.org/ihl.nsf/FULL/140?OpenDocument (accessed February 8, 2009).
42. U.K. Ministry of Defense, *The Manual for the Law of Armed Conflict*, at par. 14.10.
43. Secretary General of the United Nations Bulletin titled "Observance by United Nations Forces of International Humanitarian Law" (1999).
44. *U.S. v. Noriega*, 808 F. Supp. 791 (S.D. Fla. 1992) (indicating that a policy-based application of the laws of war is insufficient to protect the rights of General Noriega because it is subject to modification at any time at the will of the Executive).
45. A. P. V. Rogers, *Law on the Battlefield* (New York: St. Martin's Press, 1996).
46. Leslie Green, "What Is—Why Is There—the Law of War," in Michael N. Schmitt and Leslie C. Green, *The Law of Armed Conflict: Into the Next Millennium*, Vol. 71, 176, U.S. Naval War College International Studies, Naval War College, Newport,

Rhode Island (1998); U.S. War Department, General Orders No. 100, *Instructions for the Government of Armies of the United States in the Field*, April 24, 1863.
47. Max Boot, *Savage Wars of Peace: Small Wars and the Rise of the American Power* (New York: Basic Books, 2003).
48. Leslie C. Green, *The Contemporary Law of Armed Conflict*, 3rd ed. (Yonkers, NY: Juris Pub Inc., 2008), 54–55.
49. Green, *The Contemporary Law of Armed Conflict*, 29.
50. Ibid., 32.
51. Ibid., 66.
52. *Prosecutor v. Tadic*, Case No. IT-94-1-AR72, Appeal on Jurisdiction (Oct. 2, 1995), at par. 118, reprinted in *I.L.M.* 35 (1996): 32.
53. Green, *The Contemporary Law of Armed Conflict*, 64.
54. Corn and Jensen, "Untying the Gordian Knot," 787.
55. Ibid.
56. Ibid.
57. Kenneth Watkin, "Controlling the Use of Force: A Role for Human Rights Norms in Contemporary Armed Conflict," 1; Corn, "Hamdan, Lebanon, and the Regulation of Armed Hostilities," 295.
58. See, generally, Todd A. Morth, "Considering Our Position: Viewing Information Warfare as a Use of Force Prohibited by Article 2(4) of the U.N. Charter," 30 *Case Western Reserve Journal of International Law* (1998): 567.
59. Geoffrey S. Corn, "Mixing Apples and Hand Grenades: The Logical Limits of Applying Human Rights Norms in Armed Conflict," *Journal of International Humanitarian Legal Studies* 1(1) 2010: 52–94; *McCann and others v. The United Kingdom*, Judgment of 27 September 1995, 21 EHRR 97; Maj. David Bolgiano et al., "Defining the Right of Self-defense: Working Toward the Use of a Deadly Force Appendix to the Standing Rules of Engagement for the Department of Defense," *University of Baltimore Law Review* 31 (2002): 157.
60. Ibid.
61. Protocol Additional to the Geneva Convention of August 12, 1949, and relating to the Protection of Victims of International Armed Conflicts (Protocol I), June 8, 1977, at art. 51; International and Operational Law Department, *The Law of War Deskbook* (Charlottesville, VA: The Judge Advocate General's Legal Center & School, 2000), at chapter 4.
62. See supra, n. 8.
63. AP, "Pentagon Confirms Strike against Al Qaeda in Somalia," FoxNews.com, January 10, 2007, http://www.foxnews.com/story/0,2933,242500,00.html (accessed on Feb. 13, 2009).
64. Gary D. Solis, *The Law of Armed Conflict: International Humanitarian Law in War* (Cambridge: Cambridge Univ. Press, 2010), 164–167.

65. *McCann and others v. The United Kingdom,* Judgment of September 27, 1995, 21 EHRR 97.
66. See supra, n. 17.
67. Robert Sloane, "The Cost of Conflation: Preserving the Dualism of Jus Ad Bellum and Jus in Bello in the Contemporary Law of War," *Yale Journal of International Law* 34 (2009): 47.
68. Commentary, Convention (III) relative to the Treatment of Prisoners of War, Geneva, August 12, 1949 (Jean S. Pictet, ed., 1960), at 22–23.
69. Eran Shamir-Borer, "Revisiting *Hamdan v. Rumsfeld*'s Analysis of the Laws of Armed Conflict," *Emory International Law Review* 21 (2007): 601.
70. Dinstein, *Conduct of Hostilities*, 5.
71. Eran Shamir-Borer, "*Revisiting Hamdan v. Rumsfeld's Analysis*"; Corn, "Hamdan, Lebanon, and the Regulation of Armed Hostilities," 295.
72. "Remarks and Proposals Submitted by the International Committee of the Red Cross" (document for the consideration of Governments invited by the Swiss Federal Council to attend the Diplomatic Conference at Geneva, April 21, 1949), 8.
73. Ibid.
74. Corn and Jensen, "Untying the Gordian Knot."
75. Ibid.
76. Ibid.
77. Shamir-Borer, "Revisiting *Hamdan v. Rumsfeld*'s Analysis"; Corn, "Hamdan, Lebanon, and the Regulation of Armed Hostilities," 295.
78. Corn, "Hamdan, Lebanon, and the Regulation of Armed Hostilities," 295; Corn and Jensen, "Untying the Gordian Knot," 787.
79. See supra, n. 8.
80. Joint Chiefs of Staff, Joint Pub. 4–0, "Joint Logistics" (July 18, 2008); Title 10, U.S. Code, Section 3062 (a) ("It is the intent of Congress to provide an Army that is capable, in conjunction with the other armed forces, of . . . overcoming any nations responsible for aggressive acts that imperil the peace and security of the United States.").
81. Headquarters, Department of the Army, Field Manual 3–0, Operations (June 2001), at 4–13.
82. Major Mark S. Martins, "Rules of Engagement for Land Forces: A Matter of Training, Not Lawyering," *Military Law Review* 143 (Winter 1994): 34.
83. Yoram Dinstein, "Concluding Remarks on Terrorism and Afghanistan," *The War in Afghanistan: A Legal Analysis, US Naval War College International Law Studies* 85 (M.N. Schmitt ed., 2009).
84. David E. Graham, "The Treatment and Interrogation of Prisoners of War and Detainees," *Georgetown Journal of International Law* 37 (2005): 61.
85. *U.S. v. Noriega*, 808 F. Supp. 791(S.D. Fla. 1992).

86. Jay S. Bybee, Memorandum for Alberto R. Gonzales, Counsel to the President, and William J. Haynes II, General Counsel of the DoD (January 22, 2002), http://news.findlaw.com/hdocs/-docs/doj/bybee12202mem.pdf.
87. *U.S. v. Noriega*, 808 F.Supp. 791, page 1992; *Hamdan v. Rumsfeld*, 548 U.S. 557 (2006).
88. Dinstein, *Conduct of Hostilities*, 5.
89. See supra, n. 8.
90. Jay S. Bybee, Memorandum for Alberto R. Gonzales, Counsel to the President, and William J. Haynes II, General Counsel of the DoD (January 22, 2002), http://news.findlaw.com/hdocs/-docs/doj/bybee12202mem.pdf; Alberto R. Gonzales, Memorandum for the President, Subject: Decision re Application of the Geneva Convention on Prisoners of War to the Conflict with Al Qaeda and the Taliban (January 25, 2002), http://www.msnbc.msn.com/id/4999148/site/newsweek/; Donald Rumsfeld, Memorandum for the Chairman of the Joint Chiefs of Staff, Subject: Status of the Taliban and Al Qaida, [sic] (January 19, 2002), http://news.findlaw.com/hdocs/docs/dod/11902mem.pdf. In a message dated January 21, 2002, the chairman notified combatant commanders of the secretary of defense's determination. Message from the Chairman of the Joint Chiefs of Staff, Subject: SECDEF Memo to CJCS Regarding the Status of Taliban and Al Qaida [sic] (January 22, 2002), http://news.findlaw.com/hdocs/docs/dod/12202mem.pdf; President Bush Memorandum of February 7, 2002, Subject: Humane Treatment of al Qaeda and Taliban Detainees, http://www.justicescholars.org/pegc/archive/White_House/bush_memo_20020207_ed.pdf#search=%22bush%20february%207%20memo%20on%20humane%20treatment%20of%20al%20qaeda%22

2. Preventive Detention of Individuals Engaged in Transnational Hostilities

1. Roy S. Schöndorf, "Extra-state Armed Conflicts: Is There a Need for a New Legal Regime?" *New York University Journal of International Law and Politics* 37 (2005): 1. For an application of the same conceptual distinction in the field of international criminal law see Neil Boister, "Transnational Criminal Law?" *European Journal of International Law* 14 (2003): 953.
2. *Importance of the Universal Realization of the Right of Peoples to Self-determination and of the Speedy Granting of Independence to Colonial Countries and Peoples for the Effective Guarantee and Observance of Human Rights*, GA Res 34/44, UN GAOR, 34th sess, 76th plen mtg, UN Doc. A/RES/34/44 (1979), [2].
3. Charter of the United Nations, art. 73.
4. *Protocol Additional to the Geneva Conventions of August 12, 1949, and Relating to the Protection of Victims of International Armed Conflicts*, opened for signature

June 8, 1977, 1125 UNTS 3 (entered into force December 7, 1978) ("*Additional Protocol I*"), Protocol Additional to the Geneva Conventions of August 12, 1949, and Relating to the Protection of Victims of Non-international Armed Conflicts, opened for signature June 8, 1977, 1125 UNTS 609 (entered into force December 7, 1978) ("*Additional Protocol II*").

5. John Arquilla and David Ronfeldt, "The Advent of Netwar: Analytic Backgound," *Studies in Conflict & Terrorism* 22 (1999): 193, 196–97. See also John Arquilla and David Ronfeldt, eds., *Networks and Netwars: The Future of Terror, Crime, and Militancy* (Santa Monica: Rand, 2001).
6. *Geneva Convention Relative to the Treatment of Prisoners of War*, opened for signature August 12, 1949, 75 UNTS 135, art. 4.A.2(b-c) (entered into force October 21, 1950) ("*GCIII*").
7. *GCIII*, art. 4.A.2(a & d).
8. *GCIII*, art. 4.A.2.
9. *GCIII*, arts 5 & 85.
10. *Additional Protocol I*, art. 44.3.
11. *Additional Protocol I*, art. 1.4 applies to "armed conflicts in which peoples are fighting against colonial domination and alien occupation and against racist regimes in the exercise of their right of self-determination ... ," and art. 96.3 enables a people's organization to unilaterally declare itself.
12. Additional Protocol I, art. 43.1.
13. Additional Protocol I, art. 44.2 indicates that captured armed forces members accused of crimes retain their prisoner of war status.
14. Additional Protocol I, art. 45.3.
15. Additional Protocol I, art. 50.
16. Francis Lieber, *Guerrilla Parties Considered with Reference to the Laws and Usages of War*, ed. Richard Shelly Hartigan, *Lieber's Code and the Law of War* (1983), 31, cited in Sean D. Murphy, "Evolving Geneva Convention Paradigms in the 'War on Terrorism': Applying the Core Rules to the Release of Persons Deemed 'Unprivileged Combatants,'" *George Washington Law Review* 75 (2007): 1105, 1110–11.
17. As indicated by Common Article 2 of the Geneva Conventions, see, e.g., *GCIII*, art. 2.
18. Additional Protocol I, art. 1.4 applies to "armed conflicts in which peoples are fighting against colonial domination and alien occupation and against racist regimes in the exercise of their right of self-determination ...," and art. 96.3 enables a people's organization to unilaterally declare itself.
19. Additional Protocol I, art. 96.3.
20. Additional Protocol I, art. 43.1.
21. *Rome Statute of the International Criminal Court*, opened for signature July 17, 1998, 2187 UNTS 90, arts. 7 & 8 (entered into force July 1, 2002) ("ICC Statute").

22. See George H. Aldrich, "The Taliban, Al Qaeda, and the Determination of Illegal Combatants," *American Journal of International Law* 96 (2002): 891; Robert K. Goldman and Brian D. Tittemore, *Unprivileged Combatants and the Hostilities in Afghanistan: Their Status and Rights Under International Humanitarian and Human Rights Law* (2002), http://www.asil.org/taskforce/goldman.pdf (accessed Jan. 6, 2009).
23. The customary international legal status of some specific innovations that concern nonstate entities and were codified in Additional Protocol I, remain controversial among legal scholars; e.g., Article 1(4) is not considered customary: Christopher J. Greenwood, "Customary Law Status of the 1977 Additional Protocols," eds., Astrid J. M. Delissen and Gerard J. Tanja, *Humanitarian Law of Armed Conflict: Challenges Ahead: Essays in Honour of Frits Kalshoven* (The Hague: T. M. C. Asser Institute, 1991), 93, 112, cited in Ariel Zemach, "Taking War Seriously: Applying the Law of War to Hostilities Within an Occupied Territory," *George Washington Law Review* 38 (2006): 645, 658.
24. Additional Protocol I, art. 50.1: "A civilian is any person who does not belong to one of the categories of persons referred to in Article 4 (A) (1) (2) (3) and (6) of the Third Convention and in Article 43 of this Protocol. In case of doubt whether a person is a civilian, that person shall be considered to be a civilian."
25. Additional Protocol I, art. 45.3: "Any person who has taken part in hostilities, who is not entitled to prisoner-of-war status and who does not benefit from more favorable treatment in accordance with the Fourth Convention [affording protection to civilians] shall have the right at all times to the protection of Article 75 of this Protocol."
26. Murphy, "Evolving Geneva Convention Paradigms in the 'War on Terrorism,'" n. 116 (cited supra, n. 16); see also W. Michael Reisman, "The Lessons of Qana," *Yale Journal of International Law* 22 (1997): 381.
27. Murphy, "Evolving Geneva Convention Paradigms in the 'War on Terrorism,'" 1115 (cited supra, n. 16), citing numerous esteemed authorities in support.
28. *Case Concerning Military and Paramilitary Activities in and Against Nicaragua (Nicaragua v. United States of America) (Merits)* [1986] ICJ Rep 14; *Prosecutor v. Tadic* (Decision on *the Defense Motion for Interlocutory Appeal on Jurisdiction* [1995] 35 ILM 32 (1996); *Hamdan v. Rumsfeld*, 548 U.S. 557 (2006).
29. *Hamdan v. Rumsfeld*, 548 U.S. 557 (2006). The majority opinion on this point, delivered by Stevens J., did not offer further analysis of the *travaux préparatoires* or of subsequent practice in its interpretation.
30. John Yoo, *War by Other Means: An Insider's Account of the War on Terror* (Boston: Atlantic Monthly Press, 2006), 25.
31. The ICC Statute states that to be "serious violations of the laws and customs applicable in armed conflicts not of an international character" war crimes need to

"take place in the territory of a State when there is protracted armed conflict between governmental authorities and organized armed groups." As all armed conflict, including international armed conflict, takes place on some state territory, the intended meaning here is that the noninternational conflict occurs entirely in one state's territory.

32. The expansive position is also indirectly implied by commentators to be customary international law. The International Committee of the Red Cross has identified 161 rules that it considers to have achieved customary international law status. See Jean-Marie Henckaerts and Louise Doswald-Beck, *Customary International Humanitarian Law,* Volume 1: *Rules* (Cambridge: Cambridge University Press, 2005), 299. The methodology and conclusions of the study have proved controversial and drew a critical response from the United States. See John B. Bellinger and William J. Haynes, "A US Government Response to the International Committee of the Red Cross Study *Customary International Humanitarian Law,*" *International Review of the Red Cross* 89 (2007): 443.

33. Jakob Kellenberger, "Foreword by ICRC President Jakob Kellenberger" in Henckaerts and Doswald-Beck, *Customary International Humanitarian Law,* ix (cited supra, n. 32).

34. However, how human rights norms are to be implemented during hostilities has still not been settled. See John Tobin, "Seeking Clarity in Relation to the Principle of Complementarity: Reflections on the Recent Contributions of Some International Bodies," *Melbourne Journal of International Law* 8 (2007): 356.

35. Schöndorf, "Extra-state Armed Conflicts," 1 (cited supra, n. 1); Murphy, "Evolving Geneva Convention Paradigms in the "War on Terrorism," 1110–11 (cited supra, n. 16).

36. The International Criminal Tribunal for the former Yugoslavia sought to define the requisite criteria for the existence of armed conflict under Common Article 3 in *Prosecutor v. Tadic (Decision on the Defense Motion for Interlocutory Appeal on Jurisdiction)* [1995] 35 ILM 32 (1996). With regard to noninternational armed conflict, the Tribunal held at [70]: "[A]n armed conflict exists whenever there is . . . protracted armed violence between governmental authorities and organized armed groups or between such groups within a State." The Tribunal further held in *Prosecutor v. Tadic (Opinion and Judgment)* [1997] 36 ILM 908 at [562]: "The test . . . focuses on two aspects of a conflict; the intensity of the conflict and the organization of the parties to the conflict. In an armed conflict of an internal or mixed character, these closely related criteria are used solely for the purpose, as a minimum, of distinguishing an armed conflict from banditry, unorganized and short-lived insurrections, or terrorist activities, which are not subject to international humanitarian law." See also Zemach, supra, n. 23, 673–75, and Schöndorf, supra, n. 1, 11. Schöndorf observes, in note 39, that the tribunal's decision does not

address the "question of whether a state could be involved in an armed conflict with a non-state actor outside of the state's territory."

37. Additional Protocol II, art. 1.1 requires that the conflict "take place in the territory of a High Contracting Party between its armed forces and dissident armed forces or other organized armed groups *which, under responsible command, exercise such control over a part of its territory as to enable them to carry out sustained and concerted military operations. . .* " (emphasis added). See Sylvie Junod, "Additional Protocol II: History and Scope," *American University Law Review* 33 (1983): 29.

38. Additional Protocol II, art. 1.2.

39. ICC Statute, art. 8.2(d). The scope of application of this provision reflects an expansion upon the original scope of Common Article 3; that is, it applies beyond internal conflicts where a nonstate entity controls part of the territory of an affected party, to include also conflicts that are transnational or where no territory is held. This expansion can be argued to be customary international law, see Henckaerts and Doswald-Beck, supra, n. 21.

40. ICC Statute, art. 8.2(f). However, it allows that the conflict need not be between governmental authorities and organized armed groups but that it can be between such groups.

41. Nor does it require that there be control by the opposing nonstate actors over a part of the affected state's territory. The United Kingdom considered the Additional Protocol II, qualifications for the existence of an internal armed conflict with an nonstate entity, including control over territory, to be a threshold condition under analogous provisions of Additional Protocol I, for the a deemed "international" armed conflict with an nonstate entity. International Committee of the Red Cross (ICRC), *Status of Parties to Additional Protocol I, 1977–United Kingdom reservation text* (2002), http://www.icrc.org/ihl.nsf/NORM/0A9E03F0F2EE757 CC1256402003FB6D2?OpenDocument (accessed Jan. 23, 2009).

42. Anthony Cullen, "The Definition of Non-international Armed Conflict in the Rome Statute of the International Criminal Court: An Analysis of the Threshold of Application Contained in Article 8(2)(f)," *Journal of Conflict & Security Law* 12 (2008): 419.

43. The use of lethal force is legally permissible for both constabulary and military forces in prescribed circumstances. Those circumstances are still being defined for the lethal targeting by military forces of nonstate fighters. In *The Public Committee Against Torture in Israel v. The Government of Israel* [2006] HCJ 769/02 (*"Targeted Killings Case"*), the Israeli Supreme Court held that a civilian taking direct part in hostilities retains the status of a civilian but ceases to enjoy the protections granted to a civilian (at [31]) and can be lawfully targeted for attack when four conditions are met (at [40]). As interpreted in Marko Milanovic, "Lessons for

Human Rights and Humanitarian Law in the War on Terror: Comparing *Hamdan* and the Israeli *Targeted Killings* Case," *International Review of the Red Cross* 89 (2007): 373, 389:

> "1. The state must possess well-based, thoroughly verified information regarding the identity and activity of the civilian who is allegedly taking part in the hostilities; the burden of proof on the state is heavy.
>
> "2. A civilian taking direct part in hostilities cannot be attacked at such time as he is doing so, if a less harmful means can be employed. Thus if a terrorist taking a direct part in hostilities can be arrested, interrogated, and tried, those are the means which should be employed. In the words of the Court, 'Trial is preferable to use of force. A rule-of-law state employs, to the extent possible, procedures of law and not procedures of force.'
>
> "3. If a civilian is indeed attacked, a thorough and independent investigation must be conducted regarding the precision of the identification of the target and the circumstances of the attack, and in appropriate cases compensation must be paid for harm done to innocent civilians.
>
> "4. Finally, combatants and terrorists are not to be harmed if the damage expected to be caused to nearby innocent civilians is not proportionate to the military advantage directly anticipated from harming the combatants and terrorists."

See also the symposium "Are 'Targeted Killings' Unlawful? The Israeli Supreme Court's Response," *Journal of International Criminal Justice* 5 (2007): 301.

44. *Threats to international peace and security caused by terrorist acts*, SC Res 1373, UN SCOR, 56th session, 4385th mtg, UN Doc S/RES/1373 (2001).
45. See W. Michael Reisman, "In Defense of World Public Order," *American Journal of International Law* 95 (2001): 833; Thomas M. Franck, "Terrorism and the Right of Self-defense," *American Journal of International Law* 95 (2001): 839; and Yoram Dinstein, *War, Aggression, and Self-defense* (3rd ed., 2001), 213–221. But see, contra: Frédéric Mégret, "War? Legal Semantics and the Move to Violence," *European Journal of International Law* 13 (2002): 361; and *Legal Consequences of the Construction of a Wall in the Occupied Palestinian Territory (Advisory Opinion)* [2004] ICJ Rep 136.
46. *High-Level Meeting of the Security Council: Combating Terrorism*, SC Res 1456, UN SCOR, 58th session, 4688th mtg, UN Doc S/RES/1456 (2003).
47. Jonathan B. Schwartz, "Dealing with a 'Rogue State': The Libya Precedent," *American Journal of International Law* 101 (2007): 553.
48. Michael Pugh, "Legal Aspects of the Rainbow Warrior Affair," *International and Comparative Law Quarterly* 36 (1987): 655.

49. *Legal Consequences of the Construction of a Wall in the Occupied Palestinian Territory (Advisory Opinion)* [2004] ICJ Rep 136 at [138]-[142]. The Court held that self-defense arises only in response to armed attack by a state. There was dissent on this dubious point in the separate opinions of Judges Higgins at [33]-[34] and Burgenthal at [5]-[6], and by other authoritative commentators (described as the majority of authors by Gilbert Guillaume [who was recently president on the Court's bench], "Terrorism and International Law," *International and Comparative Law Quarterly* 53 (2004): 537, who have argued that the right to self-defense arises in accordance with the scale of the attacks, irrespective of whether a foreign state perpetrates them.

    The International Court of Justice held in *Case Concerning Military and Paramilitary Activities in and Against Nicaragua (Nicaragua v. United States of America) (Merits)* [1986] ICJ Rep 14 at [230] that: "the Court is unable to consider that, in customary international law, the provision of arms to the opposition in another State constitutes an armed attack on that State." As explained by Gregory M. Travalio, "Terrorism, International Law, and the Use of Military Force," *Wisconsin International Law Journal* 18 (2000): 145, 158, "this opinion suggests ... that even the active support by a state to terrorist groups would not be an armed attack under Article 51." See also Emanuel Gross, "The Laws of War Waged Between Democratic States and Terrorist Organizations: Real or Illusive?" *Florida Journal of International Law* 15 (2003): 389, 399-404.

50. Andrew Clapham, *Human Rights Obligations of Non-state Actors* (Oxford: Oxford University Press, 2006), 288.

51. Switzerland, the depository for Additional Protocol I, received a declaration of intention to be bound from a body calling itself Palestine. Yet the Palestine Liberation Organization did not name itself and the declaration was not accepted. International Committee of the Red Cross (ICRC), *Treaties by Country — Palestine* (2005), http://www.icrc.org/ihl.nsf/Pays?ReadForm&c=PS (accessed Jan. 23, 2009).

52. English language information is conveniently available for Australia and the United States, but because the primary sources of information concerning Israel's legal mechanisms are in Hebrew, information provided here is derived from secondary materials and is relatively sparse.

53. The most substantive comparative legal research to date on preventive detention for national security purposes is set out in a comparative survey of predominantly African and Asian national laws. Andrew Harding and John Hatchard, *Preventive Detention and Security Law: A Comparative Survey* (Leiden: Martinus Nijhoff, 1993).

54. These rulings are critiqued by other authors but are briefly described below in relation to hearings of habeas corpus applications brought by detainees against their detention at Guantanamo Bay. Even in its 1942, ruling in *Ex Parte* Quirin (317

U.S. 1 [1942], 31), the bench used two different terms in one paragraph to describe the status of captured German saboteurs—i.e., "enemy combatant" and "unlawful combatant": Amos N. Guiora, "*Quirin* to *Hamdan*: Creating a Hybrid Paradigm for the Detention of Terrorists," *Florida Journal of International Law* 19 (2006): 511, 517.

55. Gregory Rose and Diana Nestorovska, "Australian Counter-terrorism Offences: Necessity and Clarity in Federal Criminal Law," *Criminal Law Journal* 31 (2007): 20. Although Australia might seem isolated from such violence, it is a member of the "coalition of the willing" in Iraq, the NATO-led International Security Assistance Force in Afghanistan, and the International Security Force in East Timor, and has regional interests in the development of international norms to combat transnational violence.
56. Harding, 4 (cited supra, n. 53).
57. Office of Public Sector Information, *Magna Carta (1297) (c. 9)* (2006) UK Statute Law Database, http://www.statutelaw.gov.uk/content.aspx?activeTextDocId=1517519 (accessed Jan. 25, 2009).
58. GCIII, arts. 21, 118.
59. *Geneva Convention Relative to the Protection of Civilian Persons in Time of War*, opened for signature August 12, 1949, 75 UNTS 287, arts. 42, 132 (entered into force October 21, 1950) ("*GCIV*"). See also Additional Protocol I, art. 75.3, which requires that person interned for actions related to the armed conflict shall be released as soon as the circumstances justifying the internment have ceased to exist.
60. GCIII, art. 5: "Should any doubt arise as to whether persons, having committed a belligerent act and having fallen into the hands of the enemy, belong to any of the categories enumerated in Article 4, such persons shall enjoy the protection of the present Convention until such time as their status has been determined by a competent tribunal."
61. Amos N. Guiora and John T. Parry, "Light at the End of the Pipeline?: Choosing a Forum for Suspected Terrorists," *University of Pennsylvania Law Review* 156 (2008): 356.
62. A comparison can be made here with Australian subnational jurisdictions that have created various specialized administrative courts with powers to detain persons for the purposes of their own or the public's safety and welfare, rather than for national security purposes. Drug courts have been established in five of the six Australian states, where their main aim is to "divert illicit drug users from incarceration into treatment programs for their addiction." For example, the New South Wales Drug Court orders custodial remand for detoxification and assessment (*Drug Court Act 1998* [NSW] s 8A). The New South Wales Mental Health Review Tribunal is another specialist, quasi-judicial body with jurisdiction to make

decisions about the treatment of people with mental illness with powers that include orders for involuntary detention (*Mental Health Act 2007* [NSW] s 140).

63. An order may be made if there are reasonable grounds to suspect that a person will engage in a terrorist act, will possess a thing that is connected with a terrorist act, or has done an act in preparation for a terrorist act; and making the order would substantially assist in preventing a terrorist attack occurring (*Criminal Code 1995* [Cth] s 105.4[4]). An order can also be made if a terrorist act has occurred within the last 28 days and it is necessary to detain the person to preserve evidence (s 105.21[2]).
64. *Criminal Code 1995* (Cth), s 105.8. The definition of an "issuing authority" is set out in s 100.1(1).
65. There is provision for an unspecified number of twenty-four-hour extensions (*1995* [Cth], s 105.9[2] and 105.10[5]).
66. Specifically, federal court judges and state and territory supreme or district court judges, retired judges, federal magistrates, deputy presidents or the president of the federal Administrative Appeals Tribunal, or legal practitioners of five years' standing (*1995* [Cth], s 105.2[1]).
67. *1995* (Cth), s 105.11.
68. It is an offence for the person to refuse to be detained (s 105.4[6]).
69. *Criminal Code 1995* (Cth) s 105.37.
70. A proposition that the Law Council of Australia described as an "anathema to a system of justice which depends in significant part on the sacrosanct nature of client/lawyer communications," cited in Senate Legal and Constitutional Legislation Committee, Parliament of Australia, *Provisions of the Anti-terrorism Bill (No.2) 2005* (2005) 50.
71. *Criminal Code 1995* (Cth) ss 105.38(1) (5) and 105.50.
72. "Constitutional writs" for judicial review of executive action form part of the High Court's original jurisdiction as set out in the Constitution and cannot be ousted (*Plaintiff S157/2002 v. Commonwealth of Australia* (2003) 211 CLR 476). The *Commonwealth of Australia Constitution Act 1990* s 75(v) guarantees access to the courts where a person may seek a writ of habeas corpus or rely on the common law principles of judicial review of executive decisions (*Ruddock v. Vadarlis* [2001] FCA 1329). However, the Australian High Court has been divided on the matter of the justiciability of national security decision making (*Church of Scientology Inc. v. Woodward* [1982] 154 CLR 25). It has been suggested that substantive matters of national security themselves are inherently nonjusticiable (*Kruger v. Commonwealth* [1997] 190 CLR 1, 162).
73. Administrative Appeals Tribunal, *Security Appeals* (2009), http://www.aat.gov.au/ApplyingToTheAAT/SecurityAppeals.htm (accessed Jan. 25, 2009). It has a Security Appeals Division that reviews Australian Security Intelligence Organization (ASIO) assessments of persons within Australia.

74. *Criminal Code 1995* (Cth) s 105.51(7).
75. *1995* (Cth), s 105.51(2) and 105.52.
76. *1995* (Cth), s 105.36.
77. Within the West Bank, the legal management of detainees is similar but is under military jurisdiction. Preventive detention can be ordered by a local army commander and is subject to appeal to the local military court and then to the Israeli Supreme Court (*Military Order No. 1229* (1998)). It is beyond the scope of this paper to examine decision-making models for detention in areas subject to the principles of the international law of occupation. See Bruce Oswald, "The Law on Military Occupation: Answering the Challenges of Detention during Contemporary Peace Operations?" *Melbourne Journal of International Law* 8 (2007): 311.
78. *Emergency Powers (Detention) Law (EPDL)*, 5739–1979, S.H. 76, 33 L.S.I. 89–92 (Isr. 1979). See generally *Administrative Detention: The Legal Basis for Administrative Detention, Israeli Law,* http://www.btselem.org/English/Administrative_Detention/Israeli_Law.asp.
79. Amos N. Guiora, "Where Are Terrorists to Be Tried—A Comparative Analysis of Rights Granted to Suspected Terrorists" (working paper 07-13, *Case Research Paper Series in Legal Studies*, March 2007, 16–23).
80. 119 Stat. 2740. Detainees were initially held under the terms of a presidential order: "Detention, Treatment, and Trial of Certain Non-citizens in the War Against Terrorism," Presidential Military Order, Nov. 13 2001, 66 *Federal Register* 57833. Concerning restrictions on the military detention of citizens, see *Hamdi v. Rumsfeld*, 542 U.S. 507 (2004).
81. U.S. Government, Department of Defense, *Combatant Status Review Tribunal Process* (2006), http://www.defenselink.mil/news/Aug2006/d20060809CSRTProcedures.pdf (accessed Jan. 28, 2009).
82. Nearly 800 detainees have been detained at Guantanamo Bay at some time, and a second round of CSRT appeal review board decisions in 2007 decided that of those 572 Guantanamo detainees (being held or whose records were publicly accessible), 273 required continued detention. Others were cleared for release or for transfer to their countries of nationality, primarily Saudi Arabia and Britain. Groups of Afghans and Yemenis continue to be held because their home countries are not considered able to neutralize the threat these persons pose. About 80 of the detainees are being held pending trial. See Benjamin Wittes, *Law and the Long War: The Future of Justice in the Age of Terror* (New York: Penguin Press, 2008), 79.
83. *Detainee Treatment Act of 2005,* 119 Stat. 2740. The Act was introduced to bring national practice into conformity with the ruling of the U.S. Supreme Court in *Rasul v. Bush,* 542 U.S. 466 (2004).
84. 542 U.S. 507 (2004).
85. 542 U.S. 466 (2004). The *Detainee Treatment Act of 2005,* 119 Stat. 2740, s 1005(e), amended the *United States Code,* title 28, s 2241. See also Fiona de Londras, "The

on US Detention of Suspected Terrorists," *Journal of Conflict & Security Law* 12 (2007): 223, 226–27.
86. 128 S. Ct. 2229 (2008).
87. Wittes, *Law and the Long War*, 151 ff (cited supra, n. 82).
88. Ibid., 164–65.
89. Commission on Legal Procedures to Deal with Terrorist Activities in Northern Ireland, *Report of the Commission to Consider Legal Procedures to Deal with Terrorist Activities in Northern Ireland* (1972) Cmnd 5185; *Northern Ireland (Emergency Provisions) Act 1973* (c. 53). See also Laura K. Donohue, "Terrorism and Trial by Jury: The Vices and Virtues of British and American Criminal Law," *Stanford Law Review* 59 (2007): 1321, 1326; Steven Greer and Anthony White, *Abolishing the Diplock Courts: The Case for Restoring Jury Trial to Scheduled Offences in Northern Ireland* (Cobden Trust, 1986).
90. *R v. Boutrab* [2005] N. Ireland Criminal Court 36.
91. *Justice and Security (Northern Ireland) Act 2007 (c. 6)*. For exceptional cases that meet set conditions relating to terrorism, the Director of Public Prosecutions for Northern Ireland may issue a certificate that still requires trial without a jury.
92. Harding, 9 (cited supra, n. 53).
93. Wittes, *Law and the Long War*, 165 (cited supra, n. 82). The Foreign Intelligence Security Court was established in 1978 to oversee covert surveillance conducted for the purposes of national security within the United States, giving judicial consideration to the issue of warrants to secretly monitor the activities of U.S. persons. A similar function is discharged in Australia by the Commonwealth Administrative Appeals Tribunal.
94. Except for those involving liberation organizations subscribing under Additional Protocol I, art. 85.2. These include combatants who do not wear a uniform or carry their weapons openly (art. 44).
95. GCIV, art. 3(1)(d). Serious violations of art. 3.1(d) may be prosecuted by the International Criminal Court: ICC Statute, art. 8.2(c)(iv). Also prohibited under Common Article 3 are "(a) violence to life and person, in particular murder of all kinds, mutilation, cruel treatment and torture; (b) taking of hostages; and (c) outrages upon personal dignity, in particular, humiliating and degrading treatment."
96. However, they have not prescribed how human rights norms are to be implemented during hostilities. John Tobin, "Seeking Clarity in Relation to the Principle of Complementarity: Reflections on the Recent Contributions of Some International Bodies," *Melbourne Journal of International Law* 8 (2007): 356.
97. *R (Al-Jedda) v. Secretary of State for Defense* [2006] EWCA Civ 327 was decided in relation to military operations by the United Kingdom in Iraq, as authorized by the U.N. Security Council, and as impacted by human rights norms binding on the United Kingdom under the *Convention for the Protection of Human Rights and*

Fundamental Freedoms, opened for signature November 4, 1950, 213 UNTS 221 (entered into force September 3, 1953).
98. Wittes, *Law and the Long War*, 165 (cited supra, n. 82).
99. Ibid.
100. Harding, 9 (cited supra, n. 53).
101. In dispensing with a jury, the judicial panel might be compared with the panel that decides a court martial or a combatant status review. For example, a criminal trial under Scottish law but without a jury was employed also in the Lockerbie bombing case in 2001 to try the alleged bombers of Pan Am 103. In decision making on preventive detention, however, constraints in national constitutional jurisprudence requiring the separation of judicial and executive powers would need to be considered.
102. *Copenhagen Post*, "'Progress' Made in International Detainee Policy," June 17, 2009, http://www.cphpost.dk/news/international/89-international/45982-progress-made-in-international-detainee-policy.html (accessed Nov. 30, 2009).

3. "Jousting at Windmills"

1. Mabel F. Wheaton, *The Ingenious Gentleman, Don Quixote of La Mancha* by Miguel de Cervantes Saavedra, John Ormsby trans., VI, Ch. VI: "Of the good fortune which the valiant Don Quixote had in the terrible and undreamt-of adventure of the windmills, with other occurrences worthy to be fitly recorded" (Boston: Ginn and Company, 1893) 34.
2. As stated in the *Operational Law Handbook* (2006): "The fundamental purposes of the law of war are humanitarian and functional in nature. The humanitarian purposes include: (1) protecting both combatants and noncombatants from unnecessary suffering; (2) safeguarding the fundamental human rights of persons who fall into the hands of the enemy; (3) facilitating the restoration of peace. The functional purposes include (1) ensuring good order and discipline; (2) fighting in a disciplined manner consistent with national values; and (3) maintaining domestic and international public support.
3. François Bugnion, "The Role of the Red Cross in the Development of International Humanitarian Law: The International Committee of the Red Cross and the Development of International Humanitarian Law," *Chicago Journal of International Law* 5 (2004): 200.
4. Cervantes, Book I, Ch. XLV.
5. Curtiss F. J. Doebbler, *Introduction to International Humanitarian Law* (Washington, DC: CD Publishing, 2005), 36.
6. Jefferson D. Reynolds, "Collateral Damage on the 21st Century Battlefield: Enemy Exploitation of the Law of Armed Conflict and the Struggle for a Moral High Ground," *The Air Force Law Review* 56 (2005): 15–16.

7. Curtiss F. J. Doebbler, *Introduction to International Humanitarian Law* (Washington, DC: CD Publishing, 2005), 47.
8. George H. Aldrich, "The Hague Peace Conferences: The Laws of War on Land," *American Journal of International Law* 94 (2000): 46.
9. US Army Field Manual 27-10, *The Law of Land Warfare*, Department of the Army, Washington, DC, July 18, 1956, para. 3
10. T. McCormack and A. McDonald, *Yearbook of International Law* (Cambridge: Cambridge University Press, 2004), 41–42.
11. Michael Scheimer, "Separating Private Military Companies from Illegal Mercenaries in International Law: Proposing an International Convention or Legitimate Military and Security Support that Reflects Customary International Law," *American University International Law Review* 24 (2009): 617–18.
12. Additional Protocol I of 1977 to the Geneva Conventions of 1949, opened for signature December 12, 1977, art. 43, 1125 U.N.T.S. 3–608 (1979).
13. Ibid.
14. George H. Aldrich, "The Hague Peace Conferences," 42.
15. Additional Protocol I of 1977 to the Geneva Conventions of 1949, opened for signature December 12, 1977, art. 50, 1125 U.N.T.S. 3–608 (1979).
16. Aldrich, "The Hague Peace Conferences," 51.
17. Additional Protocol I of 1977 to the Geneva Conventions of 1949, opened for signature December 12, 1977, art. 44, 1125 U.N.T.S. 3–608 (1979).
18. J. Ricou Heaton, "Civilians at War: Reexamining the Status of Civilians Accompanying the Armed Forces," *The Air Force Law Review* 57 (2005): 170.
19. Cervantes, Book II, Ch. XXII.
20. It should be noted that this temporal requirement is one of the reasons that Israel has, to this day, refused to accede to Additional Protocol I.
21. Incarceration of Unlawful Combatants Law, 5762–2002.
22. Ibid., art. 2.
23. It should be noted that the IUCL does not specifically state that the authority of detention granted to the chief of staff is unlimited. However, a reading of the IUCL's articles, in combination, clearly sets out that detained individuals may be held until such time as the Israeli authorities determine either that the hostilities with their parent organization have ceased or that the individual in question no longer poses a security threat.
24. See Antonio Cassese, *International Criminal Law* (Cambridge: Cambridge University Press, 2008), 407, 470.
25. HCJ 769/02 *The Public Committee Against Torture in Israel v. The Government of Israel*.
26. Ibid. It thus appears that international law must adapt itself to the era in which we are living. In light of the data presented before us, President Barak proposes

to perform the adaptation within the framework of the existing law, which recognizes, in his opinion, two categories—combatants and civilians. ... As stated, other approaches are possible. I do not find a need to expand on them, since in light of the rules of interpretation proposed by President Barak, the theoretical distinction loses its sting. Vice President E. Rivein, concurrent judgment.
27. HCJ 769/02 *The Public Committee Against Torture in Israel v. The Government of Israel*.
28. Criminal Appeal 6659/06 *A and B v. The State of Israel*.
29. Ibid.
30. *Ex parte Quirin*, 317 U.S. 1 (1942).
31. Ibid., 30–31.
32. Pub. L. 107–40, 115 Stat. 224.
33. Detention, Treatment, and Trial of Certain Non-citizens in the War Against Terrorism, 60 Fed. Reg. 222 (Nov. 16, 2001).
34. US drops "Enemy Combatant Term," BBC News, March 13, 2009, http://news.bbc.co.uk/2/hi/americas/7943114.stm; Randall Mikkelson, "Guantanamo Inmates No Longer 'Enemy Combatants,'" *Reuters*, March 14, 2009; Guantanamo Bay Detainee Litigation, "Declaration of Attorney General Eric H. Holder, Jr." http://www.scotusblog.com/wp/wp-content/uploads/2009/03/holder-declaration-3-13-09.pdf.
35. Scotus Blog, "Department of Justice Withdraws 'Enemy Combatant' Definition," http://www.scotusblog.com/wp/wp-content/uploads/2009/03/doj-news-release-detainees-3-13-09.doc.
36. Cervantes, Book II, Ch. LXXIV.
37. International Committee of the Red Cross, *Interpretive Guidance on the Notion of Direct Participation in Hostilities Under International Humanitarian Law*, ICRC, May 2009.
38. Protocol Additional to the Geneva Conventions of August 12, 1949, and relating to the Protection of Victims of Non-international Armed Conflicts (Protocol II), June 8, 1977.
39. Cervantes, Book II, Ch. LXXII.
40. HCJ 320/80 *Kawasmeh v. The Minister of Defense*.

4. Direct Participation in Hostilities

1. A recent study estimates that the percentage of civilian casualties during armed conflict has risen steadily in the twentieth century, from 19 percent in World War I to 48 percent in World War II and to 90 percent in the armed conflicts of the 1990s. Ronald R. Lett, Olive Chifefe Kobusingye, and Paul Ekwaru, "Burden of Injury During the Complex Political Emergency in Northern Uganda," *Canadian Journal*

of Surgery 49(1): 51 (February 2006), http://www.cma.ca/multimedia/staticContent/HTML/N0/l2/cjs/vol-49/issue-1/pdf/pg51.pdf (accessed Oct. 1, 2009).
2. For example, see Richard D. Rosen, "Targeting Enemy Forces in the War on Terror: Preserving Civilian Immunity," *Vanderbilt Journal of Transnational Law* 42 (May 2009): 683.
3. Ibid., 690.
4. See table 3.1, p. 82.
5. See chapter 3, p. 82.
6. International Institute of Humanitarian Law, *The Manual on the Law of Non-international Armed Conflict* (hereinafter "NIAC Manual") (San Remo, Italy: International Institute of Humanitarian Law, March 2006), 10, and A. P. V. Rogers, *Law on the Battlefield*, 2nd ed. (Manchester, UK: Manchester University Press, 2004), 3 ("The great principles of customary law, from which all else stems, are those of military necessity, humanity, distinction and proportionality."). Even though this provision is stated in GPI, it is recognized to apply to both international and noninternational armed conflicts. *Prosecutor v. Tadić*, "Decision on the Defence Motion for Interlocutory Appeal on Jurisdiction," IT-94-1 (Appeals Chamber of the International Criminal Tribunal for the Former Yugoslavia 1995), ¶¶102–04, where the appellate chamber opined that the principle of distinction was so fundamental to the conduct of hostilities that it applied equally to all armed conflicts.
7. J. Ricou Heaton, "Civilians at War: Reexamining the Status of Civilians Accompanying the Armed Forces," *Air Force Law Review* 57 (2005): 168.
8. Ibid., 180.
9. Thomas M. Franck, "On Proportionality of Countermeasures in International Law," *American Journal of International Law* 102 (October 2008): 726.
10. "Protocol Additional to the Geneva Conventions of 12 August 1949, and relating to the Protection of Victims of International Armed Conflicts (Protocol I)" (hereinafter "GPI"), June 8, 1977, art. 48, http://www.icrc.org/IHL.NSF/FULL/470?OpenDocument (accessed Oct. 30, 2009).
11. Ibid., arts. 43–44.
12. Yoram Dinstein, "Unlawful Combatancy," *International Law Studies* 79 (2003): 167–70. Although the United States has signed but not ratified either of the 1977 Protocols, Michael Matheson made a statement that describes the provisions to which the United States has objections. Michael J. Matheson, "The United States Position on the Relation of Customary Law to the 1977 Protocols Additional to the 1949 Geneva Conventions," *American University Journal of International Law and Policy* 2 (1987): 419.
13. Derek Jinks notes that the "real purchase of POW status is combatant immunity and not the procedural rights protections attaching to the designation." Derek Jinks, "Symposium: The Changing Laws of War: Do We Need a New Legal Regime

After September 11?: Protective Parity and the Laws of War," *Notre Dame Law Review* 79 (July 2004): 1520.
14. Major W. James Annexstad, "The Detention and Prosecution of Insurgents and Other Non-traditional Combatants—A Look at the Task Force 134 Process and the Future of Detainee Prosecutions," *Army Lawyer* 2007 (July 2007): 72.
15. Ibid.
16. See Eric Talbot Jensen, "Combatant Status: It is Time for Intermediate Levels of Recognition for Partial Compliance," *Virginia Journal of International Law* 46 (Fall 2005): 214.
17. "Convention (III) relative to the Treatment of Prisoners of War" (hereinafter "GPW"), August 12, 1949, http://www.icrc.org/ihl.nsf/FULL/375?OpenDocument (accessed Oct. 30, 2009). Article 4 states: "Prisoners of war, in the sense of the present Convention, are persons belonging to one of the following categories, who have fallen into the power of the enemy: "(1) Members of the armed forces of a Party to the conflict, as well as members of militias or volunteer corps forming part of such armed forces."(2) Members of other militias and members of other volunteer corps, including those of organized resistance movements, belonging to a Party to the conflict and operating in or outside their own territory, even if this territory is occupied, provided that such militias or volunteer corps, including such organized resistance movements, fulfill the following conditions:"(a) that of being commanded by a person responsible for his subordinates;"(b) that of having a fixed distinctive sign recognizable at a distance;"(c) that of carrying arms openly;"(d) that of conducting their operations in accordance with the laws and customs of war."(3) Members of regular armed forces who profess allegiance to a government or an authority not recognized by the Detaining Power."(4) Persons who accompany the armed forces without actually being members thereof, such as civilian members of military aircraft crews, war correspondents, supply contractors, members of labour units or of services responsible for the welfare of the armed forces, provided that they have received authorization, from the armed forces which they accompany, who shall provide them for that purpose with an identity card similar to the annexed model."(5) Members of crews, including masters, pilots and apprentices, of the merchant marine and the crews of civil aircraft of the Parties to the conflict, who do not benefit by more favourable treatment under any other provisions of international law."(6) Inhabitants of a non-occupied territory, who on the approach of the enemy spontaneously take up arms to resist the invading forces, without having had time to form themselves into regular armed units, provided they carry arms openly and respect the laws and customs of war."
18. Dinstein, "Unlawful Combatancy," 157–60.
19. Ibid., 171–74.

20. *Ex parte Quirin*, 317 U.S. 1 (1942). See also Richard Baxter, "So-called 'Unprivileged Belligerency': Spies, Guerrillas, and Saboteurs," *British Yearbook of International Law* 28 (1951): 323.
21. "Instructions for the Government of Armies of the United States in the Field," April 24, 1863, http://www.icrc.org/IHL.NSF/FULL/110?OpenDocument (accessed October 30, 2009). The Code states:

    "Art. 20. Public war is a state of armed hostility between sovereign nations or governments. It is a law and requisite of civilized existence that men live in political, continuous societies, forming organized units, called states or nations, whose constituents bear, enjoy, suffer, advance and retrograde together, in peace and in war. "Art. 21. The citizen or native of a hostile country is thus an enemy, as one of the constituents of the hostile state or nation, and as such is subjected to the hardships of the war. "Art. 22. Nevertheless, as civilization has advanced during the last centuries, so has likewise steadily advanced, especially in war on land, the distinction between the private individual belonging to a hostile country and the hostile country itself, with its men in arms. The principle has been more and more acknowledged that the unarmed citizen is to be spared in person, property, and honor as much as the exigencies of war will admit. "Art. 23. Private citizens are no longer murdered, enslaved, or carried off to distant parts, and the inoffensive individual is as little disturbed in his private relations as the commander of the hostile troops can afford to grant in the overruling demands of a vigorous war.

    "Art. 24. The almost universal rule in remote times was, and continues to be with barbarous armies, that the private individual of the hostile country is destined to suffer every privation of liberty and protection, and every disruption of family ties. Protection was, and still is with uncivilized people, the exception.

    "Art. 25. In modern regular wars of the Europeans, and their descendants in other portions of the globe, protection of the inoffensive citizen of the hostile country is the rule; privation and disturbance of private relations are the exceptions."

22. "Convention (IV) relative to the Protection of Civilian Persons in Time of War" (hereinafter "GCC"), August 12, 1949, http://www.icrc.org/IHL.NSF/FULL/380?OpenDocument (accessed October 30, 2009).
23. Ibid., art. 4.
24. GPI, and "Protocol Additional to the Geneva Conventions of 12 August 1949, and relating to the Protections of Victims of Non-International Armed Conflicts (Protocol II)" (hereinafter "GPII"), June 8, 1977, http://www.icrc.org/IHL.NSF/FULL/475?OpenDocument (accessed October 30, 2009).

25. GPI applies to "all cases of declared war or of any other armed conflict which may arise between two or more of the High Contracting Parties, even if the state of war is not recognized by one of them. The Convention shall also apply to all cases of partial or total occupation of the territory of a High Contracting Party, even if the said occupation meets with no armed resistance." GCC, art. 2. It also includes "armed conflicts in which peoples are fighting against colonial domination and alien occupation and against racist regimes in the exercise of their right of self-determination, as enshrined in the Charter of the United Nations and the Declaration on Principles of International Law concerning Friendly Relations and Co-operation among States in accordance with the Charter of the United Nations." GPI, art. 1.4. In contrast, art. 1 of GPII states the following concerning its application:

> "1. This Protocol, which develops and supplements art. 3 common to the Geneva Conventions of 12 August 1949 without modifying its existing conditions of application, shall apply to all armed conflicts which are not covered by art. 1 of the Protocol Additional to the Geneva Conventions of 12 August 1949, and relating to the Protection of Victims of International Armed Conflicts (Protocol I) and which take place in the territory of a High Contracting Party between its armed forces and dissident armed forces or other organized armed groups which, under responsible command, exercise such control over a part of its territory as to enable them to carry out sustained and concerted military operations and to implement this Protocol."2. This Protocol shall not apply to situations of internal disturbances and tensions, such as riots, isolated and sporadic acts of violence and other acts of a similar nature, as not being armed conflicts."

26. GPI, art. 50.
27. Ibid.
28. Nathan A. Canestro, "'Small Wars' and the Law: Options for Prosecuting the Insurgents in Iraq," *Columbia Journal of Transnational Law* 43 (2004): 85.
29. The International Criminal Tribunal for the Former Yugoslavia supports this view. This is seen, for example, in *Prosecutor v. Galic,* IT-98–29-I, "Indictment," 4–6.
30. See *CNN Live Sunday*: "U.S. Helicopter Shot Down in Iraq, Both Pilots Killed; 7 Chinese Citizens Taken Hostage in Iraq," April 11, 2004 (News File 041104CN.V36 on LexisNexis), where interviewee Kelly McCann says: "We are working at a disadvantage.... The lack of uniforms, so that you can't define the enemy very well. And the intertwining of the enemy with combatants is very, very difficult. So you've got combatants and non-combatants mixed together intentionally.... [I]f you think about just the way that, for instance, the Shi'ias could basically in this area right here, thousands of pilgrims on their way into this region right here, and the mili-

tia being able to just take off the black uniforms, and blend right in, into all those pilgrims."

31. "Commentary on the Additional Protocols of 8 June 1977 to the Geneva Conventions of 12 August 1949" (hereinafter "Commentary"), comments on art. 51.3 of Protocol I, ¶1942, http://www.icrc.org/ihl.nsf/COM/470-750065?OpenDocument (accessed October 30, 2009).
32. Ibid., ¶1943.
33. Ibid., ¶1944.
34. Note that this chapter only deals with targeting standards, not with treatment standards, which do not correspond in every case.
35. GPI, art. 51.3.
36. Ibid., art. 51.7.
37. Ibid., art. 51.3.
38. See, for example, Michael N. Schmitt, "War, International Law, and Sovereignty: Reevaluating the Rules of the Game in a New Century: Humanitarian Law and Direct Participation in Hostilities by Private Contractors or Civilian Employees," *Chicago Journal of International Law* 5 (Winter 2005): 535-36.
39. There is no doubt that the nations who met during the 1970s and prepared GPI and GPII understood clearly the intermixing of fighting forces with civilians. As will be discussed in Part III, their approach was a juridical one, leading to a framework that has not been successful in incentivizing fighters to comply with the law of war, but rather has had the exact opposite effect.
40. See table 3.1, p. 82.
41. "Commentary," ¶1944.
42. To illustrate this point, assume that the military receives an intelligence report that a number of civilians are meeting at a specified location to discuss plans for a later series of attacks that will be carried out by these individuals in different locations at different times. The timeliness of the information does not allow for a military operation with the capabilities to detain those individuals, but the capability exists to target them. Pursuant to the Commentary analysis, the civilian fighters would retain their immunity from attack. Again, such scenarios add fuel to the fire of those who call for a redesignation of these fighters to be attacked.
43. International Committee of the Red Cross (hereinafter "ICRC"), "Interpretive Guidance on the Notion of Direct Participation in Hostilities under International Humanitarian Law" (hereinafter "DPH Guidance") (May 2009), 8-9, http://www.icrc.org/Web/eng/siteeng0.nsf/htmlall/direct-participation-report_res/$File/direct-participation-guidance-2009-icrc.pdf (accessed October 30 2009).
44. Ibid., 70.
45. Ibid., 67.
46. Ibid., 46.

4. DIRECT PARTICIPATION IN HOSTILITIES   241

47. Ibid., 54.
48. Ibid., 44–45 (citations omitted).
49. Lieutenant Colonel Mark S. Martins, "Deadly Force Is Authorized, but Also Trained," *Army Law* 25(1) (September/October 2001): 4–5.
50. For example, despite United Nations Security Council Resolutions 1368 (2001) and 1373 (2001) as well as the Statement of the North Atlantic Council on September 12, 2001, the International Court of Justice determined in both the *Wall* case and the *Uganda* case that armed attacks could only come from state forces, not irregular forces. See "Legal Consequences of the Construction of a Wall in the Occupied Palestinian Territory, Advisory Opinion," 2004 I.C.J. 131, (2004), ¶139, http://www.icj-cij.org/docket/files/131/1671.pdf?PHPSESSID=eea3e1c25a59cce2ac94fae955a50764 (accessed October 28, 2009) and "Case Concerning Armed Activities on the Territory of the Congo" (*International Court of Justice, Democratic Republic of the Congo v. Uganda,* Order of December 19, 2005), ¶53, http://www.icj-cij.org/docket/files/116/10455.pdf (accessed November 4, 2009).
51. ICRC, "DPH Guidance," 22.
52. Ibid., 23–24 states: "Groups engaging in organized armed violence against a party to an international armed conflict without belonging to another party to the same conflict cannot be regarded as members of the armed forces of a party to that conflict, whether under Additional Protocol I, the Hague Regulations, or the Geneva Conventions. They are thus civilians under those three instruments. Any other view would discard the dichotomy in all armed conflicts between the armed forces of the parties to the conflict and the civilian population; it would also contradict the definition of international armed conflicts as confrontations between States and not between States and non-state actors."
53. ICRC, "DPH Guidance," 26, argues that "Membership in irregularly constituted militia and volunteer corps, including organized resistance movements, belonging to a party to the conflict must be determined based on the same functional criteria that apply to organized armed groups in non-international armed conflict."
54. Ibid., 35.
55. Ibid., 34–35 states (citations omitted): "[R]ecruiters, trainers, financiers and propagandists may continuously contribute to the general war effort of a non-state party, but they are not members of an organized armed group belonging to that party unless their function additionally includes activities amounting to direct participation in hostilities. The same applies to individuals whose function is limited to the purchasing, smuggling, manufacturing and maintaining of weapons and other equipment outside of specific military operations or to the collection of intelligence other than of a tactical nature."
56. Ibid., 33.
57. *Military Commissions Act of 2006, U.S. Code* 10 (2006), § 948a(1)(i) and (ii).

58. *Military Commissions Act of 2009, U.S. Code* 10 (2009), § 948a(7)(B).
59. *In re Guantanamo Bay Detainee Litigation,* Misc. No. 08–442 (TFH), "Respondents' Memorandum regarding the Government's Detention Authority Relative to Detainees Held at Guantanamo Bay" (filed March 13, 2009), 1–3, www.usdoj.gov/opa/documents/memo-re-det-auth.pdf (accessed November 5, 2009).
60. See chapter 3, p. 89.
61. See Geoffrey S. Corn and Eric Talbot Jensen, "Transnational Armed Conflict: A 'Principled' Approach to the Regulation of Counterterror Combat Operations," *Israel Law Review* 42(1) (2009): 46.
62. See, for example, the NIAC Manual referenced earlier in note 6.
63. See Geoffrey S. Corn and Eric Talbot Jensen, "Untying the Gordian Knott: A Proposal for Determining Applicability of the Laws of War to the War on Terror," *Temple Law Review* 81 (Fall 2008): 787.
64. Exceptions to this are if members of the organization are *hors de combat* either because of wounds or because they are medical or religious personnel. "Convention (I) for the Amelioration of the Condition of the Wounded and Sick in Armed Forces in the Field. Geneva, 12 August 1949" (hereinafter "GWS"), arts. 24 and 25, http://www.icrc.org/ihl.nsf/FULL/365?OpenDocument (accessed November 4, 2009); and GPW, art. 3.1.
65. See GPW, art. 4.
66. See GPI, art. 50.
67. "Commentary," ¶1942.
68. These requirements are discussed on p. 89.
69. Of course, not all members of the military are targetable. Persons "exclusively engaged in the search for, or the collection, transport, or treatment of the wounded or sick" are non-combatants as well as religious personnel such as chaplains. GWS, art. 24. A similar rule would apply to irregular forces. But all others who are members of the force have surrendered their civilian status as part of the organization they have embraced.

5. Nonstate Actors in Armed Conflicts

1. Article 48 of the Additional Protocol I to the Geneva Conventions provides that "in order to ensure respect for and protection of the civilian population and civilian objects, the Parties to the conflict shall at all times distinguish between the civilian population and combatants and between civilians objects and military objectives and accordingly shall direct their operations only against military objectives."
2. The International Court of Justice has declared the principle of distinction a "cardinal principle constituting the fabric of humanitarian law." See *Legality of the Threat or Use of Nuclear Weapons,* International Court of Justice (Advisory Opin-

ion) (1996), para. 78. It has also been recognized as a rule of customary law applicable to all states, even to those who have not ratified the Protocol, by the International Criminal Tribunal for the Former Yugoslavia and the Inter-American Court of Human Rights. For more information see, Jean-Marie Henckaerts and Louise Doswald-Beck, *Customary International Humanitarian Law, Volume 1: Rules*, International Committee of the Red Cross (New York: Cambridge University Press, 2005), 7–8.

3. See Jensen, p. 87.
4. Jean Pictet, *Commentary: Geneva Convention III Relative to the Treatment of Prisoners of War* (International Committee of the Red Cross, 1960), 52 (hereinafter "Pictet Commentary"). At the time of drafting of Article 4, the discussion focused on whether partisans (or resistance movements) would have to meet more conditions than ordinary combatants in order to be granted prisoner-of-war status or whether such conditions should be somewhat relaxed to enable them to accede to such status. After much heated debate, it was decided to assimilate resistance movements to militias and corps of volunteers not forming part of the armed forces of a party to the conflict—a move that was regarded as an "important innovation which has become necessary as a result of the experience of the Second World War." (See Committee II, Third Meeting, April 27, 1949, Prisoner of War Convention, at 242s; and Report of Committee II to the Plenary Assembly of the Diplomatic Conference of Geneva, at 561.) That the Article was meant primarily to address the question of the legal status of partisans under the laws of war is also apparent from the fact that the Pictet Commentary not only addresses subparagraph (2) of Article 4 under the heading "Partisans," but also repeatedly refers to partisans in its analysis of the provision.
5. See Protocol Additional to the Geneva Conventions of 12 August 1949, and relating to the Protection of Victims of International Armed Conflicts ("Additional Protocol I"), Article 53(1); and Nils Melzer, *Interpretive Guidance on the Notion of Direct Participation in Hostilities under International Humanitarian Law* (Geneva, Switzerland, International Committee of the Red Cross, 2009).
6. That contractors are often regarded as a proxy of the hiring state is evident in the attacks suffered by companies over the years. In 1995 a car bomb exploded in one of the Saudi National Guards' training facilities in Riyadh. Seven employees of Vinnell died, including five American nationals. The attack is widely regarded as having been directed specifically at Vinnell's Guard training contract. The company was once again targeted in 2003, when several suicide car bombs went off near a Vinnell housing compound, and in 2005, when the company's compound in Riyadh was attacked by al-Qaeda affiliates. The repeated attacks against Vinnell illustrate the fact that the company is regarded by the enemy as an extension of the U.S. Army in Saudi Arabia, designed to advance key strategic goals of the United States.

7. Matthew J. Gaul, "Regulating the New Privateers: Private Military Service Contracting and the Modern Marque and Reprisal Clause," *Loyola of Los Angeles International & Comparative Law Review* 31 (1998): 1489; and William Hartung, "Mercenaries, Inc.: How a U.S. Company Props Up the House of Saud," *The Progressive*, April 1996. Vinnell employees also accompanied the SANG into combat at first major ground engagement of the Gulf War—the battle of Khafji (see Esther Schrader, "U.S. Companies Hired to Train Foreign Armies," *Los Angeles Times*, April 14, 2002).
8. John Mcquaid, "Citizens, Not Soldiers," *The Times Picayune*, November 11, 2003 (the hostages—Stansell, Marc Gonsalves, and Thomas Howes—were captured by the guerrillas when their surveillance plane crashed on February 13, 2003. American pilot Tom Janis and Colombian Army Sgt. Luis Alcides Cruz were shot and killed by FARC forces).
9. Consider, for example, the shooting of innocent civilians mistaken for terrorists, including that of Brazilian Jean Charles de Mennezes in London in July 2005 by the British police, following attacks on London's transportation system.
10. Geneva Convention III on the Treatment of Prisoners of War (1949) ("Third Geneva Convention"), Article 4.
11. Article 48 of Additional Protocol I, see supra, n. 1.
12. Geoffrey Best, *War and Law Since 1945* (Oxford: Clarendon Press, 1994), 24.
13. Michael Walzer, *Just and Unjust Wars* (New York: Basic Books, 2000), 42 ("[T]he general conception of war as a combat between combatants . . . turns up again and again in anthropological and historical accounts."
14. See Best, supra, n.12, 257.
15. Deut. 20:1.
16. Deut. 20:12–14.
17. Waldemar A. Solf, "Protection of Civilians Against the Effects of Hostilities Under Customary International Law and Under Protocol I," *American University Journal of International Law and Policy* 1 (1986): 117, 118 (citing Majid Khadduri, *War and Peace in the Law of Islam* (1955) 102); and Alan Rosas, *The Legal Status of Prisoners of War: A Study in International Humanitarian Law Applicable in Armed Conflicts* (Helsinki : Suoma Lainen Tiedeakatemia, 1976, reprinted 2005), 48.
18. See, generally, Saint Augustine, *City of God* (New York: Penguin Books, 1972).
19. Thomas Aquinas, *The Summa Theologica* (c. 1265), Question XL, Sixth Article.
20. Although I do not consider it in this chapter, it is certainly the case that combatant status has been characterized from the very early days by the sovereign's grant of authority to wage war. This point is appropriately noted by Jensen (p. 88) as constituting one of the main characteristics of combatant status.
21. See, for example, Synod of Charroux (989), available at http://www.fordham.edu/halsall/source/pc-of-god.html.

22. Hugo Grotius, *The Rights of War and Peace*, Books 1–3 (Natural Law and Enlightenment Classics, Indianapolis: Liberty Funds, Inc., 2005), 1439–45.
23. Jean Pictet, *Development and Principles in International Humanitarian Law* (Leiden: Martinus Nijhoff Publishers, 1985), 9.
24. Jean-Jacques Rousseau, *Du Contrat Social* (Ronald Grimsley ed., 1972) (1762), 111 (translation provided by author; emphasis added).
25. *Instructions for the Government of Armies of the United States in the Field,* General Orders No. 100 (April 24, 1863) (hereinafter "the Code" or "the Lieber Code").
26. Lieber Code, Article 155.
27. See, for example, the St. Petersburg Declaration of 1868, Declaration Renouncing the Use, in Time of War, of Explosive Projectiles Under 400 Grammes Weight (November 29, 1868), reprinted in *The Laws of Armed Conflicts: A Collection of Conventions, Resolutions and Other Documents*, eds., Dietrich Schindler and Jiri Toman, 4th Ed. (Leiden: Martinus Nijhoff Publishers, 2004), 91; the Brussels Declaration of 1874, Project of an International Declaration Concerning the Laws and Customs of War, Article 9 (August 27, 1874), reprinted in *The Laws of Armed Conflicts*, (hereinafter "Brussels Declaration"); Institute of International Law's Oxford Manual of 1880 [Laws of War on Land (September 9, 1880)], Articles 4 and 33; Convention (IV) respecting the Laws and Customs of War on Land and its annex: Regulations concerning the Laws and Customs of War on Land (October 18, 1907), available at http://www.icrc.org/ihl.nsf/385ec082b509e76c41256739003e636d/1d1726425f6955aec125641e0038bfd6; the 1907 Hague Regulations (Convention (IV) respecting the Laws and Customs of War on Land and its annex: Regulations concerning the Laws and Customs of War on Land (October 18, 1907), available at http://www.icrc.org/IHL.NSF/INTRO/195?OpenDocument ("Hague Regulations"); and the Hague Rules of Air Warfare of 1923 (Rules concerning the Control of Wireless Telegraphy in Time of War and Air Warfare, December 1922–February 1923, available at http://www.icrc.org/ihl.nsf/INTRO/275?OpenDocument, Articles 13, 16, and 34.
28. Hague Regulations, supra, n. 27, Article 3.
29. Geneva modified the Hague detention regime, distinguishing POWs from retained personnel of the armed forces (i.e., chaplains and medical personnel), see Convention (I) for the Amelioration of the Condition of the Wounded and Sick in Armed Forces in the Field, August 12, 1949. Art. 28, provides that "Personnel designated in Articles 24 (medical personnel) and 26 (staff of volunteer aid societies, including ICRC) who fall into the hands of the adverse Party, shall be retained only in so far as the state of health, the spiritual needs and the number of prisoners of war require. Personnel thus retained shall not be deemed prisoners of war."
30. Jensen supports this evolution toward a strictly membership-based approach ("To limit targeting to only those who perform a fighting function within a fighting

force does not account for the workings of a modern fighting organization that requires funding, supplies, training, and a host of other logistical support" [p. 99, this volume]; "[t]he premise that soldiers could traverse the battlefield without fear of being attacked so long as they did not act in a way openly harmful to the enemy has no basis in humanitarian law. Once an individual joins a nation's armed forces, even as a cook or court reporter, he or she immediately becomes targetable by the enemy" [p. 101, this volume]).

31. Third Geneva Convention, supra, n. 10.
32. Jensen, p. 89, this volume.
33. Third Geneva Convention, supra, n. 10, Article 4.
34. See note 4.
35. Henckaerts and Doswald-Beck, supra, n. 2.
36. Anthony Rogers, "Combatant Status" in *Perspectives on the ICRC Study on Customary International Humanitarian Law,* eds. Elizabeth Wilmshurst and Susane Breau (Cambridge: Cambridge University Press, 2008) (doubting whether Article 43 of Additional Protocol I has become customary international law).
37. Henckaerts and Doswald-Beck, supra, n. 2.
38. Incidentally, extending IHL protections to as many people as possible was one of the declared goals of the Geneva Conventions. See, generally, Commander Gregory Noone, "Prisoners of War in the 21st Century: Issues in Modern Warfare," *Naval Law Review* 50 (2004): 1, at 13; Pictet Commentary, supra, n. 4, at 38; Stanislaw Nahlik, "L'Extension du Statut de Combatant à la Lumière du Protocol I de Genève de 1977," *Recueil des Cours* (1979), 213; Diplomatic Conference, Prisoner of War, Third Meeting, April 27, 1949, p. 242; Hungarian Delegation, Joint Committee on Common Articles, First Meeting, p. 11; and Delegation of Netherlands, CDDH/SR. 41 (41st plenary meeting, May 26, 1977, p. 142).
39. Geneva Convention III on the Treatment of Prisoners of War (1949) ("Third Geneva Convention"), Article 4 (emphasis added).
40. Geneva Convention III, Article 4(a)(2) and Doswald-Beck.
41. Pictet Commentary, supra, n. 4 at 57.
42. See Henckaerts and Doswald-Beck, supra, n. 2, 15.
43. See note 39.
44. "International armed conflict" is defined as a conflict between two or more states. Cases of partial or total occupation are considered international armed conflicts as per Article 2 common to all four Geneva Conventions. To these two situations, Article 1(4) of Additional Protocol I (which has not been ratified by all states) also adds the specific category of fights against colonial domination and alien occupation and against racist regimes in the exercise of the right of self-determination.
45. The distinction between international and noninternational armed conflict has lost some of its relevance in recent years. For a number of reasons not developed here,

the international/noninternational armed conflict dichotomy fails to capture the reality and subtlety of modern warfare (see, for example, James G. Stewart, "Towards a Single Definition of Armed Conflict in International Humanitarian Law: A Critique of Internationalized Armed Conflict," *International Review of the Red Cross* 85 [2003]: 313, 314). In addition, most norms of international armed conflict are increasingly being regarded as applicable in both types of conflicts. In some quarters it has even been suggested to eliminate the distinction altogether. With respect to targeting, for example, Jensen argues that "this distinction is no longer meaningful or necessary (p. 100). This chapter takes a pragmatic stance—the distinction still exists and must be acknowledged when analyzing the involvement of nonstate actors in warfare.

46. The Rome Statute of the International Criminal Court expanded the definition of "noninternational armed conflicts" to "armed conflicts taking place on the territory of a state between two nonstate entities" (Article 8[2][f] of the Statute of the International Criminal Court, July 17, 1998, 2187 U.N.T.S. 3). It is also worth noting that an internal armed conflict may be "internationalized" if a state intervenes in that conflict or if one of the nonstate entities acts on behalf of a state.

47. Henckaerts, supra, n. 2 and Doswald-Beck at 3.

48. See *Interpretive Guidance on the Notion of Direct Participation*, supra, n. 5.

49. See Rogers, supra, n. 36, at 109 ("So there is a difference in the Study between 'combatant,' which denotes somebody taking an active part in hostilities and 'combatant status,' which implies more but does not apply in non-international armed conflicts.")

50. See, for example, René Provost, *International Human Rights and Humanitarian Law* (Cambridge: Cambridge University Press, 2002), 121 ("International law, being a system based on the formal equality and sovereignty of states, has arisen largely out of the exchange of reciprocal rights and duties between states.").

51. Examples of conflicts involving nonstate actors include the United States' global fight against al-Qaeda, Israel's conflicts with Hezbollah (2006) and Hamas (2009), the conflict between the Sri Lankan government ant the Liberation Tigers of Tamil Eelam (2009), and the growing violence pitting Pakistani forces against the Tehrik-i-Taliban Pakistan.

52. See BBC News Country Profile, Sri Lanka (August 11, 2009).

53. Provost, supra, n. 50, at 172–73.

54. George Mavrodes, "Conventions and the Morality of War," in *International Ethics: A Philosophy and Public Affairs Reader*, ed. Beitz, Cohen, Scanlon, and Simmons (Princeton, NJ: Princeton University Press, 1990), 85.

55. Provost, supra, n. 50, at 121.

56. Michael Walzer, "Moral Judgment in Time of War" in Richard Wasserstrom, ed. *War and Morality* (Belmont, CA: Wadsworth, 1970): 56.

57. See, for example, Dan Belz, "Is International Humanitarian Law Lapsing into Irrelevance in the War on International Terror?" *Theoretical Inquiries Law* 7 (2006): 97, 115 (noting that "[r]eciprocity is a vital element" in the utilitarian approach to the laws of war); James D. Morrow, "The Laws of War, Common Conjectures, and Legal Systems in International Politics," *Journal of Legal Studies* 31 (2002): 41, 43 ("Laws of war can be effective only to the extent that the parties can enforce them against one another; they must possess both the ability and the willingness to make the treaty work"); and Georg Schwarzenberger, *International Law as Applied by International Courts and Tribunals* (Vol. II, *The Law of Armed Conflict*) (London: Sweet & Maxwell, 1968), 452.
58. In support of the view that the purpose of the Conventions is mainly humanitarian, see, for example, Provost, supra, n. 50, at 137; Derek Jinks, "The Applicability of the Geneva Conventions to the "Global War on Terrorism," *Virginia Journal of International Law* 46 (2005): 165, 185; and Chris af Jochnick and Roger Normand, "The Legitimation of Violence: A Critical History of the Laws of War," *Harvard Journal of International Law* 35 (1994): 49, 56.
59. Representatives of the International Committee of the Red Cross at the 19th meeting of the Diplomatic Conference (p. 675, Vol. II) "pointed out that the Hague Convention was intended to regulate relations between States, whereas the present convention [civilians] was concerned with the rights of individuals."
60. Provost, supra, n. 50, 171.
61. Joint Committee, Second Meeting, April 27, 1949, 13.
62. Joint Committee, Fourth Meeting, May 11, 1949, 45.
63. Id. ("The Chairman noted that the introduction of a clause according to which a Party to the conflict shall be bound by the Convention only if the other Party respectively acknowledges the same obligation, raised no objections.")
64. Mark Osiel, *The End of Reciprocity* (Cambridge: Cambridge University Press, 2009), 68.
65. Pictet Commentary to Common Article 2, supra, n. 4.
66. *Assistance to Sri Lanka in the Protection and Promotion of Human Rights,* Human Rights Council 11th Special Session, S11-1 (May 27, 2009).
67. *Human Rights in Palestine and Other Occupied Territories,* Report of the United Nations Fact Finding Mission on the Gaza Conflict, A/HRC/12/48 (September 15, 2009).
68. The Grave Breaches Provisions are contained in Article 51 of Geneva Convention I; Article 52 or Geneva Convention II; Article 131 of the Third Geneva Convention; and Article 148 of Geneva Convention IV.
69. Osiel, supra, n. 64, at 73.
70. Provost, supra, n. 50, at 132 (emphasis added).
71. Ibid., 137.

72. See, for example, the American company Triple Canopy's "Commitment to Human Rights," available at http://www.triplecanopy.com/triplecanopy/en/about/human-rights.php ("As a part of Triple Canopy's commitment to conducting its operations in a legal, ethical, and moral manner, the company has adopted an organization-wide human rights policy to further inform and educate our employees. The policy states that Triple Canopy's business conduct be guided by the United Nations Universal Declaration of Human Rights and other applicable human rights documents and principles. These include the Chemical Weapons Convention, Convention Against Torture, Geneva Conventions (including Protocols Additional to the Geneva Conventions), and the Voluntary Principles on Security and Human Rights. Triple Canopy is also committed to supporting international and local efforts to combat and eliminate corruption and financial crimes. Triple Canopy operates an Employee Helpline where employees may report concerns directly to the company's senior leadership"); and the Business Ethics Policy of Armor Group, available at http://www.g4s.com/home/csr/csr-business_ethics-policy.htm ("G4S supports the principles of the United Nations Universal Declaration of Human Rights and we are committed to upholding these principles in our policies, procedures and practices. Respect for human rights is and will remain integral to our operations").

73. See, for example, Aegis's statement on its website, available at http://www.aegis-world.com/index.php/about-us/regulation-ethics-and-sector-reform ("Aegis has long been a supporter of Regulation of the Private Security Company industry. Aegis has financially supported and is a founder member of the British Association of Private Security Companies (BAPSC) which lobbies for regulation in the private sector in the UK. The BAPSC has developed, together with its members, a comprehensive Code of Conduct. Aegis is also involved in efforts by the ICRC, and the International Institute for Law and Justice at New York University to regularise the status of PSCs under International Law. Aegis believes that the sector will only benefit from improved regulation and accountability under a proper regulated system.")

74. International Peace Operations Association Code of Conduct, Preamble, available at www.ipoaonline.com.

75. Theodor Meron, "The Humanization of Humanitarian Law," *American Journal of International Law* 94 (2000): 239, 273; and *Declaration of Minimum Humanitarian Standards* (1990), available at http://web.abo.fi/instut/imr/publications/publications_online_text.htm (Meron suggests that key procedural safeguards such as proportionality and nondiscrimination be part of "minimum humanitarian standards," as well as core judicial or due process guarantees, limitations on excessive use of force and on means and methods of combat, the prohibition of deportation, rules pertaining to administrative or preventive detention and humane treatment, and guarantees of humanitarian assistance).

76. Additional Protocol I to the Geneva Conventions, supra, n. 5, Article 75.
77. Ibid.
78. This view has recently been reiterated in the *Interpretive Guidelines on the Notion of Direct Participation in Hostilities*, supra, n. 5, n.15 ("In the ICRC's view, in international armed conflict, any person failing to qualify for prisoner-of-war status under Article 4 GC III must be afforded the fundamental guarantees set out in Article 75 AP I, which have attained customary nature and, subject to the nationality requirements of Article 4 GC IV, also remains a protected person within the meaning of GC IV.")
79. See, for example, U.N. Security Council Resolution 1193 (August 18, 1998) (in the context of the Taliban's offensive in northern Afghanistan, the Security Council declared that "all parties to the conflict are bound to comply with their obligations under international humanitarian law and in particular under the Geneva Conventions"), para. 12; *The Application of International Humanitarian Law and Fundamental Human Rights, in Armed Conflicts in which non-State Entities are Parties*, Resolution, Institute of International law, Berlin Session (August 15, 1999), Article II (The Institute, aware that "armed conflicts in which non-State entities have become more and more numerous and increasingly motivated in particular by ethnic, religious or racial causes," declared that "[a]ll parties to *armed conflicts in which non-State entities are parties*, irrespective of their legal status... have the obligation to respect international humanitarian law as well as fundamental human rights," emphasis added); and Special Court for Sierra Leone, *Prosecutor v. Sam Hinga Norman (2004)*, Case SCSL-2004-14-AR72(E), Decision on preliminary Motion Based on Lack of Jurisdiction (Child Recruitment), Decision of 31 May 2004, para. 2 ("it is well settled that all parties to an armed conflict, whether states or non-State actors, are bound by international humanitarian law, even though only states may become parties to international treaties").
80. Protocol Additional to the Geneva Conventions of August 12, 1949, and Relating to the Protection of Victims of Non-International Armed Conflicts ("Additional Protocol II").
81. I should note that in my view Article 1 of Additional Protocol II does not introduce any element of reciprocity in noninternational armed conflicts. To qualify as an organized armed group to which Additional Protocol II would apply, such group must have the ability to implement Additional Protocol II. I interpret this requirement as one calling for a certain level of organization and discipline within the group—or, as the Commentary to Additional Protocol II puts it, a "minimum infrastructure" necessary to implement the law. (See Claude Pilloud, Jean Pictet, Yves Sandoz, Christophe Swinarski, and Bruno Zimmerman, *Commentary on the Additional Protocols of 8 June 1977 to the Geneva Conventions of 12 August 1949*

[International Committee of the Red Cross, Geneva: Martinus Nijhoff, 1987], para. 4470).

82. The content of these core norms has been debated in particular questions, such as how the proportionality calculation might be affected by the use of human shields by a terrorist organization or how the rules of the targeting apply to civilian-looking combatants. The limited scope of this paper does not allow for a treatment of these important questions.

83. Louis Henkin, *How Nations Behave* (New York: Columbia University Press, 1969), 47 ("It is probably the case that almost all nations observe almost all principles of international law and almost all of their obligations almost all of the time.")

84. *Interpretive Guidance on the Notion of Direct Participation*, supra, n. 5 (noting that the confusion and uncertainty as to the distinction between legitimate targets and persons protected against direct attacks has resulted in civilians being "more likely to fall victim to erroneous or arbitrary targeting, while armed forces—unable to properly identify their adversary—run an increased risk of being attacked by persons they cannot distinguish from the civilian population.")

6. Children as Direct Participants in Hostilities

1. See, for example, reports in the media about the preparation and use of child terrorists in Sri Lanka, Lebanon, Israel, and Afghanistan: "Al Qaeda Training Child Terrorists: US," *The Age*, February 7, 2008, http://www.theage.com.au/news/world/alqaeda-training-child-terrorists-us/2008/02/07/1202234020900.html (accessed August 4, 2009); Israeli Ministry of Foreign Affairs, "Participation of Children and Teenagers in Terrorist Activity during the 'Al-Aqsa' Intifada," (Jan. 30, 2003) http://www.mfa.gov.il/MFA/MFAArchive/2000_2009/2003/1/Participation%20of%20Children%20and%20Teenagers%20in%20Terrori (accessed August 4, 2009); Society for Peace, Unity, and Human Rights in Sri Lanka, "Gov't accuses LTTE of recruiting Children," www.spur.asn.au/children.htm/ (accessed August 4, 2009); "Hezbolla Establishes Child Army," Mosquewatch.blogspot,com, comment posted September 3, 2006, http://mosquewatch.blogspot.com/2006/09/report-hezbollah-establishes-child_03.html (accessed July 1, 2008).

2. A 77 Protocol Additional to the Geneva Conventions of 12 August 1949, and relating to the Protection of Victims of International Armed Conflicts June 8, 1977, article 77. (hereinafter: API). Compare with art. 1 Protocol to the Convention on the Rights of the Child on the Involvement of Children in Armed Conflict (May 25, 2000 25), calling States parties to the Protocol to prevent children under the age of eighteen from taking direct part in hostilities.

3. Supra n. 2.

4. Additional Protocol I, art. 77. 5.
5. The Coalition to Stop the Use of Child Soldiers indicates that children are recruited into armed forces in Africa, Asia, the Middle East, Latin America, and Europe. It is difficult to estimate the numbers of child soldiers for many reasons, among which is the intentional concealment of child recruiting by the leaders of armed forces and the inaccessibility of some war zones to observers. See Coalition to Stop the Use of Child Soldiers, http://www.child-soldiers.org/childsoldiers/questions-and-answers (accessed Oct. 19, 2009).
6. The core research on child soldiers conducted by Graca Machel according to the U.N. General Assembly Resolution 48/157 from 1993 was the first comprehensive report on the impact of an armed conflict on children. See http://www.unicef.org/graca/a51-306_en.pdf. Other scholarly work that followed include: R. Brett and I. Specht, *Young Soldiers: Why They Choose to Fight* (Boulder, CO: Lynne Riener, 2004); P. W. Singer, *Children at War* (New York: Pantheon Books, 2005); M. Wessells, *Child Soldiers: From Violence to Protection* (Cambridge, MA: Harvard University Press, 2006).
7. Resolution 51/77 (1996), UN Doc A/RES/51/77.
8. See United Nations Security Council, Resolution 1261 (1999), UN Doc S/RES/1261; United Nations Security Council, Resolution 1314 (2000), UN Doc S/RES/1314; United Nations Security Council, Resolution 1379 (2001), UN Doc S/RES/1379; and United Nations Security Council, Resolution 1460 (2003), UN Doc S/RES/1460; United Nations Security Council, Resolution 1539 (2004), UN Doc S/RES/1539 and United Nations Security Council, Resolution 1612 (2005), UN Doc S/RES/1612
9. API, articles 48–57. Part IV, Protocol Additional to the Geneva Conventions of August 12, 1949 and relating to the Protection of Victims of Non-International Armed Conflicts (Protocol II), 8 July 1977, articles 13–18, 1125 U.N.T.S 609, reprinted in 16 I.L.M. 1442 (1977),(hereinafter: APII).
10. Art. 51(1), API, A 13(1), APII.
11. Art. 51(2), API, A 13(2), APII.
12. Art. 51(4) API.
13. Art. 51(7) API.
14. See, for example, supra, n. 6; Singer, supra, n. 6. For an extensive analysis of these factors, see H. Moodrick-Even Khen, "Child Terrorists: Why and How Should They Be Protected by International Law," in *International Law and Armed Conflict: Challenges in the 21st Century*, eds. Noëlle Quénivet and Shilan Shah-Davis (The Hague: T.M.C Asser Institut, 2010), 262–82.
15. Wessels, 120–21.
16. Ibid., 124.

17. For a thorough analysis of the problem of direct participation in hostilities, see H. Moodrick-Even Khen, The Influence of the Combat Against Terror on the Distinction Between Combatants and Civilians in International Humanitarian Law (PhD diss., The Hebrew University of Jerusalem, 2007), 127–44 [Hebrew] (hereinafter: Moodrick-Even Khen, diss.).
18. Art. 4, Geneva Convention III relative to the Treatment of Prisoners of War (GC III), 1949, 75 *UNTS,* p. 135; Geneva Convention IV relative to the Protection of Civilian Persons in Time of War (GC IV), 1949, 75 *UNTS,* p. 287(hereinafter: GCIII).
19. Art. 44, API exemplifies this problem when it deviates from art. 4 GCIII conditions for entitlement to POW status. By demanding only that combatants carry their arms openly during a military engagement and while they are visible to the enemy during the military deployment, API facilitates the incorporation of "fighters" in the battlefield whose direct participation in hostilities is difficult to distinguish. This is one of the arguments for not becoming party to this Protocol used by states such as the United States and Israel.
20. See Orna Ben-Naftali and Keren R. Michaeli, "'We Must Not Make a Scarecrow of the Law': A Legal Analysis of the Israeli Policy of Targeted Killings," *Cornell International Law Journal* 36 (2003): 233; Nathan Canestro, "American Law and Policy on Assassinations of Foreign Leaders: The Practicality of Maintaining the Status Quo," *Boston College International & Comparative Law Review* 26 (2003): 1; Derek Jinks, "September 11 and the Laws of War," *Yale Journal of International Law* 28 (2003): 1; Asa Kasher and Amos Yadlin, "Military Ethics of Fighting Terror: An Israeli Perspective," *Journal of Military Ethics* 4 (2005): 1; David Kretzmer, "Targeted Killing of Suspected Terrorists: Extra-Judicial Executions or Legitimate Means of Defence?" *European Journal of International Law* 16, no. 2 (2005): 171; W. Hays Parks, "Air War and the Law of War" *Air Force Law Review* 32 (1990): 1; Michael N. Schmitt, "State-Sponsored Assassination in International and Domestic Law," *Yale Journal of International Law* 17 (1992): 609; Georg Nolte, "Preventive Use of Force and Preventive Killings: Moves into a Different Legal Order," *Theoretical Inquiries in Law* 5, no. 1 (2004): 111; Jordan J.Paust, "Symposium: Current Pressures on International Humanitarian Law: War and Enemy Status After 9/11: Attacks on the Laws of War," *Yale Journal of International Law* 28 (2003): 325; Kenneth W. Watkin, "Combatants, Unprivileged Belligerents and Conflict in the 21st Century," *Israel Defense Forces Law Review* (2003): 69. See, in addition, HCJ 769/02 *The Public Committee Against Torture in Israel v. The Government of Israel* (hereinafter: the targeted killings case). The decision is available at: The Judicial Authority, The State of Israel, "HCJ *The Public Committee Against Torture v. the Government of Israel*," The Judicial Authority, The State of Israel, http://elyon1.court.gov.il/Files_ENG/02/690/007/a34/02007690.a34.pdf (accessed Nov.7, 2009). For a criti-

cism of this decision, see Hilly Moodrick-Even Khen, "Can We Now Tell What 'Direct Participation in Hostilities' Is?" HCJ 769/02, *The Public Committee Against Torture in Israel v. The Government of Israel," Israel Law Review* 40(1): 213 (2007) (hereinafter: "Moodrick-Even Khen, Commentary").

21. See, for example, the recent discussion of the concept of direct participation in hostilities in the targeted killings case, paras. 34–35.
22. See a discussion of these matters and especially the temporal issue below.
23. See, for example, ICTY, *Prosecutor v. Dusko Tadic*, Case ICTR IT-94-1, Opinion and Judgment, May 7, 1997, at para. 616.
24. Only recently has the International Committee of the Red Cross published a guide to discuss this problem in depth. However, this guide—which is the joint work of experts (both practitioners and scholars)—does not have any obligatory force on any state or nonstate actor. See International Committee of the Red Cross, "International Committee of the Red Cross, Interpretive Guidance on the Notion of Direct Participation in Hostilities under International Humanitarian Law, May 2009," International Committee of the Red Cross, http://www.icrc.org/Web/eng/siteeng0.nsf/htmlall/direct-participation-report_res/$File/direct-participation-guidance-2009-icrc.pdf (accessed Nov. 7, 2009).
25. Art. 51(2), (4).
26. Art. 13(1), (2).
27. For a discussion of these questions see Parks, supra, n. 20 at 141–42; William J. Fenrick, "The Rule of Proportionality and Protocol I in Conventional Warfare," *Military Law Review* 9 8 (1982): 91, 107.
28. See, for example, Kretzmer, supra, n. 20, at 197. This question has been dealt with at length in the reports of the Expert Meeting on the Right to Life in Armed Conflicts and Situations of Occupation, organized by the University Centre for International Humanitarian Law, Geneva, convened at International Conference Centre, Geneva, 1–2 September 2005 (hereinafter "the Geneva Expert Meeting"), in the context of deciding the status of persons who participate in hostilities on behalf of an organization according to art. 14, APII. Some experts suggested that the protocol's reference to a status of "civilian" implies that there should also be a status of "fighter"—those who constitute a threat to the other party merely by their membership in the militant group. However, others objected to this view and claimed that the silence of the protocol regarding such a category (i.e., "fighters") should instead be understood as a lack of recognition of such a group. According to these latter experts, had the protocol intended to create such a category, it would have expressly defined one, as it did with the group of "civilians," in art. 14. According to this reading of the protocol, the mere participation in a group does not constitute a threat to the other party, but only specific acts of direct participation create such a risk.

6. CHILDREN AS DIRECT PARTICIPANTS IN HOSTILITIES   255

29. This is in contrast, for example, to its conclusive relevance to criminal law self-defense rules. It may be claimed that the armed conflict concept of risk is different from the common concept in the criminal law self-defense paradigm. That is, the risks to the soldiers or the civilian population may be generated at an earlier stage than the stage at which danger becomes immediate and tangible, which is the prevailing concept of criminal law self-defense rules.

30. Schmitt, supra, n. 20, at 648; Kretzmer, supra, n. 20, at 203; Georg Nolte, supra, n. 20, at 124.

31. This doctrine is widely accepted in international law. For some of its modern formulations see AP I Articles 86, 87; Statute of the International Criminal Court, Article 28 UN Doc. A/CONF/ 183/9, reprinted in 37 ILM 999 (1998), corrected through May 8, 2000, by UN Doc. CN.177.2000.TREATIES-5 (hereinafter: ICC Statute); Report of the Secretary-General Pursuant to Paragraph 2 of S.C. Res. 808, U.N. SCOR, 48th Sess., Annex, art. 7, at 38, U.N. Doc. S/25704 (1993) (hereinafter ICTY Statute); S.C. Res. 955, U.N. SCOR, 9th Sess., 3453d mtg., Annex, art. 6, at 5, U.N. Doc. S/RES/955 (1994) (hereinafter ICTR Statute); United States v. von Leeb (1948), in: 11 Trials of War Criminals Before the Nuremberg Military Tribunals Under Control Council Law No. 10, October 1946-April 1949, at 462 (1949–53) and the case-law of the ICTY and the ICTR, such as Prosecutor v. Delalic (Judgment of November 16, 1998), IT-96-21-T, 343 (ICTY Trial Chamber II),United Nations, International Criminal Tribunal for the Former Yugoslavia, "Prosecutor v. Delalic," International Criminal Tribunal for the former Yugoslavia, http://www.un.org/icty/celebici/trialc2/judgement/cel-tj 981116e.pdf (hereinafter Celebici); Prosecutor v. Delalic (Judgment of February 20, 2001), IT-96-21-A, 231 (ICTY Appeals Chamber); Prosecutor v. Akayesu (Judgment of September 2, 1998), ICTR-96-4-T, PP 486–491 (ICTR Trial Chamber I), available at http://www.ictr.org/

32. See, for example, ICC Statute, art. 25, and Kai Ambos, "Article 25," in *Commentary on the Rome Statute of the International Criminal Court*, ed. Otto Triffterer (Baden-Baden: Nomos, 1999), margin no. 9. I shall also make use of this function in the following section dealing with the prosecution of terrorist leaders.

33. Note also Daniel Statman's suggestion to define legitimate targets according to an analysis of the person's role in the organization rather than relying on the mere concept of membership. Daniel Statman, "The Morality of Assassination: A Reply to Gross," *Political Studies* 51, no. 4 (2003): 777–78.

34. A similar logic guides Ben-Naftali and Michaeli's suggestion to refer to operational leaders of terrorist organizations who are directly involved in the carrying out of terrorist acts as combatants. The consequence of such a definition is to broaden the period of time during which they should be regarded as legitimate targets, so that they may be targeted at any time throughout the entire period of their leadership. See Ben-Naftali and Michaeli, supra, n. 20, at 278, 290.

35. See also Ben-Naftali and Michaeli, *id.* The writers suggest that in reference to ordinary activists of terrorist organizations, only armed persons should be targeted and only for such time as they use their weapons. Id. at 278, 290.
36. Art. 51(5)(b), AP I
37. Some examples are the following: supra, n. 27; William J. Fenrick, "Targeting and Proportionality During the NATO Bombing Campaign Against Yugoslavia," *European Journal of International Law* 12, no. 3 (2001): 489; Parks, supra, n. 20; Kretzmer, supra, n. 20, at 200–201.
38. Eyal Benvenisti, "Human Dignity in Combat: The Duty to Spare Enemy Civilians," *Israel Law Review* 39 (2006): 81, 89, 93.
39. Kasher and Yadlin, supra, n.20, at 3.
40. The targeted killings case, supra, n. 20, para. 36.
41. Note that I do not necessarily deny the Court's conclusion, but rather claim that it lacks a general theoretical basis. For the opposite viewpoint, claiming that even civilians who are located in military installations could not be referred to as legitimate targets but that injuring them may be considered legitimate collateral damage when caused in accordance with the rules of proportionality, see Stephan Oeter, "Methods and Means of Combat," in *The Handbook of Humanitarian Law in Armed Conflict*, ed. Dieter Fleck (New York: Oxford University Press, 1995), 162.
42. See, for example, supra, n. 6.
43. Wessells, supra, n. 6, 46.
44. For an extensive discussion of this claim and the analysis of alternative ways to deal with child terrorists under the prevailing criminal systems see Moodrick-Even Khen, supra, n. 14.
45. See, for example, Case No. SCSL-04-16-T Prosecutor v. Alex Tamba Brima, UNHCR, RefWorld: The Leader in Refugee Decision Support, Prosecutor v. Alex Tamba Brima, RefWorld, http://www.unhcr.org/refworld/publisher,SCSL,,,467fba742,0.html (accessed Nov. 7, 2009) and the proceedings in the ICC against Thomas Lubanga Dyilo, Case ICC-01/04-01/06 . See International Criminal Court, ICC Prosecutor v. Thomas Lubanga Dyilo, International Criminal Court, http://www.icc-cpi.int/Menus/ICC/Situations+and+Cases/Situations/Situation+ICC+0104/Related+Cases/ICC+0104+0106/Court+Records/Presidency/Presidency/ (accessed Nov. 7, 2009).
46. This course of action is called the "differential participation model" and is accepted in most criminal law systems. See Albin Eser, "Individual Criminal Responsibility," in *The Rome Statute of the International Criminal Court: A Commentary*, eds. Antonio Cassese, Paola Gaeta, John R.W. Jones (Oxford: Oxford University Press, 2002), 782. This doctrine was also accepted by the Nuremberg Tribunal, see Charter of the International Military Tribunal (IMT), Agreement for the Prosecution

and Punishment of the Major War Criminals of the European Axis (London Agreement), 8 Aug. 1945, 82 U.N.T.S. 280, Article 7 and by the International Criminal Court for the former Yugoslavia, which determined that customary international criminal law attaches criminal liability on abettors of a criminal act. See Prosecutor v. Tadic (Case No. IT-94-I-T), Opinion and Judgment, 7 May 1997, par. 666–69. The ICC Statute also accepts this model. See A. 25(3) b, c, ICC Statute.

47. Called by the American case law "the Pinkerton rule." See *Pinkerton v. United States*, 328 U.S. 640, 646–47 (1946).
48. 4 Am. Jur. Para. 80, p. 548 and see also *Boyd v. United States*, 142 U.S. 450 (1982); 12 S.Ct. 292, 294.
49. See Art. 25(3)(a)(3), ICC Statute.
50. Wayne. R. LaFave, *Principles of Criminal Law* (St. Paul: Thomson/West, 2003), 527. The Model Penal Code rejected the Pinkerton Rule in order to restrict the boundaries of criminal liability resulting from the criminal conspiracy. See Model Penal Code and Explanatory Notes, Complete Text of Model Penal Code as Adopted at the 1962 Annual Meeting of the American Law Institute at Washington, DC, May 24, 1962, section 2.06 cmt. 6(a) [hereinafter: M.P.C and commentaries]. In spite of the wide application of the Pinkerton Rule in the U.S Supreme Court, it seems that there is no precedent for its application over large terrorist organizations. In a paper examining the question of whether members of al-Qaeda who did not participate directly in the 9/11 events should receive the death penalty, McDonnell rejects the application of the Pinkerton Rule and claims that it is unreasonable to address such criminal liability to each and every member of such a large organization. See Thomas Michael McDonnell, "The Death Penalty—An Obstacle to the 'War against Terrorism,'" *Vanderbilt Journal of Transnational Law* 37 (2004): 353, 371.
51. Peter Buscemi, "Note, Conspiracy: Statutory Reform Since the Model Penal Code," *Columbia Law Review* 75 (1975): 1122, 1152–53 (quoting Deputy Assistant Attorney General Kenney).
52. As we have seen, the doctrine of solidary responsibility of confederates takes a different view and assumes that all partners should bear the same criminal liability for an act made toward the completion of the intended offence.
53. M.P.C. and Commentaries, Section 5.02 (1), supra, n. 50.
54. Wayne R. LaFave, Austin W. Scott, Jr., *Criminal Law*, 2nd ed. (St. Paul: West Publishing Co., 1986), 488, n. 30 and the references there.
55. ICTY Appeals Chamber, *Prosecutor v. Tadic*, IT-94-1-A, Judgment, 15 July 1999, para. 229 (hereinafter: Tadic App.) It should be mentioned, though, that this test may better support the distinction between the perpetrator and the aider than the distinction between the perpetrator and the solicitor. This is because the solicitor

is in most cases as much interested as the perpetrator in promoting the common goal and hence has to be aware of it in order to induce the perpetrator to realize it.
56. Further Criminal Discussion (FCD) 1294/96 *Meshulam v. The State of Israel* [1998] 52(5) *P.D* 1, 29–30 [Hebrew].
57. Ibid., 59. My translation, H.M.E.
58. Ambos, supra, n. 32, margin No. 9.
59. Ibid.
60. *Meshulam*, supra, n. 56, at 51.
61. Ibid., 32, 63.
62. Mordechai Kremnitzer, "The Perpetrator in Criminal Law: Sketching His Figure," *Plilim* 1(1991): 65, 73 [Hebrew]. It is interesting to note that in the absence of the organizational control doctrine in the Israeli jurisprudence, the Israeli Supreme Court had to convict Adolf Eichmann as a solicitor and abettor and not as a perpetrator. Nevertheless, the Court noted the inapplicability of the concepts of solicitation and assistance to this case: "For these crimes were committed en masse, not only in regard to the number of victims, but also in regard to the number of those who perpetrated the crime, and the extent to which any of the many criminals was close to or remote from, the actual killer of the victim, means nothing as far as the measure of his responsibility is concerned. On the contrary, in general, the degree of responsibility increases as we draw further away from the man who uses the fatal instrument with his own hands and reach the higher ranks of command." See The Trial of Adolf Eichmann, Record of Proceedings in the District Court of Jerusalem, Volume 5 (State of Israel, Ministry of Justice, 1994), 2187.
63. Article 25(3)(a), ICC Statute. In contrast, in Poland, Spain, and Israel, criminal liability is inflicted on the commissioner through another only when the other cannot be ascribed with criminal *mens rea* because the other is unaware of the criminality of her or his actions or because he or she is insane, a minor, etc. See Eser, supra, n.46 at 793.
64. This concept was integrated in the Israeli Struggle Against Criminal Organizations Law [2003] *Sefer Hahukim* (No. 1894), 502 [Hebrew]. This law places a ten-year maximum punishment on anyone who manages, organizes, directs, or supervises activity in a criminal organization, either directly or indirectly.
65. *Anonymous Persons v. The State of Israel* [1997] 51(3) *P.D.* 388, 409[Hebrew]. My translation, H.M.E.')
66. A recent example from the Israeli case law is Aggravated Crime Case 1158/02 The *State of Israel v. Barghouti*, Pador 04 (4) 644 [Hebrew]. Barghouti was the leader of the *Fatah* armed branch, the *Tanzim*, and was prosecuted in Israel for several terrorist bombings that were carried out under his supervision. Although he was not an actual participant in any of these operations, he was convicted in some cases not only as a solicitor or as an aider or abettor but as the perpetrator.

7. Private Military Contractors and Changing Norms for the Laws of Armed Conflict

1. Sudarsan Raghavan and Josh White, "Blackwater Guards Fired at Fleeing Cars, Soldiers Say," *Washington Post*, October 12, 2007; Sabrina Tavernise and James Glanz, "Iraqi Report Says Blackwater Guards Fired First," *New York Times*, September 19, 2007; Steve Fainaru and Carol Leonnig, "Grand Jury to Probe Shootings by Guards," *Washington Post*, November 20, 2007.
2. Contractors, including PSC employees, were granted immunity from Iraqi law for actions taken while fulfilling the terms of their contracts under Coalition Provisional Authority (CPA) Order #17. The US-Iraq Security Pact of November 2008 superseded this order and removed contractor immunity. CPA Order Number 17 (Revised) 2004.
3. Del Quentin Wilber, "Contractors Charged in '07 Iraq Deaths," *Washington Post*, December 9, 2008; Del Quentin Wilber, "U.S. Appeals Ruling in Blackwater Case that Involved a Baghdad Shooting," *Washington Post*, January 30, 2010.
4. Gregory A. Raymond, "Military Necessity and the War Against Global Terrorism," in *The Law of Armed Conflict: Constraints on the Contemporary Use of Military Force*, ed. Howard M. Hensel (Aldershot, England: Ashgate, 2005), 12.
5. James Risen and Mark Mazzetti, "Blackwater Guards Tied to Secret Raids by the C.I.A.," *New York Times*, December 11, 2009.
6. Françoise J. Hampson, "Detention, the 'War on Terror' and International Law," in *The Law of Armed Conflict: Constraints on the Contemporary Use of Military Force*, ed. Howard M. Hensel (Aldershot, England: Ashgate, 2005), 145, n. 127.
7. Jean-Marie Henckaerts and Louise Doswald-Beck, *Customary Humanitarian Law, Volume 1: Rules* (Cambridge: Cambridge University Press, 2005).
8. Ibid., 13. On the development of the laws of war, see Stephen C. Neff, *War and the Law of Nations: A General History* (Cambridge: Cambridge University Press, 2005).
9. Louise Doswald-Beck, "PMCs under International Humanitarian Law," in *From Mercenaries to Market: The Rise and Regulation of Private Military Companies*, eds. Simon Chesterman and Chia Lehnardt (Oxford: Oxford University Press, 2007), 119.
10. Yoram Dinstein, *The Conduct of Hostilities Under the Law of International Armed Conflict* (New York: Cambridge University Press, 2004), 113–14.
11. Michael E. Guillory, "Civilianizing the Force: Is the United States Crossing the Rubicon?" *Air Force Law Review* 51 (2001): 116.
12. Christopher Kinsey, "Challenging International Law: A Dilemma of Private Security Companies," *Conflict, Security, and Development* 5 (2005): 270.

13. International Committee of the Red Cross, "International Humanitarian Law," http://www.icrc.org/Web/Eng/siteeng0.nsf/htmlall/ihl?OpenDocument (accessed Dec. 8, 2008); James Cockayne et al., *Beyond Market Forces* (New York: International Peace Institute, 2009).
14. Cockayne et al., *Beyond Market Forces*.
15. For comprehensive discussions of the private military and security industry, see P. W. Singer, *Corporate Warriors: The Rise of the Privatized Military Industry* (Ithaca, NY: Cornell University Press, 2003); Deborah Avant, *The Market for Force: The Consequences of Privatizing Security* (Cambridge: Cambridge University Press, 2005).
16. Lisa Rimli and Susanne Schmeidl, *Private Security Companies and Local Populations: An Exploratory Study of Afghanistan and Angola*. Swiss Peace. http://www.swisspeace.ch/typo3/en/publications/index.html (accessed Nov. 13, 2007), SIGIR, Agencies Need Improved Financial Data Reporting for Private Security Contractors. Report 09-005 (Arlington, VA: Special Inspector General for Iraq Reconstruction, October 30, 2008).
17. Moshe Schwartz, *Department of Defense Contractors in Iraq and Afghanistan: Background and Analysis* (Washington, DC: Congressional Research Service, September 21, 2009): 3.
18. Simon Chesterman, "Leashing the Dogs of War," *Carnegie Reporter* 5 (2008): 39.
19. UNGA, *Resolution 61/151*, December 19, 2006, http://www.un.org/ga/63/resolutions.shtml (accessed Dec 4, 2008). The debate about whether PSCs are mercenaries is beyond the scope of this study. Industry representatives consider the term derogatory and inappropriate, but some scholars point out that there is a clear connection between the traditional definition of a mercenary—which was not always pejorative—and what PSCs do. See Singer, *Corporate Warriors*, 44–48; Sarah Percy, *Regulating the Private Security Industry* (London: Routledge, for the International Institute for Strategic Studies, 2006), 14; Doug Brooks, "In Search of Adequate Legal and Regulatory Frameworks," *Journal of International Peace Operations* 2 (2007): 4; Sarah Percy, "Morality and Regulation," in *From Mercenaries to Market*, eds. Simon Chesterman and Chia Lehnardt (Oxford: Oxford University Press, 2007), 11–14; Chesterman, "Leashing the Dogs of War."
20. In theory, PSCs and their employees should be answerable under domestic and international criminal law, international labor laws should protect employees, and states employing them must uphold human rights law as well as IHL. On current PSC regulation, see Simon Chesterman and Chia Lehnardt, eds., *From Mercenaries to Market: The Rise and Regulation of Private Military Companies* (Oxford: Oxford University Press, 2007).
21. For a notable example see *Montreux Document on Pertinent International Legal Obligations and Good Practices for States Related to Operations of Private Military*

and *Security Companies During Armed Conflict* (Montreux, Switzerland: Swiss Initiative and the International Committee of the Red Cross, September 17, 2008).

22. Michael N. Schmitt, "Humanitarian Law and Direct Participation in Hostilities by Private Contractors or Civilian Employees," *Chicago Journal of International Law* 5, no. 2 (2004): 526–27; Emanuela-Chiara Gillard, "Business Goes to War: Private Military/Security Companies and Humanitarian Law," *International Review of the Red Cross* 38, no. 863 (2006): 531–36

23. Doswald-Beck, "PMCs under International Humanitarian Law."

24. The Hague Conventions stipulated four criteria that armed groups must meet to qualify for combatant status; the Geneva Conventions list six. These are the provisions common to both. Dinstein, *The Conduct of Hostilities*, 33–35.

25. Lindsey Cameron, "International Humanitarian Law and the Regulation of Private Military Companies," Basel Institute on Governance Conference Plenary Paper, February 9, 2007, p. 4.

26. Schmitt, "Humanitarian Law and Direct Participation in Hostilities," 530.

27. *Contractors on the Battlefield*, FM 3-100.21 (Washington, DC: Dept. of the Army, January 3, 2003): 1-6–1-7.

28. Guillory, "Civilianizing the Force," 140.

29. Gillard, "Business Goes to War," 533.

30. Schmitt, "Humanitarian Law and Direct Participation in Hostilities," 530, n. 77.

31. Steve Fainaru, "Where Military Rules Don't Apply: Blackwater's Security Force in Iraq Given Wide Latitude by State Dept.," *Washington Post*, September 20, 2007; Steve Fainaru, *Big Boy Rules: America's Mercenaries Fighting in Iraq* (Philadelphia: Da Capo Press, 2008), 130–31.

32. *Report of the Secretary of State's Panel on Personal Protective Services in Iraq* (Washington, DC: US Dept. of State, October 2007); Karen DeYoung, "Security Firms in Iraq Face New Rules," *Washington Post*, October 24, 2007.

33. *CPA Order Number 17*, "Status of the Coalition Provisional Authority, MNF-Iraq, Certain Missions and Personnel in Iraq," CPA/ORD/27june2004/17, http://www.cpa-iraq.org/regulations/20040627_CPAORD_17_Status_of_Coalition__Rev__with_Annex_A.pdf; Fainaru, "Where Military Rules Don't Apply;" Sharon Behn, "Unlicensed Security," *Washington Times*, September 19, 2007.

34. Discussion with PSC employee with three years experience working in Iraq, September 25, 2007; Avant, *The Market for Force*, 190.

35. Robert Young Pelton, *Licensed to Kill: Hired Guns in the War on Terror* (New York: Crown Publishers, 2006), 75.

36. Schwartz, *Department of Defense Contractors in Iraq and Afghanistan*, 10–11.

37. It should be pointed out that in early modern Europe, mercenaries operated as companies who sold their services as a group of fighters. Anthony Mockler, *Mercenaries* (London: MacDonald, 1969).

38. Cameron, "International Humanitarian Law and the Regulation of Private Military Companies," 3; Schmitt, "Humanitarian Law and Direct Participation in Hostilities," 523, n. 53; *Contractors on the Battlefield*, 1–6.
39. Risen and Mazzetti, "Blackwater Guards Tied to Secret Raids."
40. Secretary of Defense Robert M. Gates previously issued guidelines to clarify the military's oversight of contractors working for DoD on September 26, 2007, when it became clear to him that commanders were uncertain what authority they had over PSC employees. Robert Gates, "UCMJ Jurisdiction Over DoD Civilian Employees, DoD Contractor Personnel, and Other Persons Serving with or Accompanying the Armed Forces Overseas During Declared War and in Contingency Operations," http://www.justice.gov/criminal/dss/docs/03-10-08dod-ucmj.pdf (accessed November 21, 2009). Peter Spiegel and Julian E. Barnes, "Gates Moves to Rein in Contractors in Iraq," *Los Angeles Times*, September 27, 2007.
41. Doswald-Beck, "PMCs under International Humanitarian Law," 119.
42. SIGIR, *Agencies Need Improved Financial Data Reporting*, 16–24.
43. Many companies have, however, signed on to the UN's *Voluntary Principles on Human Rights*, which is intended to encourage respect by contractors for humanitarian law. *Voluntary Principles on Human Rights 2007*, http://www.state.gov/www/global/human_rights/001220_fsdrl_principles.html (accessed Sept. 24, 2007).
44. Schmitt, "Humanitarian Law and Direct Participation in Hostilities," 532–44; Guillory, "Civilianizing the Force," 130–36.
45. PSCs also provide interrogation and guard services, which raise serious questions under humanitarian law. For some discussions, see Steven L. Schooner, "Contractor Atrocities at Abu Ghraib: Compromised Accountability in a Streamlined, Outsourced Government," *Stanford Law and Policy Review* 549 (2005); David Isenberg, *A Fistful of Contractors: The Case for a Pragmatic Assessment of Private Military Companies in Iraq*, BASIC Research Report 2004, 4.
46. Singer, *Corporate Warriors*, 101–118; Joanna Spear, *Market Forces: The Political Economy of Private Military Companies*, FAFO Report 531, 2006.
47. Percy, *Regulating the Private Security Industry*.
48. Toni Pfanner, "Interview with Andrew Bearpark," *International Review of the Red Cross* 38(863) (2006); Bruce Falconer, "Blackwater's Man in Washington," *Mother Jones*, September 25, 2007. http://www.motherjones.com/washington_dispatch/2007/09/blackwater-contractors-doug-brooks.html (accessed Jan. 4, 2008).
49. Anna Leander, "The Market for Force and Public Security: The Destabilizing Consequences of Private Military Companies," *Journal of Peace Research* 42 (2005): 614.
50. Singer, *Corporate Warriors*, 180–82, 222–26.

7. PRIVATE MILITARY CONTRACTORS AND CHANGING NORMS   263

51. Leander, "The Market for Force and Public Security," 614–15.
52. Angela McIntyre and Taya Weiss, 'Weak Governments in Search of Strength: Africa's Experience of Mercenaries and Private Military Companies," in *From Mercenaries to Market: The Rise and Regulation of Private Military Companies*, eds. Simon Chesterman and Chia Lehnardt (Oxford: Oxford University Press, 2007); Kinsey, "Challenging International Law," 283.
53. This does not allow them impunity. In at least one incident, however, EO employees concerned that they could not distinguish civilians from rebel soldiers in Sierra Leone apparently obeyed a directive to "kill everybody." Singer, *Corporate Warriors*, 218.
54. Cameron, "International Humanitarian Law and the Regulation of Private Military Companies."
55. Schmitt, "Humanitarian Law and Direct Participation in Hostilities," 539.
56. "Hostile acts" have been defined as "acts which by their nature and purpose are intended to cause actual harm to the personnel and equipment of the armed forces." Guillory, "Civilianizing the Force," 117.
57. Alexander Faite, "Involvement of Private Contractors in Armed Conflict: Implications Under International Humanitarian Law," *Defence Studies* 4, no. 2 (2004): 174; Schmitt, "Humanitarian Law and Direct Participation in Hostilities," 539.
58. The December 2008 Blackwater indictment is likely to test U.S. government efforts to expand MEJA to cover contractors "supporting" the DoD mission. Moreover, the contractors' defense lawyers argue that they were acting in self-defense.
59. Faite, "Involvement of Private Contractors in Armed Conflict," 172–175; Schmitt, "Humanitarian Law and Direct Participation in Hostilities," 538.
60. Gillard, "Business Goes to War," 540.
61. Schmitt, "Humanitarian Law and Direct Participation in Hostilities," 538–39.
62. Guillory, "Civilianizing the Force," 134.
63. Pelton, *Licensed to Kill*, 143–65.
64. Schmitt, "Humanitarian Law and Direct Participation in Hostilities," 538.
65. George J. Andreopoulos, "The Impact of the War on Terror on the Accountability of Armed Groups," in *The Law of Armed Conflict: Constraints on the Contemporary Use of Military Force*, ed. Howard M. Hensel (Aldershot, England: Ashgate, 2005), 174.
66. This is not new. Concern that rival PSCs might fight each other was raised as early as 2000 with regard to PSCs associated with competing mining companies in Africa. Kevin O'Brien, "Private Military Companies and African Security, 1990–1998," in *Mercenaries: An African Security Dilemma*, eds. Abdel-Fatau Musah and J. 'Kayode Fayemi (Sterling, VA: Pluto Press, 2000), 69.
67. Cameron, "International Humanitarian Law and the Regulation of Private Military Companies," 10.

68. Lisa L. Turner and Lynn G. Norton, "Civilians at the Tip of the Spear–Department of Defense Total Force Team," *Air Force Law Review* 51 (2001); Doswald-Beck, "PMCs under International Humanitarian Law."
69. For some discussions of PSC regulation, see Caroline Holmqvist, *Private Security Companies: The Case for Regulation*, SIPRI Policy Paper No. 9, 2005, http://books.sipri.org/product_info?c_product_id=191 (accessed Dec. 9, 2009); Fred Schreier and Marina Caparini, *Privatising Security: Law, Practice and Governance of Private Military and Security Companies* (Geneva: Geneva Centre for the Democratic Control of Armed Forces, 2005); Percy, *Regulating the Private Security Industry*; Chesterman and Lehnardt, *From Mercenaries to Market*.
70. Fainaru, "Where Military Rules Don't Apply"; P. W. Singer, *Can't Win with 'Em, Can't Go to War Without 'Em: Private Military Contractors and Counterinsurgency*, Brookings Institution Policy Paper #4 (September 2007).
71. Notably, Blackwater had a reputation for acting with a sense of impunity and showing little regard for the impact of its actions on Coalition efforts to improve the broader security situation in Iraq. U.S. Dept. of Defense, "News Transcript," October 18, 2007, www.defenselink.mil/transcripts/transcript.aspx?trasncriptid=4064 (accessed Dec. 9, 2008); Steve Fainaru, "Four Hired Guns in An Armored Truck, Bullets Flying, and a Pickup and a Taxi Brought to a Halt: Who did the Shooting and Why?" *Washington Post*, April 15, 2007; Anne Garrels, "Maliki Calls Blackwater's Actions a Crime," National Public Radio, September 19, 2007, http://www.npr.org/templates/story/story.php?storyid=14527473 (accessed Sept. 20, 2007); Jennifer K. Elsea, Moshe Schwartz, and Kennon H. Nakamura, *Private Security Contractors in Iraq*, CRS Report RL32419 (August 25, 2008): 11–13; David Isenberg, "Less Lawyers, More Auditors: The Lessons of Nisoor Square," December 9, 2008, http://blog.psaonline.org/2008/12/09/less-lawyers-more-auditors-the-lessons-of-nisoor-square/ (accessed Dec. 10, 2008).
72. Schwartz, *Department of Defense Contractors in Iraq and Afghanistan*, 12.
73. Singer, *Corporate Warriors*; Avant, *The Market for Force*.
74. U.S. Dept. of Defense, "DoD News Briefing with Press Secretary Geoff Morrell from the Pentagon, Arlington, Va.," September 20, 2007, http://www.globalsecurity.org/military/library/news/2007/09/mil-070920-dod01.htm (accessed Oct. 24, 2007).
75. *Montreux Document*.
76. Colin Kahl, "In the Crossfire or the Crosshairs? Norms, Civilian Casualties, and U.S. Conduct in Iraq," *International Security* 32 (2007): 7–46.
77. Elsea, Schwartz, and Nakamura, *Private Security Contractors in Iraq*, 48. On weapons use by PSCs, see Steve Fainaru, "Guards in Iraq Cite Frequent Shootings," *Washington Post*, October 3, 2007; Richard J. Griffin, "Private Security Contracting in Iraq and Afghanistan," Statement of Ambassador Richard J. Griffin Before the House Committee on Oversight and Government Reform, October 2, 2007.

78. Griffin, "Private Security Contractors in Iraq and Afghanistan"; George Friedman, "Security Contractors: A Necessary Evil," *Stratfor*, October 9, 2007, http://www.defensetech.org/archives/003779.html (accessed Oct, 17, 2007).
79. Robert Mackey, "Taliban Blame 'Blackwater' for Pakistan Bombings," *New York Times News Blog*, November 17, 2009, http://thelede.blogs.nytimes.com/2009/11/17/taliban-blames-blackwater-for-pakistan-bombings/?scp=1&sq=blackwater%20pakistan&st=cse (accessed Nov. 20, 2009).
80. Richard Beeston, "Karzai: Private Security Companies Will Leave Afghanistan Within Two Years," *Times Online*, November 19, 2009, http://www.timesonline.co.uk/tol/news/world/Afghanistan/article6922760.ece (accessed Nov. 23, 2009).
81. Fainaru, *Big Boy Rules*, 23.
82. Mike Wessels, "Child Soldiers," *Bulletin of the Atomic Scientists* (November/December 1997): 32–39; P. W. Singer, "Western Militaries Confront Child Soldiers Threat," *Jane's Intelligence Review* 17 (2005), http://www.brook.edu/views/articles/fellows/singer20050115.htm (accessed March 28, 2005).
83. *Child Soldiers Global Report 2008*, Coalition to Stop the Use of Child Soldiers 2008, http://www.childsoldiersglobalreport.org/ (accessed Nov. 23, 2009).
84. Doswald-Beck "PMCs under International Humanitarian Law," 132–33. The U.S. DoD proposed adoption of mandatory training in IHL for all contractors supporting overseas operations in January 2008. Sebastian Sprenger, "DoD Proposes Mandatory 'Law of War' Training for Contractors," *Inside Defense.com*, January 14, 2008, http://www.defensenewsstand.com/insider.asp?issue=01102008sp (accessed Sept. 23, 2009).
85. Memorandum: Additional Information for Hearing on Private Security Companies. U.S. House of Representatives (Washington, DC: Committee on Oversight and Government Reform, February 7, 2007).
86. Chia Lehnardt, "Private Military Companies and State Responsibility," in *From Mercenaries to Market*, eds. Simon Chesterman and Chia Lehnardt (Oxford: Oxford University Press, 2007), 156–57; Leander, "The Market for Force and Public Security." Many PSCs offer intelligence and risk assessment advice, which could shape state actions that violate international law.
87. Avant, *The Market for Force*, 235–36
88. Lehnardt, "Private Military Companies and State Responsibility," 148–49.
89. Singer, "Can't Win with 'Em, Can't Go to War Without 'Em."

8. The Principle of Proportionality

1. *Ajuri v. IDF Commander*, HCJ 7015/02, para. 41 (2002) (citations omitted).
2. Protocol Additional to the Geneva Conventions of August 12, 1949, and Relating to the Protection of Victims of International Armed Conflicts, June 8, 1977,

ICRC, *Commentary*, concerning art. 48, para. 1863, http://www.icrc.org/ihl.nsf/WebPrint/470-750061-COM?OpenDocument.

3. On asymmetrical warfare, see Toni Pfanner, "Asymmetrical Warfare from the Perspective of Humanitarian Law and Humanitarian Action," *International Review of the Red Cross* 87, no. 857 (2005): 149–74.

4. *Legality of the Threat or Use of Nuclear Weapons*, ICJ, para. 78 (1996). See Vincent Chetail, "The Contribution of the International Court of Justice to International Humanitarian Law," *International Review of the Red Cross* 85, no. 850 (2003): 252–56.

5. Yoram Dinstein, *The Conduct of Hostilities Under the Law of International Armed Conflict* (Cambridge: Cambridge University Press, 2007), 115.

6. Protocol Additional to the Geneva Conventions of August 12, 1949, and relating to the Protection of Victims of International Armed Conflicts, June 8, 1977, art. 48. On distinction in the 1977 Additional Protocol II to the 1949 Geneva Conventions, see Protocol Additional to the Geneva Conventions of August 12, 1949, and Relating to the Protection of Victims of Non-international Armed Conflicts, June 8, 1977, art. 13. According to the ICRC's *Customary International Humanitarian Law*, the principle of distinction reflects customary international law in both international and noninternational armed conflicts. See International Committee of the Red Cross, *Customary International Humanitarian Law:* Volume I: *Rules*, eds. Jean-Marie Henckaerts and Louise Doswald-Beck (Cambridge: Cambridge University Press, 2009), 3–8.

7. "In so far as objects are concerned, military objectives are limited to those objects which by their nature, location, purpose or use make an effective contribution to military action and whose total or partial destruction, capture or neutralization, in the circumstances ruling at the time, offers a definite military advantage." AP I, art. 52(2). AP I defines civilian objects in contradistinction to military objectives. See AP I, art. 52(1).

8. On the principle of proportionality under international humanitarian law, see Timothy L. H. McCormack and Paramdeep B. Mtharu, "Cluster Munitions, Proportionality and the Foreseeability of Civilian Damage," in *Law at War—The Law as It Was and the Law as It Should Be: Liber Amicorum Ove Bring*, eds. Ola Engdahl and Pål Wrange (Leiden: Martinus Nijhoff Publishers, 2008), 195–97; Thomas M. Franck, "On Proportionality of Countermeasures in International Law," *American Journal of International Law* 102, no. 4 (2008): 723–34; Michael N. Schmitt, "Fault Lines in the Law of Attack," in *Testing the Boundaries of International Humanitarian Law*, eds. Susan C. Breau and Agnieszka Jachec-Neale (London: British Institute of International and Comparative Law, 2006), 292–306; Yoram Dinstein, "Collateral Damage and the Principle of Proportionality," in *New Wars, New*

Laws?: Applying the Laws of War in 21st Century Conflicts, eds. David Wippman and Matthew Evangelista (Ardsley, NY: Transnational Publishers, 2005), 211–24; W. J. Fenrick, "Targeting and Proportionality During the NATO Bombing Campaign Against Yugoslavia," *European Journal of International Law* 12, no. 3 (2001): 498–502; Frits Kalshoven, "Implementing Limitations on the Use of Force: The Doctrine of Proportionality and Necessity," *American Society of International Law Proceedings* 86 (1992): 40–45. See also *The United States Army/Marine Corps Counterinsurgency Field Manual* (2007), 247–49 (discussing the principles of distinction and proportionality in the context of counterinsurgency).

9. AP I, art. 57(2)(a)(iii).
10. AP I, art. 57(2)(b).
11. See Vienna Convention on the Law of Treaties, May 23, 1969. On unilateral declarations by national liberation movements within the context of AP I, see AP I, art. 96(3). See also Pfanner, "Asymmetrical Warfare," 160.
12. They will also remain bound, of course, by those principles of international humanitarian law that may amount to *jus cogens*. On *jus cogens* and international law, see Robert P. Barnidge, Jr., "Questioning the Legitimacy of *Jus Cogens* in the Global Legal Order," *Israel Yearbook on Human Rights* 38 (2008): 199–225.
13. *Nuclear Weapons,* para. 79, supra n. 4.
14. See ICRC, *Customary International Humanitarian Law*, 46–50.
15. Ibid., 58–62.
16. "Patton's Speech to the Third Army: 'Americans Play to Win All of the Time,'" June 5, 1944, http://www.nationalreview.com/weekend/history/history-patton-print111001.html.
17. ICRC, *Commentary*, AP I.
18. Ibid.
19. See Vienna Convention on the Law of Treaties, May 23, 1969, art. 26.
20. Ibid., art. 31(1).
21. ICRC, *Commentary*, AP I. concerning art. 51, para. 1977.
22. Ibid., para. 1978.
23. Ibid., art. 57, para. 2187.
24. Ibid., art. 51, para. 1977, 2208. See also Dinstein, *Conduct of Hostilities,* 122; Kalshoven, "Limitations," 44.
25. Schmitt, "Fault Lines," 293.
26. A. P. V. Rogers, "Zero-Casualty Warfare," *International Review of the Red Cross* 82, no. 837 (2000): 177.
27. Ibid.
28. Robert D. Sloane, "The Cost of Conflation: Preserving the Dualism of *Jus ad Bellum* and *Jus in Bello* in the Contemporary Law of War," *Yale Journal of Internation-*

al Law 34, no. 1 (2009): 111. See Gregor Noll, "Sacrificial Violence and Targeting in International Humanitarian Law," in *Law at War—The Law as It Was and the Law as it Should Be*, eds. Ola Engdahl and Pål Wrange (Leiden: Martinus Nijhoff Publishers, 2008), 212 (discussing "interpretive openness" in the context of international humanitarian law).

29. ICRC, *Commentary*, art. 57, para. 2209.
30. Kalshoven, "Limitations," 44.
31. See Eritrea-Ethiopia Claims Commission, *Western Front, Aerial Bombardment and Related Claims, Eritrea's Claims 1, 3, 5, 9–13, 14, 21, 25, and 26* (2005), 135 *International Law Reports* (2009), 608–09.
32. See Rome Statute of the International Criminal Court, July 17, 1998, art. 8(2)(b)(iv). On this analogous provision, see William A. Schabas, *An Introduction to the International Criminal Court*, 3rd ed. (Cambridge: Cambridge University Press, 2008), 125; Dinstein, *Conduct of Hostilities*, 123. According to Schmitt, the language in the Rome Statue implies the need for both contextual analysis and clarity. See Michael N. Schmitt, "Precision Attack and International Humanitarian Law," *International Review of the Red Cross* 87, no. 859 (2005): 456, n. 41.
33. See *Western Front*, 601–02; Schmitt, "Precision Attack," 457; Fenrick, "Targeting and Proportionality," 499; *Final Report to the Prosecutor by the Committee Established to Review the NATO Bombing Campaign Against the Federal Republic of Yugoslavia* (2000), para. 49; Rogers, "Zero-Casualty Warfare," 176.
34. See *Final Report*, paras. 48–52. On the *Final Report*, see Michael Bothe, "The Protection of the Civilian Population and NATO Bombing on Yugoslavia: Comments on a Report to the Prosecutor of the ICTY," *European Journal of International Law* 12, no. 3 (2001): 531–35. See also Franck, "Proportionality of Countermeasures," 735–36.
35. *Final Report*, para. 50. For some criticism of the *Final Report*'s concept of the "reasonable military commander," see Bothe, "Comments," 535.
36. See *Final Report*, para. 50. See also Fenrick, "Targeting and Proportionality," 499. Franck identifies the "problem of defining the applicable situational perspective from which to render a reasoned second opinion." Franck, "Proportionality of Countermeasures," 731.
37. See Dinstein, *Conduct of Hostilities*, 121.
38. Schmitt, "Fault Lines," 293.
39. Kalshoven, "Limitations," 44.
40. Fenrick makes a similar point. See Fenrick, "Targeting and Proportionality," 499.
41. On *hudnas* and Hamas, see Ely Karmon, "Hudna Is No Solution," *Haaretz*, January 2, 2008.
42. For some background on this, see Jonathan Schanzer, *Hamas v. Fatah: The Struggle for Palestine* (New York: Palgrave Macmillan, 2008).

43. See Asa Kasher, "Operation Cast Lead and the Ethics of Just War," *Azure*, 37 (2009), http://ww.azure.org.il/include/print.php?id=502. See also Israel Ministry of Foreign Affairs, *The Operation in Gaza: 27 December 2008–18 January 2009: Factual and Legal Aspects* (2009), 14–26, http://www.mfa.gov.il/NR/rdonlyres/E89E699D-A435-491B-B2D0-017675DAFEF7/0/GazaOperation.pdf.
44. See The Covenant of the Islamic Resistance Movement (1988), art. 7, http://avalon.law.yale.edu/20th_century/hamas.asp (stating that "The Prophet, Allah bless him and grant him salvation, has said: 'The Day of Judgement will not come about until Moslems fight the Jews (killing the Jews), when the Jew will hide behind stones and trees. The stones and trees will say O Moslems, O Abdulla, there is a Jew behind me, come and kill him. Only the Gharkad tree (evidently a certain kind of tree) would not do that because it is one of the trees of the Jews.' (related by al-Bukhari and Moslem)."). See also "On Hamas TV Friday Sermon: Calls to Annihilate the Jews, Who Are Compared to Dogs," *Middle East Media Research Institute*, April 3, 2009, http://www.memritv.org/clip_transcript/en/2080.htm.
45. Israel Ministry of Foreign Affairs, "Statement by President Shimon Peres on IDF Operation in Gaza," December 28, 2008, http://www.mfa.gov.il/MFA/Government/Speeches+by+Israeli+leaders/2008/Statement+by+President_Peres_IDF_operation_Gaza_28-Dec-2008.htm.
46. Michael Walzer, "The Gaza War and Proportionality," *Dissent*, January 8, 2009, http://www.dissentmagazine.org/online.php?id=191.
47. "Secretary-General's Statement on Continued Escalation in and Around Gaza," New York, December 29, 2008, http://www.un.org/apps/sg/sgstats.asp?nid=3637.
48. "Statement to the Security Council on the Situation in the Middle East," New York, December 31, 2008, http://www.un.org/apps/sg/sgstats.asp?nid=3641.
49. Miguel d'Escoto Brockmann, President of the 63rd Session, United Nations General Assembly, "On Gaza Airstrikes," New York, December 27, 2008, http://www.un.org/ga/president/63/statements/ongaza271208.shtml (bold omitted).
50. "UN Human Rights Experts Call for Immediate Protection of Civilians in Middle East Crisis," January 2, 2009, http://www.unhchr.ch/huricane/huricane.nsf/view01/0F804144148C59CCC12575320055A1D0?opendocument.
51. "Statement by Prof. Richard Falk, United Nations Special Rapporteur for Human Rights in the Occupied Territories," December 27, 2008, http://www.unhchr.ch/huricane/huricane.nsf/view01/F1EC67EF7A498A30C125752D005D17F7?opendocument (bold omitted).
52. See "Declaration by the Presidency of the Council of the European Union on the Violence in Gaza," December 27, 2008, http://www.ue2008.fr/PFUE/lang/en/accueil/PFUE-12_2008/PFUE-27.12.2008/PESC_Gaza_27_decembre_2008.html.
53. See Anti-defamation League, "World Leaders React to Israel's Operation in Gaza: Condemnations and Criticism," December 31, 2008, http://

www.adl.org/main_International_Affairs/World_Reactions_Israel_Gaza. htm?Multi_page_sections=sHeading_4.

54. *Report of the Independent Fact-Finding Committee on Gaza: No Safe Place*, presented to the League of Arab States (2009), 3, http://www.pchrgaza.org/files/PressR/English/2008/Report%20full.pdf.

55. *Report of the Independent Fact-Finding Committee on Gaza: No Safe Place*, presented to the League of Arab States (2009), 3, http://www.pchrgaza.org/files/PressR/English/2008/Report%20full.pdf, 125. For the Organization of the Islamic Conference's response, see Organization of the Islamic Conference, General Secretariat, Jeddah, Final Communiqué of the Expanded Extraordinary Meeting of the Executive Committee at the Level of Foreign Ministers on the Ongoing Israeli Assault on Gaza, OIC/PAL-02/EXE.COM/2009/FC, January 3, 2009, http://www.oic-oci.org/english/conf/exec/FC-exec-fm-Gaza-En.pdf.

56. See Joseph Abrams, "Protester Calls for Jews to 'Go Back to the Oven' at Anti-Israel Demonstration," *Fox News*, January 8, 2009, http://www.foxnews.com/printer_friendly_story/0,3566,477450,00.html; Soeren Kern, "Anti-Semitism Sweeps Europe in Wake of Gaza Operation," *Strategic Studies Group*, January 20, 2009, http://www.eng.gees.org/imprimir.php?id=381.

57. Israel Ministry of Foreign Affairs, "PM Sharon's Speech at Special Knesset Session Marking the Struggle Against Anti-Semitism," January 26, 2005, http://www.mfa.gov.il/MFA/Government/Speeches+by+Israeli+leaders/2005/PM+Sharon+Knesset+Speech+Against+Anti-Semitism+26-Jan-2005.htm?DisplayMode=print (continuing by stating that "[l]egitimate steps of self-defense which Israel takes in its war against Palestinian terrorist[s]—actions which any sovereign state is obligated to undertake to ensure the security of its citizens—are presented by those who hate Israel as aggressive, 'Nazi-like' steps.")

58. See Walzer, "Gaza War and Proportionality." Dinstein notes more generally in the context of international humanitarian law that "[l]egal themes like proportionality, indiscriminate warfare, or the prohibition of mass destruction weapons (to cite just a few prime examples) are bruited about—not necessarily in legal terminology—by statesmen, journalists and lay persons around the globe." Dinstein, *Conduct of Hostilities*, 1.

59. "Israel's Bombardment of Gaza Is Not Self-defence—It's a War Crime," *Sunday Times*, January 11, 2009.

60. David Kennedy, "Dinner Remarks," The New International Law Conference, Oslo, March 2007, http://www.law.harvard.edu/faculty/dkennedy/speeches/OsloDinnerRemarks.htm.

61. See Walzer, "Gaza War and Proportionality."

62. Walzer, "Gaza War and Proportionality." See Kasher, "Operation Cast Lead and the Ethics of Just War." On the *"exploitation of international legal rhetoric . . . [as] a*

major weapon in the political war to delegitmize [sic] Israeli anti-terror operations," see "The NGO Front in the Gaza War: Exploitation of International Law," *NGO Monitor*, January 21, 2009, http://www.ngo-monitor.org/article.php?operation=print&id=2251monitor.org/article.php?operation=print&id=2251.

63. On this fundamental misunderstanding, see Dinstein, *Conduct of Hostilities*, 120–21; Schmitt, "Fault Lines," 294; Schmitt, "Precision Attack," 457.

64. Interestingly, the *Commentaries* to articles 51 and 57 of AP I also make this error of assimilation. See ICRC, *Commentary*, art. 51, para. 1980; ICRC, *Commentary*, art. 57, para. 2218. On this, see Noll, "Sacrificial Violence," 213–14.

65. "UN Human Rights Experts," supra n. 50.

66. See *Human Rights Situation in Palestine and Other Occupied Arab Territories, Report of the Special Rapporteur on the Situation of Human Rights in the Palestinian Territories Occupied Since 1967, Richard Falk*, A/HRC/10/20 (2009), 6–7.

67. See *No Safe Place*, 115–16. See also Maha Akeel, "The War on Gaza: OIC Foreign Ministers Condemn Israel's Aggression; Call for International Intervention," *OIC Journal*, 9 (October-December 2008): 10, http://www.oic-oci.org/data/journals/issue9/9%20English.pdf (stating that "[t]he bombing campaign wrought extensive damage to public infrastructure and hundreds of civilian homes and businesses.").

68. This is a play of words, of course, off Justice Barak's contention that "[a] democracy must sometimes fight with one hand tied behind its back. Even so, a democracy has the upper hand." *Public Committee Against Torture v. Israel*, HCJ 5100/94, para. 39 (1999).

69. ICC, Office of the Prosecutor Response to Communications Received Concerning Iraq, February 9, 2006, 5, http://www.icc-cpi.int/NR/rdonlyres/04D143C8-19FB-466C-AB77-4CDB2FDEBEF7/143682/OTP_letter_to_senders_re_Iraq_9_February_2006.pdf.

70. Noll, "Sacrificial Violence," 213.

71. Kennedy, "Dinner Remarks." See Thomas W. Smith, "The New Law of War: Legitimizing Hi-Tech and Infrastructural Violence," *International Studies Quarterly* 46(3): 355–74 (2002); Roger Normand and Chris af Jochnick, "The Legitimation of Violence: A Critical Analysis of the Gulf War," *Harvard International Law Journal* 35, no. 2 (1994): 387–416.

72. Organization of the Islamic Conference, Final Communique, pmbl.

73. Organization of the Islamic Conference, Final Communique, para. 1 (stating that Operation Cast Lead had "claimed the lives of hundreds of civilians, injured thousands, and caused colossal destruction of homes, civilian facilities, infrastructure and places of worship.").

74. UN Security Council Resolution 1860, S/RES/1860 (2009).

75. UN Security Council, S/PV.6063 (2009), 10.

76. Supra, n. 59.

77. *Report of the Special Rapporteur*, 6–7.
78. Ibid., 7.
79. Ibid.
80. See David Horovitz, "Analysis: Counted Out: Belatedly, the IDF Enters the Life-and-Death Numbers Game," *Jerusalem Post*, February 15, 2009.
81. Ibid. A January 14, 2009, *Jerusalem Post* article had cited an earlier CLA contention that no more than one-quarter of the Palestinian fatalities in Gaza had been civilians. See Yaakov Katz, "IDF: Civilian Deaths Less Than 25% of Total," *Jerusalem Post*, January 14, 2009.
82. See IDF Spokesperson, "Majority of Palestinians Killed in Operation Cast Lead: Terror Operatives," Israel Defense Forces, March 26, 2009, http://dover.idf.il/IDF/English/News/today/09/03/2602.htm?print=true. See Intelligence and Terrorism Information Center at the Israel Intelligence Heritage & Commemoration Center, *Examination of the Number of Palestinians Killed During Operation Cast Lead Indicates That Most Were Armed Terrorist Operatives and Members of Hamas's Security Forces Involved in Fighting Against the IDF. Hamas Has Adopted A Policy of Concealing Its Casualties and Attempts to Include Them in the Overall Number of Civilians Killed*, April 7, 2009, http://www.terrorism-info.org.il/malam_multimedia/English/eng_n/pdf/ipc_e021.pdf.
83. See *No Safe Place*, 29–32.
84. See Interdisciplinary Center Herzliya, Tal Pavel, *Hamas Casualties in "Operation Cast Lead"—Final Findings and Conclusions*, April 2009, http://www.ict.org.il/Portals/0/Articles/ICT_Hamas_Casualties_Final_Report.pdf; Interdisciplinary Center Herzliya, Avi Mor et al., *Casualties in Operation Cast Lead: A Closer Look*, April 2009, http://www.ict.org.il/Portals/0/Articles/ICT_Cast_Lead_Casualties-A_Closer_Look.pdf; Interdisciplinary Center Herzliya, Tal Pavel, *Hamas Casualties from "Operation Cast Lead": Initial Findings and Conclusions*, April 2009, http://www.ict.org.il/Portals/0/Articles/ICT-Hamas_Casualties_Operation_Cast_Lead.pdf.
85. Avi Mor et al., *A Closer Look*, 14.
86. Amnesty International, *Israel/Gaza: Operation "Cast Lead": 22 Days of Death and Destruction* (2009), 1, http://www.amnesty.org/en/library/asset/MDE15/015/2009/en/8f299083-9a74-4853-860f-0563725e633a/mde150152009en.pdf.
87. See *Report of the United Nations Fact-Finding Mission on the Gaza Conflict*, A/HRC/12/48 (2009), 17. See also Amnesty International, *Israel/Gaza: Operation "Cast Lead"*.
88. *Report of the Secretary-General to the Security Council on the Protection of Civilians in Armed Conflict*, S/2001/331 (2001), 1.
89. See Tovah Lazaroff and Yaakov Katz, "UN: IDF Did Not Shell UNRWA School," *Jerusalem Post*, February 4, 2009. On this incident, see *Fact-Finding Mission*, 149–58; Israel Ministry of Foreign Affairs, *Factual and Legal Aspects*, 128–29.

90. Alan Dershowitz, "'Civilian Casualty?' That's a Gray Area: Those Who Support Terrorists Are Not Entirely Innocent," *Los Angeles Times*, July 22, 2006.
91. See Israel Ministry of Foreign Affairs, "Hamas Exploitation of Civilians as Human Shields: Photographic Evidence," March 6, 2008, http://www.mfa.gov.il/MFA/Terrorism-+Obstacle+to+Peace/Hamas+war+against+Israel/Hamas+exploitation+of+civilians+as+human+shields+-+Photographic+evidence.htm?DisplayMode=print. See also Israel Ministry of Foreign Affairs, "Hamas's Illegal Attacks on Civilians and Other Unlawful Methods of War—Legal Aspects," January 7, 2009, http://www.mfa.gov.il/MFA/Terrorism-+Obstacle+to+Peace/Hamas+war+against+Israel/Legal_aspects_of_Hamas_methods_7_Jan_2009.htm.
92. See Griff Witte, "Hamas Pulling Back Into Crowded Cities, Beckoning Israelis: For Army, Pursuit Is Tempting But Risky," *Washington Post*, January 8, 2009.
93. See Intelligence and Terrorism Information Center at the Israel Intelligence Heritage & Commemoration Center, *Civilians As Human Shields: Additional Evidence from Various Sources Demonstrating the Use Made by Hamas of Civilian Houses for Military Purposes During Operation Cast Lead—File No. 5*, February 18, 2009, http://www.terrorism-info.org.il/malam_multimedia/English/eng_n/pdf/hamas_e062.pdf.
94. See Intelligence and Terrorism Information Center at the Israel Intelligence Heritage & Commemoration Center, *The Use of Mosques For Military and Political Purposes By Hamas and Other Terrorist Organizations and Islamic Groups: According to International Laws Governing of Armed Conflict, Mosques Used for Military Purposes Lose the Special Protection Afforded Houses of Worship and May Become Legitimate Targets for Attack*, March 1, 2009, 3–12, http://www.terrorism-info.org.il/malam_multimedia/English/eng_n/pdf/hamas_e065.pdf.
95. See Intelligence and Terrorism Information Center at the Israel Intelligence Heritage & Commemoration Center, *Using Civilians as Human Shields: Additional Evidence Shows Hamas and the Other Terrorist Organizations in the Gaza Strip Established Bases, Military Installations and Rocket and Mortar Shell Launching Positions Near Schools, Some of Them Run by UNRWA (File No. 6)*, March 25, 2009, 2, http://www.terrorism-info.org.il/malam_multimedia/English/eng_n/pdf/hamas_e068.pdf.
96. Alan M. Dershowitz, "Hamas' Dead Baby Strategy," *Washington Times*, January 16, 2009. See Richard Kemp, "International Law and Military Operations in Practice," Hamas, the Gaza War and Accountability Under International Law Conference, Jerusalem Center for Public Affairs, Jerusalem, June 18, 2009, http://www.jcpa.org/JCPA/Templates/ShowPage.asp?DRIT=0&DBID=1&LNGID=1&TMID=111&FID=378&PID=0&IID=3026&TTL=International_Law_and_Military_Operations_in_Practice. Sharansky refers to this as an example of the Palestinians' "most shameful military tactic: pimping the suffering of their civilians as a weapon

of war." Natan Sharansky, "How the U.N. Perpetuates the 'Refugee' Problem: Nowhere on Earth Do Terrorists Get So Much Help from the Free World," *Wall Street Journal,* January 6, 2009.
97. Kasher, "Operation Cast Lead and the Ethics of Just War."
98. Franck, "Proportionality of Countermeasures," 764.
99. Ibid., 716–17.
100. UN Human Rights Council Resolution S-9/1, A/HRC/S-9/L.1 (2009), para. 14.
101. Ibid., pmbl., para. 1, para. 14.
102. See UN Human Rights Council Resolution S-11/1, A/HRC/S-11/2 (2009). See also Hillel Neuer and Marissa Cramer, "A Case Study in UN Hypocrisy," *National Post,* July 17, 2009; Human Rights Watch, "Sri Lanka: UN Rights Council Fails Victims: Member States Ignore Need for Inquiry Into Wartime Violations," May 27, 2009, http://www.hrw.org/en/news/2009/05/27/sri-lanka-un-rights-council-fails-victims?print.
103. "Richard J. Goldstone Appointed to Lead Human Rights Council Fact-Finding Mission on Gaza Conflict," UN Press Release, April 3, 2009, http://www.unhchr.ch/huricane/huricane.nsf/view01/2796E2CA43CA4D94C125758D002F8D25?opendocument.
104. UN Fact Finding Mission on the Gaza Conflict, "Statement By HRC President—Update on Gaza Fact Finding Mission—15 June 09" (emphasis added).
105. "Near Verbatim Transcript of Press Conference By the President of the Human Rights Council, Martin Ihoeghian Uhomoibhi (Nigeria) and Justice Richard J. Goldstone on the Announcement of the Human Rights Council Fact-Finding Mission on the Conflict in the Gaza Strip," Geneva, April 3, 2009.
106. "UN Fact-Finding Mission on the Gaza Conflict Holds First Meeting in Geneva," UN Press Release, May 8, 2009, http://www.unhchr.ch/huricane/huricane.nsf/view01/BC7C60F307A16D1BC12575B000315895?opendocument.
107. On this point, see the terse exchanges between the Fact-Finding Mission and Israel at *Fact-Finding Mission,* ann. II, 434–50 (Correspondence between the United Nations Fact-Finding Mission on the Gaza Conflict and the Government of Israel Regarding Access and Cooperation). See also Irwin Cotler, "The Goldstone Mission—Tainted to the Core (Part I)," *Jerusalem Post,* August 16, 2009; Irwin Cotler, "The Goldstone Mission—Tainted to the Core (Part II)," *Jerusalem Post,* August 18, 2009.
108. UN Human Rights Council Resolution S-12/1, A/HRC/RES/S-12/1, B, pmbl. (2009) ("*Recalling* its resolution S-9/1 of 12 January 2009, in which the Council decided to dispatch an urgent, independent international fact-finding mission, and its call upon the occupying Power, Israel, not to obstruct the process of investigation and to fully cooperate with the mission . . . ").
109. *Guidelines on International Human Rights Fact-Finding Visits and Reports (The Lund-London Guidelines)* (2009), www.ibanet.org/Document/Default.

aspx?DocumentUid=D7BFB4EA-8EB6-474F-B221-62F9A5E302AE, pmbl. The *Guidelines* are geared toward the work of non-governmental organizations but "can provide direction to all those engaged in this exercise with a view to improving accuracy, objectivity, transparency and credibility in human rights fact finding."

110. *The Lund-London Guidelines* (2009), para. 5.
111. Ibid., para. 8.
112. Ibid., para. 10.
113. Ibid., para. 23.
114. *Case Concerning Military and Paramilitary Activities in and Against Nicaragua*, ICJ, 158 (1986) (separate opinion of Judge Lachs). See *Regina v. Bow Street Metropolitan Stipendiary Magistrate and Others,* House of Lords, 1 AC 132–33 (2000).
115. See "The NGO Front in the Gaza War: Human Rights Watch," *NGO Monitor,* January 11, 2009, http://www.ngo-monitor.org/article.php?operation=print&id=2224. See also Robert L. Bernstein, "Rights Watchdog, Lost in the Mideast," *New York Times,* October 20, 2009; Noah Pollak, "Double Standards and Human Rights Watch," *Wall Street Journal,* July 31, 2009; "Examining Human Rights Watch in 2008: Double Standards and Post-Colonial Ideology," *NGO Monitor,* January 13, 2009, http://www.ngo-monitor.org/article.php?operation=print&id=2225.
116. "Gaza: World's Leading Investigators Call for War Crimes Inquiry," March 16, 2009, http://www.amnesty.org.uk/news_details_p.asp?NewsID=18109. On Goldstone, see Haviv Rettig Gur, "Analysis: The Problem With Goldstone," *Jerusalem Post,* July 6, 2009; Anne Herzberg, "NGOs Dominate Gaza Fact-Finding Commissions: Their Claims Should Be Treated With the Same Scrutiny They Demand of Israel," *Jerusalem Post,* June 9, 2009.
117. See Israel's Bombardment." "Israel's Bombardment" also contended that the "killing of almost 800 Palestinians, mostly civilians, and more than 3,000 injuries, accompanied by the destruction of schools, mosques, houses, UN compounds and government buildings, which Israel has a responsibility to protect under the Fourth Geneva Convention, is not commensurate to the deaths caused by Hamas rocket fire." See Jonny Paul, "NGO: Academic Should Quit Cast Lead Inquiry," *Jerusalem Post,* August 23, 2009; Ben Hubbard, "Goldstone: Gaza War Crimes Probe Unlikely to Lead to Prosecutions," *Jerusalem Post,* June 10, 2009.
118. See Cotler, "Tainted to the Core (Part I)"; Cotler, "Tainted to the Core (Part II)."
119. See, for example, *Fact-Finding Mission*, 17–18; Cotler, "Tainted to the Core (Part I)"; Cotler, "Tainted to the Core (Part II)," 149; 414. According to the *Gaza Report,* Operation Cast Lead was a "deliberately disproportionate attack designed to punish, humiliate and terrorize a civilian population, radically diminish its local economic capacity both to work and to provide for itself, and to force upon it an ever increasing sense of dependency and vulnerability," 408 (bold omitted).

120. See The Palestinian Information Center, "Haneyya: UN Report Clearly Condemned Israel for Its War Crimes in Gaza," September 17, 2009, http://www.palestine-info.co.uk/En/default.aspx?xyz=U6Qq7k%2bcOd87MDI46m9rUxJEpMO%2bi1s7qiZoHW7QQKojZ%2bZrbGj0movsUTpEqP2MPFV3i6U%2fRJ%2fqA7jsUS%2fVFLxRvN02A2l%2fwFzaIO1SsNkM53qMnesbZUG3fnidgZVm1nzmJBUN0a8%3d.
121. See *Legal Consequences of the Construction of a Wall in the Occupied Palestinian Territory*, Composition of the Court, ICJ (2004). See also dissenting opinion of Judge Buergenthal.
122. See Schmitt, "Fault Lines," 277–307.
123. Kemp, "International Law and Military Operations." According to Colonel Kemp, "[b]y taking these [precautionary] actions and many other significant measures during Operation Cast Lead[,] the IDF did more to safeguard the rights of civilians in a combat zone than any other Army in the history of warfare." On the significant steps that Israel has taken to investigate and prosecute alleged violations of international humanitarian law by individual members of the IDF during Operation Cast Lead, see State of Israel, *Gaza Operation Investigations: An Update* (2010), http://www.mfa.gov.il/NR/rdonlyres/8E841A98-1755-413D-A1D2-8B30F64022BE/0/GazaOperationInvestigationsAnUpdate.pdf.
124. Compare Kasher, "Operation Cast Lead and the Ethics of Just War."

9. Humanizing Irregular Warfare

1. Gabor Rona, "Interesting Times for International Humanitarian Law: Challenges from the 'War on Terror,'" *Fletcher Forum of World Affairs* 27, no. 2 (2003): 55–74, p. 57.
2. See Anthony P. V. Rogers, *Law on the Battlefield*, 2nd ed. (Manchester: Manchester University Press, 2004), for an argument for competing military and humanitarian aims; Dieter Fleck, ed., *The Handbook of Humanitarian Law in Armed Conflicts* (New York: Oxford University Press, 1995), 133, for the standard argument for balance; and Gabriella Blum, "The Laws of War and the 'Lesser Evil'" *Yale International Law Journal* 35, no.1 (2010): 1-69, for an innovative argument for bracketing the laws of war in cases of "humanitarian necessity."
3. Rona, "Interesting Times for International Humanitarian Law," 57.
4. Ibid., 57–58.
5. The rules governing international armed conflict are found in the four Geneva Conventions of 1949 and their Additional Protocol I of 1977, and the scope of application for these rules is found in Common Article 2 to the four Geneva Conventions; the rules applicable to noninternational armed conflict are found in Common Article 3 to the Geneva Conventions and in Additional Protocol II of 1977. See http://www.icrc.org/ihl.nsf/CONVPRES?OpenView (accessed Dec. 30, 2009).

6. See Rona, "Interesting Times for International Humanitarian Law," 71, n. 11. Rona also makes the point that Additional Protocol I of 1977, "Relating to the Protection of Victims of International Armed Conflicts," has 102 articles and two Annexes of 17 and 28 articles, respectively, and Additional Protocol II of 1977, "Relating to the Protection of Victims of Non-international Armed Conflict" has only 28 articles and no annexes. See http://www.icrc.org/ihl.nsf/CONVPRES?OpenView (accessed Dec. 30, 2009).
7. Modern critiques of the state and sovereignty are legion, especially in light of globalization. For examples in political theory and international relations with a bearing on international law, see Stephen D. Krasner, "Sovereignty: Organized Hypocrisy," *Stanford Law Review*, 52, no. 4 (2000): 959–86; Thomas Biersteker and Cynthia Weber, *State Sovereignty as Social Construct* (Cambridge: Cambridge University Press, 1996); James. C. Scott, *Seeing Like a State: How Certain Schemes to Improve the Human Condition Have Failed* (New Haven: Yale University Press, 1999); Bertrand Badie, *The Imported State: The Westernization of the Political Order* (Palo Alto: Stanford University Press, 2000).
8. Geoffrey S. Corn and Eric Talbot Jensen, "Untying the Gordian Knot: A Proposal for Determining Applicability of the Laws of War to the War on Terror," *Temple Law Review* 81, no. 3 (2008): 787–830, p. 788.
9. See Michael N. Schmitt, Charles H. B. Garraway, and Yoram Dinstein, *The Manual on the Law of Non-international Armed Conflict with Commentary* (San Remo: International Institute of Humanitarian Law, 2006), 2. "Non-international armed conflicts are armed confrontations occurring within the territory of a single State and in which the armed forces of no other State are engaged against the central government." By contrast, "Internal disturbances and tensions (such as riots, isolated and sporadic acts of violence, or other acts of a similar nature) do not amount to a non-international armed conflict."
10. Rona (2003): 60.
11. Ibid.
12. This is not, of course, to suggest that war prior to a changed post-9/11 security climate was somehow devoid of politics. Politics cause war, and war, as in Clausewitz's dictum, is an extension of politics. But there are historical periods of achievement in regulating the excesses and devastation of war, as with the early Hague rules (1899, 1907) and the four Geneva Conventions of 1949, so that policy—informed by the law—acts as its governing force. For the opposite argument, see David Kennedy, *Of War and Law* (Princeton: Princeton University Press, 2006); Carl von Clausewitz, *On War*, ed. and trans. Michael Howard and Peter Paret (Princeton, NJ: Princeton University Press, 1976).
13. See William Banks in this volume, p. 5 and note 2.
14. Charles J. Dunlap, Jr., "*Law and Military Interventions: Preserving Humanitarian Values in 21st Century Conflicts*," Working Paper, Carr Center for Human Rights

Policy Kennedy School of Government, Harvard University, Washington, DC, November 29, 2001: 4, www.ksg.harvard.edu/cchrp/Web%20Working%20Papers/Use%20of%20Force/Dunlap2001.pdf. See, also, C. Dunlap, "Lawfare amid Warfare," *Washington Times*, August 3, 2007, http://www.washingtontimes.com/news/2007/aug/03/lawfare-amid-warfare/. For his definition Dunlap (2001) draws on Richard K. Betts, "Compromised Command: Inside NATO's First War," *Foreign Affairs*, 80 (2001): 126–13, 129–130. See also John Carlson and Neville Yeoman, "Whither Goeth the Law: Humanity or Barbarity," in *The Way Out: Radical Alternatives in Australia*, eds. M. Smith and D. Crossley (Melbourne: Lansdowne Press, 1975). See also Richard C. Schragger, *"Cooler Heads: The Difference Between the President's Lawyers and the Military's,"* Slate.com, September 20, 2006, http://www.slate.com/id/2150050/?nav/navoa; "The Revolution in Military Legal Affairs: Air Force Legal Professionals in 21st Century Conflicts," *Air Force Law Review* 51 (2001): 293; "Lawfare, the Latest in Asymmetries," March 18, 2003, *Council of Foreign Relations*, http://www.cfr.org/publication.html?id=5772; David B. Rivkin, Jr. and Lee A Casey, "The Rocky Shoals of International Law," *The National Interest* (Winter 2000/01).

15. Dunlap, Law and Military Interventions, 4.
16. Ibid.
17. Ibid., 27. For discussion of other examples, see *NGO "Lawfare": Exploitation of Courts in the Arab-Israeli Conflict* (September 2008), http://www.ngo-monitor.org/data/images/File/lawfare-monograph.pdf; Jeremy Rabkin, "Lawfare: The International Court of Justice Rules in Favor of Terrorism," *The Wall Street Journal*, September 17, 2004, available at http://www.opinionjournal.com/forms/printThis.html?id=110005366.
18. The rise of these tactics belongs with the increasing politicization of international humanitarian law and the growth of international law generally—a development that Dunlap attributes to economic globalization and international commerce. These macrostructural economic trends require "an extensive legal architecture to function" that then "raise(s) the 'legal consciousness of the entire world community." Dunlap, Law and Military Interventions, 3.
19. Ibid., 4.
20. Ibid., 1.
21. Charles Dunlap, Jr., "Lawfare: A Decisive Element of 21st Century Conflicts?" *Joint Forces Quarterly* 54, no. 3 (2009), http://www.ndu.edu/inss/Press/jfq_pages/editions/i54/12.pdf
22. Charles Dunlap, Jr., "Lawfare Today: A Perspective," *Yale Journal of International Affairs* (Winter 2008), 146, www.nimj.org/documents/Lawfare%20Today.pdf.
23. Ibid., 147. Also see John J. Lumpkin, *Military Buy's Exclusive Rights to Space Imaging's Pictures of Afghanistan War Zone*, Space.com, Oct. 15, 2001, http://www.space.com/news/dod_spaceimaging_011015.html.

24. Dunlap, "Lawfare Today," 147.
25. Ibid., 146.
26. Ibid.
27. United Nations Human Rights Council, *Human Rights in Palestine and Other Occupied Arab Territories, Report of the United Nations Fact-Finding Mission on the Gaza Conflict,* A/HRC/12/48 (September 25, 2009), http://www2.ohchr.org/english/bodies/hrcouncil/docs/12session/A-HRC-12-48.pdf.
28. See "Protocol Additional to the Geneva Conventions of 12 August 1949, and Relating to the Protection of Victims of International Armed Conflicts (Protocol I), 8 June 1977" (hereinafter "API"), Articles 51(5)(b), 57(2)(a)(iii), and 57(2)(b), http://www.icrc.org/ihl.nsf/WebART/470-750046?OpenDocument (accessed Dec. 30, 2009); Also see Barnidge, pp. 283–84.
29. As a caveat, there is some evidence that asymmetric adversaries are trying to mitigate public perception of their use of lawfare to suggest that they too have consistent norms. See "Taliban's New Military Code of Conduct," July 27, 2009, *Al Jazeera,* http://english.aljazeera.net/news/asia/2009/07/200972775236982270.html
30. See Guy B. Roberts, "The New Rules for Waging War: The Case Against Ratification of Additional Protocol I," *Virginia Journal of International Law,* 26, no. 1 (1985): 109–70; Abraham Sofaer, "Terrorism and the Law: *Foreign Affairs* 64, no. 5 (Summer 1986): 901; Christopher Greenwood, "Terrorism and Humanitarian Law: The Debate over Additional Protocol I," *Israel Yearbook on Human Rights,* 19 (1989), 194–95. For the opposite view, see George H. Aldrich, "Progressive Development of the Laws of War: A Reply to Criticisms of the 1977 Geneva Protocol I," *Virginia Journal of International Law* 26, no. 3 (1986) and Theodor Meron, "The Time Has Come for the United States to Ratify Geneva Protocol I," *The American Journal of International Law* 88, no. 4 (1994): 678–86.
31. W. M. Reisman, "Holding the Center of the Law of Armed Conflict," *The American Journal of International Law* 100, no. 4 (2006): 852–60, p. 852.
32. Ibid., 855.
33. Reisman notes that the *jus in bello* is typically divided into absolute prohibitions ("Part B") such as torture and legal uses of force ("Part A") that, to be lawful, must reflect humanitarian core principles. The first category of absolute restrictions (e.g., poisoning wells, aggressive war) may be militarily useful, Reisman explains, but they are nonetheless always prohibited in recognition of universal humanitarian values, themselves derived from the historical record and often painful lessons learned. The second category of force, unlike absolutely prohibited activities, may be applied to adversaries as long as it is "occasioned and justified by military necessity; is proportional to that necessity; and is as discriminating with respect to combatants and noncombatants as the context allows." In fact, soldiers are "allowed a significant margin of appreciation, for this part of the law recognizes and

takes account of the complexity and variability of battle situations," and "unintended deaths and injuries caused to noncombatants are characterized as 'collateral damage' rather than war crimes and incur neither criminal nor civil liability." Ibid., 852.

34. Article 37(1) of Additional Protocol I provides that it is "prohibited to kill, injure or capture an adversary by resort to perfidy," which constitutes "acts inviting the confidence of an adversary to lead him to believe that he is entitled to, or is obliged to accord, protection under the rules of international law applicable in armed conflict, with intent to betray that confidence," including the "feigning of civilian, non-combatant status." See "Protocol Additional to the Geneva Conventions of 12 August 1949, and relating to the Protection of Victims of International Armed Conflicts (Protocol I), 8 June 1977" (hereinafter "API"), http://www.icrc.org/ihl.nsf/WebART/470-750046?OpenDocument (accessed Dec. 30, 2009).

35. While Article 44(3) of API provides that "to promote the protection of the civilian population from the effects of hostilities, combatants are obliged to distinguish themselves from the civilian population while they are engaged in an attack" or in "preparatory" military operations, it also continues: "Recognizing, however, that there are situations in armed conflicts where, owing to the nature of the hostilities an armed combatant cannot so distinguish himself, he shall retain his status as a combatant, provided that, in such situations, he carries his arms openly: (a) during each military engagement, and (b) during such time as he is visible to the adversary while he is engaged in a military deployment preceding the launching of an attack in which he is to participate. Acts which comply with the requirements of this paragraph shall not be considered as perfidious within the meaning of Article 37, paragraph 1(c)." See http://www.icrc.org/ihl.nsf/WebART/470-750054?OpenDocument (accessed Dec. 30, 2009).

36. Reisman, "Holding the Center of the Law of Armed Conflict," 857.
37. Ibid., 858.
38. Ibid., 856. See also Michael Bothe, Karl Josef Partsch, and Waldemara Solf, *New Rules for Victims of Armed Conflicts*, 244 (1982).
39. Reisman, "Holding the Center of the Law of Armed Conflict," 858.
40. Eric Talbot Jensen, "Combatant Status: It Is Time for Intermediate Levels of Recognition for Partial Compliance," *Virginia Journal of International Law* 46, no. 11: (2005–06):209–49, p. 230.
41. Ibid.
42. See Lotta Harbom and Peter Wallensteen, "Patterns of Major Armed Conflict, 1998–2007," *Sipri Yearbook 2008* (Oxford: Oxford University Press, 2008) and the *UCDP/PRIO Armed Conflict Datasets*, more generally, collected by Uppsala Conflict Data Program (UCDP), Department of Peace and Conflict Research, Uppsala

University, Sweden, and Centre for the Study of Civil War at the International Peace Research Institute, Oslo (PRIO), http://www.prio.no/CSCW/Datasets/Armed-Conflict/UCDP-PRIO/ (accessed Dec. 30, 2009); Human Security Report Project at the Human Security Centre, Liu Institute for Global Issues, University of British Columbia, *Human Security Report 2005: War and Peace in the 21st Century* (New York: Oxford University Press, 2005).

43. Reisman, "Holding the Center of the Law of Armed Conflict," 858.
44. Ibid.
45. The latter side of the equation comprises a field of actors that now rival states' authority and influence. See Peter Haas, "Epistemic Communities and International Policy Coordination," *International Organization* 46, no. 1 (Winter, 1992): 1–35; Kenneth W. Abbott and Duncan Snidal, "Hard and Soft Law in International Governance," *International Organization* 54, no. 3 (2000): 421–56 and "Why States Act Through Formal International Organizations,"*The Journal of Conflict Resolution* 42, no. 1 (1998): 3–32; José E. Alvarez, "International Organizations: Then and Now," *The American Journal of International Law* 100, no. 2 (2006): 324–47; Anne-Marie Slaughter, "Breaking Out: The Proliferation of Actors in the International System," in *Global Prescriptions: The Production, Exportation, and Importation of a New Legal Orthodoxy,* eds. Yves Dezalay and Bryant Garth (Ann Arbor: University of Michigan Press, 2002), 12–36.
46. Lester Nurick and Roger W. Barrett, "Legality of Guerrilla Forces Under the Laws of War," *The American Journal of International Law* 40, no. 3(1946): 563–83, p. 563.
47. Convention (II) with Respect to the Laws and Customs of War on Land and Its Annex: Regulations Concerning the Laws and Customs of War on Land. The Hague, July 29, 1899, http://www.icrc.org/IHL.NSF/FULL/150?OpenDocument (accessed Dec. 30, 2009). For Marten's original language (in English translation) from the Hague II debate, see James Brown Scott, *The Proceedings of the Hague Peace Conferences, The Conference of 1899:* Translation of the Official Texts, Division of International Law of the Carnegie Endowment for International Peace (New York: Oxford University Press, 1920), 548: "Until a perfectly complete code of the laws of war is issued, the Conference thinks it right to declare that in cases not included in the present arrangement, populations and belligerents remain under the protection and empire of the principles of international law, as they result from the usages established between civilized nations, from the laws of humanity, and the requirements of the public conscience."
48. Antonio Cassese, "The Martens Clause: Half a Loaf or Simply Pie in the Sky?" *European Journal of International Law* 11, no. 1 (2000): 187–216, p. 188. These include the 1907 Hague Convention IV, Preamble, Laws and Customs of War on Land, Four 1949 Geneva Conventions for the Protection of War Victims (GC I: Art. 63;

GC II: Art. 62; GC III: Art. 142; GC IV: Art. 158), 1977 Additional Protocol I, Art. 1(2) and Additional Protocol II, Preamble, 1980 Weapons Convention, but also in national conferences, military manuals, and human rights organization documents. See also Theodor Meron, "The Martens Clause, Principles of Humanity, and Dictates of Public Conscience," *The American Journal of International Law* 94, no. 1 (2000): 78–89.

49. Cassese, "The Martens Clause," 188.
50. Ibid., 187.
51. Ibid., 188.
52. Ibid., 193.
53. Rupert Ticehurst, "The Martens Clause and the Laws of Armed Conflict," *International Review of the Red Cross* 317 (April 30, 1997): 125–34. See also V. Pustogarov, "Fyodor Fyodorovich Martens (1845–1909) — A Humanist of Modern Times," *International Review of the Red Cross (IRRC)* 312 (May–June 1996): 300–14.
54. Cassese, The Martens Clause, 212. Scott, *The Proceedings of the Hague Peace Conferences,* 546. Article 9 of the draft Declaration of Brussels 1874 (which did not result in any international treaty): "The laws, rights, and duties of war apply not only to armies, but also to militia and volunteer corps fulfilling the following conditions: (1) That they be commanded by a person responsible for his subordinates; (2) That they have a fixed distinctive emblem recognizable at a distance; (3) That they carry arms openly: and (4.) That they conduct their operations in accordance with the laws and customs of war. In countries where militia constitute the army, or form part of it, they are included under the denomination army."
55. Ian Frederick William Beckett and John Pimlott, *Armed Forces and Modern Counter-insurgency* (Sydney, Australia: Croom Helm Ltd., 1985).
56. "Francs-tireur," *The Oxford English Dictionary,* 2nd ed., 1989, OED Online, Oxford University Press, December 14, 2009, http://dictionary.oed.com/cgi/entry/50089445.
57. General Erich Ludendorff, *Ludendorff's Own Story, August 1914–November 1918* (New York: Harpers, 1919).
58. G. K. Chesterton critiqued the London-released book in the September 13, 1919 issue of *Illustrated London News*, noting that Ludendorff's "military measures were often very effective," but "without being a fool when he effects his measures, he becomes a most lurid and lamentable fool when he justifies them," *The Collected Works of G.K. Chesterton: The illustrated London News, 1917–1919* by G. K. Chesterton, George J. Marlin, Lawrence J. Clipper (San Francisco: Ignatius Press, 1989), 533.
59. Chesterton, *The Collected Works of G.K. Chesterton,* 533.
60. Ibid.
61. Beckett and Pimlott, *Armed Forces and Modern Counter-insurgency,* 2.

62. Ibid.
63. Ibid.
64. Ibid.
65. Ibid., 3.
66. Beckett and Pimlott presciently note that "this latter campaign" also "illustrates the difficulty of troops trained for conventional warfare adapting to anti-guerilla tactics and the vulnerability of troops tied to fixed railway supply lines in difficult terrain occupied by the guerillas, " Ibid.
67. Cassese, "The Martens Clause," 195.
68. Ibid.
69. Ibid.
70. Ibid.
71. Beckett and Pimlott, *Armed Forces and Modern Counter-insurgency*, 2.
72. Ticehurst (1997), http://www.icrc.org/web/eng/siteeng0.nsf/html/57JNHY (accessed Dec. 20, 2009).
73. Cassese, "The Martens Clause," 192.
74. Joseph Raz, "Elements of a Theory of Norms," *The Concept of a Legal System* (Oxford: Clarendon Press, 1970), Ch. III., 44–69.
75. Martha Finnemore, "Are Legal Norms Distinctive?" *New York University Journal of International Law and Politics* 32, no. 3 (2000): 695–703, p. 695. In international policy-based literature norms are defined as "describ[ing] collective expectations for the proper behavior of actors with a given identity" and thus differ from ideas or values in being collectively or socially shared and intersubjective rather than individually held. Peter J. Katzenstein, ed., *The Culture of National Security: Norms and Identity in World Politics* (New York: Columbia University Press, 1996), p. 5, 21, describes norms as "spontaneously evolving, as social practice; consciously promoted, as political strategies to further specific interests; deliberately negotiated, as a mechanism for conflict management; or as a combination, mixing these types." As Martha Finnemore and Kathryn Sikkink point out in "International Norm Dynamics and Political Change," *International Organization*, 52, no. 4 (1998): 887–917, p. 894, norms regularize state and nonstate behavior, limit the range of choice and constrain action, and create social order and stability.
76. Audie Klotz, *Norms in International Relations: The Struggle Against Apartheid* (Ithaca, NY: Cornell University Press, 1999), 14.
77. Friedrich Kratochwil and John G. Ruggie, "International Organisation: A State of the Art on an Art of the State," *International Organization* 40, no. 4 (1986): 753–75.
78. Finnemore, "Are Legal Norms Distinctive?" 699.
79. Across the disciplines and subfields of international relations, political science, and law, constructivism has focused on different issues: domestic structures, norms and identities, norms and legitimacy. For philosophical roots in sociology,

see John Ruggie, "What Makes the World Hang Together? Neo-Utilitarian and the Social Constructivist Challenge" *International Organizations* 52 (1998): 855. See also Thomas M. Franck, *The Power of Legitimacy Among Nations* (New York: Oxford University Press, 1990) and Myres S. McDougal and W. Michael Reisman, eds., *International Law Essays: A Supplement to International Law in Contemporary Perspective.* (Mineola, NY: Foundation Press, 1981).

80. Finnemore, "Are Legal Norms Distinctive?" 699.
81. W. Michael Reisman, "Assessing Claims to Revise the Laws of War," *American Journal of International Law* 97, no. 1 (2003): 82–90.
82. Ibid., 90.
83. Ibid.
84. Ibid. Although doctrines may or may not conform to international law, they "do contribute to minimum order by stabilizing the expectations of all actors," making clear the "consequences of certain types of action and thus aid in avoiding adventures and mistakes."
85. The *Memorandum for Alberto R. Gonzales, Counsel to the President: Re: Standards of Conduct for Interrogation under 18 U.S.C. §§2340–2340A*, Prepared (August 1, 2002) by Jay S. Bybee, Assistant Attorney General at the Department of Justice's Office of Legal Counsel (OLC), as a response to a CIA query on detainee interrogation tactics directed to the OLC by White House Counsel to the President, Alberto R. Gonzales. Experts believe it was principally authored by OLC Lawyer John Yoo, after he left the Department of Justice, see: http://fl1.findlaw.com/news.findlaw.com/nytimes/docs/doj/bybee80102mem.pdf; http://www.gwu.edu/~nsarchiv/NSAEBB/NSAEBB127/. The Memo was intended to provide the CIA with authoritative legal opinion on permissible interrogation tactics for al-Qaeda detainees—with obvious implications for torture rules in general.
86. Bybee takes on a larger legal conceit, delimiting *habeas corpus* standards: "As we understand it, this question has arisen in the context of the conduct of interrogations outside the United States." The context for the *habeas corpus* restriction is Presidential Military Order: Detention, Treatment, and Trial of Certain Non-citizens in the War Against Terrorism, *The White House*, November 13, 2001, which shifted authority from the courts to the executive branch in the power to detain suspects suspected of terrorism (as unlawful combatants), including indefinitely holding detainees without charges, a court hearing, or legal consul. The Supreme Court in *Hamdi v. Rumsfeld* (542 U.S. 507, 2004) reaffirmed U.S. citizens' right to seek writs of *habeas corpus* even if designated enemy combatants; the Supreme Court in *Hamdan v. Rumsfeld,* 548 U.S. 557 (2006) rejected Congress's attempts to displace the courts of jurisdiction over *habeas corpus* appeals by detainees at Guantánamo Bay and declared Military commissions in this application as lacking

the "power to proceed because its structures and procedures violate both the Uniform Code of Military Justice and the four Geneva Conventions, signed in 1949," specifically Common Article 3.

87. Christopher B. Shaw, "The International Proscription Against Torture and the United States' Categorical and Qualified Responses," *Boston College International and Comparative Law Review* 32, no. 2 (2009): 289-304.

88. *Boumediene v. Bush*, 128 S. Ct. 2229, 2240 (2008), Justice Kennedy at 2259 (quoting *Marbury v. Madison*, 5 U.S. (1 Cranch) 137, 177 (1803)).

89. Since the norm literature in international relations describes several schools of thought, it is worth noting that norms, collective understandings of appropriate behavior by international actors (states and nonstates), are important to those with one of two broad perspectives: realists, who see norms as a function of the distribution of power among states in the international system, and idealists (liberal, neoliberals), who believe norms account for the behavior of international actors. Within liberal frameworks, four theoretical traditions dominate: the English school; neoliberalism, or transnationalism; international regime theory; and social constructivism.

90. M. Cherif Bassiouni, "Legal Control of International Terrorism: A Policy-Oriented Assessment," *Harvard International Law Journal* 43 (2002): 83, 99.

91. Formalized in Article 5 of the Statutes of the International Red Cross and Red Crescent Movement, elements of this role include the following: undertaking the "tasks incumbent upon it under the Geneva Conventions, to work for the faithful application of international humanitarian law . . . in armed conflicts and to take cognizance of any complaints based on alleged breaches of that law" (5.2c), and "to work for the understanding and dissemination of knowledge of international humanitarian law applicable in armed conflicts and to prepare any development thereof" (5.2g), in "Statutes of the International Red Cross and Red Crescent Movement," http://www.icrc.org/Web/eng/siteeng0.nsf/htmlall/statutes-movement-220506/$File/Statutes-EN-A5.pdf.

92. ICRC Publication 2008 ref. 0923, *Increasing Respect for International Humanitarian Law in Non-international Armed Conflicts,* http://www.icrc.org/web/eng/siteeng0.nsf/html/p0923?opendocument (accessed Dec. 30, 2009) ICRC Report (hereafter).

93. Foreword, ICRC Report.

94. See UN resolution 54/109 (adopted December 9, 1999) International Convention for the Suppression of the Financing of Terrorism.

95. Dunlap (2008): 150, quoting Richard C. Schragger, *Cooler Heads: The Difference Between the President's Lawyers and the Military's*, Slate.com, September 20, 2006, *available at* http://www.slate.com/id/2150050/?nav/navoa.

96. Article 38 of the Statute of the International Court of Justice lists the sources of international humanitarian law as international conventions or treaties; international custom as evidence of a general practice accepted as law; the general principles recognized by civilized nations; and "judicial decisions and the teachings of the most highly qualified publicists of the various nations, as subsidiary means for the determination of rules of law."

Contributor Bios

WILLIAM C. BANKS is an internationally recognized authority in constitutional law, national security law, and counterterrorism law. Banks has helped set the parameters for the emerging field of national security law since 1987, co-authoring the two leading texts in the field, *National Security Law* and *Counterterrorism Law*. Banks is Professor of Public Administration in the Maxwell School at Syracuse University and director of the Institute for National Security and Counterterrorism (INSCT), a joint research initiative of the Maxwell School of Citizenship and the College of Law at Syracuse University. In 2008, Banks was named the College of Law Board of Advisors Distinguished Professor at Syracuse University, where he has been a member of the faculty for more than thirty years.

ROBERT P. BARNIDGE JR. is Lecturer at the School of Law, University of Reading, UK, where his scholarly and teaching interests include public international law, international humanitarian law, international human rights law, and terrorism. Barnidge received his JD from the University of North Carolina at Chapel Hill, his LLM in Public International Law from the University of Amsterdam, and his PhD from the School of Law, Queen's University Belfast. He is a member of the University of Reading's Liberal Way of War Programme, funded by the Leverhulme Trust.

GEOFFREY S. CORN is Professor of Law at South Texas College of Law in Houston Texas and a retired U.S. Army Lieutenant Colonel. Before his academic appointment, Corn was a Special Assistant to the U.S. Army Judge Advocate General for Law of War Matters—the Army's senior law-of-war expert advisor. Additional U.S. Army assignments include tactical intelligence officer; supervisory Defense Counsel for the Western United States; Chief of International Law for U.S. Army Europe; Professor of International and National Security Law at the U.S. Army Judge Advocate General's School, and Chief Prosecutor for the 101st Airborne Division.

Professor Corn's research expertise and publications focus on the law of armed conflict, national security law, and criminal ethics, and he has recently authored *The Laws of War* and the *War on Terror* (Oxford University Press). Corn received his JD from George Washington University School of Law and his LLM. from the Army Judge Advocate General's School. He has received advanced military training at the U.S. Army Command and General Staff College, in JAG, Military Intelligence Officers Courses, and at the U.S. Army Officer Candidate School.

DAVID M. CRANE is Professor of Practice at Syracuse University College of Law and an expert in rule of law, international criminal law, national security, and international war crimes. Before his academic position, he was founding Chief Prosecutor of the Special Court for Sierra Leone, appointed by the Secretary-general of the United Nations. In this position Crane was responsible for indicting the first sitting African head of state in history, President Charles Taylor of Liberia, for war crimes and crimes against humanity. Professor Crane served for more than thirty years in the U.S. federal government in such positions as Director of the Office of Intelligence Review, Department of Defense Inspector General; Assistant General Counsel for the Defense Intelligence Agency; and Waldemar A. Solf Professor of International Law at the Judge Advocate General's School, U.S. Army. Professor Crane holds a JD from Syracuse University. For his service to humanity, Case Western Reserve University recently awarded him an honorary Doctor of Laws degree. Before his departure from West Africa, Crane was made an honorary Paramount Chief by the Civil Society Organizations of Sierra Leone.

RENÉE DE NEVERS is Associate Professor of Public Administration at the Maxwell School of Citizenship and Public Affairs at Syracuse University. Previously, de Nevers taught at the University of Oklahoma and was a Program Officer at the John D. and Catherine T. MacArthur Foundation. She has also been a research fellow at the Belfer Center for Science and International Affairs, the Center for International Security and Cooperation and the Hoover Institution at Stanford University, and the International Institute for Strategic Studies. She received her Ph.D. from Columbia University. Her work has been published in a range of journals, including *International Security, International Studies Review, Political Science Quarterly*, the *Washington Quarterly*, and *Survival*. She co-authored *Combating Terrorism*, with William C. Banks and Mitchel Wallerstein, and is the author of *Comrades No More: The Seeds of Change in Eastern Europe* (MIT Press, 2003).

ERIC TALBOT JENSEN is Associate Professor, J. Reuben Clark Law School, Brigham Young University, where his teaching and scholarly interests include public international law, U.S. national security law, criminal law, the law of armed conflict, and international criminal law. Before this academic position, Jensen spent twenty years in the U.S. Army, serving in various positions, including chief of the Army's International Law Branch; Deputy Legal Advisor for Task Force Baghdad in Iraq; Professor of International and Operational Law at The Judge Advocate General's Legal Center and School; legal advisor to the U.S. Contingent of UN Forces deployed to Skopje, Macedonia; Legal Advisor in Bosnia in support of Operation Joint Endeavor/Guard. Jensen received his JD at the University of Notre Dame Law School and his LLM at the Judge Advocate General's Legal Center and School and Yale Law School.

HILLY MOODRICK-EVEN KHEN is a Professor of Public International Law at Sha'arei Mishpat College, Israel. Moodrick-Even Khen's research and teaching focus on international humanitarian law, international criminal law, and philosophical-juridical interdisciplinary scholarship. Before her present appointment, Moodrick-Even Khen was a visiting professor at Northwestern University. Moodrick-Even Khen's current scholarly writing includes modernizing the international laws of armed conflict, addressing the influence of terrorism on the traditional distinction between combatants and civilians (published by the Sacher Institute for Legislative Research and Comparative Law at Hebrew University), the duties of occupying states, and criticism of targeting killing.

DANIEL REISNER is a partner at the Tel-Aviv law firm of Herzog, Fox & Neeman, where he heads the firm's international law, defense, and homeland security practice. Before entering private practice, Reisner served for nineteen years as a military lawyer, specializing in international and operational law. Between 1995 and 2004 he served as the head of the IDF's international law department, serving as the senior Israel government lawyer for security- and international-law-related issues. Between 1994 and 2000, Daniel Reisner served as a senior lawyer and negotiator for the Israeli government's peace negotiation teams with both Jordan and the Palestinians, advising prime ministers Rabin, Peres, Netanyahu, Barak, and Sharon, and participating in all the negotiation sessions and summits, including Amman, Wye River, Taba, and Camp David. Concurrent with his legal practice, Reisner currently teaches at three leading Israeli academic institutions and continues to advise the Israeli government on the Israeli-Arab peace process.

DAPHNÉ RICHEMOND-BARAK became Professor of Law at the Radzyner School of Law at the Interdisciplinary Center, Herzliya in 2009. Richemond-Barak holds a Maîtrise from Université Panthéon-Assas (Paris II), a Diploma in Legal Studies from Oxford University (Hertford College), and an LLM from Yale Law School. She was awarded the Fulbright Scholarship and was a recipient of the European Commission Scholarship, the Hertford College Prize, and the Oxford Prize for Distinction. At the IDC, Richemond-Barak also teaches in the BA and MA programs of the Lauder School of Government, Diplomacy, and Strategy. Before joining the IDC, Richemond-Barak served as a clerk at the International Court of Justice and worked as an attorney in the New York office of Cleary Gottlieb. Richemond-Barak has acted as a private counsel for international law firms and as a legal adviser to several states, including the government of Colombia in its territorial dispute against Nicaragua before the International Court of Justice.

GREGORY ROSE is Associate Professor with the Faculty of Law at the University of Wollongong, Australia, and a Research Fellow at the Institute for Transnational and Maritime Security. His research interests include international law and its application to terrorism, noninternational armed conflict, and environmental issues. Before his academic appointment, Rose was a practicing international lawyer at the Head of the Trade and in the Environment and Nuclear Law Unit at the Legal Office of the Australian Department of Foreign Affairs and Trade. Rose also has extensive experience in training officers in the Royal Australian Navy in legal aspects of maritime security and in offering counterterrorism law training courses to government officials in South East Asia.

CORRI ZOLI is a research professor at the Institute for National Security and Counterterrorism (INSCT), a joint research initiative of the Maxwell School of Citizenship and the College of Law at Syracuse University. Zoli's scholarly and teaching interests include national and international security, international humanitarian and human rights law, and the role of cultural issues in security studies. Zoli completed her PhD at Syracuse University and has an area specialty in the Middle East.

Index

Abu-Bakhr, 112
adaptation of traditional laws and customs of war, 2–3, 10–11, 16; appearance of, 13–15; conceptual tools for, 12; Obama and, 235n26
Additional Protocol I to the Geneva Convention (GPI; 1977), 16, 17, 18, 224n24, 226n41, 239n25; application of, 223n13, 224n18; Article 1(4), 247n44; Article 37(1), 281n34; Article 44(3), 282n35; Article 48 quoted, 243n1; on children, 134–35; civilian fighters under, 241n52; civilians under, 91, 93, 101; combatant status under, 47–48, 73–74, 88, 110, 115–17, 190, 196–99; controversy over, 224n23; creation of, 7–8, 240n39; humanitarian protections under, 124–25; Israel's rejection of, 235n20; Israeli Supreme Court on, 77; nonstate entities and, 46, 50, 54–55; POW status in, 83, 224n25; on principle of distinction, 87; on principle of proportionality, 172–76; on release of internees, 229n59; Switzerland and, 228n51; United States and, 237n12; ununiformed combatants under, 232n94
Additional Protocol II to the Geneva Convention (GPII), 226n37; application of, 239n25; creation of, 240n39; criminalization of violations of, 50; direct participation and, 137; reciprocity under, 126, 251n81; triggering of international humanitarian law under, 51; United Kingdom and, 226n41
Aegis: combatant status of, 117; as responsible firm, 249–50n73
Afghanistan: armed conflict in, 98, 118; Guantanamo detainees from, 232n82; military contractors in, 12–13, 108, 156–57, 165–66; NATO forces in, 229n55; Taliban offensive in, 250n79
al-Malki, Riyad, 182
al-Qaeda: affiliates of, 244n6; as detainees, 206, 286n85; laws of war and, 124, 128; network structure of, 10–11; as prototypical nonstate actor, 10; status of members of, 8; September

al-Qaeda (*continued*)
11 attacks by, 258n50; United States vs., 7, 9, 26–27, 43, 248n51; as unlawful combatants, 89, 98
Amnesty International, on Operation Cast Lead, 183
Angola, private security companies hired by, 159
Annan, Kofi, 183
Arab Center for the Development of the Rule of Law and Integrity (ACRLI), 209
armed conflict, 23–32, 3, 239n25; categorizing of, 13–14, 52; death and destruction in, 175, 181; defining of, 15, 225–26n36, 242n52; distinction of law enforcement from, 33–36, 38; laws of, 1, 5, 40–42, 194, 210; under Geneva Conventions and Protocols, 6–7, 223n11, 224n18; modern, 86; nonstate entities in, 45, 47–50, 52, 54, 61, 68–69, 81, 106–29, 190, 193, 198–99; private military contractors in, 150–68; Red Cross and, 287n91; as term, 215n13. *See also* internal armed conflict; international armed conflict; noninternational armed conflict; transnational armed conflict
armed forces: captured, 223n13; minimal organization of, as criterion for application of laws of war, 7; retained personnel of, 246n29; of states, under Hague Conventions, 4–5
arms: provision of, to terrorists, 228n49; requirement to carry openly, 6, 16, 232n94, 253n19, 282n35
Article 43 of Additional Protocol I to the Geneva Convention, combatant status under, 2, 18

Article 44 of Additional Protocol I to the Geneva Convention, combatant status under, 2
Article 77 of Additional Protocol I to the Geneva Conventions of 1949: child soldiers under, 252n2; direct participation and, 137
asymmetric conflict: definitional dilemmas in, 11–12; as nonwar, 7; parties to, 2; proportionality in, 172; transnationalism of, 9–10
asymmetric strategy: definition of, 214n2; laws and customs of war in, 2; politicized humanitarian war as part of, 19
asymmetric warfare, 1, 6; absence of rules governing, 7–8, 9; as challenge to international humanitarian law, 188; extension of international humanitarian law to, 9–13; international law and, 208–9; lawfare and, 193–96, 207–8; legal regulation of, 8; low-intensity, 3; private security companies in, 161–65
Australia, 228n52, 231n73; courts of, 230n62, 230n70, 230–31n72; forces of, in Iraq, 229n55; preventative detention and, 56–57; surveillance in, 232n93
"Authorization for Use of Military Force against Terrorists" (AUMF; 2001), 78

Baghdad: Green Zone in, 194; IEDs in, 102. *See also* Nisoor Square incident
Ban Ki-Moon, 179
Barak, Aharon, 171
Barnidge, Robert P., 19, 193, 195, 197
Barrett, Roger W., 199
battlefield, 14, 165–68, 198; children on, 134–35, 141–42, 148; combatant sta-

tus on, 196; contemporary or modern, 45, 133, 136, 190; guidelines for modern, 4; legal, 9, 210, 211; nonstate actors or entities and, 46–55, 116, 117, 119; nontraditional participants on, 12, 16–17; private security companies on, 151–52, 155, 157, 164; regulation of, 25, 26, 30, 43, 191; terrorists on conventional, 24; traditional objectives on, 2, 193
Beckett, Ian F. W., 201, 203–4
belligerents: under *jus in bello*, 5; nonstate actors as, 3, 6, 7, 193; private security companies as, 160–61; unprivileged, 9, 88, 152, 161, 164, 197, 200
Best, Geoffrey, 111
Bin Laden, Osama, on killing of noncombatants, 11. *See also* al-Qaeda
Blackwater Security: Baghdad Nisoor Square incident and, 12, 150–51, 156, 157, 165; blamed by terrorist groups, 166; combatant status of, 117; indictment of, 264n58; in Iraq, 160–61; sense of impunity of, 265n71
Brockmann, Miguel d'Escoto, 179
Bush, George W., administration of: global war on terror of, 8–9, 43–44; memoranda of, 222n90; preemptive self-defense in, 206; Presidential Military Orders of, 78; interrogation memo and, 286n85; response of, to September 11 attacks, 8; U.S. Supreme Court and, 58–59
Bybee Memo, 206–7, 222n90, 286nn85–86

California Microwave Systems, 109
Callwell, C. E., 202
Cassese, Antonio, 200–201

Central Intelligence Agency (CIA): Blackwater and, 166; Bybee memo and, 206; detainee interrogation tactics and, 286n85; in Iraq, 157
chaplains, 71, 243n69; under Article 33, 73; POW status of, 246n29
Chesterton, G. K., on Ludendorff, 202, 284n58
children: definition of, 133; as human shields, 141, 148; as protected category, 111–12. *See also* child soldiers
child soldiers: under Article 77 AP I, 252n2; criminal liability and, 136, 141–49; as irregular participants in modern conflicts, 3, 12, 18, 133–34, 165–67; recruitment of, 134, 142, 252n5; in Sierra Leone, 250–51n79; as terrorists, 135–36, 148–49
Chinkin, Christine, 187
CIA. *See* Central Intelligence Agency
civilians: blurring of lines between soldiers and, 3, 7, 135–36, 241n52, 251n84, 263n53; casualties among, 1, 236n1; collateral damage and, 256n51, 281n33; combatants distinguished from, 72, 107–8; deaths of, in Gaza, 273n81; definitional dilemmas of, 12, 99–100; definition of, in Additional Protocol I, 224n24; as direct participants in combat, 87, 89, 91–93, 101–3, 141; Hamas's use of, 19; as irregular participants in modern conflicts, 3, 17; under Lieber Code, 238–39n21; mistaken for terrorists, 244n9; private security companies as, 72, 151, 155–58; protection of, 5, 18, 69–71, 85–86, 93, 113, 137, 140, 152, 282n35; status of, 13, 47, 74, 90–91, 97, 227n43, 235n26, 255n28; targeting of, 2, 14, 86, 94, 198,

civilians (*continued*)
    241n42; terrorist use of, 109. *See also* distinction
civilians accompanying the force (CAFs), 153–54; private security companies as, 157, 158, 160
civil war, 27; as noninternational armed conflict, 6, 7
Civil War, American, 90, 113
Clausewitz, Carl von, 194, 201, 279n12; Eurocentric concept of war of, 4–5
coalition operations, 32
Coalition Provisional Authority, 161, 259n2
Coalition to Stop the Use of Child Soldiers, 252n5
Cold War, 7, 16, 46
collateral damage, 70–71, 256n51, 281n33; international law and, 140; proportionality principle and, 180; as result of Operation Cast Lead, 180–82; war crimes vs., 281n33
colonial regimes, 32, 202; fighters against domination by, 7, 46, 200, 223n11, 224l8, 239n25, 247n44
combatants, 58, 75–78, 87–90, 93, 97–99, 103–7, 200, 281n33: civilians distinguished from, 72, 107–8, 128, 135, 152–53, 184; operational leaders of terrorists as, 256n34; targeting of civilian-looking, 251n82; terrorists as unlawful, 286n86. *See also* combatant status; lawful combatants; unlawful combatants
combatant status, 13, 71, 229n54, 235n26; changing criteria of, 196–99; combatants vs., 247n49; criteria for, 155, 261n24; definitional dilemmas of, 12, 73–75, 80, 85, 88, 99–100; direct participation and, 97; "fixed distinctive symbol" of, 2, 16; for *francs-tireurs*, 201; functional test of, 8; under Geneva provisions, 6, 47–48, 109–11, 114–18, 128; under Hague Conventions, 4; private security companies and, 109, 151–52, 155–59; POW status and, 17, 73–75, 80; state sovereignty and, 245n20; of terrorists, 12. *See also* Combat Status Review Tribunal; distinction; lawful combatant status
Combatant Status Review Tribunal (CSRT), 58, 99, 231–32n82
combat operations, 5, 6, 8, 31–32, 33, 40; in Afghanistan, 24; British, in Iraq, 233n97; against nonstate entities, 15, 226n37; regulation of, under Article 3, 9; regulatory framework for, 28, 30; transnational, 26. *See also* military operations
command structure, 117; nonhierarchical, of al-Qaeda and other terrorist networks, 11; of nonstate entities, 13; responsible, 6, 226n37, 239n25, 258–59n62
Common Article 3 to the Geneva Conventions on noninternational armed conflicts, 9–10, 31, 126, 208, 226n39; applicability of, 162; as catch-all formula, 49; detainee protections under, 191; detention hearings and, 60; humane treatment obligation under, 125; as limited framework, 50; LOAC paradigm and, 26–28; prohibitions under, 233n95; serious violations of, 52
compliance, 31–32, 84, 171, 195, 198–99; assessment of, 81; common standard of training and operational, 25, 30; with criteria for lawful combatant status, 8; enforcement of, 74, 115; of individuals, 90; with humanitarian

INDEX 295

law and laws of war, 1, 11, 39, 42, 173; noncompliance and, 11; international norm creation and critical tools of, 205–9; nonreciprocal, 122; nonstate entities and, 79, 80; of nontraditional forces, 47; partial, 2; "policy is enough" argument and, 41; reciprocal, 79; of states, 5; as tactical vulnerability, 190
conflict paradigms, evolution of, 3
constructivism, 205, 285n79, 287n89
Control Risks Group, in Iraq, 161
Convention Against Torture and Other Cruel, Inhumane, and Degrading Treatment or Punishment, 206, 249n72
Copenhagen Process on the Handling of Detainees in International Military Operations, 62
Corn, Geoffrey S., 15–16, 54, 192, 289
counterterrorism, 33–36, 114; challenges of, 136; children and, 133, 141, 148; extraterritorial law enforcement paradigm and, 24, 40; legal framework of, 23–25, 30, 39; military operations for, 15–16, 41, 42, 43; in Sri Lanka, 185; targeting and, 138; terrorists disguised as civilians and, 136; U.S. policies on, 8
Crane, David, 17, 87–90, 93, 114, 290, 267n6; Reisner and, 86, 88, 93, 94
criminal law. *See* law, criminal
cultural objectives in war, commonality of, 2
Customary International Humanitarian Law, 118, 174, 225n32

death penalty: children and, 134; for terrorists, 258n50; decolonization, 16; Protocol I and, 7

Declaration of Brussels (1874), 201, 284n54
de Nevers, Renèe, on military contractors, 18, 72, 290
detainees, detention, 230n68; al-Qaeda and, 206; changing rules for, 14; under Common Article 3, 191–92; at Guantanamo Bay, 9, 18, 229n54, 231–32n82, 286n86; human rights and, 60–61; indefinite, 286n86; interrogation of, 286n85; under Israeli law, 235n23; judicial review of, 59–60; Military Commission Act of 2006 and, 98–99; presidential order on, 78, 231n80; preventive, for national security, 56–59, 229n53, 231n77, 250n75; terrorists and, 260n63; treatment of, under international humanitarian laws, 5, 6, 7, 15, 62–63, 211; U.S. Supreme Court on, 27, 55. *See also* prisoners of war
Detainee Treatment Act of 2005, 58, 232n83, 232n85
"Detention, Treatment, and Trial of Certain Non-citizens in the War Against Terrorism" (presidential military order, 2001) 78
differential participation model, 144, 257n46
Dinstein, Yoram, 33, 40–41, 177; on Article 48 of Additional Protocol I, 172; on conditions of lawful combatancy, 89; as *jus belli* scholar, 24; on principle of distinction, 29
direct participation in hostilities, 17, 86–87; by children, 18, 135–38, 141; by civilians, 86–87, 91–97; defining, 101–5; by private security companies, 158–61, 164; terrorist leaders and, 138–39

distinction, 74, 106–11, 258n55; under Additional Protocol I, 243n1; challenges of, 92, 103, 126, 196–97, 251n84; early formulations of, 111–14; ICRC on, 267n6; International Court of Justice on, 243n2; in noninternational conflicts, 118–19; as principle of humanitarian law, 2, 6, 7, 16–18, 29, 100, 104, 236n6; rejection of, by al-Qaeda, 10; states forced to violate, 19; violations of, 148. See also uniforms

doctrine, doctrines, 29, 46, 255n31; of civilian protection, 90; of command responsibility, 138; counterinsurgency, 201; definition of, 206; international law and, 286n84; of irregular warfare, 202; of organizational and functional control, 138, 143, 145–47, 258n62; of solitary responsibility of conspirators, 142, 258n52; of warfare, 208

domestic law. See law, domestic

Dunlap, Charles, 209–10, 280n18; on lawfare, 193–94

DynCorp, combatant status of, 117

Eichmann, Adolf, 258–59n62
Elaraby, Nabil, 188
enemy, enemies, 9, 47, 48, 69, 84, 99, 109, 202; in armed conflict, 33, 37; civilians as, 140, 162; Guantanamo detainees as, 9, 58; inhumane treatment of, 119; lawful combatant, 43, 56, 61, 79; under Lieber Code, 96, 238n21; before Middle Ages, 4, 111–13, 191; rights of, 80; submission of, 87, 101; targeting by, 90, 101, 160; as terrorists, 34; transnational, nonstate entity as, 7, 25, 39; as unlawful combatant, 58, 78, 98. See also combatants; lawful combatants; unlawful combatants

Eritrea-Ethiopia Claims Commission, 177

Falk, Richard, 179–80, 182
FARC (Fuerzas Armadas Revolucionarias de Colombia; Revolutionary Armed Forces of Colombia), 109, 244n8
Finnemore, Martha, 205, 285n75
Foreign Intelligence Surveillance Court (United States), 60, 232n93
Fourth Geneva Convention for the Protection of Civilians in Times of Armed Conflict (GCC; 1949): administrative detention under, 77; application of, 239n25; civilians and, 90; POW treatment and status in, 224n25; violations of, 1, 277n117
francs-tireurs under international law, 200–204
functional control, doctrine of, 138, 143, 146–47

Gates, Robert M., 163, 262n40
Geneva Convention, Common Article 1, on reciprocity, 123–25
Geneva Convention, Common Article 2, 25, 29; armed conflict and, 43, 191–92; reciprocity in, 121–24, 127, 129
Geneva Convention, Common Article 3, 25, 191–92, 208; direct participation and, 137; on international armed conflict, 26–28, 43, 52; on noninternational armed conflict, 125–26, 162; nonstate actors and, 49
Geneva Conventions and Protocols: as accepted by all states, 210; applicability of, in Afghanistan armed

INDEX

conflict, 250n79; civilian fighters under, 241n52; civilians under, 69, 137; combatant status criteria under, 47, 109–11, 114–17, 128, 199, 261n24; Common Articles of, 6; detention of combatants under, 56; devaluation of, 10; goals of, 246n38; Gonzales on, 9; humanitarian protections and, 38; "Grave Breaches Provisions" of, 122–24; Israeli Supreme Court on, 76–77; 1949 revisions of, 6, 16, 36–37, 42; nonstate groups under, 3, 6, 48, 128; POW status and, 55, 56, 101; private security contractors under, 18, 109; reciprocity and, 120–27, 129; violations of, 286n86; warfare under, 108. *See also* Additional Protocol I to the Geneva Convention; Additional Protocol II to the Geneva Convention; Article 77 Protocol Additional to the Geneva Conventions of 1949, and relating to the Protection of Victims of International Armed Conflicts; Fourth Geneva Convention for the Protection of Civilians in Times of Armed Conflict; *and under individual articles*

Germany, 200, 203; combatant policy of, 115; doctrine of commission of, 146; in Franco-Prussian War, 201–2; law doctrine of organizational control, 143; law of war policy of, 219n39

global war on terror: Bush administration's, 8–9, 43, 78–79; laws of war and, 192; skepticism toward, 23. *See also* war against terrorism

Goldstone, Richard, 122, 186–87; report of, 193, 195

Gonzales, Alberto, on Geneva Conventions, 9, 286n85

Graham, Lindsey, 194

Green, Leslie, *The Contemporary Law of Armed Conflict*, 32–33

Grotius, Hugo, 112–13

Guantanamo Bay detainees: children as, 18; combatant status designation of, 9, 58; CSRT and, 231–32n82; habeas corpus hearings of, 229n54, 286n86; military commission procedures and, 9; presidential order on, 231n80. *See also* detainees, detention

guerillas, guerilla warfare, 106, 119, 128, 201, 204; counter-, 202, 284n66; Hezbollah as, 75; 1960s–70s movements of, 115; in South Asia, 108; status of, 117, 199. See also *francs-tireurs* under international law

Guidelines on International Human Rights Fact-Finding Visits and Reports, 187, 276n109

Guillory, Michael, 161

Gulf War, private contractors in, 244n7

habaes corpus: Bybee on, 286n86; detention of terrorists and, 58–59, 229n54, 230–31n72

Hague Conventions Respecting the Laws and Customs of War on Land; civilian fighters under, 241n52; civilians under, 69; combatant status criteria under, 113–14, 261n24; *francs-tireurs* under, 201–3, nonstate groups under, 3; POW status under, 246n29; preamble to, 200; states under, 4–5, 248n59. *See also* Martens Clause

Hamas, 183; civilians used by, 19, 184, 195; Israel vs., 122, 248n51, 270n44; Operation Cast Lead and, 178–79; propaganda of, 188; rockets fired by, 277n117

297

Henkin, Louis, 127, 251n83
Hezbollah, 115; civilians used by, 19, 195; as nonstate combatants, 75, 115; Israel vs., 1, 17, 24, 26, 27, 28, 248n51; recruitment of children by, 18
hors de combat, 5, 71, 104, 125, 242n64
hostages, 125, 233n95, 244n8
hostile acts, 37, 92; civilians and, 14; as criterion for application of laws of war, 8; definitional dilemmas of, 12; definition of, 264n56; lawful, 88; specific, 95
humanitarian standards, minimum, 124, 129, 250n75
human rights, 23, 56, 84; community, 14; declarations of, 69; experts on, 179; groups focused on, 187, 188; lawyers for, 191; norms and standards of, 34, 205–9, 211, 225n34, 233n96, 233n97; obligations of, 43; protections, 9, 60–61, 149, 234n2; private security companies and, 123; state security vs., 191–93; treaties of, 50. *See also* United Nations Human Rights Council
human rights law: armed conflict and, 50, 60–61; discourse of, 140; violations of, 186
Human Rights First, 205
Human Rights Watch, 187
human shields, 19, 108, 135, 198; children as, 18, 133–34, 136, 141, 148; Hamas's use of, 184, 195; Hezbollah's use of, in Lebanon, 1, 2, 195; Liberation Tigers of Tamil Eelam's use of, 122; terrorists' use of, 251n82

ideology as basis of transnational groups, 14, 136

Incarceration of Unlawful Combatants Law (IUCL; Israel), 76–77, 235n23
incentives for compliance to laws of war, 11, 86, 95, 98, 110, 119, 152, 240n39; disincentives and, 80–81, 190, 198; ineffectiveness of, 107; positive, 2
insignia rule, 6, 16, 197; under Declaration of Brussels, 284n54; partial compliance to, 2. *See also* distinction; uniforms
Institute for National Security and Counterterrorism (INSCT), Syracuse University, 2, 289, 292
Instructions for the Government of Armies of the United States in the Field (1863). *See* Lieber Code
insurgency, insurgencies, 163; counter-, 201, 202; domestic, 45; as internal armed conflict, 7; in Iraq, 98, 164, 194; membership in, 12; modern, 204; Rose on, 16. *See also* insurgents
insurgents, 7–12, 121, 162, 198, 210; affording protected status to, 9; children recruited by, 166–67; detention of foreign, 58; human shielding by, 19; in Iraq, 150, 157, 164; local support for, 165; prosecution of, under domestic criminal law, 10, 16; targeting of diplomats by, 152; training of, 94; as unlawful combatants, 89, 160; unmarked from civilians, 2. *See also* insurgency, insurgencies
Inter-American Court of Human Rights, 243n2
internal armed conflict, 6, 7, 32, 191, 219n39; Common Article 3 and, 49, 50; internationalization of, 247n46; noninternational armed conflict vs., 279n9; regulation of, 41

INDEX

international advocacy organizations, 2, 199
international armed conflict, 6, 23–32, 219n39, 226n41; definition of, 247n44; adherence to Geneva Conventions in, 123; noninternational armed conflict vs., 100, 191–92, 247n46; principle of distinction in, 267n6; regulation of, 41, 49, 50, 191; *Tadic* ruling and, 32; threshold criteria for, 12
International Committee of the Red Cross (ICRC), 23, 242n53, 242n55, 254n24; civilian protection and, 91, 100; on combatant status, 82, 97–98, 99, 118, 199; *Customary International Humanitarian Law*, 267n6; definition of international humanitarian law and, 5, 225n32; on "direct participation in hostilities," 86, 95–96; Geneva Conventions and, 49, 92, 287n91; as guardian of international law, 207–8; on Hague Convention, 248n59; Montreux Document and, 164–65; on POW status, 250n78; preventative detention and, 58; regulation of private security companies and, 250n73; triggering threshold of international armed conflict and, 6–7, 36–37; war crimes and, 225n31
International Court of Justice (ICJ), 187, 188, 228n49, 241n50; Advisory Opinion on Nuclear Weapons, 204; Common Article 3 and, 49; on distinction principle, 172; human rights and, 61; on international humanitarian law, 174; Statute of, 287n96
International Criminal Court: armed conflict and, 52; on children, enlistment of, 166; nonstate entities and,

48; on right of states to self-defense, 54; Rome Statute (1998), 50, 52, 143, 146, 177, 181, 247n46
International Criminal Court for the Former Yugoslavia (ICTR), 145, 255–56n31
International Criminal Tribunal for the Former Yugoslavia (ICTY), 32, 145, 219n39, 225–26n36, 236n6, 255–56n31, 257n46; Common Article 3 and, 49; distinction principle and, 243n2
international humanitarian law. *See* laws and customs of war; principles of humanitarian law
International Institute for Counter-Terrorism (ICT), at Interdisciplinary Center, Herzliya, Israel, 2, 183
Interpretive Guidance on the Notion of Direct Participation in Hostilities (DPH Guidance), 95–100, 118–19
interrogation of prisoners, 9, 14, 227n43, 286n85, 286n86; changing rules for, 14; by CIA, 206; military contractors and, 12, 263n45. *See also* detainees; detention; prisoners of war
Iraq, 240n30; al-Qaeda in, 98; British military operations in, 233n97; civilian deaths in, 181; "coalition of the willing" in, 229n55; lack of reciprocity in, 119; lawfare in, 194; military contractors in, 12–13, 259n2, 265n71; private security companies in, 108, 117, 150–51, 156, 164–66; Status of Forces agreement with U.S., 156
irregular forces, 3, 19, 104, 241n50; children as, 133, 135; as combatants, 17; destructiveness of, 117; in international law, 199–204; lawfare used by, 195–96; as networked cells, 17, 46;

irregular forces (*continued*)
nondistinctiveness of, POW status of, 17, 81; targeting of, 97, 103. See also *francs-tireurs* under international law

irregular warfare, 94, 162, 198, 210; abuses in, 44; of nonstate combatants, 3

Israel, 229n52, 259n64; accusations against, 178–84, Additional Protocol I and, 234n20, 253n19; civilian deaths and property damage by, 273n81, 277n117; criminal liability in, 259n63; Eichmann trial in, 258–59n52; Gaza and, 178–88, 195; Hamas vs., 122, 248n51, 270n44; Hezbollah vs., 1, 17, 24, 75, 248n51; Interdisciplinary Center in Herzliya, 2; IUCL in, 235n23; Lebanon vs., 195; legitimate self-defense of, 272n57; preventative detention in, 57–58; Supreme Court of, 76–77, 84, 145–47, 227n43, 231n77, unlawful combatants and, 75–79. See also Operation Cast Lead

Israel Defense Force (IDF): in court, 171; in Operation Cast Lead, 182–83, 188–89, 277–78n123, 291

Jahangir, Asma, 179, 180
Jensen, Eric T., 17, 192, 198, 246n30, 247n45, 290–91; on combatants, 114, 245n20, on distinction principle, 108
Jilani, Hina, 187
jus ad bellum, 25, 36–39, 210; norms in, 205–9, 211; state interests under, 5
jus cogens, 268n12
jus in bello, 89, 211; compared to *jus ad bellum*, 5, 26, 36–39; definition of, 1; Dunlap on, 209–10; Reisman on, 281n33; as state-centric, 191, 192, 199

Karzai, Hamid, 156–57, 166
Kemp, Richard, 188, 277n123
Klotz, Audie, 205

Lachs, Manfred H., 187
law, criminal, 6, 15, 16; differential participation model in, 257n46; liability under, 258n50, 258n52, 259n63; private security companies under, 261n20; self-defense rules under, 255n29; terrorism under, 8, 10. See also law enforcement

law, domestic, 7, 16; private security companies under, 18, 261n20; terrorists prosecuted under, 10; unlawful belligerents prosecuted under, 9

law enforcement, 15, 16, 52, 54; asymmetric attacks and, 11,44; in Australia, 59; extraterritorial, 24–25, 33–36, 39–40, 43; framework of, 26, 42; nonstate entities and, 14–15; state power and, 38; terrorism and, 10, 33

lawfare, 281n29; definition of, 1; as symptom of changing equilibrium between security and humanitarian goals, 193–96; as tool of asymmetric strategy, 19, 198, 207–8, 210

lawful combatants, 9, 85, 88, 93–94, 200; distinction between unlawful and, 86, 89–90, 104; *francs-tireurs* as, 203; under Hague Conventions, 4. See also unlawful combatants

lawful combatant status, 201; criteria for, 8; definitional dilemmas of, 12; under Geneva provisions, 6; private security companies and, 162; requirements of, 89, 103

Law of War Program (U.S. Department of Defense), 15, 25, 28

INDEX

laws and customs of war, 171–72, 219n39, 225n32, 284n54; adaptations to, 2; adequacy of, 3; children and, 133–36; civilians and, 87, 90–92; codification of, 283n47; combatant status under, 152–54, 196–99; compliance of nonstate entities with, 54, 80–81; conflict types and, 29; counterterrorist operations and, 42; direct participation and, 137; functional nature of, 233–34n2; humanitarian norms in, 205–11; as international humanitarian law, 4, 5; lawfare in, 193–96; noncompliance of nonstate entities with, 79, 190; noninternational armed conflict and, 126–27; nonstate entities under, 83, 85, 108–9, 115; partial compliance to, 2; politicization of, 2, 14–15, 19, 280n18; principles of, 6; private military contractors under, 150–51, 158–61, 167–68; problems in, 67–68; proportionality under, 139–41, 172–73, 180–81; reciprocity in, 106, 119–29, 248n57; state sovereignty vs. humanitarian norms in, 191–93; threshold criteria for triggering, 6, 39, 42; traditional, 111–13

Lebanon, 1, 24, 26, 195

legal instruments, international, 5, 14, 108, 114; politicization of, 3, 19

lex specialis, 5, 210

Liberation Tigers of Tamil Eelam, 118, 122, 185, 248n51

Lieber Code, 29, 90, 113, 238–39n21

Lieber, Francis, 48, 90, 96, 113. *See also* Lieber Code

Ludendorff, Gen. Erich, 202, 284n58

Machel, Graca, 252n6

Martens Clause, 190; irregular fighters and, 199–204

Martens, Fyodor Fyodorovich, 200, 203. *See also* Martens Clause

Maxwell School of Citizenship and Public Affairs, Syracuse University, 2, 289, 290, 292

mens rea, 134, 142, 148, 259n63

mercenaries: definition of, 157; in early modern Europe, 262n37; private security companies and, 154, 159, 163, 261n19

military advantage, 140, 227n43; in Additional Protocol I, 137; child terrorists and, 133; civilians and, 19, 179, 184; direct or definite, 173–77, 181, 267n7; disadvantages and, 3; proportionality and, 103, 195, 196; targeting and, 93; terrorists and, 138

military commissions, 56; Guantanamo detainees and, 9, 286n86; Hamdan and, 27

Military Commissions Act, 98–99

Military Extraterritorial Jurisdiction Act (MEJA), 158, 264n58

military necessity, 2, 5–6, 36, 41, 68, 123, 191, 195, 196, 236n6; asymmetric tactics and, 19; balance between humanitarian law and, 5, 25, 29, 87; current rules of, 69–71; destruction of property and, 179; in history, 32, 203; military objective and, 36; targeting and, 100, 101, 103; terrorism and, 35, 43

military objective, 25, 38, 41, 109, 193, 267n7; in Additional Protocol I, 87, 137; civilian objective vs., 125, 128, 172, 243n1; compromise of, 1; deadly force used against, 33, 34; human

military objective (*continued*)
shielding of, 135; military necessity and, 36; private security companies and, 164
military operations, 24, 28, 31, 40, 158, 186; applying rule of laws to, 38, 68, 210–11; Corn on, 54; distinction principle in, 135; under General Protocol I, 91–92; human rights in, 61; lawfare and, 194; military necessity and, 69; under Protocol II of 1977, 51; rules for governing conduct of, 5, 8; targeting during, 87, 100; against transnational terrorism, 15, 23, 25, 33–36, 42–43; under status-based rules of engagement, 44. *See also* combat operations; counterterrorism
militia, militias, 237n17, 240n30, 242n53; combatant status of, 116, 153; as distinguishable from civilians, 136; POW status of, 110, 243n4; private security companies and, 155; under Declaration of Brussels, 284n54
minimum humanitarian standards, 29, 124, 129, 250n75
Model Penal Code, 257–58n50
Montreux Document, 164–65
Moodrick-Even Khen, Hilly, 3, 18, 166–67, 291
moral authority, 11, 68
Moreno-Ocampo, Luis, 181
Muslims, 112, 209; al-Qaeda and, 11; Jews vs., 270n44; pilgrimages of, 240n30

national liberation movements, 46, 47, 50, 55, 199, 268n11; as covered by international law, 210, creation of Protocol I and, 7, 48
national security, 63, 68; humanitarian protections vs., 4, 19, 190, 191; jurisdiction and courts, 59–60, 61; national legislatures and, 55; preventive detention for, 45, 57–58, 59, 62, 229n53

NATO (North Atlantic Treaty Organization): Afghanistan and, 229n55; Kosovo and, 177, 194
Nevers, Renée de, 18, 72, 290
Nisoor Square incident (Baghdad), 12, 150–51, 156, 157, 165. *See also* Blackwater Security
noncombatant immunity, 11, 112, 113, 233–34n2; as core principle of humanitarian law, 10
noncombatants: in armed forces, 115; combatants and, 30, 39, 182, 198, 233–34n2; distinction and, 111, 113, 116, 152, 155, 199, 281n33; protection of, 69, 197; targeting of, 208
noncompliance, 11
nondiscrimination as minimum humanitarian standard, 250n75
nongovernmental organizations (NGOs), 12, 158, 187, 205
noninternational armed conflict, 7, 50, 79, 100, 128, 225n31, 225–26n36; Additional Protocol II and, 83, 91; al-Qaeda vs. United States as, 9; civil war as, 6; combatant status in, 152; Common Article 3 and, 9, 125; definition of, 279n9; detainees in, 62; distinction principle, 267n6; international armed conflict vs., 191–92, 247n45; nonstate actors in, 118–19; proportionality principle in, 180; reciprocity principle in, 126; in Rome Statute, 247n46; threshold criteria for, 12
nonstate actors, entities, and groups, 11, 14, 26, 27, 48, 52, 53, 63, 79–81, 196, 242n52, 250–51n79; action against,

INDEX

68; asymmetric warfare and, 9; as belligerents, 193; child soldiers and, 134; conflict between states and, 23, 31–32, 73, 75, 120; control of territory by, 226n39; controversy concerning, in Additional Protocol I, 224n23; examples of, 248n51; exclusion of, by Geneva provisions, 6; humanitarian law and, 7, 14–15, 18, 47, 50–51; international norms and, 205; lawful combatant status and, 85–87, 111; laws of war and, 107, 109, 127, 191–93, 202; military operations against transnational, 15, 33; in modern armed conflict, 3, 106–30, 198, 199; noncompliance with humanitarian law by, 110; in noninternational armed conflicts, 9, 118–19; norms and behaviors of, 285n75; private security companies and, 151, 159; responsibilities of, 54; in warfare, 108, 247n45. *See also under names of specific groups*

nonstate combatants and fighters, 3, 9, 115; aiding and abetting of, by states, 12; challenges to humanitarian law posed by, 72, 95; exclusion of, under Geneva Conventions, 6; partial compliance and, 2; POW status and, 82, 86, 88, 104, 114; Protocol I and, 7–8; regulations of, 190; rights of, 49–50; for self-determination, 13, 223n11

Noriega, Gen. Manuel, 219n44

norms, 4, 16, 32–33, 54, 107, 122, 128, 176, 208, 286–87n89; alternative, 199; of armed conflict, 61, 62–63, 126; baseline, 29; challenges to, 2; changing, 204; creation of, 50, 205–6; of humanitarian law, 13–14, 19, 55, 124, 127, 129, 191–93, 196, 210; international, 14, 19, 47–48, 81, 140, 194, 209; legal, 45, 53, 76, 78, 106, 207; values vs., 285n75

Northern Ireland: Diplock courts in, 59–60; terrorism in, 232n91

Nuremberg Tribunal, 257n46

Nurick, Lester, 199

Obama, Barack, administration of, 79, 99

occupation, 201, 208; alien, 223n11, 224n18, 239n25; foreign, 46, 50; as international armed conflict, 247n44; under international humanitarian laws, 5, 231n77; of Iraq, 150; occupying power and, 90, 211; of Palestine, 179, 185, 188; resistance to, 203; of territory, 55, 110, 116

Operation Cast Lead, 185–88; civilian casualties and property damage from, 273n73; *Gaza Report* on, 277n119; proportionality principle in investigations of, 172, 177–84, 188–89; protection of civilians by Israel during, 277n123; reciprocity and, 122

organizational control, doctrine of, 143, 145–47, 258n62

Osiel, Mark, 123

Oxford Manual of the Laws of War on Land, 30

Pakistan, 166, 187, 248n51

Palestine Liberation Organization, 228n51

Palestinians, 179; civilian suffering and deaths of, 182, 183, 275n96, 277n117; in Gaza, 182–83, 185–86, 273n81; as refugees, 184

paramilitaries, 3, 16, 45, 46, 47, 53, 167; Irish, 60

partisans, 108, 114, 199, 201, 211, 243–44n4

Patton, George S., 175

Peres, Shimon, 178, 291
Pictet, Jean, Commentary of, 122, 125, 243–44n4
Pimlott, John, 201, 202, 203–4
Pinkerton Rule, in U.S. Supreme Court, 143, 257n47, 257–58n50
political violence, 48, 52; Australia and, 56; continuum of, 16; Israel and, 55, 57; organized, 53
politics, 211; as basis of transnational groups, 14; of Cold War, 16; domestic, 167; international law and, 171; language of war and, 215n13; power, 14, 206, 207; public opinion and, 185; war and, 193, 194, 279n12
postconflict settings, 13
prevention of unnecessary suffering, 2
principles of humanitarian law, 7, 28, 31–40, 44, 82, 120, 122, 174, 204, 210, 268n12, 281n33; application of, 40–42; counter-terrorism and, 25; historical, 15, 18; listing of, 2, 4, 6, 71–73; nonstates and, 80; proposed, 8; rejection of, 10; states' compliance with, 28, 29–30, 79; targeting, 95, 100. *See also* distinction; military necessity; military objective; noncombatant immunity; prevention of unnecessary suffering; proportionality; protective parity; reciprocity; self-defense
prisoners of war (POWs), 71, 237–38n17, 250n78; combatant status and, 73–75, 80, 88–89, 104, 110, 152–54, 197; criteria for obtaining status of, 7, 115, 128, 224n25, 253n19; Gonzales on interrogation of, 9; Hague Conventions on, 114; humanitarian standards and, 124, 211; Jinks on, 237n13; nonstate entities and, 49, 55, 81, 86, 118; partisans as, 243n4; privileges of, for terrorists, 12; status of, 11, 17, 223n13, 229n60; treatment of, under international humanitarian laws, 5, 6. *See also* detainees, detention
private security companies (PSCs), 150–51, 160, 162–66; in Afghanistan, 156–57; in asymmetric conflicts, 161; as civilians, 72, 155–58; combatant status and, 117; international humanitarian law training for, 266n84; in Iraq, 156, 259n2; as irregular participants in modern conflicts, 3, 12; laws of war and, 108–10, 154–55, 158–59, 161; MEJA and, 264n58; as mercenaries, 261n19; reciprocity and, 119, 123–24, 126; regulation of, 250n73, 262n40; as rivals, 264n66; as victims of terrorism, 244n6. *See also under names of individual companies*
proportionality, 139–41, 272n58; in asymmetric warfare, 12, 195; balancing test of, 174–77, 184; collateral damage and, 256n41; direct participation and, 103; in Operation Cast Lead, 178–81, 188–89; as principle of humanitarian law, 2, 6, 7, 19, 29, 172–74, 185, 236n6, 250n75, 251n82; problems with, 174–75
protected sites, 12
protections of international humanitarian law, 2, 4, 9, 100, 118, 148, 149, 191, 193, 197, 209, 210; al-Qaeda and, 27; of civilians, 5, 6, 18, 227n43; extension of, to nonstate entities, 14; Geneva Conventions and Protocols and, 38, 77, 125, 128, 137; minimal, 127; nonstate actors and, 68; private security companies and, 155, 160–64; for women and children, 111–12. *See*

also children; civilians; lawful combatant status; noncombatant immunity; prisoners of war
protective parity, 8
Provost, René, 123
public relations war, 19

racist regimes, 223n11, 224n18, 239n25, 247n44
Ratner, Steven, 205
reciprocity, 13, 119–20, 128–29, 248n57; absence of, 16–27; Additional Protocol II and, 251n81; in international law, 106, 120–26; lack of, by nonstate entities, 54, 79–80, 124; in noninternational armed conflict, 126–27
reform of international humanitarian law, 14, 94
Reisman, W. M., 196–97, 199, 206
Reisner, Daniel, 17, 85–86, 88–90, 93–94, 99, 104, 114
Report of the Independent Fact-Finding Committee on Gaza: No Safe Place, 179, 180–81, 183
religion, 14, 58, 107, 112, 115, 118, 124, 128, 178, 243n69; battlefield objectives and, 2; conflict based on, 270n44. *See also under names of specific religions*
resistance movements, organized, 110, 237n17, 242n53; lawful combatant status of, 200; militias and, 153; against occupation, 201, 203; POW status of, 243n4
retained personnel, POW status of, 246n29
Revolutionary Armed Forces of Columbia (FARC), 109, 244n8
Richemond-Barak, Daphné, 3, 18, 47, 48, 54, 197, 291–92
Roberts, Adam, 29, 219n35

Rona, Gabor, 191–92, 215n13
Rose, Gregory, 3, 16, 34–35, 292
Rousseau, Jean-Jacques, 113
Rwanda: ethnic conflict in, 118

sabotage, acts of, 13, 90, 229n54
Saint Augustine, 112
sanctuary for terrorists, 12
Saudi Arabia: car bombings in, 244n6; Guantanamo detainees from, 232n82; National Guard of, 244n6
security. *See* national security
self-defense, 68, 138, 161; of Blackwater, 264n58; of Israel, 272n57; preemptive, 206; right to, 53, 160, 201, 228n49
self-determination, right to, 13, 223n11, 224n18, 239n25, 247n44
September 11, 2001, terrorist attacks, 7–8, 53, 95; al-Qaeda and, 8; armed conflict provoked by, 43; effect of, on military policy, 41; U.S. response to, 23, 78
Sharon, Ariel, 179, 291
Sierra Leone, 263n53; child soldiers in, 142, 250–51n79; private security companies hired by, 159
soldiers, 2, 30, 108, 112, 113, 140, 145, 210; on battlefield, 101; as combatants, 110, 152, 191; lines between civilians and, 3, 72, 163; state, 6, 80, 164; uniforms and, 71, 114, 139. *See also* child soldiers; lawful combatants; prisoners of war
Sri Lanka, Liberation Tigers of Tamil Eelam in, 118, 122, 185, 248n51
state-centrism of humanitarian law, 4–10, 209; conflict framework of, 24; fixed terminology of, 14; of *jus in bello*, 191, 192, 199

states, sovereign, 4, 7, 12, 18, 205–11, 242n52; asymmetric warfare and, 8; compliance of, to international treaties, 1; under Geneva Conventions, 5–6; inability of, to enforce domestic laws, 10; international law and, 248n50; international law protection of civilians by, 1–2; Martens Clause and, 201, 203–4; norms and behaviors of, 285n75; obligations of, toward international law, 167–68, 173–74; obligations of, toward private contractors, 13; as parties to Hague Conventions, 5; POW status for, 11; reciprocity and, 119–20, 122–23; right of, to self-defense, 53–54, 228n49; security of, vs. humanitarian norms, 191–93, 209

status designation categories: under humanitarian law, 9, 12; legal, 4; modernization of, 8; new, 17

Switzerland: Montreux Document and, 164–65; Additional Protocol I and, 228n51

Syracuse University, College of Law, 2, 289

Taliban fighters, 17, 248n51; in Afghanistan, 250n79; as Guantanamo Bay detainees, 9; as unlawful combatants, 89

targeting: changing protocols for, 14, 256n33; of children, 135, 141; of civilians, 1–2; under international humanitarian laws, 5, 100–101, 211; of irregular forces, 17; lawful vs. unlawful combatants and, 86, 98, 103; on modern battlefield, 97, 246n30, 251n82, 251n84; of nonstate fighters, 227n43, 247n45; of terrorists, 137–38, 256n34, 256n35

terrorism, 8, 226n36; car bombings as, 244n6; civilians and, 94, 136; combating, 18, 140; domestic criminal law and, 10, 16, 144; Lockerbie bombing as, 53, 233n101; in Northern Ireland, 232n91; prolonged campaigns of, 3; state-sponsored, 24; transnational, 17. *See also* al-Qaeda; global war on terror; terrorists; war against terrorism

terrorists, 109, 141, 166–67, 260n63, 286n86; Additional Protocol I and, 7–8; affording protected status to, 9; children as, 133–36; classification of, under humanitarian law, 12, 192; criminal responsibility of leaders of, 142–49; detention of, 77; under Geneva Conventions, 117; human shields used by, 251n82; under Israeli law, 227n43; leaders of, 138–39, 256n34; misidentification of, 244n9; Palestinian, vs. Israel, 272n57; Pinkerton Rule and, 258n50; reciprocity and, 119, 124, 126; recruiters, 102, 136, 142; state support of, 228n49; targeting of, 256n35

Third Geneva Convention: on combatant status, 114–16, 128; quotations from 237–38n17

threshold criteria, 15; considerations of, 11; for international and noninternational armed conflict, 12, 215n15; for triggering laws of war, 6–7, 226n36

Ticehurst, Rupert, 204

torture, 123, 124, 206, 281n33; Bybee Memo and, 206; convention against, 249n72; presidential military orders on, 78; prohibited under Common Article 3, 233n95; Yoo memo on, 286n85

INDEX

transnational armed conflict, 38, 40, 41, 45, 50, 54, 100; Common Article 3 and, 49, 52; norms for, 62–63
transnational terrorist networks, 24, 25, 36, 87, 94, 192: international humanitarian law and, 23, 40, 129; international humanitarian war and, 7, 93; states vs., 17
Travers, Desmond, 187
Triple Canopy, 161, 249n72
Turku Declaration of 1990, 124

Uniform Code of Military Justice, 27, 157–58, 286n86
uniforms, 71, 115, 135, 136, 155, 197, 240n30. *See also* distinction; insignia rule
United Kingdom: Additional Protocol II and, 226n41; forces under authority of, 31; Guantanamo detainees from, 232n82; Lockerbie bombing and, 233n101; PSCs in, 249–50n73; terrorist attacks in London, 244n9; military operations in Iraq by, 233n97; use of private security companies by, 155, 159; *United Kingdom Ministry of Defense Manual for the Law of Armed Conflict*, 29
United Nations (UN): Charter of, 5, 46, 239n25; children involved in armed conflict and, 134; compounds of, 277n117; Operation Cast Lead and, 179, 182; private security companies and, 154–55; report of, on impact of armed conflict on children, 252n6; *Voluntary Principles on Human Rights*, 263n43
United Nations Fact-Finding Mission on the Gaza Conflict, 178, 185–88

United Nations Human Rights Council, 122, 123; declarations of, 125; reports to, 182; Resolution S-9/1, 185–87
United Nations Security Council, 211, 233n97, 250n79; Resolution 1373, 53; Resolution 1860, 182
United States, 163, 228n52; Additional Protocol I and, 253n19; in Afghanistan, 118; al-Qaeda vs., 26–27, 43; counterterrorism policies of, 8–9, 43; defense principle of, 221n80; enemy combatants and, 78–79, 88; in Iraq, 156, 259n2; law of war policy of, 219n39, 219n40, 219n44; lawfare and, 193–94; military policies of, 25, 29, 115, 206; preventive detention in, 58–59; use of private military contractors by, 150–52, 155–60, 164–67; unlawful combatants and, 98–99
U.S. Congress: "Authorization for Use of Military Force against Terrorists," 78; establishment of armed forces by, 221n80; jurisdiction over Guantanamo detainees' *habeas corpus* appeals and, 286n86
U.S. Department of Defense: guidelines for contractors with, 156, 157–58, 262n40; international humanitarian law training for contractors with, 266n84; Law of War Program of, 15, 25, 28; use of private security companies by, 164–65
U.S. Supreme Court: *Boumediene v. Bush* in, 59; Common Article 3 and, 49; on conflict with al-Qaeda, 7, 9; *Ex parte Quirin* in, 78; on foreign detainees, 55; *Hamdan v. Rumsfeld* in, 27, 225n29, 286n86; *Hamdi v. Rumsfeld*, 58, 286n86; Pinkerton Rule and, 257–58n50; *Rasul v. Bush* in, 232n83

unlawful combatants, 68, 70, 83, 88, 89–90, 93, 97–99, 154, 160, 229n54; definition of, 12, 94, 100, 103; Guantanamo Bay detainees as, 9; in Israel, 58, 75–77; modernized view of, 86, 87, 104, 105; terrorists as, 286n86; in United States, 78

Vienna Convention on the Law of Treaties (1969), 175
Vinnell: in Gulf War, 244n7; repelling Saudi rebels, 109; terrorist attacks against, 244n6
volunteers, 47; corps of, 54, 110, 116, 209, 237n17, 242n53, 243n4; under Declaration of Brussels, 284n54

Walzer, Michael, 8, 178, 180
war: European concept of, 4–5; between states, 238n21; as term, 215n13
war, laws and customs of. *See* laws and customs of war
war against terrorism: Bush administration's, 8–9; international humanitarian law and, 7, 85. *See also* global war on terror
war crimes, 7; child enlistment as, 166–67; civilian death as, 181, 281n33; in Gaza, 186; Hamdan and, 27; ICC and, 142, 225n31; private military contractors and, 151, 160; protection of persons accused of, 125; regime of, as negative incentive, 11. *See also* International Criminal Tribunal for the former Yugoslavia; Nuremberg Tribunal
weapons: under international humanitarian laws, 5, 69; of mass destruction, 272n58
Wittes, Benjamin, 59, 60, 61

Xe. *See* Blackwater Security

Yemen, Guantanamo detainees from, 232n82
Yoo, John, and Bush torture memo, 286n85

Zoli, Corri, 19–20